DODO

by Dodo Lees

Other Books Recorded and Edited by Clive Murphy

AUTOBIOGRAPHIES

THE GOOD DEEDS OF A GOOD WOMAN
The Memoirs of an East End hostel-dweller
BEATRICE ALI

BORN TO SING
The Memoirs of an East End mantle presser
ALEXANDER HARTOG

FOUR ACRES AND A DONKEY
The Memoirs of a lavatory attendant
S.A.B. ROGERS

LOVE, DEARS!
The Memoirs of a former chorus girl
MARJORIE GRAHAM

OIKY
The Memoirs of a pigman
LEN MILLS

AT THE DOG IN DULWICH
The Memoirs of a poet
PATRICIA DOUBELL

A STRANGER IN GLOUCESTER
The Memoirs of an Austrian in England
MRS FALGE-WAHL

A FUNNY OLD QUIST
The Memoirs of a Gamekeeper
EVAN ROGERS

FICTION

SUMMER OVERTURES
FREEDOM FOR MR MILDEW
NIGEL SOMEONE

DODO

by Dodo Lees

Originally Recorded and Edited by Clive Murphy

Printed in 1993 by
The Self Publishing Association Ltd
Units 7/10 Hanley Workshops,
Hanley Road, Hanley Swan,
Worcester.

British Library Cataloguing in Publication Data

A catalogue record for this book is available from the British Library

ISBN 1 85421 190 0

Designed and Produced by Images Design and Print Ltd
Printed and Bound in Great Britain by Hartnolls Ltd, Bodmin, Cornwall.

Contents

PART ONE – CHILDHOOD DAYS,	13
Chapter One – Born With a Silver Spoon,	15
Chapter Two – Halcyon Days,	22
PART TWO – TEENAGER,	33
Chapter Three – A Polyglot Teenager – Brussels and Munich,	35
Chapter Four – Debutante,	42
Chapter Five – Germany and the War Clouds Gather,	46
PART THREE – WARTIME ENGLAND,	55
Chapter Six – The War – England,	57
Chapter Seven – Wartime London,	65
Chapter Eight – Engaged,	75
Chapter Nine – Fate Steps In – France,	78
PART FOUR – FRANCE 1944-45,	81
Chapter Ten – Normandy,	83
Chapter Eleven – Paris Just After the Liberation,	89
Chapter Twelve – With The Maquis,	96
Chapter Thirteen – Into Germany With My Regiment,	104
PART FIVE – PEACE,	121
Chapter Fourteen – Peace,	123
Chapter Fifteen – Working for the Quai d'Orsay,	130
Chapter Sixteen – America!,	133
Chapter Seventeen – America Again,	140
PART SIX – LABOUR POLITICIAN,	151
Chapter Eighteen – Fleet Street,	153
Chapter Nineteen – Parliamentary Candidate,	162
Chapter Twenty – Fighting Lancaster,	172

PART SEVEN – A START IN MARRIED LIFE – MALTA, 179

Chapter Twenty One – Marriage, 181

Chapter Twenty Two – H.M.S. Battleaxe – Malta, Egypt and Cyprus, 193

Chapter Twenty Three – Dom Mintoff, 201

PART EIGHT – NAVAL LIFE, 207

Chapter Twenty Four – More Following The Fleet, 209

Chapter Twenty Five – Rome, 213

Chapter Twenty Six – Back in England, 222

Chapter Twenty Seven – H.M.S. Lagos, 227

PART NINE – AN EASTERN ODYSSEY, 231

Chapter Twenty Eight – Singapore and Hong Kong, 233

Chapter Twenty Nine – Australia, 240

Chapter Thirty – Journeying Back to England: Johore, Trinco, Iran and Malta, 247

PART TEN – FAMILY LIFE IN DORSET AND THE MED, 259

Chapter Thirty One – A Home of my Own, 261

Chapter Thirty Two – Back to the Med – Beirut and Gozo, 271

PART ELEVEN – SOUTH AMERICA, 277

Chapter Thirty Three – Off to Caracus!, 279

Chapter Thirty Four – The Hovercraft and the Earthquake, 289

Chapter Thirty Five – Snowy, 297

Chapter Thirty Six – More Caribbean Excitement, 306

PART TWELVE – SWAN SONG, 329

Chapter Thirty Seven – Sons, 331

Chapter Thirty Eight – Back to Venezuela, 336

Chapter Thirty Nine – Malta and Mintoff, 338

Chapter Forty – Settling down in Dorset, 347

Epilogue – By Chipps Selby Bennett, 359

The Times Obituary, 362

Outline Family Tree, 363

Index, 365

List Of Illustrations

Dodo, 10

Trokes Coppice, Lytchett Minister, Dorset, 17

Howard, 75

The Ambulancières, 118

Jean de Villèyre, 125

Gerald Paul, 127

Monique and Carroll in Portofino, 139

Monique and François on holiday in Portofino, 1947, 139

Photograph used during canvassing, 1950, 146

International Seminar Compiègne, 1950, 167

Leaving the Church, 182

Wedding Reception, Whatcombe House, 18th April, 1953, 183

Dodo on her Wedding Day, 185

Jamie's Christening, Lulworth Castle, 1954, 190

Dodo with Jamie, 1954, 191

With the Pope, 214

London, 1957, 221

A photograph taken of the family before leaving for Caracus in 1966, 265

Dodo and family, 1961, 269

On board the French liner *Flandres*, 1966, 282

On the beach at San Andres, 309

Hugh and Antonia Fraser at Canaima, 320

Chipps and Dodo with Officers of the Venezuelan Navy on board H.M.S *Zest*, 326

4th June at Eton, 1970, 332

Jamie and 'Scilla's wedding, 1978, 349

Chipps and his grandson, Andrew, 1988, 351

Dodo and Porfirio, 355

Slepe Green, 1992, 361

Dedication

For Chipps

Part 1

Childhood Days

Chapter 1

Born With A Silver Spoon

I always call myself a cockney because I was born in a London nursing home within the sound of Bow Bells. I was christened Dolores, but I've always hated that. So I've always been called Dodo. The date was April the 20th 1920. Oddly enough, Hitler and Charlie Chaplin were born on April the 20th, too.

My father, nicknamed Berry, was Captain Bernard Percy Turnbull, the third son of Sir Elliot Lees; the 2nd baronet, Uncle Jack's older brother, Tom, was killed at Gallipoli. My father and mother were married in 1919 after he returned from serving in the war with the Dorset Yeomanry. When he died in 1922, he had just been appointed Commissioner of Police in Lagos. The High Commission there gave him a huge party as soon as he arrived. The next day a bullet went wide of the target during shooting practice and shot him in the hand, and the doctor who operated gave him too much anaesthetic and killed him. I was two at the time. Mike, my brother, was one. Bumble, my sister, was on the way.

The following year my mother – her name was Mary – dedicated me to the Virgin Mary, so I never wore anything but blue and white until I was seven when I made my First Communion. She dedicated Mike to the Sacred Heart, so for three years he never wore anything but red. The Lees family was Protestant, though my great-grandmother, Bernada Mejia de Turnbull, Sir Elliot's mother, was from Puebla, Mexico, and my grandmother, Granny Bee, Lady Florence Lees née Keith, was converted to Catholicism before she died. But my mother's side of the family – her father was a Radcliffe and her mother was a Weld – were all terribly religious Catholics. The Welds are an old Catholic family – Robert the Wild landed in England during the Norman Conquest – and their places in Dorset have always been Lulworth Castle and Chideock Manor. In fact, the Welds and the Radcliffes never changed their religion in the Reformation: among my ancestors there are forty martyrs who were hanged, drawn and quartered.

My Godfather was Humphrey Weld of Chideock Manor, the brother of my grandmother Maud Radcliffe, and my First Communion was at Chideock in the family chapel. I remember my mother giving me afterwards a dress of orange chiffon embroidered with white edelweiss. Being used to nothing but blue and white, I adored that dress: I wouldn't take it off: I wanted to wear it to bed. I was vain already, you see, at the age of seven. Not that I didn't pray and pray and go to Holy Communion and make novenas and say my rosary with a gorgeous amethyst rosary given to me by my Godfather, the rosary given to him by Pius X, the Saintly Pope. Uncle Humphrey and Gaga, my grandmother, were the children of Sir Frederick Weld, the Governor of the Straits Settlements and Western Australia and Tasmania.

I think I remained fairly religious until I was seduced at the age of twenty-five – I'd even make novenas to get a boyfriend. I still go to church on Good Friday and Christmas Eve, generally at Lulworth Castle, and Jamie and Bruce, my two sons, have been brought up as Catholics and were christened there, though Chipps, my husband, is Protestant.

My great-great-grandmother Weld used to have George III down to stay at Lulworth for the sea bathing because it did his madness good. After one of his visits, he said to her, "We would like to give you a present. What would you like?" thinking she'd say, perhaps, a diamond tiara, but she said, "I'd like a chapel." Well, of course, that was absolutely forbidden before the Catholic Emancipation Act but, as had given his word, he said, "all right. You may make a chapel if you make it look like a folly." She did, and it's absolutely lovely. It has a dome and it looks like a summer house in the garden – it's the only Georgian Catholic church in England and it's quite unique.

A hundred and fifty years ago, Thomas Weld the then owner of Lulworth Castle was widowed. His children were now grown-up and he became a priest. Within a few years he was a Cardinal in Rome, perhaps the only Cardinal to have had a perfectly legitimate family!

It was always great fun for us as children when we went to lunch with Cousin Herbie at Lulworth Castle. You pressed a bit of the panelling and the floor opened and you could play in the priest's secret hiding hole. The priest at Lulworth now also does the church at Wool and the chapel at Bindon Abbey. Lulworth Castle was built out of the stones of Bindon Abbey and the Abbot cursed it and said it would be destroyed by fire – because of the curse Gaga Radcliffe always slept in the housekeeper's annexe instead. And Lulworth was burned down.

Sir Joseph Weld is the present owner and, with the help of the Heritage Trust, is keeping it propped up, but his predecessor, Herbie Weld, was living there at the time of the fire. I was eight and was staying in Ireland with the Boylans at Hilltown near Drogheda. I remember that holiday because I once saw a figure come in to my room. I was simply terrified and I screamed and Mummy came up and held my hand and stayed with me until I went to sleep. The next day I was moved to another room. My mother didn't approve of night lights – she thought they were habit forming – so she left the door slightly open and the light on in the passage. But I went on screaming, pretending I'd a pain, and my appendix was taken out as a result. I was paid back in kind.

I've seen ghosts all my life. In fact ghosts are one of the reasons I pray. Though I'm not absolutely a hundred per cent convinced there's a God, I think there must be something out there. Why would I see ghosts otherwise? I'm now more like a French Catholic: "Born, married and died in the Church". I try to keep to the rules of Catholicism. For instance, I would never divorce. And I was once in charge of a little boy while his parents were away from home, and he fell down the stairwell from the top storey. I called a doctor immediately but, before he came, because I knew the boy hadn't been baptised, I poured some water from a cup over his head, made the sign of the cross and said, "I baptise thee in the name of the Father and of the Son and of the Holy Ghost. Amen."

Trokes Coppice, Lytchett Minister, Dorset.

My first memory is of sitting on my father's knee in the library at Trokes Coppice and pulling out his eye-glass. Granny Keith, the wife of my grandfather Sir Elliot Lees, left Letterawe, her place in Loch Awe, to my father and he sold it to build Trokes. So Trokes may look like an old house, but it isn't. It was built, when I was born, with old bricks and old tiles, and my mother put in lovely beams from a part of Christchurch Priory which was falling down. It has two acres of land and the most divine view over Poole Harbour and it's a mile from South Lytchett Manor which then belonged to my Uncle Jack (Sir John Lees the 3rd Baronet), who was married to Madeleine Lees née Pelly, my Aunt Maddy. Because of my father's death, which greatly affected my life – I spent a great deal of my youth at Lytchett Manor with Uncle Jack, Aunt Maddy and their seven children, Kath, James, Ros, Anne, Tom (the present baronet), Jane and Mary Gabriel. We were all well known for living in one another's pockets. People would say, "It's an awful bore having the Lees' to Hunt Balls and things because they do nothing but dance with each other and talk amongst themselves in a gang." Mary Gabriel died in 1961. She wasn't entirely normal, but I loved her dearly and she was very fond of me. I have a definite affinity with that sort of person. I don't draw away from mental defectives or the physically handicapped, and I like old people, too.

My mother was very good-looking: tall and fair with one blue eye and one brown. I have always missed not having a father, yet I joined with my sister and brother in persuading her not to marry again. When I was about ten, she went on a cruise to the Bahamas with Sir Philip and Lady Colfox of Simondsbury Manor in Dorset. They were close friends of my parents. "Uncle" Philip was the "Father of the House of Commons". He and Uncle Jack more or less acted as our guardians, helping my mother with her investments and so on. Anyway, on this cruise, my mother met a very rich American whom she rather fancied, and he was frightfully in love with her and he asked her to marry him. When she got back to Trokes, she was toying with the idea and she said to us, "Would you like it if I married again?" We were absolutely horrified! We said, "But no, Mummy! You had the most perfect marriage with Daddy. We would hate you to put anybody in his place!" I think one of the reasons why none of us has been divorced is that all our lives we've believed that marriage should be a marvellous thing like our parents. Their marriage was always a honeymoon. I don't think it would ever have gone wrong. My mother told me afterwards she thought it was meant that she shouldn't remarry and that my father, who she would meet again one day, was influencing her from heaven.

My father's death left her quite well off, though with taxes and so on her income gradually dwindled. She helped to run the Catholic Needlework Guild in Exeter and the Women's Institute in Lytchett Minster; she was also on the Board of Governors of the Cornelia Hospital, founded by Cornelia – Lady – Wimborne, which became Poole General, the first National Health hospital to be opened by Nye Bevan after the Second World War. But, apart from good works, and religion of course, her main interest was gardening. In fact, she became such a good gardener and the garden at Trokes was so marvellous that friends with big gardens asked her to landscape theirs.

My Aunt Vivian Pleydell-Railston (not a real aunt but a great friend of my parents) asked her to design her garden at Whatcombe House. Aunt Vivian was a talented sculptress and in return for my mother's work she made her an exquisite china figure of me aged fourteen – she later made a statuette of Anton Dolin in *Firebird* and gave it to me as a wedding present because of my love of dancing. It was Aunt Vivian who, when my brother married and my mother gave him Trokes, allowed her to go and live in Shepherd's Cottage, a Domesday house in the grounds of Whatcombe.

The head gardener at Trokes was called Pope – how apt for the head gardener of a very Catholic family! – but the man who really taught my mother all she knew about gardens was Dance, the head gardener at Lytchett, a terrific chap, an ex-guardsman with a marvellous wax moustache. He was very interested in bees. He had a glass-fronted hive where you could see what the Queen Bee and the other bees were doing. I think that's one of the reasons I adore bees so much. Among other gorgeous things, Dance grew the most wonderful muscatel grapes in Lytchett Manor's huge great greenhouse. They were out of this world: they were the most divine grapes I think I've ever eaten in my life in any country. The vines, alas, died during the war because there was no fuel to heat them.

My mother also played the violin beautifully – she was a member of a London orchestra before the war. And she was rather good at producing plays. The playwright Trevor Wood asked her to produce pre-London try-outs of two of his plays – *The Dream Children* and *Mother Earth* – in the big Hall at Lytchett Manor.

Oh, and my mother was a terrific bird person, which is probably why I'm a terrific bird person. And why I hate cats. I adore all creatures, except cats and spiders, but particularly birds. I use a whistle taught me by the Sultan of Johore in the Malayan jungle – I quite often whistle it to Porfirio, my parrot, and he whistles back. I wanted to look at some wild orchids and the Sultan said, "I will teach you a whistle. Whistle it and you will be completely safe. In Malayan it means 'Lords of the Jungle, I come in friendship, not in enmity. Please be good to me and mine'." So he taught me this whistle and, whenever I've gone through the jungle in South America or anywhere else, I've never been attacked by a snake or any other animal.

I suppose, by today's standards, my childhood at Trokes Coppice was *très snob* with nanny, cook, parlour maid, tweeny, gardeners and governess, not to mention the same sort of thing on a grander scale at South Lytchett Manor where I spent so much of my time. Trokes, unlike Lytchett, had no wings but it had a nursery side with children's bedrooms, a nanny's bedroom, bathrooms and a nursery.

All through early childhood, winter and summer, there were lots of parties with conjurors and cakes and dancing and charades and, hunt-the-slipper. The great "fun" parties were given by Admiral Drax whose estate, Charborough, was next to the Lees', on board enormous ships, generally in Portland. Children's parties are well known in the Navy. You give one wherever you go in every port. The sailors are marvellous at looking after children. They give you rides up and down on the guns and play all sorts of games with you, and take you all over the ship. In 1927 there was a party on board Admiral Drax's battleship H.M.S. *Marlborough* at Portland. They had a large paddling pool in the middle of the deck, with an electric current running through it that made your hand tingle when you put it in the water. The pool was mostly full of pennies but, in the middle, there were half-crowns. Electricity doesn't seem to affect me much, so I took my shoes off, got straight into the pool and was picking up all the half-crowns, when Nanny insisted on my putting them all back again and told me to get out. So I was in disgrace for that, and I thought it very unfair. Nanny could be a real old tyrant. I think my mother was terrified of her. But she never beat us. The nanny at Lytchett Manor beat my cousins!

When Nanny died, the cook, came with us on holidays and looked after us. She used to pray every evening outside the summerhouse where she thought she'd seen the Virgin Mary – she thought it was like Lourdes. Our great joy as children was to camp out there in summer. My mother used it for making chocolates which she sold to friends. My mother always thought she was poor, though she left £160,000 in full when she died in 1980. During the Thirties she really pulled in her horns and only employed Maggie, as cook-housekeeper, two maids and one gardener. I suppose she was fussing because she had to bring up three children without a husband.

Our first governess was Paddy, a terrific old Irish spinster. I remember I slept in her room for a time instead of in Mike's, but that didn't work because I couldn't bear her snoring so I got a room of my own. You see, I was a nervous little girl, I was what my mother-in-law later used to call "tickety-boo", and, because of her snoring, I simply couldn't sleep. I said to Mummy, "I must have my own room!" and she said, "No. Then I won't have a second spare-room." The next day I made snooks at Paddy and my mother beat me on the bottom with a hairbrush, though not very hard. Early next morning, while Paddy snored like mad, I flitted: I ran away. Now my mother had started a pigsty at some stage to make money. Somebody had said, "You buy a pig and have some piglets and then you sell them for vast sums." Well, the plan failed – they all got swine disease or something – so there was this pigsty at the end of the garden, completely empty, and I went and hid in the pigsty. I stayed there till about midnight, with the whole of the police force of Dorset looking for me. At midnight I sneaked in to the kitchen and said, "Maggie, can I have some food?" My mother, of course, instead of punishing me and smacking my bottom again, fell on me and hugged me. It does show I was a bit spoilt, because I then got my own room and my mother decorated it exactly the way I wanted it.

Chapter 2

HALCYON DAYS

I'll tell you, now, about some of the family houses we stayed at throughout my childhood.

When I was about five I was taken to New Hall. This was a convent where my grandmother Gaga's younger sister, Aunt Angie, was a nun. Every night, huge spiders came out of the panelling of my room and I was absolutely terrified. That's when my phobia about spiders began. The nuns thought in some way they were the soul of Anne Boleyn. New Hall was once Anne Boleyn's home, you see.

I also stayed at Harrowden with Lord Vaux who was married to my mother's favourite cousin, Freda Radcliffe. Lord Vaux had horrible chins that went down to his tummy and I think he liked little girls, you know what I mean, because he was always taking me for walks in the wood and chafing me with a stick. He never had any children of his own and he led Cousin Freda an awful dance. But, being a Catholic, she spent most of her time in the chapel, and never looked at another man.

A nicer holiday was spent in Ireland at Mount Nugent, the home of my Lees Great Aunt Kitty, Lady Nugent of Farren Connell. Mrs. Joe, her housekeeper, used to tell us fairy stories and we went boating and I learned to walk on stilts and I saw baby owls, little white fluffy things in the barn and I was taught by a man called Freddy, who'd been out in India, how to make baskets out of apple prunings.

I also went to Rudding Park, Harrogate, my mother's old home, several times – once, when I was about seven, alone with my grandmother, Gaga, to give my mother a rest. This was when I saw my first ghost. Gaga was put in a big room with a four-poster bed and I slept in a sort of small powder closet off hers. Of course, in those days, there was no central heating so there was a fire in each room as we were guests – I was only allowed one in my bedroom at Trokes when I had a cold. Suddenly I saw a girl standing in front of the fire in a white ball dress. She was still there when I went to sleep. The next day at breakfast, I said to my Great Aunt Cathy, "Who was the pretty girl in a white dress who came into my room last night to warm herself?" Aunt

Cathy looked at my grandmother and said, "Heavens! she's seen the ghost!" It was an ancestral cousin of ours who'd burned to death after standing too close to the fire in a white ball dress.

Then there was Allerton, where I stayed with my Cousin William, Lord Mowbray and Stourton. He was a pigeon fancier so, because I loved birds, I spent a lot of time with him in the dovecot. He lived alone with a hoard of servants and a personal chaplain for his chapel. Later, the Pope removed this right because William kicked the chaplain down some stairs. The only inconvenience at Allerton was that everyone – guests and servants – had to parade at 7.00 a.m. each day before Mass for Cousin William to inspect everything from our dress to the state of our teeth and nails.

I shan't list everywhere I went but I think I should mention Carlton Towers and Traquair House. Carlton Towers, near Goole, belonged then to my Cousin Mona, Baroness Beaumont, and her husband Bernard, Lord Howard of Glossop. Their eldest son, Miles, is now Duke of Norfolk. The names of all eight children began with M – Miles, Michael, Marigold, Martin, Miriam, Miranda, Mirabel and Mark. Their nanny couldn't bear our nanny. Marigold was my age and we subsequently "came out" together. As a child she came to stay at Trokes. She made jokes like, "Look! There's a man running down the garden with a bear behind!" which I thought terribly old hat. She wasn't a terrific friend of mine. I was very much thrown at her.

Traquair House, Innerleithen, belonged to my cousin, Arthur Maxwell Stuart. It's the oldest inhabited castle north of the border – Mary Queen of Scots stayed there frequently. The main gates are never opened. The family vowed that they would never be opened until a Stuart was once again upon the throne of Scotland. The late Queen Mary, when she went to lunch with Cousin Arthur, wanted to drive through them, but Cousin Arthur firmly said that they were rusty so this would be impossible. She got her own back later by admiring his favourite bit of Dresden and he had to give it to her.

My favourite cousin at Lytchett Manor was Aunt Maddy and Uncle Jack's elder son, James. He was born in 1920 like me, and would now be the 4th baronet had he survived the war. We used all to stay at Knoll House, Studland, the home of Lady Margaret Drummond-Hay, the Duke of Hamilton's daughter and a cousin of Aunt Maddy's. There was usually no one else on the beach and, one morning, James and I went for a swim before breakfast. When we camc back, I said to Nanny, "There was a man on our beach!" and Nanny said, "It doesn't belong to you! The foreshore belongs to the country!" At Studland, once – I must have been about seven – we came across Dr. Grantley Dick-Reid, the pioneer of natural childbirth, teaching Agatha McCarthy relaxation exercises on the sand as she was expecting a baby. I had been a bridesmaid at Agatha's wedding a few years before. She was the actress Agatha Kentish who once did *Mary Rose* in London, and she married Desmond McCarthy who eventually became an admiral. By an extraordinary coincidence he was also Chipps' first Captain when he was a midshipman in the battleship *Anson* during the war. I loved Desmond McCarthy madly: I thought he was God's gift to little girls.

Anyway, I copied and learned Dr. Grantley Dick-Reid's exercises there and then and have done them all my life in times of stress, even in war-time leaning up against a tree.

They renew you terrifically. You clench your toes and let them go. You clench your calves and let them go. You clench your thighs and let them go, You clench your tummy and let it go. You clench your arms and let them go. You clench your face. And then you flop.

Another place where we swam was up at Beacon, above Lytchett, where there are two lovely pools, the colour of sapphire. It's really the most romantic place. When I was older, I used to take all my boyfriends up there and play to them on a piano accordion I bought in Bournemouth. Since I was a child I'd ride up there and take my clothes off and swim and dry in the sun before riding home. I remember an awful-looking woman arrived once, when we were children, with a frightful husband in a Rolls. We were having a picnic with Aunt Maddy, and we were wandering around practically naked. The woman got out of the car and said to Aunt Maddy, "Who are these dreadful people picnicking at our favourite place?" and Aunt Maddy said, "I'm most frightfully sorry but, you know, I'm afraid it does actually belong to me." "No, it doesn't!" said the woman. "It belongs to Lord and Lady Lees of Lytchett Manor!" Aunt Maddy said nothing, she just giggled.

Uncle Jack, who was Joint Master of the South Dorset, taught me to ride. I was hunting at the age of three – Nanny or Uncle Jack's groom, Toop, used to lead me on a donkey called Charmaine. As a girl I simply adored the excitement of getting dressed and getting my pony ready and going out across country, not knowing if there was barbed wire or a ditch on the other side of a fence – it was the hunt I enjoyed most, not the meet and hanging around outside a cold covert. If my mother wanted to punish me and didn't let me hunt for a month for losing, say, my third mackintosh – that was the punishment that really mattered. In latter years I've hunted Chipps' horses but now I can't see well enough. Quite often I go on foot and I generally know where the fox is going. If I holler a fox then the various Masters that Chipps has whipped-in to, would bring hounds to me. They know that it's true.

Chipps lives for hunting. When he dies the whole of the South Dorset will be at his funeral, I'm sure. I do hope I'm dead already.

I had my first pony, Barebones, when I was four. He would pull the trap when Nanny drove us to Mass in Poole. Then we had a darling pony called Bluebird, who lived to be thirty-one. Bumble and Mike weren't really crazy about riding, but my mother bought me Diamond, an absolutely gorgeous white Arab, so that I could go out with Mike. Diamond was as good as gold with me and would do anything. But Mike was frightened of it; and once it bolted with him and my mother got rid of it without telling me. This was when I was about thirteen and it was one of the most awful things that she ever did to me. I came down one morning to feed Diamond at crack of dawn and he was no longer there. It was the first time I had a heartbreak. To give her her due, my darling mother, she thought that, if he bolted with Mike, he might bolt with me. I said, "Mummy! Mummy! How could you do that to my darling Diamond?! You've broken my heart!" so she immediately bought me another pony called Sunshine who I grew equally fond of. I *was* spoiled, you see!

Sometimes, as a teenager, I reduced my mother to tears by going out with too many men, sunbathing in the nude and wearing too much lipstick.

Actually, my mother was very *avant garde* about make-up. When I developed acne she took me to Cyclax in London to have a facial and to find out what was the best make-up for me to use. But this was when I was fifteen and she didn't allow me to make-up before then, so I used cochineal for my cheeks and lips and blue paint for my eye-lids and talcum powder for my nose. The talcum powder looked ridiculous because I've always tanned up in the summer, but it was part of growing up.

As a very young child, I had long curly hair and slept in ribbons. Later I wore plaits and ringlets. Then, at sixteen, I insisted on cutting my hair short because my mother wouldn't let me put it up and it was right down to my bottom. She cried, of course, but eventually gave in – my mother always gave in. She took me to Wimborne and I had it chopped off. Unbeknownst to me, she kept it and, years later when I went with Chipps to South America, she found it in the roof of Shepherd's Cottage and I had it made by Raymond into the dark hairpiece which I wear to this day.

It was at Pony Club, and private dances, when I was thirteen, fourteen, that I began to be interested in boys. We danced cheek to cheek, and I was madly in love with one and then with another. Uncle Jack was the Father of the Pony Club. He practically invented it and wrote the first book about it. He literally used to do cavalry drill with us in the park at Lytchett, only without saddles and bridles so we'd ride entirely with our knees. He had a proper horse-box, not a trailer, and he'd take me off with Sunshine to meets, gymkhanas and hunter trials and things where I won cups. Also in my teens, I'd go fly-fishing and shooting with Mike. But I hated taking fish off the hook and picking up pheasants. I was very squeamish.

In fact, I leant, as a child, rather towards the artistic – dancing, acting, painting, playing the piano – rather badly – reading. *The Incomparable Bellaires* I adored – it's a Powder and Patch story. And the *Just William* books, and *The Irish R.M.* – one of the two women who wrote that was some sort of relation. I practically know all of Jane Austen by heart. If I'd had a daughter I'd have called her Elizabeth Bennett after my favourite heroine. My favourite book of all is still *Destiny Bay* by Donn Byrne. Mummy gave it to me. It's an enchanting book, full of Irish feyness. Thackeray is another author I loved as a child, and I've since read all of Evelyn Waugh, Nancy Mitford and Graham Greene.

I haven't read *The Seven Pillars of Wisdom* by T.E. Lawrence – 'Lawrence of Arabia' – but Aunt Maddy took me to tea with him in 1935, not long before he died. She was very interested in Arab religions and she had a bee in her bonnet about the 'World Conundrom', Jews taking everything over. His house was near Bovington Camp. It was so spartan that there wasn't an inside loo. When it was announced that he'd been killed in a motorbicycle accident at Gallows Hill, Aunt Maddy said it was a plot and that he'd been spirited away by the Government to the Middle East to organise the Arabs. The white man organising the Arabs turned out to be Glubg Pasha, but my aunt was always convinced it was Lawrence; and that there was nobody in his coffin in the old church at Wareham.

I started ballet lessons at the age of seven. The classes were held in the Long Room of Charborough Rark, Admiral and Lady Drax's place which bordered literally upon ours: the Drax's land begins where ours ends. Kay de Voss would come down from her ballet school in London and put the Drax girls and daughters of local friends in line and make us do the positions. We wore party clothes and there was always a pianist. We even had a *barre*. Dor Drax is my age and, then, she was my height so she was next door to me in the line. She pinched my bottom and I said to my mother, "Dor does hurt! She digs her nails right in!" Mother told me to pinch back and I did and she never pinched me again and we're the greatest friends now.

Sometimes Miss de Voss brought star pupils, such as Sarah Churchill, Margot Fonteyn and Beryl Grey, and she'd single me out to dance with them because I was good enough. I danced with them twice at Lytchett in a troupe provided by Miss de Voss for charity fêtes organised by Aunt Maddy. I was so keen on ballet that I'd go out into the garden at Trokes in the evening, take my shoes off and dance on my toes on the grass – which is one of the reasons I've such bad feet. Mother thought my dancing was so pretty that, when she had a lunch party, she'd say, "Dodo, do a little dance for us!" She was awfully proud of me. One night, Nanny caught me dancing in front of the mirror, stark naked and covered with mother's talcum powder. But we didn't just do ballet at Charborough: we did Spanish dancing, the waltz, the polka and reels. I adored the fast waltz – the Viennese. When I was eleven, I grew too tall for serious ballet. I grew and grew and grew, and there's no man who can lift you up if you're too tall. I was six foot, my present height, by the time I was sixteen! I got to know Margot Fonteyn quite well. We shared a boyfriend after the war and I spent one Christmas with her in London. We were to met again in South America.

Our first governess at Lytchett was Lakey, a Protestant cousin of Aunt Maddy's, who left to marry a South African millionaire. We were rather a handful, actually. Because we were very fond of her and didn't want her to go, we sang, "He said that he loved her, but oh how he lied, oh how he lied . . ." Then we had a Miss de Winter, also Protestant, who left to become a nun. She was Welsh, very red-faced, a sweet person. Next Aunt Maddy started a school in the house, moving in term-time to Post Green, and I was taught there by a Miss Tilliard – Tillywhim, we called her – as well as by a woman called Mrs. Smith in Lytchett Minster village. Mrs. Smith tried to teach me Maths. I remember vaguely doing fractions and decimal points and things, but I didn't understand them then and I can't say I understand them now, though I'm good at mental arithmetic and can work out costings in my head to the nearest penny.

I adored the school at Lytchett Manor, and was there for about a year as a day-girl. It was a private school, a cosy family sort of school which was much sought after as a boarding school for girls up to the age of thirteen. Tillywhim was the headmistress, and Aunt Maddy muscled in and gave lectures on religion. The sad thing is, it was at its full capacity of about a hundred and booked up for several years and just beginning to pay when it had to be shut down at the start of the war because it was so close to the cordite factory at Holton Heath. Then, when Uncle Jack died in 1955, it was sold to the Dorset County Council to pay taxes, and became a Secondary Modern and, later, a Comprehensive.

Unfortunately, Tillywhim didn't think I concentrated enough – I was bothering too much about my ponies – and, at the age of thirteen, I was sent to a I.B.V.M convent, St Mary's at Sheringham in Norfolk where there were only twelve pupils. The extraordinary coincidence is that, after the war, the convent moved to Shaftesbury and became very large and took in a number of Protestant girls; my daughter-in-law, Scilla, was educated there and was even taught the Moonlight Sonata by Mother Teresita, the nun who taught it to me. I adored St Mary's as much as Lytchett Manor, but I only lasted one term, the summer term. The nuns read our letters and a boy who went to the same church rather fancied me and sent me a note via the milkman which was pounced on. And then my cousin Ros had written in my autograph album "How odd of God to choose the Jews" and I was hauled up in front of the Reverend Mother over that. She asked who had written it and why and, when I said Ros wasn't a Catholic, she was a Protestant, she was furious and wrote to my mother who took me away. When we got home I asked my mother was it true what a girl called Myra McGrath had told me, that "to have a baby, your daddy goes inside your mummy's tummy". Mummy got frightfully red and embarrassed and said, "Darling, it's just like the Blessed Trinity. The Father, the Son and the Holy Ghost are united." Well, I was just as wise as before because I thought Myra had been talking nonsense. And even when I became a very sophisticated deb I wasn't sure of the actual details.

The next term, I was sent to a school I hated. This was a very expensive convent near Ware in Hertfordshire, I think, called Pole's, where we had mauve uniforms and a grey coat and hat. Everything was frightfully institutionalised and impersonal, and the nuns were tartars. The only thing I really liked was the netball which I was good at. I couldn't sleep because I was put in a room with a girl who snored, so I left after six weeks. After only three weeks I'd hitch-hiked all the way to my grandmother, Gaga, in London. She put me up for the night at her house in Duke Street, Mayfair, fed me and that sort of thing; but she immediately rang up my mother who came up in the Lanchester and took me back to Pole's again, though I explained I'd been put in a room with three girls and one of them snored and that I couldn't sleep at night. Well, if you don't sleep for three weeks at that age, it's awful! The funny thing is that I snore now and Chipps doesn't.

I had to see the Reverend Mother and I was put back into this room with the girl who snored, and who never stopped snoring, so, after three days, I rebelled and Uncle Jack temporarily took me back to Lytchett. I think he was on my side, actually, as he didn't much care for Catholicism.

A third time, I hitch-hiked up to London again in a lorry and Gaga rang my mother and said, "Don't send her back to that place. We'll let her live here with us for a while instead." And that, apart from being "finished" later in Brussels and Munich, was the end of my formal education!

So I had a wonderful "informal education", however brief, with Gaga and

Grandpa Radcliffe. Chipps' stepfather always said I should have gone to university. But I don't think I'd have been any good at all I'm not at all academic, though I've read since the age of five. But experience educates you, too. And knowing intelligent people. And you can only really understand a country if you go there, and I've travelled a great deal. I speak a little Maltese six languages in all, if you include English.

Gaga spoke sixteen languages; including two Chinese dialects! This was because she'd followed Grandpa, a British Army Officer, all around the world. He spoke Mandarin Chinese. Here at Slepe Green I've two Peking temple dogs a mandarin gave him. I call them Pride and Prejudice. He married Gaga when she was seventeen. They had two children – Mummy first, and then a son, Arthur, who was killed in the First World War. Arthur was her ewe lamb. She wore black from the time of his death till the day she died. Grandpa was the son of Sir Joseph Radcliffe of Rudding Park in Yorkshire and his mother was Katty Doughty Tichborne of the famous Victorian "Tichborne Trial".

Katty Doughty Tichborne of Upton Park got engaged to Roger Tichborne, the heir to the Tichborne estates, but was sent abroad by the family because they were first cousins. He disappeared for twenty years when a claimant came forward saying he was Roger. My great-grandmother didn't recognise him and this was used to prove that he was a fraud. She said in court, "You would recognise your own fiance, wouldn't you?" Roger had left her some money in his Will and, when the claimant said it was because she was expecting his – the claimant's – child, my great grandfather had to testify that she was *virgo intacta* when he married her. With the money Roger Tichborne left her, she built St Mary's, the Catholic church in Poole where Chipps and I were married. After the trial, Queen Victoria insisted on Hogg, the claimant, having extra years in prison for the insults to Lady Radcliffe.

Before I was born; Gaga went to Lourdes because she had something wrong with her spine. She was cured, so, every year when they were in Europe, until they were very old, Grandpa went with her to Lourdes on a pilgrimage. When he was younger, he carried people in and out of the water. Later, he helped to hold the canopy over the bishop.

While I stayed with them in London, Grandpa and Gaga took my education in hand themselves, making sure I attended lectures at the British Museum, the Natural History Museum, the Victoria and Albert, the Tate and the National Gallery. I remember there was a very good man who lectured on Rubens at the National Gallery. I've always been interested in art. My mother had sent me to an art class in Wimborne where I learned how to sketch in charcoal, and I'd spent several weekends water-colouring with my old

Aunt May Weld who lived in Childeock village.

Grandpa was a Fellow of the London Zoo. He'd take me there on Sundays when it was shut to the public. After lunch in the Fellows' Dining Room, I was allowed to feed the serpents while he played bridge with his cronies. A boa constrictor used to wind itself around me. The keeper would say, "That snake do wait for you on Sundays, Miss Dodo". Wild things have always loved me, perhaps because I treat them as human beings.

I returned to Trokes at the end of spring. During that summer – it was 1934 and I was fourteen years of age – my attitude to life changed or, rather, a seed was sewn which subsequently changed the course of my life completely: I became more aware of just how privileged I was.

I don't think I had ever taken my privileges for granted – none of us had. When I was six and seven I used to sit high in the fork of a tree at the end of the garden and, with Mike helping me, write stories in an exercise book about poor girls getting richer. And I played a game called Pig Girl with my cousin Kath. She was the Princess and I was the Pig Girl, though I did always marry the Prince! And a few years later when I was staying in Ireland at Mount Nugent with Aunt Kitty, I asked Mrs. Joe, her housekeeper, "Are the people in Ireland very poor?" because I'd noticed so many people travelled by cart instead of by car. She said, "Yes, they are very poor, but we're all right at Farren Connell because Lady Nugent looks after us." I said, "But what about all the other people who aren't in Farren Connell?" I remember that quite clearly. You see, I was conscious of politics from a very early age, and conscious of the class difference and the responsibilities of being richer. And I always wanted the servants to have a better life. Well, not the servants, because they were well treated and very happy, but poor people and the unemployed. I was also becoming conscious of people like us getting poorer and I was more or less aware that they were nicer to their employees than the *nouveaux riches* who were getting richer.

What clinched the political ideas that were forming in the back of my mind as a child was a holiday in 1934 with my cousin Nettie and her husband Herman Salvin at Croxdale Hall near Durham. Croxdale Hall was a gorgeous place with tennis courts, and boats on a lake with wild raspberries all round it.

Nettie fascinated me. She was a prison visitor and did other good works, and, when we stayed with her, she and Herman had just had to close down part of Brandon Colliery so she was doing everything in her power to find workers alternative jobs. She had even taught them how to grow bulbs in pots to sell at the side of the Great North Road to supplement their dole. I remember thinking it was rather awful for lusty great men to have to do this, and I asked her one day, why it was we all had such comfortable houses with our own servants while such men at the end of the valley were unemployed. She said, "I suppose it's partly due to the unkindness of human nature." Her self-critical remark worried me. I wanted to have some contact with these working folk. Nettie, of course, was Conservative, but she wasn't the kind of stupid Conservative like most of my mother's friends, who said, "It's a waste of time giving miners council houses with baths. They'll only put coal in them!": Nettie, a very Christian woman, was in her way a Socialist.

One day I asked her if I might go down the mine before it was closed and she arranged it with the foreman. I had to wriggle on my tummy and then stand up and then go down again for ages and ages in dark sort of caverns. I remember the poor pit ponies. I remember my horror at the sight of men who, for tripping and crawling and wielding pickaxes underground, had only been paid peanuts and were now out of work. I came out of that coalpit determined to join the Labour Party when I grew up.

Part 2

TEENAGER

Chapter 3

A Polyglot Teenager – Brussels and Munich

My teens were rather sexy. Up till then I preferred ponies to boys, preferably riding them through thunder and lightning. My first real kiss was when I was thirteen. It was rather dramatic, actually. My mother used to have some of Mike's Avisford friends to stay at Trokes during the summer holidays. Mike's team played against Mark Bond's team and Uncle Philip Colfox's, The Bonds are a very Dorset family and lived at Tyneham. Mark Bond, who went on to be a general, was Mike's age and very good at cricket. This particular year, John Hunt was on Mike's team – you know, Sir John Hunt who became Secretary of the Cabinet in 1973. Also on Mike's team was Peter Farmer, a very good-looking boy who fancied me. One morning Peter kissed me on the mouth as I was coming out of the bathroom. I was awfully startled. Mike happened to come round the corner and see all this, and knocked him out. We didn't tell my mother why he'd done it, so he just got ticked off for scrapping.

My real love at this time was James, my first cousin. He didn't kiss me till I was fifteen. We were sitting on a stone bench in the Blue Garden at Lytchett Manor. After kissing me, he said, "If we go on sitting on this stone bench, we'll get piles." I said, "What are piles?" He said, "Don't you read your Bromo?" – in those days one spent endless hours in the loo reading what was written on Bromo loo paper.

James and I always swore that, if neither of us was married to someone else by the time we were twenty-eight, we'd marry each other. But, he was in the Special Boat Service in the war and died after being wounded during a raid on an island off the coast of Yugoslavia. When hostilities were over, and with Tito's permission, Aunt Maddy visited the Countess whose *château* was used as a hospital where James and the wounded Italian who actually shot him were nursed. According to the Countess, everyone thought at first that the Italian was going to die and that James would live, but it was the Italian who recovered. When Aunt Maddy asked how to find him, the Countess told her all she knew was that he was now a garage mechanic in Milan. Well, there are a lot of garages in Milan, but Aunt Maddy went to all of them, and found him and he gave her James' signet ring with the Lees' crest on it. Apparently James had said to him, "If you can find my mother after the war, give her my ring." When a memorial was put up to James in the family church in Lytchett Minster, Aunt Maddy paid the fare for this Italian to be present at the service of dedication. The Countess came too – and, as a result, the Italian Government gave her a medal, specially struck, because of her forgiveness.

As a matter of fact, at the very time when James must have died in Yugoslavia, I saw him in my crystal ball looking frightfully happy and walking down a sun-drenched street. Gaga Radcliffe was psychic and I'm psychic, too. Gaga not only knew that the Abbot of Bindon Abbey's curse of fire on Lulworth Castle would have effect, she foresaw the deaths of my fiancé and Bumble's first husband, and, like me, she saw ghosts all over the place. She said once to my Lees Aunt Bessie Oldfield who lived at Uddens House near Wimborne, "What's the name of the redheaded parlour-maid?" and Aunty Bessie said, "But the red-headed parlour-maid drowned in the lake last year!"!

I started reading hands and cards and looking in a crystal ball during my teens. To begin with, I told hands. I did it instinctively with my own interpretations, more or less as a joke. And then I found that what I said was true. I feel it in my head. It's the same with tarots or ordinary cards. They're a medium. I literally used to see people in the crystal ball, though whether I could now, being so blind, I do not know. They say you can tell fortunes in a glass of water, but I've never tried. With tarots and ordinary cards things come surprisingly into my head. I've a book called *Napoleon's Book of Fate* which gives the tarot readings, but I don't go by them much.

When my son Bruce was at Harrow, I told fortunes with my crystal ball at one of its Christmas Fairs. I wore a Spanish dress and a comb and mantilla, and sat with my parrot, Porfirio, under an eerie sort of light in a tent marked Fortune Teller. There was a queue half way down Harrow: I'd a longer queue than anybody else, including the Teas. No less than three men have come up to me at parties since and said, "Do you remember telling my fortune at Harrow with your crystal ball? You were absolutely right! Everything came true!" But I've always rather restricted the use of it. It's a great strain and you often see unpleasant things too clearly. I've sometimes looked in it for myself, but that's supposed to be awfully unlucky.

In Spring, 1935, I went to Brussels. My mother took me to improve my French. She thought that what I'd learned at school and with Grandpa and Gaga wasn't enough and that I needed some further education.

The very first evening, we went to dinner with Marie Louise de Meeus, Comtesse de Meeus, at her lovely little *château* in the Bois de la Cambre.

Marie Louise was a Silzer cousin of mine on my mother's side. She'd invited Baron Eduard de Marmol, a dapper army officer, as a match to sit next to me at table. Over liqueurs, he asked my mother could he take me on to a ball at the *château* of the Duc d'Urcels. Her reply was immediate: "Certainly not, my dear Eduard! Dodo's not 'out' yet!" I was only fifteen, you see, and he was of marriageable age, about twenty-two. He said goodnight to me and gave me great sort of eyes and I gave him great sort of eyes, and, next day, looking very glamorous in his uniform, he called on me at the *pension* and obtained my mother's permission to take me for a drive through the Bois and down the Meuse Valley – he didn't tell her he was going to show me the Manneken Pis! When, after ten days or so, his mother, the Baronne, asked my mother to agree to my marrying Eduard as soon as I was of age, she was absolutely horrified. She said, "Catholics of *bonne famille* may still arrange marriages in Belgium. We don't do it any more in England!"

My mother then returned to Trokes after arranging for me to stay two months at 115, rue Belliard, the beautiful house of Jean and Marie Renkin whose daughter, Nanette, was to come to Trokes the following Easter in exchange. Jean Renkin was an advocate in the Ministry of Justice. His late father had been the first Minister of the Belgian Congo, and then Prime Minister at the time of Leopold II. The house was enormous and full of the most frightfully valuable objects from the Congo, and, as Marie was from Northern France, the food and wine was marvellous. Almost every evening there were dinner parties to which were invited Belgian high society, including people from the Court surrounding King Leopold, and eminent servicemen and members of the Chambre des Deputes. Visiting politicians came too. Leon Blum, who the following May became the first Socialist prime minister of France since 1870, came four nights running and discussed at length his political problems. I was agog in view of my growing Socialist ideals. By day, the Renkins took me to museums and picture galleries. But, best of all, they took me to debates in the Chambre which I soon understood easily – after hearing no English for three weeks, I was dreaming, let alone speaking, in French.

Back in England, I made sure I visited the House of Commons whenever we were up in London. Aunt Mamie Colfox would gossip downstairs with mother while I listened to debates from the Ladies' Gallery. It was all rather dull compared with the Chambre in Brussels where they threw ink pots at one another. Uncle Philip, if he happened to drift in, just sat at the back making cat's cradles.

After leaving the Renkins, I stayed for a month in Brussels with Vicomtesse d'Hendrecourt whose job, among other things, was to jolly well teach me French and polish my grammar. She succeeded. I left Brussels speaking the language perfectly. Otherwise, it was a matter of dances and the opera and trips to the Ardennes Forest. One or two week-ends, I went on shooting parties with my cousin, Baron Raymond Snoy at Château L'Hermite, near the battlefield of Waterloo. Everyone stood in a ring round a wood and the cross-fire was at any level. I was scared stiff. My next door neighbour offered me a cigarette from a case with a hole in it. "*Ça m'a sauvé la vie!*" he said. When Chipps and I were married and his ship H.M.S. *Battleaxe* was at Ostend, I took him to lunch with Raymond who afterwards showed him the battlefield of Waterloo. Chipps is crazy about history so they made great friends, talking military tactics and things . . .

I returned to spend Christmas, 1935, in Dorset and enjoyed telling everyone I'd actually flown. Uncle Philip persuaded my mother to let me use the Sabena airline, it was frightfully exciting. Mike, at the insistence of Uncle Jack, had been allowed to go up with my cousin James for ten minutes when Sir Alan Cobham brought his Air Circus to Tarrant Rushton while my mother said her rosary, but I'd never been in an aeroplane before and was sure most of the other young people I knew hadn't either. I intended to boast about the experience on Christmas Day at Lytchett Manor and at all the parties and dances given by friends. I think I was embarking on an over-confident phase of my life: I knew I was pretty, and "You're vain!" and "You"re too sure of yourself" were constant leg-pulls. But I've never had many enemies because I'm not malicious and I don't gossip and I don't mind having the mickey taken. I know, and always have known, my limitations: with me, everything hangs out.

The people I wanted to impress most were the Rhodes Scholars (before the war, Lady Frances Ryder used to arrange for scholars paid out of the Rhodes Scholarship Fund to stay in country houses for Christmas and Uncle Jack and Aunty Maddy always had half a dozen at Lytchett). I flirted with them like mad. They were the first grown-up young men I ever danced with. Family Christmases were terrific. We went to Midnight Mass on Christmas Eve. Then we all went over to Lytchett from Trokes for lunch. After lunch, our Best and Marsden cousins and some of the tenants came to tea and, in between lunch and tea, there was football on the lawn, sometimes thirty a side. Then there'd be this enormous tea in the Great Hall where Dance, the gardener, had marvellously garlanded the chandelier, the bannisters of the gallery, and the huge Christmas tree from which we all received presents. Then at Trokes, in the evening, after dinner for family and friends, we played Murder and Charades. Always Murder and always Charades. Such fun.

In 1936 I went to Munich. My mother wanted, indeed I wanted, my

German to be as proficient as my French, so I went there for three months I went to the "finishing" school of Gräfin Rex – as Munich was then the smart place to go. The Gräfin had a big flat in, I think, the Hapsburgher Strasse and, as she had no money, she took in girls. I went with Tina Douglas Roberts and a friend of hers, Diana Malden. Tina and I were friends already (she was the prospective heiress of Brigton, Douglastown in Angus.) A couple of other girls were being "finished" by the Gräfin, too, and an artist called Michael Brockway – he became rather a boyfriend of mine, actually – was staying in the flat as a lodger. Iris Mountbatten was with a Gräfin elsewhere and everyone from the two establishments got to know each other. We were properly introduced to counts and princes but preferred picking up boyfriends for ourselves.

A Fraülein was employed by Gräfin Rex to teach us German and we went to the usual picture galleries and museums and so on. Opera was what we adored most. Wagner. Gorgeous, gorgeous Wagner. The Munich Opera was the best in the world. Oh, it was unbelievably good. Hitler saw that it was. I mean, Hitler's great thing was the Munich Opera.

The Gräfin owned a chalet in Garmisch Partenkirchen where we were supposed to learn to ski. Apart from being taught awfully badly, I was too tall and had awful skis, so I didn't learn properly till I married Chipps. The chalet had been decorated by a Theosophist. The rooms were different colours – mauve, green, pink, purple, yellow. One night we all thought we saw a ghost which turned out to be the lover of Baby, the Gräfin's daughter. In Munich, Tina and I did see a sort of napkin floating across the bedroom floor. We were so frightened we spent the night in the same bed. We told the Gräfin all about this and she gave us a certain amount of stick for sleeping together, but she soon realised we didn't know what she was talking about.

Munich, of course, was full of Nazi troops and officers. We went to a musical comedy one evening. The star was Willy Fortcht. One scene took place in a Bavarian chalet. The door opened and in came Willy, holding up his hand in the Nazis salute. All the good Nazis in the audience rose to their feet and yelled, "Heil Hitler!" Willy then turned the palm of his hand at the sky and said, *"Ich glaube es wird regnet."* – "I think it's going to rain." In another scene he came on stage as a hotel porter, holding a shoe. Spitting on it after each phrase, he said, *"Ein Reich!"*, spit, *"Ein Land!"*, spit, *"Ein Führer!"*, spit, polished it and then walked off. I gather such satire resulted in the Gestapo eventually arresting him . . . One last story about Munich. Almost every afternoon we seemed to end up at the Carlton Teeraumer where there was always a table with a card on it saying RESERVIERT FÜR DEN FÜHRER. Michael Brockway took this one day and stuck it on my coat as we left and let me walk through the streets, past all the rival S.S. and S.A. (the "brown shirts") Nazi guards, without telling me.

The summer after I returned from Munich, our cousin, Molly Shaw-Stuart who had married lan Forbes of Rothiemay Castle, Bannfshire, persuaded my mother to let me attend the coming-out dance of her step-daughter, Rose, though I wasn't due to come out myself till 1938, the following year. Molly was a Catholic and Ian Forbes had been a Protestant widower of the right ilk, but she converted him and his four children – two boys and two girls – to Catholicism. Rose, the youngest and only a year or so older than me, wanted to be a nun, and eventually became one, but Molly said, "To be sure you don't want to get married, you must do a season first." I went up by overnight train, with a lovely new dress in my suitcase. I was so excited it wasn't true.

Rothiemay Castle is frightfully romantic, with turrets and towers and a moat, and I was given a small bedroom leading to a larger one which had a wardrobe where I could hang my clothes. The larger room opened on to a picture gallery which was locked at the other end. There was no access to it except through my little room which was off a staircase in one of the towers. As the dance was to be the next night, we went to bed fairly early and I read a bit before undressing. I then changed into my nightie and, when I went into the other room to hang up my clothes, I saw a woman in a black dress with a white collar sitting on the bed. Thinking it was a housemaid, I said, "Hello!" Then, seeing her sad expression and realising there was no way a maid could have got there, I took fright and rushed upstairs calling for Rose who let me spend the rest of the night with her and promised to change my room next day. Her father said to me at breakfast, "I hear you saw 'the lady' last night, but you can't have because I've had the house exorcised!". I laughed it off and said I must have been imagining things. But I wasn't imagining things and I learned later of the legend that, if the lady, Mary Queen of Scots, appeared at Rothiemay, there would be no male heir of the present occupant and the castle would pass to another branch of the family. Well, both of Ian Forbes' sons became monks and the castle did pass to another branch of the family. Because I saw "the lady", the legend came true: there was no male heir.

Recently years later, here at Slepe Green, I had a ghost too. My 'friend' lives in the room we use as an office – Jamie's room when he was a little boy. He is my great, great friend and I love him dearly. I've only seen him once – a sort of white foam – but I hear him walk down the stairs and I feel him and I hear him breathing. He looks after me and he protects the house. He loved Jamie – Bruce and the *au pair* never felt him, but Jamie did. He doesn't like Chipps, so Chipps won't stay here on his own without the lights on and the doors locked – he's terrified of anything like that. But our ghost is very, very benign except during alterations. When I was first doing up the kitchen, the painter from Wareham said, "Your house is haunted. I'm not going to work hereafter dark. Something opens the kitchen door and breathes down my neck." You see, this house was the Manor of Slepe cum Cockamore – the garage was the tithe barn – and he must think of himself as its guardian. In days gone by he must have saved the house from being burnt as there are traces of a fire behind the beam behind the old fireplace. He also woke me up once when I was having a zizz and literally made me go downstairs. I found that the *au pair* was in the kitchen and hadn't noticed that the electric fire behind a cushion on which Bruce, who was very small, was lying was switched on. The cushion was just going to catch fire, and I was able to switch it off. I talk to him like I do to Porfirio, my parrot. After my mother died, when Chipps was away and I was alone one night, sitting with my feet up watching television, terribly unhappy and miserable because I adored my mother, I heard him coming downstairs and suddenly I felt a terrific sense of relief. I said to him, "Well, I suppose you're in the same place as Mummy." He's terribly on my side, but he doesn't like being disturbed. I can feel him now. He knows he'll be mentioned in my book. You're going to be in a book, my friend. Yes, You're listening to me, aren't you? You won't mind that, will you? You'll find that rather fun . . .

Anyway, Rosie's coming out dance was glamorous and wonderful, and I was allowed to stay for the subsequent series of Northern Meetings. Men in kilts or white tie and tails. Women with tartan silk sashes over the shoulders of their gorgeous dresses. Waltzes, rhumbas, tangos and, of course, every sort of Scottish dance, night after night till dawn . . . I returned miserably to England, wishing I wasn't still a sub-deb, and immediately succumbed to flu. Then my beloved grandmother, Gaga, came to my rescue yet again. She suggested I go with her for a fortnight to recuperate on the Isle of Wight. We stayed at Bonchurch convent, a finishing school next door to the home of my cousin Mary Weld-Blundell, the former mistress of Lulworth, and her husband Alfred Noyes, the poet, with whom we lunched almost every day.

There was a German girl called Irmgard Ercklentz staying at the convent to learn English. She was terribly nice and she was terribly pretty with green eyes and bright red hair, and she was amusing and intelligent and sexy, and we clicked like crazy. Her mother was dead. Her father, a famous physician, was immensely rich and she lived with him and her brother, Hima, in Breslau, Silesia. We became the greatest friends and promised we would write to one another often, and I swore I would visit her in Breslau soon. Irmchen, my darling Irmchen, a catalyst in my life, was killed in the war. But I did visit her, as you shall hear.

Chapter 4

Debutante

In 1938 1 came out and did the season. It was all the greatest fun, though I thought it frightfully immoral because of my Socialism.

To be a deb you were in *The Times'* list of people giving dances, and all the people giving dances invited the other people giving dances to their dances, unless they thought they were too non-U. My mother picked and chose a bit, but I still went to a dance almost every night for the whole season in London during the week and in country places during the weekend. In London I stayed with Gaga. Before each dance, there would be a dinner party somewhere for us debs plus partners, and your dinner hostess – people like my cousins Cicely Stourton and Baroness Beaumont and Mrs. de Pentheny O'Kelly – would act as your chaperone for the evening, but she generally got rather dozy about two o'clock so, unknown to her, you'd then whizz off to a nightclub such as the Paradise or the Nut House. I was what used to be called an awful cock-teaser, because I was so innocent. As you danced to all the lovely old tunes – not those shrieking things we have now – you'd feel something happening to your partner but you didn't really understand what it meant.

I had a most divine dress which Gaga bought me at Harrod's. Red chiffon. It sort of clung and it had a sort of frill all the way down the front and it was rather *décolleté*. I was always known as "the lady in red". "The fellows are crazy for the lady in red" was my theme song in that dress. It was a huge success. I dressed quite well, actually. Do you know what my dress allowance was? A pound a week! My darling mother gave me a pound a week from when I was fifteen till the day she died! You can't say I'm a kept woman, let's face it!

My mother gave my coming-out dance at Trokes on a Friday in July. June Pleydell-Railstone, the daughter of Aunt Vivian, gave hers at Whatcombe House on the Saturday. My mother was going to have it at Lytchett Manor and then she decided, as her garden was so marvellous, she'd rather have a large marquee at Trokes. The dance was heaven, with a lovely three-piece band.

That was when I met my first real boyfriend, John Sherbrooke, who was a cousin of Aunt Vivian's and staying at Whatcombe as a match for June. We went out in the rose garden and I told his fortune and we fell in love. That night, and the following evening at Whatcombe, we danced cheek to cheek. He was tall, good-looking, and very intelligent. He was learning to be a solicitor in London and his parents lived in Hertfordshire. He'd been in Vienna and he really did the Viennese waltz beautifully. Quite often at debs dances we would dance long after everybody else had stopped to have lemonade or champagne: we'd just go on dancing, round and round and round. He could make me reverse and everything. Our arguments about politics seemed to make us even more in love.

Years later, he told me he had always been frightfully worried about being a virgin. Then, just before the war, he was coming back one night from his office and a darling old tart looked at him and said, "Do you want something?" and he said, "Well, yes. I rather do." And she initiated him. Chipps was still a virgin at twenty in the navy. When he was going in to Crete in those little torpedo boats with supplies for the guerillas, he thought, "How awful to be killed without ever having made love to a girl," so, soon afterwards, he deliberately lost his virginity to a Frenchwoman, a friend of his mother's, when he was on leave in London. They went out to dinner and, when they came back and had a nightcap, she said, "Come and say goodnight to me." She'd put all her sexy undies on the table lamps. He got the message.

Being a deb is jolly hard work. You go to the hairdresser. You go to get clothes. There are cocktail parties, lunches, dinner parties, dances, Ascot, Henley, Wimbledon, Lords . . . John and I went several times to Lords. I knew Lords well. I first started going there when, I was about eight. Grandpa who'd played for the Yorkshire Gentlemen, took me and he'd fall asleep while I watched. I'm very interested in cricket still, though, frankly, I don't think I quite understand the meaning of "silly mid-on" . . .

During all this, I was "presented", by Aunty Mamie – Lady Colfox. Uncle Jack was on duty as a member of the Bodyguard. I had a white dress with a long train and three feathers on my head. I seem to remember I also had a lovely fan. And Harold Hood, a boyfriend, introduced to me by Cicely Stourton, gave me rather a nice sort of vanity thing for my powder and lipstick and cigarettes. You could hang it on your little finger or round your wrist. Aunt Mamie and Mummy and I were driven to the Palace by Uncle Philip's chauffeur and, when we got there, I wasn't quite sure if I could curtsy with Harold's bag on me, so I gave it to Uncle Jack to look after. You were ushered through one room after another until you reached the Throne Room where you did a deep curtsy in front of King George and Queen Elizabeth who smiled at you. I could do my curtsy beautifully, no hassle, because I was a dancer – I can do it still. Other friends had to practise for months. After the presentation I was dying for a cigarette, but I couldn't find Uncle Jack. I finally asked one of the equerries, "Do you know where Sir John Lees is? He's got my bag." With the bag safely returned to me, I went in to the buffet. The lobsters were delicious. Oh yes, a frightfully funny thing. At most of the deb parties, you'd get the same food, provided by Lyons, who also provided the Palace and – we were awfully naughty – we'd make marks on the aspic round the quails and recognise them at the next party, and I do remember recognising one of these marks at Buckingham Palace!

That summer, Aunt Maddy decided she wanted a swimming-pool for the school at Lytchett so she got my seven cousins and Mike and Bumble and me and the Georges and the Mansels and various other Dorset young friends to dig a hole in the old orangery, and the estate workers concreted it in and put in the plumbing and a second-hand pump. It was ready in July, and Prunella Stack was invited to open it. Prunella Stack ran the Women's League of Health and Beauty, started by her mother, and was a friend of Douglo Clydesdale the flier, who later became the Duke of Hamilton. Aunt Maddy, after asking Douglo to fly Prunella down, announced the occasion to the press. They landed at Hurn and, for some reason, I was alone at Post Green, the dower-house, when suddenly this gorgeous girl appeared. I chatted her up and made great friends with her and gradually various members of the family drifted in as well as Douglo and a sort of professor who said, "Lady Lees met me on a bus in Bournemouth and asked me to come to the celebrations." Aunt Maddy and Uncle Jack were nowhere to be found so we agreed we'd better start lunch. We had begun helping ourselves to vegetables, while waiting for Uncle Jack to carve the meat, when the professor said, "I'm awfully glad to see that you're vegetarians. Lady Lees is a wonderful woman." We thought, "Oh my God! What has Aunt Maddy been saying now? We'd better support her," so we didn't cut ourselves any meat and, when the meal was over, the professor announced, "We will now lie down – that is good for the stomach" and he promptly lay on his tummy on the dining-room floor. Giggling like mad, we all did the same and, just at that moment, Dance, the head gardener, passed the window and, thinking twenty people had been poisoned, rushed off to call the doctor! . . . That was my first sight of Prunella Stack. Wearing a heavenly swimsuit, she opened the pool during the afternoon by making a perfect dive. A few months later she married Douglo's younger brother, David, in Glasgow Cathedral.

After the London season, I went to Scotland for the balls and Northern Meetings. The Georges of Organford Manor had a daughter, Anne, who was a deb, so I stayed at their other house in Skye. Then I stayed with Tina

Macmillan Douglas in Angus, then with Di Malden in Aberdeenshire. You take your house party to the public dances. Certain people go and certain people don't. It's snobbish, you see.

The final Meeting was at Inverness where I stayed with the Stuarts. This was literally just before Munich – Chamberlain had flown out to see Hitler. I'll never forget how we'd been dancing our reels and Dukes of Perth and so on and then, after midnight, the men who were in the army or in the reserve left one by one. It was like the Duchess of Richmond's ball before Waterloo. We were dancing sixteensomes with about fourteen women and two men. The only men left were those in tail coats – you know, diplomats, and people at Oxford and that sort of thing. Though I was supposed to be staying for another few days, I asked Elizabeth Mansel to drive me back to Gaga's in London. I then went straight to the House of Commons and sent a green card in for Uncle Philip, who said I could sit in the Ladies' Gallery from where I heard that extraordinary speech of Jimmie Maxton, the Labour M.P. who was afraid of what would happen to London under a German bombing and had no faith whatever in Chamberlain's negotiations. This little man, with his wizened figure and his shock of hair, was a frightfully good speaker, and he was saying, "We will creep into our holes like rats to die!" Rather dramatic.

Chamberlain returned and the false peace began. I went, one evening, to a cabaret starring Tommy Trinder. I remember him waving a piece of paper and saying, "I saw chalked up on the wall 'Chamberlain Has Gotta Go' so I went and brought back this!" It was funny and yet terrible. I mean we were all relieved by Munich but it wasn't right to let down the Sudetenland Czechs.

Chapter 5

Germany and the War Clouds Gather

For quite some time I had wanted to be a writer – for idealistic reasons: to save the workers, to save the world. I would have done that sort of writing for nothing, but now, because I desperately wanted to visit Irmchen Ercklentz in Silesia, I thought it would be rather nice to write for money. Debs don't earn. With the help of Gaga, I'd been O.K. for clothes during the season – she rather undermined Mummy by buying them for me. My pound a week allowance just about covered having my hair done and getting the odd bottle of sherry at seven pounds and six shillings for my boyfriends, and I mended the ladders in my stockings with a thing like a fish-hook . . . Anyway, in 1938, I needed to earn my fare to Silesia and I decided to do so by writing newspaper gossip. I was already politically motivated. Fleet Street wasn't a foot in any door: it wasn't part of my eventual plan to help people. But I liked men and I was having innocent fun and, to get to Germany, I knew I could at least write fun stories about the parties I went to and the people who were at them.

Ivor Lambe had a gossip column called "Lambs Tales" in the *Daily Mirror.* at that time. Though I'd never met him before, I put on my most fetching dress and a hat I made out of an artificial rose and a few wisps of net and I climbed the back stairs of the *Daily Mirror* building in Chancery Lane, asked, "Can I see Ivor Lambe?" I walked into his office, and this darling cuddly bear took one look at this pretty girl in a nice hat and said, "Oooh!" and offered me a cigarette. I said, "Look! I want to earn a lot of money to get to Silesia to stay with a German girlfriend of mine. I'm a deb and I can get you the odd story." I think he fancied me, because he asked me out to lunch and, by the end of lunch, said he'd pay me on space. I said, "O.K., but don't say who wrote the stories and don't pay me till I've made enough to get me to Germany." I made a similar arrangement with Jack Garbutt, the news editor of the *Sunday Express.* He literally picked me up in Fleet Street and, when I told him I was working for Ivor Lambe part-time on space and why, he said, "Well, you'd better work for us, too." Jack was madly in love with me. He even followed me down to Trokes once and my brother decided to chuck him out.

I came rather a cropper with the *Sunday Express.* I'd been invited to the wedding of David Douglas-Hamilton and Prunella Stack, and Jack asked me to do a piece on this and, as well as a photographer, sent a top journalist to help me. The night before the wedding, while David was having his stag party, I had dinner with Prunella and her girlfriends, and she showed us all the presents and, amongst them, was the most gorgeous mink coat from Aunt Nina – "Aunt Nina" was how her future mother-in-law, the duchess, was known to the Lees. Now this mink coat astonished me because Aunt Nina was a great defender of wildlife and terribly anti-vivisection and that sort of thing – she even had sham ermine on her peeress's robes. So I mentioned this in my article and the article hit the front page. There was then, of course, a frightful row because in fact the mink was false. I was called into the editor's office and told that the duchess was suing and that I must ring her lawyers personally. I said, "I wouldn't dream of ringing! I can't let anyone know I wrote the article!" In the end the paper settled out of court and printed an apology. The experience jolly well taught me to check my facts before rushing into print. Rather good training.

By February 1939, I'd earned enough to travel to Germany, just in time for the beginning of *Faschingzeit* when everybody gets drunk and dresses up in fancy clothes and there are dances in the streets and marvellous parties. I went to my mother who no way wanted me to go there at this uncertain period and was frightfully worried about Hitler. I said, "Darling, I know I'm not twenty-one yet, but I want to see Irmchen and I speak fluent German and I've earned my ticket and enough for pocket money as well!" Gaga was super and backed me up and said I must be allowed to spread my wings and my mother, as usual when she recognised a *fait accompli,* caved in and gave permission. She said, "All right, you can go. But promise me that if there's any political problems you'll come straight back. Send me a telegram saying you've got flu and Uncle Jack will come out to fetch you." So with six copies of *Bei mir bist du schön* hidden in my case amongst my undies I left for Dreslau. Irmchen had told me in a letter that *Bei mir bist du schön* was her favourite song and that every self-respecting German of our age would want to hear it, as it had been banned by the Nazis.

I was eighteen and thrilled to be travelling alone across Europe by over-night train. After Berlin some good-looking S.S. officers with black uniforms and a skull and crossbones on their hats boarded the train, and I let one of them flirt with me. He asked all sorts of searching questions. Was it true that many of our Royal Family were of Jewish descent? Was Prince Albert the illegitimate son of a Jew? I didn't know and I didn't much care. I wasn't absolutely crazy about Jews, not having any Jewish blood myself, so the questions didn't really interest me. Of course, Aunt Maddy and many others in England had the World Conundrum theory that Jews were out to dominate the world. She said that Goebbels was a Jew and Hitler was probably part Jewish. She had even started a movement called "The Peace Aim" saying we mustn't fight Hitler – or Italy or Russia – and that we must all be friends and refuse to be manipulated by a Jewish international mafia which was trying to make us fight as part of its campaign to take eventual world control. She believed that the only way to beat the "Conundrum" was through peace and prayer, and lots of people helped her to distribute free pamphlets setting out these views.

Needless to say, when war broke out, MI5 got very interested and we thought she'd be had up under Section 18 (b) and put away in the Isle of Man. But they came to interview her and saw that she was a completely innocent Christian, in no way connected with Admiral Barry Dunville's "The Link", or Moseley, or any other pro-Fascist organisations. It was said, however, though never proved, that George Pitt Rivers, who was very pro-Hitler and lived at Hinton, near Salisbury, had planned to be Gauleiter of Dorset after a German landing at Studland, so he was put away.

Irmchen and her father and her brother, Hima, met me at Breslau and drove me to their luxurious flat at 115, Hohenzollern Strasse.

"Unpack and have a quick rest!" said Irmchen. "We're going out tonight for *Fasching*."

Two princelings picked us up at seven o'clock. One was dressed all over with ears of corn and poppies and grass seeds. He was an officer in the 8th Cavalry Regiment and I never knew him as anything but *Der Frühling* (which means Spring). The other, who was introduced to me as *Hoheit* – "Highness" – turned out be be Prince Hima of Schleswig Holstein. With them and a boy called Peter, a member of the Hitler *Jugend,* I danced all through every night of Carnival fortnight, and, by day, we'd often ride horses over the Silesian countryside. Banned or no, *Bei mir bist du schöln* became our signature tune at one of the smart nightclubs and we were always greeted with the music on arrival. Peter took me once to his camp and taught me how to shoot with a revolver at a passing cardboard figure. Most of the young people I met were great admirers of Hitler, and I must admit I was a bit pro him myself when I saw the marvellous houses going up everywhere in place of slums. Everybody seemed prosperous. O.K., Hitler said, "Guns before butter" but there was lots of butter around, and you could get substitutes for whipped cream.

During the whole of my visit, one of the few people I met who expressed doubts to me, a foreigner, about Nazi-ism, was Irmchen's elder brother, a doctor, another Peter, and that was in the privacy of his home when he had Irmchen and myself and his brother Hima, who had by now fallen in love with me, to dinner and bridge one evening. Our fourth was a fellow doctor called Rudi and, a few days later, I saw Peter in the street and said, "How is Rudi?" Peter looked around both ways and whispered, "I'm afraid he's gone to Dachau. He is, as you probably realised, a Jew." I hadn't realised anything of the kind and I didn't know what "going to Dachau" meant. When I brought the subject up at dinner somewhere, I was cut short with, it's a *Konzentrationlager* and what about it? You had them in South Africa!"

A few months later, I was in a nightclub with Irmchen and her brother, Hima, and Peter, our Hitler *Jugend* friend; when a young man in the cubicle next to ours suddenly produced a revolver and shot himself. The Gestapo were called and the place surrounded, but Peter produced his Hitler *Jugend* card and managed to get us out by a back door. I was trembling and couldn't stop crying. Though Peter said he must have done it because of an unhappy love affair, I suspected it was because he was a Jew. I was beginning to have real doubts about the glorious Nazi revolution. I became aware of *Juden* notices and of a definite anti-Jew campaign.

After *Fasching*, I continued to go to dances and to parties, of course, but I also went skiing and did a certain amount of painting – paintings of my own and as pupil assistant to Paul Mayer-Speir, Irmchen's brother-in-law, who was restoring the dome of a baroque church with the most gorgeous *trompe l'oeil.* Hima took me skiing in the Riesen Gebirge Mountains where we stayed at the Peterbaude Hotel. I skied with Hima down to Spindemuhle in the Sudetenland where we explored the machine-gun emplacements preserved by the Nazis after Munich to prove what lengths the stubborn Czechs had gone to in their abortive attempt to withstand the Greater Reich. Nailed to a shed was an anti-British poster with a very realistic picture of Indians being shot out of the mouths of canons. Underneath was a long description of the atrocities of Clive of India, followed by excerpts from British newspapers deploring Nazi treatment of the Jews. In thick black letters were the words: *solche beispiel britisher friedenspolotik und sie wollen uns morale prechen* – such an example of British peace politics and they want to preach morals to us. On another outing I was rescued from a snowdrift by Conrad Henlein, Hitler's Gauleiter of the Sudetenland. We flirted rather and, at the hotel afterwards, I gave him one of my watercolours of the Schneekoppe.

On the Ides of March there was to be a dance at Oels Castle, the home of Wilhelm, "little Willy", the Kaiser's son. The Ercklentzes were taking me there after a large dinner party to which they'd invited various Princes and Princesses and Archdukes and King Boris of Bulgaria, a former patient of

Irmchen's father. Irmchen, who ran the flat, ran everything, asked me how many quarterings I had so she'd know where to seat me at table. Well that, to me, was a joke. We never bother about that sort of thing in England, not even in the diplomatic world, unless it's a royal function. But I rang up my mother who told me my quarterings on the Weld and Radcliffe side numbered sixteen. She was still terribly worried, though, about the war situation and said I must forget about the dinner party and forget about the dance and come home immediately. I told her I'd no intention of missing either the dinner party or the dance, and I rang off. Two hours later I received a telegram from Uncle Jack, saying, "Return at once." Not even Uncle Jack, though, could frighten me, given the prospect of exquisite German men, including Hima, dancing me off my feet till dawn.

I didn't think I was in any danger and I was dead right, because I went to see the Consul in Breslau who said, "There's no need to worry. There are very few English in Silesia. Only you, a few governesses, three students at the university and my secretaries and me. If there's an emergency, my aeroplane's big enough to take us all out." So I rang up Jack Garbutt of the *Sunday Express* and told him to get in touch with my mother and say the Consul was looking after me. I didn't dare to dictate any stories to him. I didn't want to be interned as a spy. After all, I was really just a deb, staying with Irmchen and having a wonderful time . . .

Anyway, to this terrific dance I went – candles everywhere, Ribbentrop champagne. And, exactly as at the dance at Inverness at the time of Munich, I noticed that, by midnight, the men who'd asked me to dance three dances were telling me they'd got to go. They were, of course, driving in their Mercedes to the frontier as part of Hitler's final assault on the Czechs.

I'd become infatuated with Irmchen's brother, Hima. Actually, John Sherbrooke and Hima were rather similar – they were both tall and handsome; they were both blue-eyed and fair; and they both had S.A., which is what we called sex appeal. My millions of fiancés were always tall and handsome. I couldn't ever contemplate small men except to like as friends.

Anyway, Hima had a girlfriend in Prague called Bianca who was Jewish and had an eleven year old daughter, so I agreed to hitch-hike down with him to see if they were all right. Many of the streets of Prague were full of troops or lines of departing refugees, but some were surprisingly empty. With our German and British passports we felt quite safe although they hadn't been stamped at the frontier which officially didn't now exist. The main door of the block of flats where Bianca lived was locked and, although we rang and knocked for half an hour, there seemed to be no one around. Hima said, "Let's have dinner somewhere and then we'll ring her up. Perhaps she is frightened or perhaps she has gone away." We went to a restaurant. The French and English parts of the menu, including *rosbif,* had been crossed out and substituted with Czechoslovakian, which brought home to both of us what the Czechs must think of Deladier and Chamberlain.

After dinner, we rang Bianca and she answered in a whisper. She was waiting for us at the main door and led us up to her flat – her daughter was already sleeping. She gave us coffee and liqueurs. Then Hima said, "If Dodo lent you her passport, could you get it back to her?" She said, "I will find out. We have a Jewish organisation here. I will let you know soon." Hima and I stayed at her flat for about a week. We wandered through Prague and out into the surrounding countryside. After a few days, Bianca said, "I will take your passport tonight. God willing, you will get it back within three days."

She packed, and left during the night with her child. Four days later, at breakfast-time, the telephone rang. A voice told Hima to come downstairs. He went down and returned with my passport. I heard later that Bianca had boarded a train with her daughter and, when they came to the Austrian frontier, she had taken her along the corridor and into a lavatory. She then put on dark glasses and hid the child under her skirts. When the Customs banged on the door, she opened it and held out my passport. She had long hair in a bun and, as mine was shoulder-length, she had let it down and taken it up in a page-boy bob. Seeing a British passport, the officials just looked at it cursorily, stamped it and didn't bother her any more.

Hima and I then bummed our way to Bulgaria, intending to stay with King Boris. In fact we stayed instead with an extraordinary old Bulgarian princess – terribly grand in a huge *château* with lots of servants. I had an entire suite of enormous great rooms all to myself! The *château* was frightfully cold and yet the princess and her servants ponged. When, the first night, I asked for a bath, the maid went and ran one. And when, the next morning, I asked for a bath, the maid went and ran one. Ditto that night and the next morning. The third night, she looked at me in horror and said, "Do you underland, Fraulein, that every time you ask for a bath we have to cut down a tree?

Back in Breslau, I found a pile of frantic letters and telegrams from my mother and Uncle Jack. Also a letter from Jack Garbutt, asking me to reverse charges and give him stories. I showed this to Hima. He said, "If you are thinking of marrying me, you'd better not!" I was vaguely thinking of marrying him, though he was ten years older, so Jack Garbutt still didn't get his stories.

My return fare to England was booked from April 19 via Berlin and Brussels where I wanted to stay again with the Renkins. It was so sad, saying goodbye to Irmchen. She was a darling and I loved her dearly and we were great friends and we'd had such fun together. During the war she was in the Red Cross and she managed to get letters to me through the Bulgarian diplomatic bag until, at the end of the war, the Russians walked in to Silesia and blew up her ambulance by mistake.

Hima came with me to Berlin and stayed not at my hotel but with a friend. That evening there was a queer blood-red sign in the sky like an evil omen. We arranged to meet the next day – April 20, my birthday and Hitler's. We went down to the *Unter den Linden* and waited for the fly-past, the speeches and the parade. The crowd was absolutely massive. It was disciplined and without humour, not like the jolly English crowds I knew in England that cracked jokes and dropped orange peel while waiting, say, for the Coronation procession.

Hitler appeared on his podium with Goering, Goebbels and his other henchmen. When he stood up to speak, everyone went "Heil!" There was something almost religious about their adoration. Their cheers were deafening. For four and a half hours, guns and tanks and cavalry and infantry moved past that still figure with its outstretched arm. They would have gone through fire and water and hell for the man. Somehow I realised that England *would* go to war with Germany and I didn't want to believe it because all my German friends were so pro-English and we loved each other so much.

As it happened, we met Heinrich Hohenzollern, a descendant of the Kaiser's. He asked if we'd like to go to the official reception afterwards. *"Natch,"* we said, "Love to." So he took us along. We went through hundreds of people in an enormous hall to a smaller room behind for chosen guests. Suddenly Conrad Henlein, who'd rescued me from the snowdrift in the Riesen Gebirge Mountains said, "Would you like to meet the Fuhrer?" I said, "Yes, I would because it's my birthday too." "In that case, he'd love to meet you because he believes in the stars and also he liked your painting."

After wishing one another Happy Birthday, Hitler and I talked together for about a quarter of an hour. He was small with strange eyes – all the men of power I've ever known, Dom Mintoff included, have had strange eyes – but he didn't look frightening. I told him I was nineteen that day and a deb. He asked what I thought of Germany. I said his slum clearance programme had impressed me. When he said he knew I painted, I thought, "Yes. Badly like you," but I only said, *"Ein Bischen."* He then asked me if I liked music. I told him I liked Beethoven and was simply mad about Wagner. "When I was fifteen," I said, "my grandmother gave me a book of Wagner Operas with all their stories beautifully illustrated. And when I was in Munich I went to hear

Wagner at . . .' He cut me short. "I prefer Mozart," he said. Well, I bet nobody else knows *that!* Hitler was always supposed to be mad about Wagner. But that's what Hitler said to me, his birthday mate! Then we sort of drifted. I mean, with important people at a party, you realise the talk is at an end and you turn to someone else. His parting words were, "If you were born on the 20th of April, you should be a good orator!" Coming from the lips of the Fuhrer himself, I often remembered this remark when, in later years, I lectured in the United States and stood for Parliament.

Next day, Hima travelled with me as far as Cologne where we had lunch together and went to see the cathedral. He said, "Stay! Don't go back! Marry me!" and gave me his signet ring. I was tempted to return with him to Silesia but I merely put the ring on my engagement finger, made sincere but immature promises and continued on to Brussels alone. I'm afraid I was to get engaged very often in those days without quite meaning it.

Jean and Marie Renkin and Nanette and all the family pumped me about Germany and were absolutely horrified that I'd spoken to Hitler. When I told their son Paul, who was very political, all about my German friends and the fun I'd had, I thought he'd murder me. He said, "Dodo, how can you say anything nice about those brutes?" French speaking Belgians were anti-Nazi almost to a man. They thought they'd be next after Czechoslovakia.

My cousin Raymond Snoy – the one whose shooting parties I went on in 1937 – was General of the Artillery in the Belgian Army. His English wife, Enid, had fled back to England to find a house for herself and their children because Raymond was so sure there'd be a war and, as I was his cousin by marriage, he asked me to act as hostess at several of his official receptions. I soon became aware what a very divided country Belgium was. Some of the Flemish were pro-German, you see. Indeed, I have a theory that King Leopold was, too, because his girlfriend, Madame de Rethy, was Flemish and, when the Germans invaded Belgium in 1940, her father had a very convenient car accident and failed to get the right message to the right place at the right time. My Uncle Alan – Sir Alan Brooke, later Lord Alanbrooke – was the second husband of Aunt Ben (Benita), the widow of my Uncle Tom, and he attended a briefing with King Leopold and the Belgian generals. Unbeknownst to them, he understood every word of their quick colloquial French – he was bilingual, having been brought up in Pau. So, realising their intention was to undermine General Gort's plan to make a stand, he withdrew his troops. Thus they got out at Dunkirk . . . The Blitzkreig of 1940 and the evacuation from Dunkirk are history, but that's the reason they happened as I understand it! . . .

In May 1939 I returned to England where my second season as a deb was more fun than ever. I had another dance at Trokes and June Pleydell-Railston had another dance at Whatcombe. Waltzing again with John Sherbrooke, who had joined the Territorials, rather watered down my passion for Hima; though, wearing his signet ring around my neck as a keepsake, I could imagine I was still in Silesia if I closed my eyes. To this day, one dance in London remains vividly in my mind. It was at the Mayfair and was given for Val Cole. Her father spared no expense – I believe he made his fortune selling radio-sets. There were wigged footmen, three bands, unlimited champagne and wild strawberries flown specially from France. Leaving with John afterwards, I saw some men and women, huddled together on the pavement. They were shabbily dressed and there was hunger in their eyes. I realised that the price of two strawberries would have meant a meal for them, and that the cost of a bottle of champagne would have bought them a pair of shoes. When I said this to John, he replied, "Dodo, it's not as simple as that." I knew he was right, but I felt so ashamed.

In August, Hima rang me at Trokes to say he was coming over. My mother was terribly anti-German and, rather than be in the same house, went to stay with Aunty Mamie Colfox, leaving us in the charge of Maggie, our old cook, who chaperoned us like a lynx. Again, Hima asked me to marry him. He said, "There's bound to be a war. I'll leave Germany. I'll become English. I don't intend to fight for Hitler." I said, "Hima, I simply *can't* marry you. I'm no longer in love," and I gave him back his ring. He asked me to keep his English currency till the war was over, and returned to Silesia. I never saw him again. He was killed during the bombing of Hamburg in 1943.

I was already helping Aunt Maddy to scrub and furnish stables and cottages on "Lees Land" to provide accommodation for about thirty children evacuated from London. Some were only babies in their mothers' arms. Most came without any parent at all. They were sweet, but not very house-trained at first. Many, in fact, fell in love with the countryside and, when they grew up, decided to work on the land.

On Saturday, September 2nd, the Stringers gave a dance at their home over near Wimborne for their son Brian and my cousin Kath, his fiancée. The night was hot. The sky was alive with summer lightning.

John said, "It must be ack-ack," and we all laughed. War was in the balance – we'd given Germany an ultimatum. I couldn't bear the thought of fighting against Hima and Irmchen: I kept saying loudly, "There *isn't* going to be a war! There *isn't* going to be a war!" But, in church next morning in Wimborne, the priest announced from the pulpit that war had been declared, and, strangely, just when his announcement ended, an air-raid siren blew.

Part 3

Wartime England

Chapter 6

THE WAR – ENGLAND

I tried to get into the F.A.N.Y.s. I was too late. I tried to get into the A.T.S. I was too late. I tried to get into the W.A.A.F. to be a parachutist. I was too late. I tried to get into the W.R.N.S. I hadn't the qualifications. My mother said, "Couldn't you be a Land Girl like your Cousin Kath, or work in a factory or join the Red Cross?" I said, "I think I'm too squeamish to be Red Cross, but I'll try it. Perhaps I can drive for them or something" – I'd been taught how to drive by Air Marshal Bonham-Carter who had lost a leg in the First World War. So I went and did my Red Cross training in Poole with the idea that after I'd passed the exam and done the necessary two weeks practical nursing in a hospital, I'd drive or pack parcels or go into administration. Well, I did my two weeks in the Cornelia Hospital and, from the first moment, I adored it! I wasn't a bit squeamish, and it pleased me to know that, though I was in the war, I was saving lives instead of killing – I'm very pacifist at heart.

I was now a mobile V.A.D., you know, the Voluntary Aid Detachment, called the "Virgins are Desperate" by our boyfriends. If you were "Mobile", you could be moved all over England to nurse in military hospitals. The other sort generally nursed in a civilian hospital. My cousin, Mona Beaumont, had turned Carlton Towers into a convalescent home for the military and I wanted to join her troop but, because it was the Phoney War and she didn't yet have any inmates, she didn't have a job for me. So I decided to stay in the Cornelia. Sister Thomas of the surgical ward thought I was more likely to be a good nurse than the average V.A.D. who mostly did rather menial tasks like taking round the coffee and dealing with the bedpans, so she taught me how to do dressings, how to give injections, how to assist in the theatre. I really was nursing as opposed to being just a hospital orderly. I learned an awful lot, and the surgical side interested me enormously. I also liked the smart navy blue uniform and the fact that, because I was usually on day duty, I could go out at night to parties.

Masses of amusing people were arriving on the scene. The Grenadiers came down, as well as various Gunner regiments and the 10th Hussars and the 60th Rifles and the Rifle Brigade. It was the greatest fun – just as gay as the season, actually. We danced most nights at the Branksome Towers or the

Royal Bath, or dined at the Norfolk. John Sherbrooke was away in France and I had a new boyfriend called Ian Farquhar who was in the Grenadiers. I met him at a party given by my cousins, the de Pentheny O'Kellys, at Uddens. He used to come round to Trokes in his tank and station it in the field and tap our telephone and say, "Hello! I'm in the field. I've come for a glass of sherry." I'd look out of my window, and there was this tank. Later I had another terrific boyfriend called Bill, in the S.O.E., you know, Special Operations Executive, who I met at Blandford Camp. My mother knew the Colonel there and I was introduced to this divine Bill – I can't remember his surname. He was frightfully tall and good-looking, Irish actually, in one of those funny Scottish Border regiments that wear trews. He was one of those who risked their necks in the raid on Lofoten where the Germans were making heavy water.

The first winter of the war, my mother got up a Concert Party, roping in Aunt Vivien, – Mrs. Pleydell-Railston – to help her. In one of the many houses on her estate, Aunt Vivien had somebody staying called Yootha Phillips. Yootha had been an actress and a dancer and she was very good at arranging choreography and teaching people how to dance. We also had a very good girl, Betty Comyns, to sing for us. She'd a marvellous voice and was known as the Pocket Battleship because she was so tiny and full of fire. There was rather a shortage of boys, but we had two masters from Canford School near Wimborne. Both could act and one of then wrote a lot of our sketches. I wrote a lot of them, too. For instance, there was one where I played the part of a wife who, still in her dressing-gown at breakfast, has a blazing row with her husband before he leaves for the office – he wanted eggs and bacon for breakfast instead of cornflakes despite the rationing. A short time later the husband returns full of remorse to beg his wife's forgiveness. She is sitting reading the newspaper with her back to the door, and he walks quietly up to her and runs his hands over her and kisses her passionately on the mouth. With her eyes closed in ecstasy, she says, "Only one pint today, thank you, milkman!" This always brought the house down as the part being easy to learn was usually played by the Commanding Officer. The 10th Hussars were based at Gaunts House, Wimborne, and I remember a randy Major doing it with me and, of course, when he crept in and put his hands over my eyes and gave me this terrific kiss, there were yells and shouts from all his soldiers: "Go on Major! Go on! Give her another!"

My mother played solos on her violin. I did a Spanish dance. And so on. With an interval, the show lasted about an hour and a half. It was very professional and my mother rehearsed it in the drawing-room at Trokes. We went all over the South – to lots of Air Force places, to the Gunners in a marvellous fortress near Portsmouth, to H.M.S. *Daedalus* at Lee-on-Solent, to Bovington, Lulworth, all the camps round here . . . Everywhere.

The extraordinary thing is that, once or twice, I played the Milkman Sketch with Chipps Selby Bennett, my future husband – although he was then only a rather precocious thirteen.

Chipps' real name is Harry, the first name of Andy Bennett, his mother's second husband, but, during his childhood, a Basque cook always called him Chippo, a Basque endearment, and this eventually became Chipps – Selby is a name that has been passed down on his mother's side, the Ormand side, for generations . . . Anyway, at the start of 1939, Chipps' mother, Kitty, was living with her third husband, Geoff Pittar a former Secretary of I.C.I., in Dorrea, her father's lovely old house in Saint-Jean-de-Luz, a coastal watering town in the South of France on the Spanish border. Dorrea had been in the family for twenty-five years but, guessing that France would be overrun, they decided to buy somewhere in England, especially as Geoff was only just beginning to recover from TB And the doctors said that, though he couldn't go into the army; farming – "growing for victory" – would do him good. So Geoff bought Slepe House and the two hundred acres and the cottages and things all around, including Slepe Green, my present house, which was then used as a farm worker's cottage.

That summer, I had met Chipps at Beacon – where the lovely pools and the gypsies were. I was nineteen and he was thirteen and just about to go to Marlborough. My cousin Tom and I were up at Beacon for a swim one day and we saw these strangers, a man and woman and this boy, on what was really Lees' property. Tom said, "Oh God! I wanted to bathe in the nude today. But, I know what I'll do, Dodo, I *will* bathe in the nude and perhaps they'll go away!" So in he plunged and the Pittars didn't mind a bit, in fact they thought it a huge joke. Then my mother met Kitty at Lady Drax's and liked her very much and made friends with her and took her under her wing and introduced her to everybody. She even invited Geoff to start the local ARP (Air Raid Precautions) with her. In fact, my mother rather launched the Pittar's. In those days being a divorcee was still frowned on, so such a person as Kitty, three times married, would have found it hard to get to know people. But the fact that my mother, who was Catholic and very anti that sort of thing, introduced her to everybody led to people saying that she must be O.K.

During his Christmas holidays from Marlborough, where he was now beginning to swot for his Navy Exam, I met Chipps again, because my mother needed men for the Concert Party and he was always coming to Trokes to rehearse. He was terribly good-looking but I thought he was too hairy and *far* too precocious, *far* too sexy: I wasn't yet interested in anybody sexy who was younger than me. This schoolboy didn't turn me on at all. No way.

Lytchett Manor had been taken over by the army (anti-aircraft) – Aunty Maddy and everyone had moved to Post Green – and they gave hops occasionally for the officers and nearby people. I remember Chipps asking me at one of these hops to dance a waltz. I said, "Chipps, *can* you waltz?" He was frightfully upset. He said, "Of course I can. We started but, half way round the room, being used to dancing with John Sherbrooke who really could dance, I said, "Let's go and sit it out."

I didn't see Chipps again till 1950 when he was twenty-four, six foot four and a Lieutenant on leave from the Navy. By then I considered him very attractive and we started a romance and married three years later . . .

I went on duty at the Cornelia at nine in the morning and came off at six, five days a week. My mother lent me the Lancaster but, nine cases out of ten, I hitched a lift from Mr. Stacey who owned the Upton Garage and now owns the Upton Oil Company. As a nurse I got special petrol coupons, so I was able to save them for going to parties.

I must tell you rather an extraordinary story about Geoff Pittar, my future step-father-in-law. When he was in command of the Lytchett Minster platoon of the Home Guard he arranged for an exercise, a sort of manoeuvre between Lytchett Minister and Lytchett Matravers. Unfortunately live instead of sham ammunition was put into their shotguns, and Dance – you knows the gardener at Lytchett Manor who taught me all about bees and was a great, great friend – Dance was a sergeant for Lytchett Minister and he was peppered, wounded quite badly. Well, Lytchett Matravers and Lytchett Minister were rivals, loathed each other like poison, and everybody said, "This is going to be simply terrible. Lytchett Minister will think this was done on purpose," whereas it was only because poor Geoff Pittar muddled up the cartridges. Anyway, darling old Dance was brought to the Cornelia and ushered into the surgical ward; Sister, Thomas said, "Come over here, Nurse Lees, and treat this patient. He's been wounded." I rushed over and I saw Dance. He opened his eyes and said, "Oh Miss Dodo! Thank goodness you've come to look after me!" and, in the days that followed, I nursed him back to health.

But in May/June 1940 came Dunkirk, and our hospital soon filled up. I was going off duty one evening when a casualty arrived – the captain of a Dutch ship sunk by the Germans coming in to Poole Harbour. He was in a very bad way, dying practically, and one of his legs had to be amputated because of gas gangrene – he'd been in the water for some time. Sister Thomas asked me to stay, so I phoned Maggie, the cook, to tell her I'd be late home. The captain was taken to the theatre and, after the surgeon had operated, his heart stopped. The surgeon said to me, "Nurse, go and get the Adrenalin. I'll inject into his heart." I said, "It will take a few minutes because it's in the outside cupboard, sir." "It doesn't matter," he said. "I think it's too late anyway. But we'll try." So I rushed out and got it, gave it to him, and he injected into the heart and the man recovered. In those days we didn't have "intensive care". There was just one surgical ward with a fish-kettle in which we boiled the instruments for twenty minutes, and I don't remember a single case of cross-infection.

Anyway, I was assigned to look after this captain who could only speak Dutch and a little German and could not speak a word of English. Actually, he couldn't speak for ages because he was in a coma but, when he came to, I started talking to him in German. One day I said to him, "Can you remember anything about your accident?" He said, "Except for the dive-bomber coming over, all I can remember is seeing myself on a table and your voice saying, 'It will take a few minutes because it's in the outside cupboard sir,' and another voice saying, 'It doesn't matter. I think it's too late anyway. But we'll try.'" Now how did he understand what was said if he didn't speak English? I asked him to describe the sensation of looking down at his own body. He said that he felt very happy – *sehr glüklich* – and he could hear lovely music; he didn't want to go back into his body but he felt it was his duty to do so as there were certain things he still had to do in this life.

I wrote the story up for a local newspaper and had a lot of letters back, one or two from doctors. The experience, apparently, was not uncommon, but this case was different in that the captain could understand a language he didn't know. He got better and ran off with one of the night nurses and I believe went to the Bahamas. His name was Captain Posthumous.

The phone rang one evening when I got back to Trokes. It was Paul Renkin, Nanette's brother who had volunteered for the army as soon as Belgium was invaded. He said, "I've just landed in England. I was evacuated at Dunkirk." I said, "You must come to stay at once." So he stayed with us until his regiment was re-established and he could join the Belgian Paratroops – he was killed in the Ardennes in 1944. The night he arrived at Trokes, he came to see our Concert Party perform in Blandford. Before the show he came to my dressing-room just as I was putting on my dress, mantilla, comb and castanets in preparation for my Spanish dance. He said, "Dodo, you don't look well!" and I must say I did feel very hot. Afterwards, as we were having a drink in tha Crown Hotel, he said, "You know, Dodo, you've got measles!" And it was absolutely true. I was covered with spots! Ian Farquhar rang me up the next day from his tank and said he was taking me out to dinner, but, instead of taking me out to dinner he came and sat on the end of my bed with Paul, commiserating. Luckily they'd both had measles. I never had any of the childish diseases when young, probably because I never really went to school.

Aunt Ben, Lady Alanbrooke had a lovely story about Uncle Alan, then only a Lieutenant General, after Dunkirk. He was absolutely whacked, as you can imagine, when he got back to their home at Hartley Witney, as he hadn't slept for nights, and was going up to London to see Churchill in a few hours. Their son was practising the piano with his nanny, and Aunt Ben said to her, "Do you think that he could do without his lesson today? The General is so tired and must have some sleep." "Certainly not, my Lady!" said the nanny. "The child's routine can't be interrupted!" So poor Uncle Alan, unable to sleep, came down to help Aunt Ben with her bees and, forgetting to put his bee things on, was frightfully badly stung. Churchill took one look at his swollen face and hands when he arrived for their meeting and said, "Good heavens! Are they using poison gas as well?"

Next, of course, was the Battle of Britain, partly fought out in front of our eyes over the Isle of Purbeck. At week-ends Maggie used to give us lunch on the lawn and we'd watch the dog-fights. It all had a kind of sick fascination. It was a matter of Goodies and Baddies. How we cheered when the Baddies lost and a German plane plummeted! Yet, in my heart, I was horrified to think that this was the death, perhaps, of one of my boyfriends from Munich or Breslau.

Michael Lees* , my brother, was in the Dorset Yeomanry as Daddy had been, and he was getting frightfully bored with staying put in Dover while everybody else was going abroad, so he became a parachutist. Then, after service in the Middle East and Egypt, he volunteered for the S.O.E. and was parachuted in to Yugoslavia where he blew up trains with the Chetniks for Mihailovich in German occupied territory. Later, he was dropped into Piedmont in Northern Italy from where he managed to get some of the Italian Resistance over the mountains to Nice. His last assignment was to shoot Kesselring in Reggio Emilia. The idea was that he'd dress up in a Don Camillo type soutane, shoot Kesselring when he came to Mass, run through the aisle and out to where there'd be a horse waiting to get him up into the mountains. Unfortunately, Kesselring had been replaced by a General who didn't go to Mass, so Mike had to go in with the Partigiani and raid his H.Q. and, unfortunately, the General badly wounded him! He still has trouble with one leg.

Mike and I were great friends when younger, though we have had rows since. He's married with two children. He married Gwen in Bari before being dropped into Northern Italy – she was a F.A.N.Y. there. After the war he

---

* Died 1992

went into business. Actually, Mummy gave him Trokes that's when Mummy went to live in Shepherd's Cottage, the pretty Domesday thatched cottage belonging to Aunt Vivien. But he then sold it to our sister Bumble's mother-in-law, "Atty" (Jean) Curtis, the wife of General "Squeaker" Curtis, and he and Gwen now live in Courtmacsherry, Co. Cork, where they grow the best strawberries in Ireland and let out Holiday Homes on the estate for shark fishing. Everything they touch turns to gold. They've a little house in Milton Abbas, here in Dorset, where they spend the winter. They have lots of friends and relations in Dorset and Mike, though he shoots his snipe in Ireland, likes to shoot pheasant over here.

In 1941 my mother moved up to London and shared the Maxwell Stuarts' flat in Westbourne Terrace where she looked after Bumble who was working for Jay Llewellyn (Lord Llewellyn) in the Air Ministry. She also arranged for the evacuation of Grandpa and Gaga who, after leaving Duke Street, had settled down in 12, Claridge's House, next door to Claridge's – they'd always preferred to live in Mayfair as they could go to morning Mass at Farm Street. My mother now got them into a boarding house in Lyme Regis. Grandpa, actually, died there soon afterwards, aged eighty, cutting down a tree for the local priest, and Gaga died in 1944 after Mummy moved her back to London to a convent. Darling Gaga was divine. Completely white-haired and dressed in black, she didn't smoke and she practically didn't drink, except masses of coffee, but she adored all my boyfriends and my boyfriends all adored her. Her attitude when I was a deb was, "Why shouldn't she have fun?" Mummy didn't know I went to nightclubs but she did. I'd once got back to Duke Street from a dance in Lichfield. It was late morning, and all she said was, "Goodness! That nightclub must have lasted a long time!"

The next night I went to a big party somewhere with Pat Britten, a friend in the Grenadiers. Someone I'd never met before chatted me up and said, "Have a cigarette." I said "Oh, thank you so much. I'd love one." and passed out. Pat took me back to Gagas where I was put to bed and didn't wake up for two days. Whatever drug it was in that cigarette, it didn't give me a trip: it knocked me out. it completely put me off drugs for life, though we were given Benzedrine in the French Army when we had to keep awake for nights on end and, after marrying Chipps, I used to take some with me when I was following the fleet around the world.

My children have never been interested in drugs either. Jamie, when he was fifteen, went to a barbecue at Ramla in Gozo – Ramla is an enormous, gorgeous, red sandy beach, the biggest in the Maltese Islands. He said to me next day, "Mummy, you can't imagine what it was like. There were all those bodies on lilos on the sand having fixes and copulating." Drugs, then, were rife in Malta. One of the things I did there was help Dom Mintoff to get rid of the pushers. After 1971, we refused to allow yachts into any of the harbours unless they'd been through Valletta and the Customs first. Till then drugs were coming in to Dwejra, in Gozo, for instance, and left in a cave for picking up by another boat which took them to Marseilles for processing . . .

At the start of the war, my sister, Bumble was Jay Llewellyn's PA. Jay who was a Minister and producing Spitfires and things in the Ministry of Aircraft Production under Beaverbrook, was a friend of ours being the then owner of Upton House – you know, the former home of my great grandmother, Katty Doughty Tichborne. Then she went into the W.R.N.S., ending up as an officer, a torpedo attack instructor for destroyers. After the war she was Sir Fitzroy Maclean's PA on his mission to screen for war crimes the displaced persons, including Chetniks, held in Italy. Well this is all rather funny really, because during the war my brother Mike was parachuted in to Mihailovich and Fitzroy was parachuted in to Tito. And I was Socialist and Fitzroy was Conservative, and I was to stand against him as M.P. for Lancaster. Not only that, Fitzroy married a distant cousin of mine, Veronica Fraser, a deb who came out with me and whom I knew very well indeed.

Chapter 7

WARTIME LONDON

Early in 1942 I moved to my mother's flat in Westbourne Terrace in London because I'd decided to become a proper nurse and do the necessary training in London. My mother had allowed my first cousin Alice Dilke, née Best, who was expecting a baby, to stay at Trokes for nothing, provided she, with Maggie the cook, looked after me. The matron of the Cornelia gave me a good chit so I went to St Thomas's and asked if I could join. But I failed the interview there, and instead went to Bart's who took me on at their Preliminary Training School near Harrow where I did a crash course lasting six weeks.

This was all very different from the happy-go-lucky atmosphere of the Cornelia. The sisters were tyrants and we had to wear an extremely unbecoming uniform with uncomfortable thick starched collars and caps at absolutely the right angle with no hair showing. No late nights with boyfriends or anything: it was nose to the grindstone. But I was fascinated by the medical side, and we even learned about plumbing and sewage which I found very useful in after years when I had to cope with Dom Mintoff's sewage problems in Malta. Part of the course involved helping a midwife deliver babies born at the drop of a hat and at a minute's notice any time of the day or night in the East End. We always took a large piece of carbolic soap to catch the bugs which were on the walls, in the bedding, everywhere. We delivered on newspaper – usually the *News of the World.* Newspaper is fairly sterile.

I passed the Prelim but, as I'd found the discipline a bit much – I was quite unused to it – and as I didn't want to wait another two and a half years to do my Final – who knows, the war might be over by then – I thought it best to go back into the Mobile V.A.D. So I wrote to Mona Beaumont, my cousin Baroness Beaumont, the mother of the present Duke of Norfolk. She said, "Why not work for me here at Carlton or somewhere else up North." Well, I naturally wanted to be near London so I said, "Could I go to the Queen Alexandra's Military Hospital at Watford?" – the Q.A.M.H. had been moved from Millbank to Watford to escape the bombing. She said, "Oh, there's a queue to go there. I'll never get you in." Every V.A.D. in England, you see, wanted to be posted to the Q.A.M.H. I had several ex-deb friends who were who were nursing there, but they'd all pulled strings.

At a loose end, I got a job in Selfridges in the Letter Order Department, the L.O.D. Typing in L.O.D. forms was money for jam. We were paid two pounds and fifteen shillings a week – a fortune as the V.A.D. pay was under a pound and a lot of that was taken for laundry. It was great fun. Pat Britten was on guard at St James's Palace, and he used to ask me there several times for lunch. I'd say to Miss Spencer who was in charge of the department, "Can I possibly have a bit more than an hour for lunch because I'm going to lunch On Guard?" She'd say, "Stay as long as you like and tell me all about it afterwards!" She thought it a great joke. She hadn't met an ex-deb before. Billy Hartington, Lord Hartington, the oldest son of the Duke of Devonshire, was often at these lunches with Kick Kennedy, Jack Kennedy's sister, Katherine. They were unofficially engaged but were getting an awful lot of opposition because his family, the Devonshires, were very Protestant and didn't approve of Irish Catholics, and the Kennedys wouldn't allow her to be married in a Protestant church. Eventually they did marry and he was killed in the war and she was killed in an aeroplane disaster. She was a pretty, fun person and my first American girlfriend.

My mother was now running a Catholic Hostel for Service girls somewhere off Belgrave Square and was living between the flat in Westbourne Terrace and the Ladies' Carlton. One evening when I got home I found her having a drink with a man who was a complete stranger to me. She said, "This is Captain Maxwell Knight. He wants to have a word with you." When she'd gone out into the kitchen, he said, "I'm from MI5. We think you can be of help to us. Will you come and have a drink with me tomorrow evening at my flat in Dolphin Square? If so, you must not divulge a word of what I say to you, not even to your mother."

I went to Dolphin Square. Captain Maxwell Knight mentioned the name of a Russian living in London with a high semi-official position and with diplomatic privileges. Did I know him? Well, I'd danced with him at "The 400". He had a reputation as a playboy and had often made passes at me. Would I find out where he banked? I agreed to try. It was a marvellous challenge.

I rang the Russian and said, "Aren't you ever going to take me again to 'The 400' "Tonight?" he said. "All right," I said. "Tonight." So off we went to "The 400" and, physically revolting though he was, I let him dance with me cheek to cheek. For quite some time afterwards we danced and dined at the best places. He seemed to have unlimited funds and I'm afraid I led him on unashamedly. One evening he asked me out and I said, "Darling, I'd love to. The thing is I'm dining out with a friend called Harold Hood who's bringing me up some eggs from the country." In fact Harold (Sir Harold Hood) – he was in an Anti-Aircraft Regiment in Bristol – did this whenever he came up, and eggs were like gold, you were only allowed one a week. "Would you like some eggs?" I said. "You'll have to pay for them." "Of course I'd like them and of course I'll pay for them!" he said. So I went out to dinner with Harold. Jimmy Kennedy was there too, Jimmy Kennedy who wrote "The Isle of Capri", "Red Sails in the Sunset" and "We're Going to Hang Out the Washing on the Siegfried Line". Actually he wrote that song "How I love the kisses of Dolores, Aye aye aye, Dolores" about me. This annoyed me enormously as although Dolores is my real name, I hate anybody to know that I was christened Sorrow as I'm not a sorrowful person. Dodo was the name of a favourite doll of my mother's.

Anyway, Harold turned up with an enormous box of four dozen eggs and Jimmy gave me a very expensive-looking French paste clip which I danced with my suspected Russian spy – at Claridge's as it happens – I was able to tell him I'd four dozen eggs waiting for him at home and, when he dropped me there, I gave them to him saying, "Would you mind paying for them by cheque because I'm overdrawn at my bank?"

Even now I can't tell you all of this story. Chipps used to ask me about the scar in my leg from a revolver bullet, but I was sworn to secrecy.

I duly delivered the cheque to Maxwell Knight at Dolphin Square and he seemed very pleased. I said, "You can now jolly well do something for me in exchange." "Like what?" he asked. I said, "Like getting me into the QA Military Hospital at Watford as a V.A.D.!" Three days later Mona Beaumont rang me up and said, "I've had a telephone call from the War Office. You're being posted to Watford next week."

I couldn't, of course, tell my mother how I'd wangled it. I doubt if she even missed the eggs. She'd always been rather vague, was usually thinking of something else and answering "Yes, darling" and "No, darling" though she wasn't really listening – she only really listened if you were telling her something about the garden or the family. There's a marvellous story about her losing umbrellas in London during the war. She'd lost about eight and, one day, she got on a bus to go and collect them at the Lost Property Office and, getting off, picked up the umbrella of the man sitting next to her. He seized it and said, "That's my umbrella! You're stealing my umbrella!" Mummy said, "I'm terribly sorry. I thought it was mine." She went to the Lost Property Office, collected her umbrellas, got back on the same bus going the other way, and the man whose umbrella she'd picked up by mistake was on it too. He said, "You've had a good day today, haven't you, madam?"

I worked for about three months as a V.A.D. at Watford. Then the whole Q.A.M.H. was moved to the R.A.M.C. Hospital at Shenley, near Radlett in Hertfordshire, because Watford was too small for the number of casualties. At Shenley I shared a room with Madeleine Maxwell Stuart, Barbie Crichton, Hilary Lee, Margaret Dennison Pender and Moggy Lyttleton. We were all great friends and had been debs together and knew the same people, though a few were just too young to have been presented before the war started and it was stopped. We filled in for each other to get the maximum time-off possible, and soon found where we could get over the wall at night. If ever Matron, who was rather a stickler, suspected that one of us was missing fron the ward, someone else would swear she'd just seen her in the sluice room when, in fact, she was probably already on her way to the bright lights.

We were supposed to be on the ward at seven in the morning, so breakfast was at six thirty, but my mother gave me a Valor stove to heat our Arctic room, and we discovered that, by putting a kettle on it at night with six eggs in, the eggs were coddled by the morning and the water was hot enough for coffee. In this way, we didn't have to get up until six forty-five when, of course, it was a mad rush. Many is the time Barbie and I wore each other's dresses and aprons as she also was six foot tall. It's rather funny that Madeleine was the one who eventually married John Sherbrooke, isn't it? – their eldest son is my godson.

John Sherbrooke went to France with the Royal Horse Artillery and was taken prisoner at the time of Dunkirk and named me as being entitled to send him the official Red Gross postcard. Madeleine used to stand over me and make sure I sent it. She wouldn't let me go out to dinner till I had. Sometimes I used to send him my chocolate ration which was good for my figure. He did his Articles with other solicitors in prison and became a full-blown solicitor before he got out, so he didn't waste those five years. He also ran a racing book for his fellow prisoners – he *loves* racing- He's the senior partner of the firm in which my son, Jamie, now works.

The war was beginning to hot up and convoys of ambulances appealed regularly with badly wounded men. I loved every minute of the work, especially, as usual, the surgical side, and I knew that I was doing something worthwhile. You had your routine of making beds, taking the temperatures, doing the dressings, and giving medicines and injections under supervision. You were paid with an army Pay Book. You were like men in the army, only you had special status because you'd volunteered. You had one half day off a week and one full Sunday once a month. After a month of night duty you got a week-end off.

The V.A.D.s were all very popular. The patients thought that we were great fun and that we worked very hard, which we did. They called me Dizzy. Anybody who was able to get out of bed always helped me do my chores like bumping the floor. They'd even polish the brass buttons on my coat and skirt before I went out so that I'd look nice for my boyfriends. You were never out of uniform. Occasionally, though, I'd slip in to the flat at Westbourne Terrace and put on a glamorous blouse. You wore the Red Cross uniform for nursing – pale blue dress, white hat and a white apron with a red cross on it, and went out in a very smart navy blue hat and navy blue coat and skirt and white shirt and black tie. To dance you'd just remove your coat and hat. I mostly hitch-hiked up to London and was generally taken back by taxi. In those days it was quite safe to hitch-hike. You could get into a lorry perfectly happily: you never thought twice about it. Drivers always stopped when they saw you in uniform. The whole atmosphere of my time at Shenley was fun. When I didn't hitch-hike, I usually caught the first or the last train to Radlett Station where I parked a bicycle painted bright red with orange handlebars, known by the station master as the "Pride of the Line", for travelling the further stretch. All I can say is that as V.A.D.s we played jolly hard but, bleary-eyed or not, we worked jolly hard too.

The V.A.D.s' Madame was Lady Margaret Illingworth. The Matron, of course, was in charge of the whole hospital but she never interfered with us without discussing it with Maggie first. Maggie, a tall, massive, imposing creature, was married to Cyril Illingworth who was in the 60th Rifles so I knew her quite well as they used to stay with Uncle Jack at Lytchett. When I arrived, she was quite pleased to see me and we had a sort of chat. The others said she was frightfully ferocious, and certainly if she heard you'd been climbing over the wall, you might get a rocket, but fair enough . . .

I had various boyfriends – Harold Hood, Tommy Redfern, Doric Bossom, Tim Haley . . . I kept getting re-engaged. That's the sort of life it was. Because I didn't sleep with anyone, they asked me to marry them. They were just going abroad and you said "Yes" because you thought they were going to be killed and they usually were. Tim Haley, a Catholic, actually took me down to see his parents. He was very good-looking, and danced and played the piano beautifully. My mother got a letter from his mother saying, "Dodo must really either marry him or not make him so miserable. It's too unkind. He's going abroad." He was killed, poor darling . . .

I'd be taken out to dances at the Café de Paris, before it was bombed, or the Lansdowne Club or the Berkeley or the Mayfair, and then we'd go on to "The 400" which was very sort of up-market. By that I mean I'd have to go with the member and they were very picky and choosy about who their members were. But there weren't so many yobs around then – they were all in the army! A chap called Rossi ran "The 400". It was red plush and very romantic, with very low lights and a marvellous band with a marvellous saxophone. Of course we didn't *always* go to "The 400": sometimes we went to "The Nuthouse" which was the greatest fun. It was the sort of place where you'd sing The Lambeth Walk to different words:

Any time in Leicester Square
All the boys and girls down there
you'll find them all
Just a-doing the Pansy Walk – oi!

With their hand upon their hips
Where they fasten up their zips
You'll find them all
Just adoing the Pansy Walk – oi

There's a big one they call Queenie
And a little one called Rene
And a massive Ovaltini
High, wide and handsome
If at you they wink their eye
Don't you stop as you rustle by

Or else you'll be
Doing the Pansy Walk.

Everywhere was so jokey and friendly despite the rationing and the danger. A friend of Bumble's husband, a flier, once gave me a banana which I wore round my neck on a ribbon at "The 400" to make people jealous as they hadn't seen one for years. There never, strangely, seemed to be any shortage of wine: there must have been enormous stocks.

Of all my boyfriends, Doric Bossom was the most extravagant. I received a telegram from him one day while on ward duty at Shenley. It said, "Gorgeous glamorous creature – can't wait to take you out to dinner soonest – ring me tonight – reverse charges – would sign my name only that would cost a penny more."! I had just met him at a cocktail party and we had an ecstatic flirtation. He always took me back to Shenley in a taxi because he wanted to neck. His father was the architect, Sir Alfred Bossom who became a life peer in 1965. Queen Mary is reputed to have said, "Bossom? What a strange name. Neither one thing nor the other." Doric's dead now. He came into my life quite often. For instance, when I was in New York, he took me to Harlem.

I remember at Shenley that a repatriated pilot was brought in, very badly wounded, from Germany. He would normally have gone to an R.A.F. hospital but we were experimenting with a new drug called Penicillin so he was sent to us. He told me that a pilot friend of his had been nursed in Silesia by a Red Cross girl called Irmgard Ercklentz. I was able to talk to this friend on the telephone. It was wonderful to hear that Irmchen was well and beautiful as ever and adored by her patients. It gave me a warm feeling to hear of her first hand. After all, we were both Red Cross nurses and the Red Cross is international so she wasn't one of the enemy.

We'd moved to the R.A.M.C. Hospital at Sheyley toward the end of '42 and I was there till February '44. It had been a hospital for loonies and the loonies were fenced off in their section of the hospital to make room for the military. The V.A.D.s lived with Lady Margaret and her kingpin, Miss Dean, in a Victorian house – I suppose the original house of Shenley Park – with the various hospital blocks scattered around. Here we looked after ourselves, occasionally doing House Duty which meant cooking, – cleaning, washing up, and so on, instead of nursing. You could see the loonies exercising behind wire, and you'd hear about them second-hand. One poured petrol over himself and set it alight. One thought she was the Duchess of Hamilton, Aunt Maddy's Aunt Nina. She walked up and down all day tearing her hair and saying, "You must call me 'Your Grace'." I've a fondness for loonies. Any good nurse wants to heal, and likes people who are ill in mind or body. It's in you, like loving a child is natural to a mother. Occasionally a loony would escape, but the Army tended not to put out an alarm call so as not to frighten the A.T.S. girls. One nurse was murdered while I was there. I used to bicycle back very quickly on the Pride of the Line at night when I wasn't in a taxi.

Because the whole place had been a loony bin before we arrived, most of the wards consisted of cubicles with peepholes in the doorways and there were rows of lavatories with stable type doors revealing knees and shoulders. The sister in our psychiatric ward was dottier than the patients. One day she called me into her office and said, "Nurse Lees, I think you take sexual pleasure out of doing the surgical dressings." Well, when you're doing surgical dressings, you don't think of the patient as a man even, though of course you had your favourites and some of them were attractive. There was a walking patient, a very attractive Glaswegian sergeant called Jock, I allowed to kiss me behind the haystack once or twice. I certainly had a fancy for him and he for me and he used to scrub tables and floors for me. But none of us took sexual pleasure in doing surgical dressings. One V.A.D., though, became terribly stout and we told her to go on a diet. Then she started having a baby and Maggie had to trot her off to the A.T.S. ward and make the father marry her – a soldier from the barracks where the anti-aircraft guns were.

The officer in charge of the hospital was Colonel Wallis. He was ex-Indian Army and a terrific tartar. When it was Colonel's Inspection of the ward, my goodness you bumped it. He'd go down on the floor and run his finger along to find if there was a speck of dust. You had to make all the patients, however ill, lie to attention in their beds. I liked him very much, actually, and he rather liked me because he thought I was a good nurse, whatever I did in my off-time. He once put me on night duty in charge of a ward, which was rather unheard of for a V.A.D. This particular ward was the ward where the Night Superintendent always came to have her supper about midnight after she'd done her rounds. She was in charge of all nurses and my friends said, "Oh my God, Dodo, you're going to have a most ghastly time! She's an absolute bitch – she really is – and she hates V.A.D.s." I remember the first thing I said to her was, "Can I go to the loo?" She looked rather surprised and said, "Yes". I then tore down the corridor and rang everyone to tell them they could put their feet up and take their caps off as she was having supper.

When I got back I told her how inconvenient it was being on night duty that week as I was missing two cocktail parties and two dinner dates. She was very snooty about this and said something about not wanting to interfere with my social activities. Then I told her I wanted to go to the Fourth of June at Eton with lan Farquhar who'd been to school there, so I might be rather sleepy when I came on duty afterwards. I went to the Fourth of June and I then went on night duty and, when she came in at twelve o'clock for her supper, she said, "Nurse, there's an empty cubicle over there. Go and have a kip, and I'll look after your ward."

From that moment we made the greates of friends. In fact, I had a Christmas card from her for years. Frankie Wallis was her name – the same surname as the Colonel – and she taught me more than anyone since Sister Thomas at the Cornelia. She even taught me how to give an intrafemoral injection, and she also let me do a blood transfusion under her supervision and watch a doctor doing a lumber puncture. Later, in the front line in France, when there was no one else to give anaesthetics, or emergency treatment for which I was certainly not officially qualified, I would thank her profoundly in my heart for giving me the skill that I needed. By teaching me, she saved many French lives.

During the entire war I only went down into a shelter once and that was one night at Shenley when the bombs were coming too jolly close. On the instructions of Colonel Wallis, Maggie took all the V.A.D.s off duty to a shelter and the next day, after a very uncomfortable night, we all went to her in a delegation – the debs and the girls in the next room to us, about twelve of us – and I spoke for them all, saying, "Madam, we cannot go on duty at seven o'clock in the morning and work all day until sometimes half past nine at night if we're not going to have a night's sleep. Please can you make sure that we never spend a night in a shelter again." And, you see, she was a very good commandant, because we never had to do it again, though there were bombs all the time.

I can't explain, but somehow the bombs were very beautiful: the whole of London was lit up with incendiaries. Of course you thought of the people being killed, but it was exciting and everybody was so friendly, so determined to stick this thing out. The general atmosphere was "We're all in this together", there was no backbiting; everybody was on each other's side. That was the lovely thing about the war. A bomb fell on the Ladies' Carlton and I went round there with my ankles deep in broken glass to see if my mother was all right, and an old lady of about eighty was sweeping the entire street and she gave me a cheery greeting and said, "That blasted Hitler's done it again!" And I was in a bus one evening going down Park Lane and a bomb fell and the blast made the whole bus swivel round and pushed it right into the park, and the woman next to me didn't scream or anything, she just turned to me and said, "It does take your mind off the war, don't it, luv?"

The blackout, too, was a bit of a problem. I sometimes stayed with a great friend of mine called Anne Fane whose mother-in-law had lent her a lovely house in Shepherd's Market. The staircase was very dark so we always used to put the light on during the day when we went upstairs and forget to turn it off when we came down again. When we got back at four or five in the morning, there'd be police at the door so we'd have to invite them in, and generally the taxi driver too, and give them a cup to coffee. Shepherd's Market is a very attractive part of London and full of tarts who, assuming we were tarts as well, used to lean out of their windows and shout that we'd get them bombed.

Miss Jones was a woman who came down to Shenley from the War Office with a plan that all V.A.D.s must become military orderlies like the A.T.S. and wear khaki. Well, we were under military discipline, but we had our own special privileges, our own special corps, running our own house, wearing our own Red Cross uniform and travelling first class by train like officers when we had a pass for leave.

As I told you, we didn't even mess with the A.T.S. – or with the Q.A.s if it came to that, though they would have been far too snooty to mess with us as they considered we were nothing and they were queen bees. We only took orders from them because they were trained nurses. Some of them were terrific snobs. For instance, one Q.A. said to me that she wouldn't dream of scrubbing a floor, she'd use a mop. I said, "It's much quicker and easier this way. I don't mind going down on my hands and knees." What's the difference between that and giving bedpans, I ask you? And the Matron, whenever she passed me in the corridor, used to say, "You won't get your stripe until you cut your hair!" – I had long flowing hair to my shoulders and stuck my cap on top. I'd just say, "Yes, Matron" and pass by. I never cut my hair because my boyfriends wouldn't have liked me to. After Colonel Wallis put me on night duty in charge of a ward, Maggie said to Matron, "You must give Nurse Lees her stripe now," so I got it just the same. That was rather a victory for Maggie. Maggie was always on our side, you see . . .

Anyway, Miss Jones came down from the War Office dressed in Khaki and with several pips on her shoulder and asked us to sign away our special status and integrate with the Army. I didn't see why the Mobile V.A.D.s should be bulldozed in this way when we'd volunteered for the Red Cross. The Red Cross nurses who nursed in civilian hospitals and the ones who packed parcels and ran canteens and did this, that and the other, were going to continue as before – after all, the Red Cross wasn't going to fold up. I was very indignant, so I formed a Trades Union and said to all the girls, "Look, you mustn't sign! Refuse to sign and then it won't go through because the hospital can't run without us. If we all refuse, Matron will never be able to replace us and, if this happens at Shenley, I bet you none of the other hospitals will sign and we'll be sort of pioneers." So they all said yes, they wouldn't sign; but when it actually came to the point, only one or two didn't: I was let down.

I, of course, refused to sign and, in February '44, was moved temporarily to an Army Officers' Convalescent Home in Hempstead, a smallish house behind the Spaniards Inn with about ten patients and a rather nice sister in charge and one other V.A.D., Madeleine Maxwell Stuart, stayed behind at Shenley and, in fact, looked after Doric Bossom when he came in, wounded. And, later, when John Sherbrooke came back from prisoner of war camp she looked after him, too, and they later became engaged.

Chapter 8

ENGAGED

It was at this point, when I was nursing in Hempstead and almost twenty-four, that I met the man to whom I became properly engaged and intended to marry, – Sir Howard Frank. Howard's father was of the estate agents, Knight, Frank and Rutley, married his secretary Nan, and Nan bore him two sons; Howard and Robert, the present Sir Robert Frank. When he died Nan married Air Marshal Sir Arthur Coningham, always known as "Mary" Coningham – he, was a New Zealander: "Mary" comes from Maori, you see – and had a daughter called Jane by him. Nan and Mary had a home in London and at Lepe, near Beaulieu. I still wear the sapphire engagement ring Howard gave me.

Howard

We met in Claridge's, at the reception after Ian Farquhar's wedding in the Guards' Chapel. I got the day off, naturally, and the whole thing was the greatest fun. I knew everybody – Kick Kennedy, Andrew Devonshire, Charlie Rutland . . . Two tall, good-looking young men in the Grenadiers were standing, talking to one another at Claridge's, and one of them came up to me and said, "Who are you?" I said, "Dodo. I'm a friend of Ian's." He said, "Well, I'm Howard Frank, and this is Peter Rawlinson." For Howard and me, it was instant love, love at first sight, something chemical, spiritual, telepathic. I forgot all the other boys I'd been engaged to and flirted with, including John Sherbrooke.

Howard said, "I'm going to another reception downstairs," and I said, "I haven't been asked," and he said, "That's all right, I'll say you are my wife." He then said that he was taking me out to dinner that night and I said, "I'm already dining with Brigadier Bruce-Haye" – Brigadier Bruce-Haye and I were great friends. He was married and just had a little yen for me, that's all. Howard said, "It's *got* to be tonight. I'm joining my regiment in Yorkshire tomorrow." So I rang Beloved – I always called Bruce-Haye "Beloved" – and I said, "Beloved, I've been asked out to dinner by somebody I've just fallen madly in love with! May I go?" He said, "Of course you may go, Dodo! I'll take you out another evening instead."

By this time, Howard had left and, though he had given me his telephone number, I'd forgotten his name! I rang the number and discovered I was talking to the porter of a block of flats. I said, "I want to speak to somebody but I don't know his name!" He said, "What's he look like?" I said, "He's tall and fair and he's a Lieutenant in the Grenadier Guards." "Oh, that's Sir Howard Frank," he said, and he put me through. Howard said, "Well, can you come out?" I said, "Yes! I'll meet you at the Berkeley at half past seven." And I was waiting at the Berkeley, a little after half past seven, and was just getting cross and about to leave and wishing I was going out with Bruce-Haye, when Howard arrived and said "Sorry, darling, I've been to a cocktail party." We went to dinner at the Mirabelle and then danced at "The 400" where "Night and Day" became our tune. At about three o'clock in the morning, he took me in a taxi back to my Nursing Home and I crept in, hoping I wouldn't wake Sister. He was twenty-one and I was twenty-four, and we'd decided we'd get married.

When Howard next came down to London, I rang up my mother at the Ladies' Carlton and said, "I'm bringing somebody I'm going to marry." Though she was dying to marry me off really, she was rather apprehensive who it might be. But, when Howard and she met, they got on like a house on fire. She was disappointed he wasn't a Catholic, but only a few of my boyfriends had been Catholic – even John Sherbrooke wasn't a Catholic – and she herself had married a Protestant. So I imagine she didn't mind very much. That night Howard took me to the Mirabelle to be vetted by Nan, his mother, and Mary Coningham, his step-father, who was just back from fighting in North Africa with Monty – they were together again later in the Invasion of France. Mary was a very attractive and amusing chap, I must say. I remember he went up to the band leader – Paul Raymond who now runs all those porn clubs – and asked him did he know "Lily Marlene". Well, he didn't, so Mary sang it and the band played it for us and we danced to it. When I think of my first meeting with Howard's mother and step-father, I always think of "Lily Marlene".

Nan thought I was just one of Howard's flirtations. However she did come and meet my mother, but they were merely polite to each other as they didn't have much in common. Mother would have let me marry Howard tomorrow, but Nan said that, though we could get engaged, we mustn't announce it till after the Invasion in which Howard's regiment was to take part. She said that, if he survived the first battle, he could put it in the papers and we could then get married in the Embassy in Paris, possibly, when he was on leave, or after the war. She told me afterwards she was terrified he might give me a baby and then get killed. That's understandable, but I wish she had let us marry. I would like to have had his baby.

Howard, however, considered the arrangement reasonable and he bought me a ring and we went about together and most people knew we were engaged though it wasn't in the papers. The Sister at the Convalescent Home was awfully kind. In fact, thanks to her, I had a very happy engagement. Whenever Howard was in London she gave me time off. She adored young love and she adored me, this newly engaged girl. Howard and I would talk on the telephone for hours: he got through pounds and pounds. I remember him ringing once to say he'd be arriving from Yorkshire on an evening when I was dining with Harold Hood, who wanted to marry me himself, so the three of us dined together. We told Harold the situation and he accepted it and went home. Howard and I then went on to "The 400" where we couldn't bear to leave each other so he missed his train. In the hiatus between "The 400" closing and the morning train we sat in the hall of Grosvenor House among the women hoovering. We just sat there on a sofa, holding hands, unable to kiss and hardly talking, but so happy to be together. I had sometimes vaguely wondered if, to be as near as possible to Howard, I might go to France with the Invasion. I was, now determined to get there somehow. But how?

Chapter 9

Fate Steps In – France

Fate was on my side. One April afternoon in 1944 I was walking on a day off through Belgrave Square on my way to see my mother at the Ladies' Carlton when I noticed the *Tricolore* flying above the headquarters of the Free French Red Cross. Sat behind a desk, was the President, the Comtesse de Salis. "Do you need a nurse for the Invasion?" I asked. "I have four years' experience." She looked at me in astonishment and said, "Do you know, it's a most extraordinary thing, but soon after the Invasion we're sending a team of seven out to France and one of the nurses has just rung up to say that she's got appendicitis! If you can get an Exit Permit to go instead of her, it would be much less trouble for me than searching England for another French nurse."

Well, to get an Exit Permit just like that in the war wasn't easy. So I rang Uncle Alan who was now C.I.G.S. (Chief of the Imperial General Staff), and I asked him how to obtain one. He said, "Dodo, I don't like nepotism but come to dinner on Friday and I'll seat you next to Ernie Bevin who may be able to help." So I went to dinner with Aunty Ben and Uncle Alan where I sat next to Ernie Bevin, the Minister of Labour and former Trades Union leader. He turned to me during the soup and said, "There must be some reason why I'm sitting next to a pretty girl and not an old boot. Tell me now, and then we can relax and enjoy ourselves!" I said, "I want an Exit Permit to go to France with the French Red Cross after the Invasion." He said, "Come to my office on Monday morning and you shall have it."

And that's how I got to France, and was able to follow Howard. All through seeing a flag in Belgrave Square on my day off! Now isn't that Fate? Call it God taking a hand, if you like. We, ourselves, have a certain amount of control, but God intervenes sometimes.

Officially I was now an "ambulance driver with nursing experience" in the Free French Red Cross, and I was happy to leave the British Red Cross here and the Convalescent Home in Hempstead because, hanging over me, was the threat of being bulldozed into the British Army. The only other English girl in the team was Anne Swinton Lee, a tall adventurous blonde three years younger than myself, whose father, Brigadier Stanislake Swinton Lee, soon became Head of British Civil Affairs in Paris. Anne, who up till now had been doing code work at Bletchley, was an "ambulance driver", and, because we rather clicked, we moved together into the home of a friend of mine, Evelyn Northcroft, at 115, Harley Street. The joke was that, though Anne was an *ambulancière*, she didn't yet know how to drive: she'd never, in fact, driven in her life! But the French Red Gross didn't know that – I didn't know that – and, when the American Red Cross delivered a Dodge station-wagon to Headquarters in Belgrave Square, the Comtesse de Salis said to us, "Well, you'd both better drive it and get used to it," so we got in and I said to Anne, "You drive first," and she said, "O.K. Which are the gears?" and I showed her, and off we started with a terrific bump, bump, bump, bump. We went – and this was the most hair-raising thing that happened to me in the whole war, literally – we went round Hyde Park Corner and, when we'd almost hit about sixteen Army vehicles, buses and God knows what, I said, "How long have you driven for?" She said, "I've never driven." I said, "Well, I think I'd better take over and drive back until you've had some practice in the country." It was nerve-wracking. You can't imagine. But she was always very brave, Anne. She got the Croix de Guerre before I did.

Howard's regiment had by now moved down to Brighton but as I now had a military uniform and a pass (Brighton was in a restricted area), I could sometimes meet him there.

Do you remember "*Pistol Packin' Momma?*" Everybody in the Mirabelle used to sing, "Lay that Dodo down, Frank! Lay that Dodo down!" And Rossi, at "The 400", asked me to ask "Mary" Coningham, Howard's step-father, to get him into the Services as a cook. I didn't ask Mary, because in no way did I want Rossi to leave "The 400"! Howard and I were at Haywards Heath once, waiting to change trains, and there was a train standing at the station and another one coming in the other direction, and Howard shouted, "My God! They're going to crash!". I really believed him and I cried, "Oh darling!" and I hung on to him. "Sucker!" he said. He was always playing such tricks on me, but he was a very poetic person, a very sort of idealistic person.

One day we went to lunch with Mary and Nan. Monty, Field Marshal Lord Montgomery, was coming, too; he and Mary had these enormous great working caravans at their headquarters in Sussex. Mary said, "I'm going to pull Monty's leg like mad." They didn't frightfully like each other. For one thing, Mary drank dry martinis and champagne cocktails and Monty didn't drink at all.

And Mary was an ebullient sort of person and Monty wasn't. So Monty arrived and Mary immediately said, "Have a champagne cocktail, Monty!"

and Monty said, "Good heavens, you know I don't drink!" and asked for a lemon juice or something. And then Mary said, "I say, Monty, your double's behaving awfully badly in Gibraltar. He's drunk all the time and he's been over to La Linea twice to play polo and he stays in a brothel every night." Monty was absolutely furious. The rest of us giggled like mad. It was naughty of Mary. Actually, towards the end of the war in Europe, his relationship with Monty deteriorated completely.

Then over dinner one evening, "Beloved" Bruce-Haye said to me, "Look, Dodo, as Head of Civil Affairs, I can get you into the Grand Hotel at Eastbourne so you can see Howard even more often. D-Day is imminent and the South Coast is sealed off to civilians but, if you come down with a French Red Cross pass and in uniform, I'll find you a room." So in navy blue French battledress and armed with my pass I went down and stayed at the Grand Hotel, Eastbourne, towards the end of May, and Howard would drive over, or send a soldier, to take me back to Brighton.

We invaded on June 6th. I didn't go till July and on the 5th June Howard rang me up and said, "I can't fetch you tonight. There's a panic on." Well, I didn't fuss. I knew something important was going on from the amount of landing ships that were collecting. In fact, that evening I thoroughly enjoyed myself. We all went down to the quay at Eastbourne where the Welsh Guards were starting to embark and there was much dancing and farewell kissing: we didn't go to bed that night at all and, the next morning, when a gang of us went up to the roof of the hotel, we saw the first buzz bomb flying over with its eerie chug, chug, chug, chug, and soldiers shooting at it with a Bofors gun. I then went back to London. What would have been the point staying in Eastbourne now that Howard had left?

So, after June 4th, 1944, I never saw Howard again. Soon afterwards I dined with Harold Hood and, when I got back to Harley Street, Evelyn Northcroft said, "Howard phoned. He's staying with his mother at Lepe." I rang Nan immediately, and she said, "Oh, I'm so sorry, Dodo. During a respite, Howard came over in the bomb bay of Mary's Mosquito and they had dinner here and now they've gone back." Howard had rung me and I could have got on a train and gone straight down to Lepe and seen him, and, instead, I was out with Harold Hood! He was sweet, Harold Hood, and madly in love with, me but, because of him, I never really said good-bye to Howard.

Part 4

FRANCE 1944-45

Chapter 10

Normandy

So it was summer, '44, and I was in London, at 115, Harley Street, waiting with Anne Swinton Lee to go to France.

Every morning we said to the Comtesse de Salis, "When are we going? When are we going?" and she said, "Look at the news. I simply don't know." You see, for quite a while it was really thought we'd be thrown back into the sea. There was great German opposition. Pegasus Bridge was supposed to be taken in twenty minutes and it took three weeks. And Caen was very heavily defended, and Monty refused to go in until it was bombed. The. irony was that an awful lot of civilians were killed and looking after civilians was part of what we were meant to be doing. But, if we couldn't get to them, how could we look after them?

There were seven in our unit. One was Colonel Guillemand, a "doctor". The rest of us were nurses, except for Anne who was an ambulance driver, in the charge of a sort of matron. Anne and I talked English to one another, but we talked French to everyone else. The American Red Cross had given us a real ambulance in addition to the Dodge station-wagon. The ambulance held two stretchers on the top and two on the bottom. The Dodge held two stretchers and supplies and luggage. I planned to take my piano accordion. When, eventually, I left the Free French and joined the Paris French Red Cross as an *ambulancière*, I used to sit on the bonnet of my ambulance and play French army songs as we went into battle.

Il y a des filles sur toutes les routes
Aujourd'hui comme à demain
Et ça suffit que tout le monde s'en foute . . .

All very naughty.

Suddenly, one day in July after the Battles of Caen and the Falaise Gap, we got a telephone call to say we were leaving that night. I was thrilled, thinking it quite likely that Howard and I would meet and get married.

We were driven to a clearing station. I don't know where, everything was very hush, and there were no signposts and I've no bump of locality anyway. I do know that, when we reached this camp, it was pouring with rain and the whole place was knee-deep in mud! We spent a night in tents and, the next evening, Squeaker Curtis, my sister, Bumble's father-in-law and the General in charge of logistical arrangements for the launching of the Invasion in the Southampton area, came into my tent with his A.D.C. to say good-bye to me and wish me luck. He was able to tell my mother that I'd left for France and that I was in good form.

We were then driven to a hospital ship at Southampton, and sailed for Normandy. Believe it or not the passport officer came in to stamp our passports. I thought it was extraordinary going to invade France with a stamped passport. It was a very rough crossing. I'm never sea-sick but Anne was sick the whole time. One pleasant incident: a darling sailor called Jock gave me a really thick cable-stitched wool jersey, knitted for him by his old aunt in the Hebrides. I wear it to this day.

We landed in Arromanches at Mulberry, that extraordinary port made with huge landing-stages taken over in sections with the Invasion, and were herded into a camp at Bayeux. Then our unit assembled somewhere on the way to Falaise and we drove to the Duc de la Rouchefoucault's Château de Versainville which had been designated partly as a hospital. Almost all the roads and bridges had been bombed so our maps weren't much use to us. The apples were ripening and I remember Anne and I stopped at an orchard and, while the others went in search of omelettes, (in England our ration had been one egg a week) we sat under a tree and gossiped and ate apples and I played my accordion.

This was a happy interlude during a journey in which, ever since Arromanches, my chief impression was the overpowering smell of death – the death of humans as well as of hundreds of cows whose corpses I saw rotting in the fields. Most of the invasion force had moved on towards Belgium, but the Poles were still fighting pockets of Germans in the woods, and the Germans at Bordeaux still held out. Le Havre was still occupied. It was, of course, was bombed to Hades in September by Mary Coningham's 2nd Tactical Air Force. There were practically no Germans left there by then, but Monty never wanted to lose a soldier, that's why he was so popular – so, from a civilian point of view, it was over-bombed. The extraordinary thing is the majority of the French never resented that. On the contrary, wherever the English went, the French welcomed them.

Anyway, our unit commandeered an empty section of the *château* where Anne and I, when we weren't working or messing, kept rather to ourselves.

The windows of our room had been blown out and the floorboards were bare and there was no furniture, but we had our stretchers and we had blankets, and we filled every inch of space around us with rhododendrons picked in the grounds. Of the wounded that constantly arrived many were farmers – and their workers – who'd insisted on their sacred *moisson* – harvesting, though they knew their fields were mined.

After a few days, Colonel Guillemand asked Anne and me to use the Dodge and the ambulance to move a group of nuns and old people to a *château* rather like ours. The nuns had run an Old People's Home at Falaise and, when this was bombed, they and the old people had been evacuated to the safety of a farmer's barn. There were about thirty of them all told so we had to make several trips. The first batch was the nuns – all except one who stayed behind putting things in boxes. After ferrying the old people, we returned in the Dodge for the remaining nun and the boxes, which the farmer helped us to load. But of the nun there was no sign. Suddenly I noticed part of a veil slipping out of one of the boxes. She had hidden there so as not to be left behind! I said, "Oh my *mère*, you mustn't sit in a box! You must sit in front with us!" So she came and sat in front, telling her rosary all the way as she'd never been in a car before.

Next day Anne and I drove to service our vehicles at the 12th L.O.C."The 12th Lines of Communication Unit", in Caen – this included greasing the nipples, always called "tits". We went up to, the office of Colonel Eric Williams, the chap in charge, to see if there were any letters. There weren't and I'd been hoping for one from Howard. Eric immediately started flirting with me, then took us into the bar for a drink, saying, "No need to do the tits yourselves. I'll get my men on to them," and the men – sweet, English Army, Montgomery's Army – were naturally delighted to help two pretty English girls. We made great friends with Eric who promised to take us one day for a meal in Trouville. This was something to look forward to. Apart from a daily litre of wine, our rations mostly consisted of spam, baked beans, powdered eggs, powdered milk and coffee, though we could get extras, such as fresh bread and milk, as gifts from farmers or by buying them with the pound or so a week we were paid in special money printed for the Invasion.

Actually, compared with England, there seemed to be lots of food in Normandy – we'd thought everybody would be starving. The farmer who had sheltered the nuns and the old people invited Anne and me to his daughter's wedding, and the food had to be seen to be believed. It was laid out for about forty people on a huge table in the barn of his pretty old farmhouse, with everything you could imagine: pork, lamb, beef, eggs, cakes, cheeses, masses of wine . . . Incredible! The wedding breakfast went on all day, literally.

There wasn't much conversation, just solid serious eating and drinking, but every now and then one of the party got up, made a little speech and then sat down again.

I said to Anne, "I think we'd better make a little speech, too," so I stood up and said how good it had been of the farmer to look after the nuns and the old people; and how pleased we were to be in France; and how we loved France so much; and how we were so glad to have been able to liberate them or rather, I tactfully added, help them to liberate themselves. Then someone made another little speech thanking us for liberating them and saying that, when they saw the Royal Air Force coming over, they always cheered and clapped, whereas they ran when they saw the Germans and the Americans whose aim was not so good. I thought this a marvellous thing to say as our Air Force had killed so many of them. Anyway, it was a very joyous occasion – and so unexpected after the recent fighting.

Once, on our way back from a trip to the 12th L.O.C. to grease our "tits" and collect any letters, we saw a little blue Renault at the side of the road with a very pretty girl in French Red Cross uniform standing by it. She hailed us down and said in perfect English but with a slight American accent, "Can you possibly give me some petrol?" We said, "Of course!" and got some out – we always carried huge enormous *bidons* which we used for petrol, water, wine, everything. Her name was Monique de Nervo, Baronnne de Nervo. Her unit was based in Paris and she lived in Neuilly with her parents, but she was on a swan because Paris had been liberated on August 25th. She had a huge sense of humour and was very attractive and sophisticated. We giggled together and enjoyed ourselves and hoped we'd meet again. I never thought we *would* meet again: I never realised what an important part Monique was to play in my life.

Our second meeting was when Anne and I next went in to the 12th L.O.C.

As usual the soldiers rushed up and said, "Hello, sweeties, we'll grease your tits for you!" and up we went to Eric Williams who, after giving us a gin and tonic, handed us each a pile of mail. I was in the best of form. But the very first letter I opened was from Bumble and it said, "My darling, I'm so sorry for you. I know exactly what it's like" – of course she did, because her husband, Dick, had been killed in the R.A.F. in the spring. But till then I didn't know that Howard had been killed, and in the same sheaf there was actually a letter from Howard which he'd written to me a long time before. I soon heard in a letter from Nan that he'd been killed on September 10th on the Leopold Canal in Belgium and that Mary had immediately sent a dispatch rider to tell me this, but the dispatch rider was killed before getting through. And when Ian Farquhar wrote and said, "We got the gun that killed Howard,"

I found it no consolation because I just thought some German girl would probably be going through what I was going through.

Meanwhile, on this dreadful day, I was opening other letters, including the one from Howard which contained a poem. There was one of consolation from my mother. Others were from V.A.D.s and boyfriends saying things like, "How are you?" and, "We do envy you."

I was devastated. I couldn't believe what had happened. Howard and I were so close I thought I would have *known* when he was killed. I thought I would have seen him or heard him singing "Night and Day". Watching me cry, darling Eric said, "Look, we'll go in the jeep to Trouville for that meal I promised you. You just cry and cry and cry. It doesn't matter. I don't mind." Eric was a sweet person. I mean, he was a married man and he flirted a bit because I was a girl, but it was an easy sort of flirt, you know, not serious.

When we got back from Trouville – Anne had come, too – who should be sitting near the ambulance, waiting for her Renault to be filled, but Monique! I rushed up to her with tears pouring down my cheeks and I said, "My fiancé has been killed!" Putting her arms around me, she said, "I'll make you a cup of tea. One day you will wake up and you'll see the grass is green again, but it'll take time." Monique is a lovely person.

That night at Versainville I cried and cried and cried in Anne's arms in that little room full of flowers. The next morning I went to Holy Communion in a church nearby. That gave me a bit of comfort. But I was desperately miserable. I thought my life was at an end.

It virtually took me eight years to get over Howard's death: until I married Chipps in 1953 I didn't want to put anybody in his place. But I had boyfriends and I had lovers and I was as flirtatious as before – you can be heartbroken and, though something has been taken away from you, you can still do things and talk to people and live a life. The only psychological difference Howard's death *did* make was that, if I couldn't marry the love of my life, it didn't matter to me if I remained a virgin. Till then I'd wanted to have the perfect marriage like my mother. My seduction about nine months later wouldn't have happened if Howard had still been alive.

People have suggested that I now wanted to get into the front line of the fighting because I didn't care whether I lived or died. That isn't so. I had hoped to be in the front line to be near to Howard and to be doing something useful. So did Anne and we got our chance: Edwina Mountbatten came to inspect the hospital with my cousin, Joe Weld, Colonel Sir Joseph Weld of Lulworth Castle. We all had lunch in the mess and I asked Edwina to help us. She turned to Buddy d'Allières, the head of the French Red Cross – the *Croix*

Rouge that had been under Pétain throughout the war – and asked him if he'd fix it. Fix it he did and, within about a week, Anne and I were transferred and reporting for duty at the *Croix Rouge* Française in Paris. Anne had to stay at some cold Y.W.C.A., though her father's H.Q. was the Crillon Hotel. I was luckier: I stayed in the house at 33, rue de Graviers, which Mary Coningham had requisitioned for his Paris H.Q.

Chapter 11

Paris Just After The Liberation

Thirty -Three, rue des Graviers was a marvellous, divine house in Neuilly, looking over the Bois de Boulogne. It had been requisitioned from André Dubonnet of apéritif fame, a collaborator now in Frèsnes Prison, and was now in the charge of André Jocet, Mary's French Liaison officer – Mary and Nan were in Brussels – and run by an old married couple called Jean and Marie. André was a most amusing man whose play *Elizabeth Femme sans Hommes* had a great *succès* in Paris at the end of the war.

Marie was instructed to show me up to the top floor flat which had belonged to France, André Dubonnet's daughter. Everything was as France had left it. Her dressing-gown, even, was on the bed and her scent was on the dressing-table. I'd never seen a flat like it – blue glass everywhere, a loo you could see out of but not into, a pink radiogram . . . The only time I'd ever seen a pink radiogram before was when Noël Coward took me to drinks as a deb with Princess Marina, the Duchess of Kent. I saw a third one later in Germany under strange circumstances.

I'm sure this flat at 33, rue des Graviers was the one described by Nancy Mitford in *The Pursuit of Love*, the one Fabrice (Gaston Palewski) kept the girl in. It had an extraordinary picture window which could be opened in summer for sunbathing. Downstairs, too, was gorgeous – exquisite pictures, a magnificent jade collection, a marvellous cellar . . . Here I was in absolute luxury after so much discomfort and the smell of death.

Marie brought me tea and, soon afterwards, I heard a squeak of laughter and in came André Jocet with Monique de Nervo, the Red Cross girl I'd met twice in Normandy. She rushed up to me, flung her arms around my neck and said, "Isn't it absurd! André, who I've known since I was a child, appeared at this cocktail party and said, 'You won't believe what happened to me today. The Air Marshal has invited his late stepson's fiancée to stay. She and another six foot English girl have joined the *Croix Rouge*, hoping to cross the Rhine with the French Army.' I said, 'Is she called Dodo!' and, when he said 'Yes,' I said, 'Take me there at once!'"

So that's how I met Monique again, Monique, who became my greatest friend and a catalyst throughout my life, and is godmother to my son, Jamie. And when André Dubonnet came out of prison and was respectable again, his daughter, France, met Monique and they became friends and Monique is godmother to her daughter Marie! Isn't it all extraordinary? In the days that followed I learned that Monique's father was the Baron de Nervo, the head of the French steel *cartel* and, later, President of Le Polo, and that she lived with him and her mother and her sister, Claudia, in a lovely house in Neuilly with a gorgeous garden. Her mother, like mine, was a wonderful gardener owning (which is very unusual for the heart of Paris) a real English garden with a herbaceous border. She kept hens and a cow there during the war.

Monique was twenty-three, about eleven months younger than me. She had had a huge coming out ball and was a great social success and, in 1939 when she was just eighteen, she had married the Comte de Baudry d'Asson. She was in two minds about him. On arrival at the church, her father said to her, "Do you really want to go through with this?" and she thought, "Well, here I am in my wedding dress, with five hundred people waiting for me. I can't get out of it now."

So she married him and it wasn't a success. He made her go to Communion every morning and he wouldn't let her see any of her friends. Kinky, you see, and frightfully jealous. Eventually he shut her up in his castle and she escaped back to her parents in Paris by climbing out of a window . . .

Anyway, after meeting Monique again in Paris, I went with Anne next day to the Red Cross. We were told that the French First Army was fighting its way from Provence, where they had landed, up towards Besançon. We were soon to be sent there with twenty-two other *ambulancières*. A Madame René would be in charge of the convoy and there'd be two of us to an ambulance. Anne and I would be attached to a battalion of the *6ième R.I.C. (Regiment d'Infantrie Coloniale)* of the *9ième D.I.C. (Division d'Infantrie Coloniale)* which was part of the First French Army under Général de Lattre de Tassigny. The commandant of our battalion was Pierre Langlais – later Colonel Langlais, the hero of Dien Bien Phu – and the colonel of the regiment was Colonel Dessert. We were given our very smart new uniforms – pale blue *calot* (forage cap), skirt and belt and jacket with silver buttons (designed by a couturier) and had our hair done in a Pompadour with lovely curls.

We certainly looked very nice, and an enormous party was given for us with all the Press there. These two English girls were an absolute gift as propaganda, you see. We made the front page of all the papers in France. Later, of course, when we were with the army we wore khaki and the dark blue *calot* of the *9ième D.I.C.*

We remained in Paris for about a month, and reported daily to the *Croix Rouge* where the king-pin was Madame de Peyerimhoff, and her second in command the Comtesse de Foucauld. Both were rather masculine, but I just thought, when they came to inspect us in their jackboots, that they were terribly nice.

Actually, an awful lot of the *ambulancières* were considered to be lesbians. Up till now I didn't quite realise what a lesbian was. I knew about pansies – my brother, Mike, had told me about that when he was a schoolboy, and I'd some boyfriends in the Foreign Office. But I'd never had a pash on a woman in my life and I didn't realise *women* did it. Once at Sheringham, the nice convent I went to as a child, I couldn't open the door of the loo and Mary McGrath, the girl who told me the facts of life, climbed over and showed me how to work the lock. Well, it was perfectly innocent but a nun came in at that moment and led us to the Reverend Mother for an explanation. Mary explained that she'd climbed over to help me open the door. It didn't occur to me what the fuss was about. It was the same in Munich that time when the Gräfin Rex gave me stick for jumping into bed with Tina Douglas Roberts because I thought I saw a ghost. We hadn't "done" anything and to do anything never dawned on us. So, until I was twenty-four and I joined the *Croix Rouge Française*, I honestly didn't know what being a lesbian, let alone a practising lesbian, meant.

Anyway, Anne and I reported daily to Headquarters and went off on a very intensive driving and maintenance course each morning and afternoon, messing between-times in the *popote*. I'm hopeless at cars now – I wouldn't know the petrol filter and I can't even change a wheel -but I got through the exam, though everything went in one ear and out the other as with our less intensive course in London. Finally, we had to take a driving test, before being given the driving licence issued to the French Army on the strength of which you would get an international licence for life.

Our examiner in Paris was Henriette Vieilhomme, a woman of about thirty-three, with lovely red hair, and so, so pretty in this gorgeous uniform which made you look too glamorous for words. She passed us, and I didn't see her again till I met her by chance shortly after the war. My boyfriend at the time, Jean de Villèyre, said one day, "I'm taking you to lunch with a very beautiful woman," and we went to 88, rue Michelange and had lunch with Henriette. She said to me, "You're English and you're in the French Army. I took two English girls for their driving exam before they went into battle, and one of them was called Dodo." I said, "Well, that's me!" She said, "I didn't think your driving was good enough, but it would have been too sad not to let you pass!"

Of course, we roared with laughter and I made very great friends with Henriette and her husband, Paul, and I often stayed with them. Her maiden name was Kiefer. She owned a fair amount of property, and her father was a well-known Alsatian doctor, practising in Paris. Paul is Jamie's godfather. He's tall, good-looking and very, very intelligent. He's a great wine man, and adores his wine. When he came to stay here at Slepe in '58, after Bruce, my other son, was born, he went round to the Cock and Bottle at Morden and found wines in their cellars which he said couldn't be bought in France since before the war. He's a *Gérant d'Affaires*, the French equivalent of a Chartered Surveyor. The extraordinary thing is that, throughout the war, he looked after the office of Chipps' uncle Pat Selby Ormond, my mother-in-law's only brother.

Pat was a lawyer in Paris. My father-in-law, Andy Bennett, was an international lawyer, too – he had been a partner of Pat's and took his *License ès Droit*, but subsequently became Chief Justice of the Sudan, a High Court Judge in India and a Q.C., and then a judge at the International Restitution Court in Germany.

In the evenings, Anne and I usually went our separate ways. Through Monique and André Jocet I was introduced to *Tout Paris,* who were very sophisticated, very amusing, very well dressed, mostly rich, and some of whom had collaborated. There was the ball at the *Cercle Interallié* after the parade in honour of Churchill. And, of course, cocktail parties and dinner parties. And visits to night clubs – Chez Susy Solidor in particular, where Susy had marvellous paintings of herself, many in the nude, all the way round the walls. One of Susy's songs was *The Peach*. She took a peach, and sang:

Je la prends
Je la susse
Je la sens . . .

making it into a very sort of dramatic act of love.

At one cocktail party I met Gaston Palewski, de Gaulle's Chef de Cabinet, or Private Secretary, and known by those who didn't like him as the *émimence grise* of France. He was of Polish extraction and very charming, though his face was covered with pockmarks. He was fascinated to see an English girl in French uniform, and we had a long talk because he was a great *résistant*. He said, "You must come and have dinner with me in my flat in the rue Jacob." I said, "Well, I'd love to." "Tomorrow," he said. "I hear you tell fortunes." I suppose Monique had told him. "You must tell mine." So the next day I went to have dinner with him in the rue Jacob.

After a very nice dinner *à deux*, I told his fortune and we talked about this and that, and then he said, "Buddy d'Allières tells me your fiancé's just been killed." Buddy d'Allières, you'll remember, was the head of the French Red Cross whom the marvellous Edwina Mountbatten had asked to enlist me. Later on, he was Chef de Protocol for the Prince of Monaco.

Of course, I was terribly, terribly sad and I burst into tears, and he put his arm round me and comforted me and poured me a glass of wine. He said, "Life seems completely empty for you now, Dodo, but, you know, you can love three people in your life. I have."

I've always remembered that, and I have, in fact, loved three people in my life – Howard, completely and on sight; Carroll Fitzgerald in a sort of infatuated way; and Chipps. I was engaged to Carroll for two years until Mummy persuaded me to break it off. Funnily enough he lives now in a villa in Xlendi, Gozo, where I have my other house (He died in 1988.) But when Gaston spoke to me I didn't think I'd ever love anybody again. I felt that I would flirt, perhaps I would sleep, but I would never love.

Gaston became a very great friend of mine and, whenever I was in Paris, I had dinner with him in the rue Jacob. There was a very dramatic evening in '47 or '48 when de Gaulle was in the wilderness at Colombiers and Gaston had just accepted a job from Faure or Gouin, whichever was then Prime Minister. In the middle of dinner a motorbike arrived with a letter from de Gaulle saying, *"La France peut vous pardonner, mais moi jamais."* So he gave up the job. Despite this, I don't think de Gaulle did ever forgive him. He was sent as Ambassador to Rome, but he was never given a really good *political* job again.

There's a lovely story about Gouin. When, as Prime Minister, he went to lay the wreath at the Arc de Triomphe, it happened to be the time the Americans were sending in maize flour as part of Marshall Aid. The Americans think this flour is a great delicacy but the French hated it, loathed it, so all the way along the Champs Elysees the crowd was shouting, "*Pain, Gouin! Pain, Gouin!*" What made it even more amusing was the fact Gouin actually did waddle rather like a penguin!

I had some trouble in the Champs Elysées, too. Monique's mother, Madame de Nervo, had a little electric car which charged itself up in the garage at night. She used to lend it to me to help me get around as there was hardly any petrol and half the *métros* didn't work. it was a terrifying thing to drive because it went very slowly in first, very slowly in second, very slowly in third and then faster in fourth, so you had great difficulty judging your distance and not being knocked into by the army vehicles whizz-banging everywhere. Needless to say, I ran out of power several times half way up the Champs Elysées and had to be pushed home.

During this time, Mary and Nan came back to Paris – Mary from the front and Nan from Brussels. We had a reunion and Nan gave me Howard's cigar case and his last letter to her in which he said, "Give Dodo all I have that she wants. Mary said, "Nan had Howard when she was scarcely out of the schoolroom. She loved him not only as a son but as a companion. It's very hard on her." I said, "Yes. It's very hard on me, too!" Anyway, they were both very sweet to me and we had many nice evenings together.

Then Monty came back for the great parade with de Gaulle – the Victory Parade. Monty persuaded Eisenhower not to let Mary take part, but to have Air Marshal Tedder, who was further up in the hierarchy, instead. O.K., but Tedder wasn't in the Invasion with Monty. I don't think Eisenhower liked Mary very much, and Mary always used to talk of Eisenhower rather pejoratively and say, "He signs his Christmas cards 'E' as if he was God or the King." So Mary went straight back to the front and Nan went straight back to Brussels. Before leaving, Mary said to me, "Use my car, Dodo, as much as you like" – his Air Marshall's car and Jim, the sergeant who drove it – "to go shopping or to go to parties. Do with it what you want."

Well, on the day of the parade, I decided to go shopping and, obviously on purpose, Jim didn't take the Air Marshall's flag off the bonnet. We drove around Paris in this Air Marshall's car with the Air Marshall's flag on the front, with me sitting in the back wearing my French uniform and my French *calot*, and, somehow, Jim got into the procession behind Eisenhower and Tedder and Monty right down the Champs Elysées. Of course the French went wild because they loved the Royal Air Force, they loved the 2nd T.A.F.: I got more cheers than anybody. It was the most divine surprise.

Mary came back to Paris the following weekend. By then Anne and I were on alert to join the *6ième R.I.C.* which had come up from Africa via Corsica and Elba. There hadn't been much fighting till they reached Besançon where we were to join them. It was all High Command stuff. Anita Leslie has written about it. Anyway, Mary said to me, "Before you leave for the front, would you like to come with me to see Nan and your friends, the Renkins, in Brussels? I'll take you in the bomb bay of my Mosquito." I said, "I'd love to!" and went to ask Madame de Peyerimhoff's permission and she said, "You won't be leaving for Besançon till Tuesday. You must be back in Paris on Monday."

So I took off on the Friday and went to stay with Nanette and her mother and father. It was terribly exciting to find them still in their old house after all they'd been through, and to sleep in my old room. Paul, who had stayed with us at Trokes at the time of Dunkirk, had been killed in the Ardennes, but in war death doesn't prevent you having fun as well. Brussels was so gay and happy, having just been liberated. Everybody was thrilled to have the English there: they couldn't do enough for you. People were giving you flowers, giving you champagne, giving you everything. Compared with Caen and any of the places I saw in Germany later, Paris and Brussels, apart from the odd gaping hole, had been left standing – including the Manneken Pis! Nan was staying in the R.A.F. Hostel and I went to see her there and talked to all the airmen.

I *had* to return on the Sunday, and the plane couldn't take off because it was too misty so Mary sent me back in a sort of station wagon with a driver. We'd just got beyond the frontier when a drunken French farmer came haring round a corner almost opposite a police station and crashed into us, and I was thrown unconscious out onto the ground. This was a sad incident. When I came to I was given a cup of coffee by a policeman (the farmer had been arrested) and, later, when I went through my rucksack, I discovered that some very nice pearls and a very pretty gold bracelet with a watch on it left to me by Gaga were missing. I've always, suspected the police of stealing them. Thank God, though, Howard's ring was still on my finger.

Chapter 12

WITH THE MAQUIS

Our twelve ambulances travelled towards Besançon in convoy. I went with Madame René who did most of the driving; Anne was with someone else. Amongst our number were two duchesses, a countess and a marquise. Most of us in fact were of *bonne famille*. I remember Fafa de Langallerie and Jacqueline de Chargière in particular. All mucked in, none of us minded the discomfort. Some whose name began with a "de" didn't mind not washing, either!

We spent that night lying on our stretchers in a barracks in Dijon because one of our engines seized up and had to be repaired. During the night I developed the most terrific sore throat and temperature and earache. Next day we moved off towards Besançon which we reached at about midnight. I was shivering and my head and eyes ached abominably. The city had been liberated and the Army had advanced that morning. The huge citadel was silhouetted against flashes of artillery fire to the north. We spent the night – two to a big double bed – in a former brothel.

My partner was an *ambulancière* with short cropped hair and a deep voice and, next morning, the others were giggling and asking what had happened, to which I could honestly say "Nothing" as we had both slept. As a matter of fact she later *did* seduce rather a pretty fluffy little *ambulancière* with blue eyes and the Army sent both of them back to Paris in disgrace.

Though the fighting army had moved on, soldiers of every kind and colour had remained in Besançon and were hurrying through the narrow streets. We saw Goums mounted on mules and Arab stallions, their lean dark faces surmounted by turbans and their bodies draped in what looked like brown fishnet which Anne called their *chemises de nuit*. The faces of the Zouaves contrasted strikingly with their scarlet *chechias,* a sort of fez cap, and *fourragères* (lanyards). We ourselves were in khaki and navy blue *calots. Calots* of varying colours were also the distinctive mark of the French Army, some of whom were in British or American battledress as they hadn't enough uniforms of their own.

My earache was so bad by now that Madame René decided I should be left to recover with a darling old farmer and his wife somewhere beyond Besançon while the other *ambulancières* drove north – it would be relatively easy for me to get a lift later to the front line. Unfortunately, cows lived in the farmhouse rather like they do in Gozo, and there were huge gaps in the floorboards of my room and things crept up and crawled all over my sweating body. But I felt too ill to care, just took the pills prescribed for me and drank the steaming *tisanes* tasting like senna pods, brought to me by the farmer's wife.

* When I was up and about, Colonel Barthelet *(nom de guerre* Boulaya*)* called at the farmhouse and asked me to tea. It was the first I had heard of the famous Maquis Chief, hero of the Franc-Comptois F.F.I., (Forces Francaises de l' Intérieur) who has since become a legendary figure through George Millar's book. He came that same afternoon to collect me for dinner. The romantic Colonel Boulaya was the picture of quiet respectability, in a grey suit and with a good-humoured smile and thinning fair hair. His wife, comely and kind, reminded me oddly of a red-haired gypsy who had once been my friend. They lived in a modern, delightfully furnished flat which had been lent to them by Maquis sympathisers after their own house and furniture had been destroyed by the Gestapo. In the drawing room there was a huge painting of Hitler, hung upside down, with the legend "Captured from Gestapo Headquarters by Colonel Barthelet of the Franc-Comptois F.F.I.,". I thought that my host in his well-pressed grey suit belied his dashing reputation, almost as much as my own dirty battle-dress contradicted my play-girl past.

One evening after about a week, when I was very much better, the farmer's wife came-upstairs to me and said, "There are some visitors for you." I was quite unprepared for the three sinister looking villains who were waiting for me. They introduced themselves as Captain Roco, George and Marco. The captain had an apache cap pulled down over his swarthy face and various murderous-looking weapons distributed about his person, barely concealed by a dark grey overcoat. George was good-looking in an aesthetic way and quite young, had two days growth of beard, a ragged coat and a pair of German uniform-trousers. I found out afterwards that these were the only ones he possessed and I never discovered what he had been wearing before he killed the German who had owned them!

The third member of this odd trio was dressed like a villain in a third-rate

---

* Some of the passages that follow have been taken at Dodo's request, from an account she wrote immediately after the war.

melodrama. Little Marco was an Italian with flashing black eyes, a curling moustache and he had hung a wicked looking knife round his neck on a thong. Only the sombrero hat was missing. He was dirty and ragged, obviously not a prosperous villain, but nevertheless I felt sure that any self-respecting maiden would undoubtably swoon if she should meet him in a dark alley. "How sweet," I thought. "They are just like small boys dressing up as robber bandits!" I wondered whether they looked as respectable as Boulaya when dressed in their best clothes.

"We believe there's an English nurse living here," said one. "Yes," I said. "That's me." He said, "We're from the Marquis. We've fifteen wounded in the mountains above the Swiss border across enemy lines. We need someone to look after them as we have no-one to nurse them."

I said, "Well, I'm not a doctor, but I can certainly nurse them. I'll do my best." The farmer's wife gave me a knapsack for my *trousse de secours* (medical case), and a big coat to protect me from the cold and to disguise my uniform.

We went a certain distance by lorry, then jettisoned the lorry and got onto bicycles which were in the back. Then, after bicycling to the mountains, we jettisoned the bicycles and walked – I presume the lorry and the bicycles were picked up by others afterwards.

Everybody always says to me, "How brave you were to cross the lines into *German-occupied* territory to help the marquisards." Well, I only saw a German patrol once during the journey and even then it was quite far off on the other side of a chasm. I was with Roco, their leader, one of the three who had come to the farmhouse to find me. *"Avec ta taille et ton accent il faut dire que tu es Alsacienne,"* he said. "Pretend we're a loving couple out for a evening stroll". He was only about five foot, and it isn't very easy to try and walk lovingly with someone who only comes up to your *nombril.* However, thinking we were peasants, the patrol merely shouted some ribaldries and then ignored us.

Roco was a fascinating character. He had been a *voyou* in Marseilles and his mistress was unfaithful to him, so he shot her lover and was imprisoned and expected to be guillotined. The gaoler – this was during the occupation, of course – said to him the night before his execution, "Do you believe in God?" Roco said, "No." He was a Communist, you see, one of the F.T.P. (*Francs Tireurs et Partisans*), that part of the Maquis who wanted to run France as a Communist State once she won her freedom. Anyway, the gaoler then said, "Do you believe in anything sufficiently to swear on?" "I'll swear," he said, "on the head of my mother." "Will you swear on the head of your mother," said the gaoler, "that if you knock me out and take my keys you will join the Maquis, because I think you'd be much more use to France in the Maquis than dead?" "Yes, I'll swear to that," said Roco and he escaped and was now, in charge of this particular group in the *réseau*, consisting of both F.T.P. and F.F.I., the non-Communists.

Chipps always says that I got my first *Croix de Guerre* for living with forty men in a mountain hut. Well, I did live with forty men, but I slept nearer to the fifteen wounded and everyone was awfully sweet. I mean, they treated me like a queen and never made a pass or anything: they even rigged up a blanket so that I had a bit of privacy.

Every so often some of them would go down to blow up a train or whatever and collect information left for them between the leaves of a telephone book in a certain kiosk. A lot of this information was collected by a charwoman who worked at the German headquarters. She would leave it in a different pre-arranged place each day where a small boy would pick it up. He would go to the goods train and take the last carriage where he hid and got out when the train slowed down where the Maquis were waiting for him.

One day he was hiding in the carriage when, suddenly, the S.S. came on to the platform. They ordered a complete search of the train. The little boy was terrified. They started at the beginning by the engine and went thoroughly into every carriage down the train. When they came to the one before the last, the station master, who was on our side, rushed forward and said, "The train must go or it will be late and then there is a danger of it being blown up." So they left the last carriage. When the Maquis collected him, the little boy was still shivering with fright and I think he must have had his first taste of *pastis* at that moment.

Several people have asked whether I was frightened during my sojourn behind the lines. I can truthfully say that it was among the most comfortable and happy of all my adventures. I was treated like a queen by the Maquis troupe, who waited on me hand and foot and, although the knowledge of danger was there, the joy of helping these brave people, even with so few amenities, was well worth it.

Picture four and twenty brave men huddled in the rough timber hut up the mountain, which served as the Resistance headquarters and secret wireless station, eating their supper. Some lay on straw mattresses against the wall. Others ate standing up, leaning against their guns by the door and glancing out from time to time to watch the rising moon as they gnawed their raw sausage and stale bread. Outside amongst the crooked firs the remainder of the contingent of forty *Franc Tireurs et Partisans* lay hidden along the snow-spattered path, keeping watch.

Inside the hut the air was thick with the smoke of black *gauloises* cigarettes. The little band of dirty, unshaven, ragged men came from all walks of life. There was a duke, a postman, the son of a rich industrialist, an elderly night-watchman, a young escaped prisoner of war, an artist and several men from the nearby steelworks. Roco sat in the middle of the hut at the only table working out a code message. They were drinking champagne – Pol Roger '38, stolen from a captured German lorry.

It was the quietest hour, when the Maquis relaxed, chatting and drinking before their Night Operations, while the watching guards gave them the illusion of security.

"How goes it, *mon vieux*?" the Duke asked Roco.

"*Ça va*!" answered the Southerner, turning his swarthy countenance into the light of the smokey oil lamp. "They want to know in London why we haven't sent any information lately. As if we hadn't other things to do!" He lit a black cigarette and spat a few bits of tobacco onto the floor. "It seems the pansy-boys of the R.A.F. don't know what to bomb these days. They make me tired. Why can't they bomb the German women and children if they've nothing better to do? Like they did to ours. My God, they don't know what war is, over there."

"I imagine they want a more useful target now that the second front has started in Normandy," said George. "These V.1 and V.2 installations, for instance. The German radio says they're causing havoc in London."

The oil lamp by Roco's hand flickered as the door was pushed wide open and a guard came in. Dressed in German army boots, corduroy trousers and a woman's fur jacket, he dwarfed the little old lady whom he was half pushing, half dragging over the threshold. Her hair stained with sweat, her clothes torn, her wrinkled face gleaming whitely in the half light, she stumbled into the room. She seemed to be at the end of her tether.

The guard saluted Roco and parked his rifle by the table. "I found this old hen coming up the secret path," he said. "She seems half dead, but I thought I'd better not take any chances, so I brought her here myself. Not that she looks dangerous!" He laughed brutally. "I don't suppose there'll be any need for the spy routine. The old tart doesn't look as though she could dig her own grave."

One of the engineers supported the old lady to an upturned packing case and forced some brandy down her throat. There were murmurs among the men, who had all stopped drinking and turned towards the newcomer. Two of them spat. A few laughed. A young boy with a pink and white face and soft down on his upper lip offered her a cigarette, which she refused with a weak wave of her be-ringed hand. Roco had not said a word.

Suddenly the postman spoke. "My God! It's not possible!" He pushed the lamp under her face. "Yes, it's Madame la Comtesse." He shook his head unbelievingly and waved the lamp backwards and forwards. "No wonder she's tired." He pushed the guard aside and went over to her. He handed her his bread and meat. "She must have climbed all the way without food. It's two days walk from her *château*."

Roco got to his feet. Small and tough though he was, the lamplight made him tower above her. Very deliberately he bowed. The old lady's eyes gleamed up at him and the silence was thick amongst the waiting men as they sensed the bond between these two. Gently Roco helped her to her feet. It was as though he did not wish to have her at a disadvantage. The Countess drew herself up and looked him straight in the eyes. She smiled and her hand moved up to straighten her hair, with a gesture that was almost coquetry. She swayed a little but her voice was firm and crystal clear.

"I came here to find you, Captain Roco, because I want you to do me a favour. I want you to send a message to London to tell the R.A.F. to send a squadron to bomb my park. My gardener – who is one of you – will verify that this is not a trap. I believe that the Germans are building something secret in my garden. Before they started to wall it in, I got a glimpse of the machine they are assembling. It looks like a small aeroplane – or a large bomb. It is guarded night and day."

She drew a sheaf of photographs out of her *fichu* and laid them on the table in front of Roco. Her manner became practical. "These are aerial photographs of my property," she explained. "They were taken by a friend of my son's a long time ago. I have marked in red ink the exact location of the German barracks and the Officers' Mess. In green ink I have marked, as near as I can, the spot where they are building this machine."

In her enthusiasm she was indifferent to the bruises and discomfort of her tired body, even to her soaked clothes that were clammy and cold. Her eyes were eager and her hands that held out the photos to Roco were alive in their carved whiteness. She was stronger than the tough little band of men – their combined power was as nothing compared to the determination in her wiry, delicate frame. The men were silent. Roco looked at the small figure who represented all that he had ever hated in this world – wealth and capitalism, the old order out of which had been born his sad education amongst the slums and prisons of Marseilles. His voice was a challenge as he told her, "Your information can be very useful, Madame. It may be worth your tiring journey. But think well before you ask me to send this message. If the R.A.F. come and bomb your park, they will almost certainly destroy your castle too."

He sat down at the table and said in a whisper so that the men could not hear him, "Although you may not believe me, Madame, I know how much that means to you. After all, it's the only thing you have left."

The old lady drew herself up proudly. Her voice rang clearly through the mountain hut, but she spoke to Roco alone, "I think that's a very small price to pay for France."

Her park was bombed and the German weapon destroyed, but the *château* was not touched. Marvellous R.A.F.!

So I was living with these men in the mountains. It was snowing, but our hut was under the pines and we'd plenty of fuel for a fire. We were never short of food: we regularly collected *saucisses*, bread, cheese and wine given generously by peasants in a village down below. One thing we *did* need was penicillin – one of the men had been shot in the stomach and he was very ill. I had a syringe in my *trousse de secours* and I knew about penicillin because we had used it at Shenley. "I must have penicillin," I explained, and it was agreed that, with two *Maquisards* to guard me, I should walk by mountain paths and cross the Swiss frontier at Delle where there was a hospital. The journey took a day and a half. A doctor, after examining my British Passport, gave the penicillin I needed. Very Swiss, he charged an exorbitant sum and made me sign a receipt! He knew that it would never be paid for but at least he had a signature and a British passport number.

There was one small incident of which I was totally ignorant until afterwards. Roco, who had been guarding the hut, caught sight of a German sniper who had aimed his gun at me while I was taking in a wounded patient. The little Italian shot him before he had taken proper aim.

I learnt later that some of the money to support the *Maquis* came from François Louis-Dreyfus who had been in the French Air Force at the beginning of the war: When the Germans took Paris, being from a well-known Jewish family, he realised he was not safe in France so he got away to Buenos Aires where his family owned the grain monopoly and a fleet of ships. He asked to send money through Switzerland to help the *Maquis* funds and years later, when he became engaged to my friend Monique, we went to Switzerland to find his agent, Monsieur Boulot.

Monsieur Boulot was very Swiss! François asked him to describe his journeys to Alsace to deliver the money and he replied, "I used to read and memorise the instructions and then, as ordered, I would burn them and write them all down in my diary."

Monique and I could hardly suffocate our giggles. However, the money got through and Monsieur Boulot was never caught.

My *Maquisards* intended to go to the front whose whereabouts I now had to try and find myself. They laughed and talked optimistically of numbers they intended to kill when they became real soldiers at last. Poor brave little *Maquis*! How many were broken or killed, I wonder, in the bloody battles of the Colmar Poche by the well-trained, well armed "*Schleuhs*" of whom they were so contemptuous in the first flush of victory?

Chapter 13

Into Germany With My Regiment

Reluctantly I said good-bye to my *Maquisards* and made my way to Montbeliard where I reported at its old castle, the headquarters of the First French Army. There I was shown into a small office and, not having slept for about four days, I sat on a chair in one corner and fell fast asleep. I woke to find a frightfully good-looking man staring down at me. "Good heavens!" he said. "What are you doing in my office!" I said, "Oh, *mon Lieutenant*," I was rather tired, "I've come to beg a lift so as to re-join my regiment – the *6ième R.I.C.*" "Well," he said, "I shall always remember you because I'm not a lieutenant, I'm a two star général."

He was Général de Linares who, after that, I always called *"Mon général deguisé en lieutenant"* when he stopped his jeep to chat with me. Anyway, on this occasion, because earache was bothering me again, he arranged for a jeep to take me to Boncourt, a small Alsatian village whose school, the one undamaged building, had been taken over as a Casualty Clearing Station. Just as I arrived, they were preparing a patient for operation. It was an *ambulancière* with a bullet in her stomach, and I was terrified it might be Anne. At Boncourt, while being treated myself, I helped as a nurse before being transferred to the Casualty Clearing Station at Mulhouse.

When I remember the Alsace Campaign nowadays, I do not think of the mud and blood, the intense cold and the thrill of danger, nor the spit of machine gun bullets keeping pace with my racing heart, but I remember the personality of Captain Pierre d'Aimbert, the doctor of the *9ieme D.I.C.* against the plaintive leitmotif of 'Lily Marlene'. It is odd that, although I have always hated the idea of war and death, I look back on those days almost with regret. The friendliness, the unselfish bravery, above all the fact that we were all in it together, brought me closer to the minds of my associates than I had ever been with my peace-time intimates. Since then how often have I longed for the easy camaraderie of those shared hardships, and dangers!

At Mulhouse, I did see Anne again whenever she brought back casualties. But, because of my earache – it was otitis developing into a double mastoid – I didn't join her at the front. This was just as well as another nurse was needed at the Clearing Station desperately. The place was absolute chaos.

Ambulances were coming in continuously, groaning patients lined the corridors and we had to operate day and night. Half the time I was helping the surgeon, half the time tending the wounded with dressings and injections. Despite the blood and smell and horror we did what we could, using sheets and blankets as dressings, scrubbing down any old table for use as an operating table.

There was a German, obviously one hundred per cent Nazi, who kept swearing at us and tearing off his dressings, and shouting, "I want to die for the Führer! I want to die for the Führer!" Finally I yelled at him in German – he was upsetting other patients – "Well, if you want to die for the Führer, this is the last time I'm putting these dressings on! You can bloody well *die* for the Führer! I shall leave you to do it! In fact I'll help you!" He didn't take his dressings off again.

The men coming in to us at Mulhouse were from the Battle of the Colmar Poche. That battle seemed to go on for *ever*. The French lost thousands but, every time a man was lost, somebody new wanted to join and, as a result, that pocket was held. And in Von Runstedt's counter-offensive the French held their line: it was the Americans, the 7th Army, who dropped back.

People always say the French did nothing in the war. My goodness, I know otherwise. They were marvellous. From wherever they were liberated, there was an influx of young conscripts and ex-*Maquisards* who picked up uniforms from the dead – they'd even use the boots of the German dead when they thought they were of better quality.

The padre of our regiment was a terrific morale booster. I didn't meet him at the front till after Christmas, and I sometimes met him at the Mulhouse Casualty Station when he came back during a lull in the fighting to give extreme unction. He was a Catholic Monk – a Benedictine, I think. Knowledge of his presence, here and later at the front, consoled me. Those who died were often in a state of grace due to his ministrations.

We had moved up to Altkirch. Our new quarters looked grim and foreboding. Shelling was going on quite violently when we arrived and the town looked deserted and derelict, with very few houses intact. Some of the people were hostile and all the children spoke German or the Alsatian dialect. The snow had thawed slightly and I felt as though I was walking over a badly iced chocolate cake, the dark frozen mud crinkling and giving under my worn boots. I thought that it looked even more desolate than the battered towns of Normandy, as the wintry sun made blood red pools out of the melted snow.

The C.C.S. was established with the usual efficient bustle and one of the German prisoners brought me the welcome news that the post had arrived.

This was an unusual event and, as soon as my work was finished, I abandoned myself to the voluptuous pleasure of skimming through a huge pile of letters, some dated four months back, accentuating my cut-off state.

There were several rambling documents from my mother, the unaccustomed staccato typing being almost as illegible as her spidery handwriting, but they brought a warm comfort and a nostalgic vision of home. I could imagine her sitting in the library, glints from the setting sun picking silver threads out of the gold of her hair, tapping out the letter with two fingers on the hated machine which her family and friends had bullied her into buying, her tongue going round and round her lower lip, rather like a small boy concentrating on his homework. She would be worrying about us all, I knew – wondering where I was now and whether I was wearing enough underclothes; thinking about Mike and his guerrilla troops behind the lines in northern Italy, and Gwen, his new wife, who had just flown home; thinking about Bumble, her "baby" twenty-year-old widow, who was far away in Malta.

Poor Mummy, she had a queer unsettled nomad family for one who was deeply rooted in the soil of her Dorset garden and I wondered again for the hundredth time whether our Spanish grandmother had slipped a little gypsy blood into our veins . . .

During that Christmas of 1944 my ear was so bad I was told to go back to Paris and have it looked at by a specialist. I went by ambulance, driven by a girl who also needed some sort of special treatment. When we arrived, I was put on a stretcher on a floor in the Headquarters of the French Red Cross. A specialist then examined me and said he must operate, but I told Madame de Peyerimhoff I'd prefer an English surgeon and I arranged through André Jocet, Mary Coningham's liaison officer, for Mary to lend me his Mosquito back to England.

Meanwhile Monique nursed me at her home in Neuilly. She put hot compresses on my ears and her doctor gave me some homeopathic pills. When she drove me to Le Bourget where the pilot was waiting with Mary's plane, there was a thick, thick fog and nothing was taking off because visibility was too near. I lay on a stretcher and she stayed with me till evening when the pilot said, "I don't know what to do. The Air Marshal needs his plane tomorrow morning." As it would have been criminal to ask him to stay – he needed the plane for action Monique took me back to Neuilly and continued nursing me till Anne's father, Brigadier Swinton Lee, got me into the American Hospital. There they gave me penicillin and almost cured me without an operation.

I'll always remember that, during Christmas, a stick of bombs was dropped on Paris, I do not know why or where. It wasn't very near the American Hospital, but you could hear the thump. The American doctors thought it was probably a German airman with a grudge. The point of the story is that all the American patients and the doctors and the nurses dived under the beds, every single one of them, including the cases who shouldn't be out of bed. I was in bed and I didn't move: I just went on reading my book.

After Christmas I flew back to England in a French Air Force Dakota from Le Bourget to Croydon. From Croydon I went down to Trokes which my mother had let to Bumble's mother-in-law, Atty Curtis, the wife of General "Squeaker" Curtis who had seen me off to France. There, an old faith healer friend of Aunt Maddy's put his hands on my ears and miraculously took the remaining pain away.

It was now January and I was rearing to get back to France. We'd taken Strasbourg and were waiting to cross the Rhine into Germany. I packed my kit and went up to London and stayed at my mother's hostel and reported for duty at the French Red Cross in Belgrave Square where I was told I could leave from Croydon the next day – again on a French Air Force Dakota.

I decided, before leaving, to pay a visit to Daisy Carter, the well known fortune teller, in St. John's wood. A loquacious old Cockney, she first gave me a *spiel* about her illustrious clients and how my friend Ernie Bevin came to her regularly. Did I want tarot, hands or the crystal ball? I said I'd have the lot, and what she told me turned out to be amazingly true. Except one thing. She said I'd write a famous book that would have three words in the title. As I want this one to be called "Dodo", it can't be that. I wasn't in uniform and she didn't know me from Adam but she said, "You're in uniform and you're in the uniform of another country and you think you're returning to that country tomorrow but you're not, there'll be a delay. You *will*, however, get back and you will cross a river with dark men wearing red hats. You'll be commanded by a little man who looks like a bear and, after going through fire and hell with him, he will ask you to marry him."

Well, I didn't go back for three days because of engine trouble, I crossed the Rhine with the Zouaves of the *9ième D.I.C.* and I went through the Battle of Freudenstadt, commanded by Colonel Aumeron, later General Aumeron, who proposed to me after the battle and he did look like a bear: I called him "*mon petit ourse*".

The army train from Paris to Strasbourg was so packed somebody had to lift me up and put me through a window. Strasbourg, of course, now that it was liberated, was the greatest fun with plenty of good food and it was there that Colonel Dessert awarded me my first Croix de Guerre for my work with the *Maquis*. The Palme, or Bar, came later, for rescuing wounded from minefields.

The French were very proud to have got to Strasbourg first. They'd shouted at the Americans when they came in, "You're a bit late, aren't you chums?" Before crossing into Germany, General de Lattre de Tassigny gave them a pep talk saying, "No fraternisation at all. These are our enemies. They've murdered your women and children. They've destroyed entire villages and towns. Fight to the death, but no fraternisation!" And all the troops said, "Fraternisation? We won't fraternise! We'll get their guts! We'll get their balls'" Then, as soon as they arrived and there was a peaceful moment, they were giving sweets to the children and poking the girls. Too funny. De Lattre de Tassigny himself, of course, didn't like women.

It is a strange feeling going into battle. I don't believe I shall ever forget the morning that we crossed the Rhine: it was quiet and cold and I wondered what was in store for us, how many casualties we would have and would the lines of communication be too long to get them back to the Casualty Clearing Station in time? We were going back to Irmgard's country. She had said to me before the war in our teenage language, "Though rivers of blood may flow between our two countries, our friendship will build a bridge." And it *has* built a bridge though she is now dead, killed by the Russians in Silesia.

The crossing was unforgettable. We had worked for this for so long. Lives had been given that we might reach this broad river with its swift current and the unknown power waiting for us on the far bank. Lives had been taken that the river might no longer be a boundary, that the dragon awaiting us might be killed or put in chains.

We crossed at Speyer, north of Strasbourg, where the *9ieme D.I.C.* had waited for two months knowing that they had only to show themselves to provide a shot from the opposite bank. Although we had the minimum of assault craft, the casualties were surprisingly low. Perhaps the Germans had not expected us to attempt it. My fellow *ambulancière* at the time was a girl called Christianne Deschelrins – Anne had crossed already. I was the driver.

The Americans had issued us with trousers, but I was the only girl who could fit into them! As part of our K rations, also supplied by the Americans – delicious bars of vitamin-filled dark chocolate, cigarettes, matches, sachets of sugar, sachets of lime juice, sachets of Nescafe, tins of ham and egg pie, tins of spam, loo paper – we were issued with French Letters, so Desch and I blew them up and tied them on a bit of string to our ambulance like balloons; we crossed the Rhine trailing them behind us. This, I assure you, was very good for the French *poilus*' morale.

The deformed hulk of the old bridge lay in two pieces, tipped drunkenly against the sky. It wasn't easy driving over our hastily erected pontoon. It swayed and rocked in the current as we drove slowly into Germany, accompanied only by stray shots. It was curiously sad this unexpected lack of resistance. In most of the derelict villages, the men saluted and the women curtsied, servile and terrified. Once an old woman spat at us as we drove past and a little further a prosperous looking man saluted. "I liked the first greeting best," I said, surprised. "Yes," said Desch, "I suppose you'd call the man a *collaborateur*. How odd it sounds to use that term when describing a German!"

We drove straight to Karlsruhe for the forest in between had been taken by the *23ième* regiment and the road was no longer exposed to gunfire. The convoy stopped only once and we got out of the ambulance, glad of the chance to stretch our legs and spend a penny. Inhibitions are hard to lose. All the way up the road there were Frenchmen, Arabs, Indo-Chinese, and neither Desch nor I had ever managed to conquer our civilised upbringing, so we slunk away in search of a bush, not caring about the possibility of mines and only wishing that the Commandant had not chosen a clearing for the halt.

Before we had gone far he shouted out: "*Nom d'un pipe, qu'est ce que vous faites là*? You know very well you are forbidden to leave the road! Do you want to be blown up by a mine or shot by a sniper? What are you doing anyway?" We both blushed scarlet. "Well, come back at once and behave like anyone else! No one's watching you, *nom de Dieu*!" he said furiously and I knew that he was blaming it all on my English upbringing. The French, who simply pee anywhere handy, think the English terribly hypocritical about that sort of thing. There is much to be said for their point of view!

After we had eaten, I took the wheel. Keeping exactly fifty yards behind the truck in front of you is a difficult business when passing through such beautiful country. It was twilight when we reached Karlsruhe, which lay derelict and deserted, with some of the houses still burning.

We spent a few hours kipping in our ambulance and then were roused by the Commandant. There was no one awake in the village, except the medical contingent and a few sleepy Indo-Chinese guards. One of them challenged us sharply, his finger on the trigger.

"Oh dear, I've forgotten the password again," said Desch, so I hissed

"Kiss" at him. He looked at me suspiciously and I saw that he did not understand my accent.

"Keeeess," Desch interpreted for me. His yellow face crinkled as he smiled and told us, "Switch your lights off and drive with your 'code' lights only. There are a lot of snipers out and the road is covered by gun-fire." He let us through.

"These little yellow men frighten me more than the Germans," Desch whispered to me as we drove to the dressing station. "I always think they are going to let off their rifles, whether I've remembered the *mot de passe* or not, just for the fun of it!"

Desch and I went to church the next morning. It was dark and cold and every inch of standing-room down the aisle was crowded. Hostile, frightened eyes gazed at us, seeing in us the destroyers of their homes, the invaders of their country. I was not sure that I liked the feeling of being a conqueror. "Only Nazis appreciate that," Desch commented when I told her of my sensation of guilt.

We rejoined the medical team and the *9ième D.I.C.* fought its way to Rottweil, before which there was quite a bloody battle as the town was held by S.S. troops. The only two buildings that seemed to be standing were two factories. We put our stretchers in one of the factory offices and ate the remainder of our rations before going to sleep. There was no water of any sort and the sanitary arrangements weren't working, the result being rather more unpleasant than usual. Desch had a bottle of *eau de cologne*, but I was so filthy after all the dust and mud that my skin and hair were engrained with dirt and I felt that I would never be clean again. It is bad for the soul to be really dirty, until one reaches the lousy stage, when it is no longer degrading, merely inevitable. We cleaned our teeth with white wine out of Jaqueline de Chargière's water flask.

Desch and I were picking wounded off the field of battle and we had made so many journeys to the casualty clearing station we had lost count. We had little morphia syringes which you stuck in the arms of the wounded and the dying and then threw away. One man. called to me in German, as I approached, "Don't touch me! I'm mined!" The Germans wired their own wounded to mines so as to blow us to smithereens when we picked them up! I gave him some morphine and left him as there were minesweepers following.

There was a frightfully brave doctor, a lover of Anne's actually – he was half her size but he adored her. Well, he walked across a minefield and wouldn't let the *brancardiers*, the stretcher bearers, come with him. He tended those on the ground by himself and then waited for the mineclearers.

He got a *Croix de Guerre* for that.

At first Desch and I had Senegalest stretcher bearers. One used to get us water in our tin hats so we could wash. Then he always stayed out of the ambulance and turned his back, though I invited him inside as it was so cold. This suited my *pudeur,* however. The Senegalese were eventually sent home because they were turning blue with cold and dying like flies. So we mostly had North African Arabs and Indo-Chinese cooks and Goums and Moroccans and Zouaves.

We arrived in Rottweil where, on entering a derelict house, I found a child eating a candle because of the fat it contained. At Rottweil the doctor told me to go into a factory and set up an operating table in preparation for further fighting. We had a doctor, a couple of Arab nursing orderlies and four stretcher-bearers – that was the medical unit. The Indo-Chinese cooks were marvellous. To supplement our K rations they shot chickens and so on which, in the French Army was not called stealing, it was called "requisitioning". The doctor was a white Frenchman, but the man who paid us was a black lieutenant whom we saluted. There was no snobbery in the French Army – and no colour bar either . . .

I went into a room of this factory to make it into an operating theatre. I removed some blueprints off a table and scrubbed it down. I then removed more blueprints off some shelves where I started arranging the medical supplies. Suddenly, I noticed a man hiding in a corner. I don't know what made me do it, but I went straight away to the drawer of a desk which was covered in blueprints also. There was a revolver in it. I grabbed the revolver and pointed it at the man and waited till an orderly arrived. I shouted to the orderly, "Call some soldiers! This man must be taken prisoner!" and he turned out to be a Russian civilian working at this place on research for an atom bomb. Lord Linlithgow's brother, George Scott, who was in Intelligence and who I hadn't seen since Grenadier parties in London, arrived in Grenadier uniform about an hour later, the only English uniform I'd seen since Normandy, and told me what an important thing I'd done. Afterwards, when the war was over, a French pilot "requisitioned" a Junkers and flew me back to Paris for a weekend. We gave George a lift. The manoeuvres of our French pilot terrified him. Poor George, he was taking aspirins and swigs out of a whisky bottle all the way!

I was attached to the Zouaves for the Battle of Freudenstadt. This time I was with Anne, though we were often kept apart. I'm sure the French thought these two six foot Amazons were spies, Lesbian spies. Much as I love them, there's a deep mistrust, you know, amongst the French about the British. They think we're all out to kill Joan of Arc again . . . There was a particular corner of the valley road which the Army couldn't get past because of a gun manned by Germans, Anne and I were hanging around smoking till tanks or the Air Force arrived to blow it up. I played an army song on my squeezebox and soon we were all singing:

Il y a des gars sur toutes les routes
Aujourd'hui comme à demain
Et ça suffit que tout le monde s'en foute
Il y a des gars sur touts les chemins.

Later it becomes unprintable. Our regiment had originally been Marines and its little song was:

Nous sommes les soldats de la marine
Et nous avons dans la poitrine
Le coeur d'un matelot
Et celui d'un soldat,

While we were singing, along came some Americans dishing out K rations and chatting us up and so on and so forth. Then suddenly machine-gun fire rang out from the other side of the gorge. Needless to say, the Americans went down flat on their faces much to the amusement of everyone else who merely carried on singing as before.

We were waiting to go round the guarded corner when Evelyn Irons, the war correspondent, appeared out of the blue and interviewed Anne and me for the *Evening Standard*. The article, when it was eventually published, read:

> "Striding along the road in the Black Forest, beside a broad mountain torrent, were two splendid Amazons in khaki. One was a blonde and the other a brunette, and both had striking good looks. They were each six feet tall, and in addition, towered a foot higher, because they wore the high scarlet chéchia of the Zouaves. I stopped and stared and wondered what on earth these two were doing in the French Front as ambulancières with the French Red Cross.' . . . 'The blonde who wore the red and green ribbon of the *Croix de Guerre* was Anne Swinton Lee from London, twenty-one-year-old daughter of Mrs. and General Swinton Lee, who was Civil Affairs Chief in Paris. The other was Dodo Lees from Dorset who was twenty-five yesterday.

> They showed me the American ambulance van which they had driven with the French Army since they joined the troops in the battle for Alsace. There was a bullet hole in the right hand side of the windscreen. The bullet whizzed through when Anne was driving alone along a snowbound road near Mulhouse. The ambulance is left-hand drive and the bullet passed clean through the front, without touching the wounded, and emerged through the back."

The Zouaves attacked the next day and drove the enemy down the mountain pass which was our only line of communication. On one side the pines rose steeply to the sky line, on the other a precipice dropped sheer to the river. The road wound through the valley, dropped down to the river, then climbed again, a perfect white target for snipers and, for the first time, we knew the terror of being hunted at night by the German *Maquis*.

Every day the Casualty Clearing Station got further away, until our evacuations took three hours or more and, as the number of casualties increased, we were seldom off the road, snatching our meals out of tins and sleeping when we could. Our reception in the villages was different now and the civilians, some of them women, fired from their windows and from behind the shelter of the trees.

The battle was quite fierce and it was chaos ferrying the wounded to the Casualty Clearing Station. Anne and I just went back and forth and back and forth until the battle was over. Everything in Freudenstadt seemed to be on fire. We went into one burning house to see if anybody was left in there alive and found nothing but corpses. The owner, obviously a Nazi, had shot himself after slitting the throats of his wife and six children.

Ali, our Arab orderly, noticed a rather nice leather case with gold topped bottles in it and said to me, "Look! For you, Missy!" I said, "No, no, no! That's loot! We mustn't loot!" Later, when we were further down the street, we saw a Moroccan carrying the case away and Ali said, "*You* could have had that Missy!"

The casualties at Freudenstadt really were terrible. One night I had to take four of them back to the Clearing Station all alone. The lines of communication had been getting longer and longer but I knew roughly the route I should be taking. I was driving only with my side lights when I heard Howard's voice from the empty seat beside me saying, "Darling, I'll be with you always. Now stop." I stopped, got out of the ambulance and I went round with my torch and I found that the bridge I was about to cross was no longer there, I was on the edge of a chasm! A minute later and we'd have been in the river below.

After the victory celebration, when Colonel Aumeron presented us with our *chechias,* Anne and I (probably the only two women in the world who have the right to wear one), had to make our own way back to join our regiment. We had our maps but bridges marked on it had been blown up and we kept getting lost. The snow had melted. It was a hot day in April, and we were dying of thirst and we asked at a farmhouse for glasses of water. The farmer's wife went down to the cellar and brought us up a jug of ice-cold delicious cider. We drove on. Suddenly we were going through a forest – we looked at each other. I said to Anne, "Have you got a pain? I've got a pain." She said, "Yes. An awful pain." I said, "My God! We've been poisoned!" So we stopped the ambulance and made a map showing where the farmhouse was and where we were now, and I wrote a letter to my mother and Anne wrote to *her* mother and, after we'd done all this, we found we were perfectly all right again. The pain had obviously been due to drinking acid cider on an empty tummy, but we'd had quite a fright.

As we went deeper into the Black Forest, I realised why it had gained its sinister reputation. The dark trees closed in on us relentlessly and there was no mercy in the depths of the bottomless pools that lay beneath great crags of jagged rock. Gnomes, wizards, werewolves, could all be imagined in those eerie surroundings. Many of the people were hunchbacks and I saw women with goitres and other disfigurements. It was an intensely romantic country, which lent itself to the dark deeds of the medieval stories and, sometimes at night, as we drove through the silent pines, Anne and I had to talk and sing to keep our courage up, feeling that the danger of battle was far less frightening than this lonely stillness.

In spite of the beauty of the landscape, there was an atmosphere of leashed evil, which spoke of Wagner and Hans Anderson and the witch in Hansel and Gretel. It was a strange country, this land of contrasts which the French had come to capture from the greater evil of Nazism.

At a place which, I think, was called Zell, I was paired again with Desch. And again the communication lines got longer and longer as we were advancing so quickly and the Germans were giving in. We would arrive in a town and the officer would always take the best billets leaving us to sleep in our ambulance with the wounded. Once, when I'd had enough of this, I told Desch to drive back with the casualties on her own while I looked for a pad. "I speak German," I said. "I'll get a pad not only for us but for the whole Medical Team." As soon as she'd gone, I went into a rather modest looking house backing onto a high mountain of the Black Forest, a sort of workman's house, about three flights. A beefy man came to the door. He was in old clothes, but didn't seem at ease in them. He had the air of someone prosperous.

I said, "I am requisitioning rooms for two *ambulancières* and their Medical Team. I would like to see over your house, please."

He glared at me and took me upstairs. The first room he showed me was his children's bedroom. "Have this. My children will have to sleep with me and my wife." "For heaven's sake," I said, "I'm not going to take the beds away from your children!"

At that his attitude changed completely. He said, "Well, if you promise me on your honour that you will not reveal that you stayed with me, I can provide space for all of you." We were seven – Desch and myself, the doctor, the orderly and two stretcher-bearers and the Arab orderly. I couldn't believe there'd be space for everyone. But he took me to a kitchen cupboard with a broom and a hoover in it, and he pressed a button and the whole of the back opened and, there, in the heart of the mountain, was a drawing-room with air conditioning and gorgeous carpets and marvellous furniture including a pink radiogram like the Dubonnets had in the rue des Graviers. It was a real luxury apartment because, beyond that, there was a gorgeous bedroom and another room with deep freezes where a maid was ironing. So we all slept in this sort of hide-out. Not only that, we were given a marvellous dinner of *pâté de fois gras* and God knows what. I suppose he was a leading Nazi who had got his hide-out prepared, or he was a big business man. Anyway we had a comfortable night and didn't say anything about it. Sometimes the Germans could be nice.

On one occasion, I drove behind the lines into a deserted village where there were no lights except in one house so I assumed it had been occupied by the Germans. I knocked at the door to ask how we could get back to the French Army and found myself face to face with a German corporal who pointed his revolver straight at my tummy. But I asked my question – in German – "Where is the French Army?" All he did was shake his revolver at me, so I retreated backwards to the ambulance, got in and, in my panic, stalled the engine. The German rushed down the path, waving his revolver. I was certain he was going to shoot. Instead he shouted, "Don't go that way! The German Army is that way! The French Army is that way!" Back at H.Q. I proposed a toast to him.

On the way to Tuttlingen we found another billet: a German farmwife let Desch and me sleep in her own bedroom. I said, "We've only got four hours. Will you wake us, please?" She woke us after about three and a half hours and we went downstairs. Breakfast was all ready on a table at which a young man, her son, was sitting in German Army uniform. "You speak German," she said. "Will you advise my son, Hans, what to do? He's been on leave and he's due to rejoin his regiment." I said, "My dear lady, I can certainly advise you. He can't possibly rejoin his regiment. We've taken this part of the region and you're entirely surrounded. You must burn his uniform, put him in civilian clothes, put a bandage round his leg and set him to do simple household tasks. Otherwise, he'll be a prisoner of war as sure as eggs is eggs."

We were now advancing quickly. Desch and I stopped in a town and found ourselves a billet where there was one bedroom with two officers' rucksacks on the beds. I said to Desch, "Look, they always take the best billets. Let's put the rucksacks in the living-room next door where there are two perfectly comfortable sofas." So we went out and had something to eat with the others and came back and went to bed and locked the door. We had to be up at four. At two, there were furious bangings on the door. We paid no attention. At half past three, when in uniform again, we went out to join our ambulance and there was a furious little man in pyjamas shaking his fist at us saying, "How dare you take my room? I am a General!" I couldn't resist saying with my English accent, "I'm afraid I don't salute generals in pyjamas!" and we went out quickly before he arrested us.

The siege of Lahr was our last big battle. After that the *9ième D.I.C.* continued to 'mop up' the remains of the German Army in Wurtenburg, Baden, and the Black Forest – as far south as Basle and east towards Bregenz on the Lake Constance. We captured the notorious concentration camp of Charnier. Many French patriots had met with torture and death there, but we found some of the victims still alive. Then we went south towards Todmoos where the scenery became more alpine. We advanced up to a hundred kilometres daily, stopping for a few hours in each town as it surrendered, sometimes moving on again in the middle of the night. Most of the troops had requisitioned bicycles to quicken their pace. When they broke down, we put them, bicycle and all, into the back of the ambulance, which was, of course, the most popular method of transit. Once I saw a lazy N.C.O., a friend of ours, puncture his tyre with his tie-pin so that he could have a free ride! It was a more leisurely war this, and one could take time off for lunch. At last the Germans were on the run.

I then rejoined Anne. For a short time we were attached to the Goums, a very romantic regiment with a fierce reputation amongst their enemies. The N.C.O. had a beautiful Arab stallion and the belief amongst his soldiers was that he was the only man who could ride it. Anne and I got up early one morning and had a good gallop. He was as quiet as a lamb. It didn't do much for the N.C.O.'s *kudos* but the soldiers were our slaves from then on. It was a contrast to the war we had hitherto known: billeted in comfort on the Germans and living off the land whenever our rations failed to catch up with us. On the whole the civilians were now resigned to the fact that Germany had lost the war and only longed for the bloodshed to cease. In the more remote parts of the German Alps they still believed in Goebels' picture of the Allies and many of them were terrified of us, believing that we had come to murder them and take their food away so that they would starve during the winter.

The regiment went up to a sanitorium in the mountains. There was little fighting. At one point we saw a group of Germans who wanted to give us their arms. As we were officially not allowed arms in our ambulance, although we did have a revolver hidden for emergencies, we told them they must wait for the soldiers to come up, who would take them prisoner. They included two generals.

We rejoined the regiment at the sanitorium at St. Blasien, where we spent the night. The nurses and doctors were all very dour and were obviously Nazis. In the morning Commandant Langlais commandeered their ambulance, so Anne drove it and I drove ours. Half way up the mountain I saw to my horror that Anne's wheel had come off and her ambulance was poised terrifyingly over the brink of the road, almost falling into the chasm. I stopped my ambulance and rushed forward, opened the door and said, "Get out quickly!" which she did and we went on in our ambulance. We were both convinced that some of the staff at the sanitorium had loosened the wheel purposely and, but for the grace of God, it could have killed Anne.

From Lindau the regiment made its way towards Brigenz on the Austrian border, with no opposition at all. I was thrilled to go back into Austria, but Eisenhower didn't want the French to take Austria. He wanted the Americans to go in there, so we were told by de Lattre de Tassigny that the regiment had to go back to Tuttlingen which we reluctantly did.

When peace was declared we were billeted at Trossingen but our *popote* and regiment were in Tuttlingen, Our Commandant, Pierre Langlais, took Anne and me and another officer up to the hospital in the mountains above a lake when he went to interrogate its chief doctor who had the reputation of being very Nazi. I was to act as interpreter.

The doctor kept shouting, "We're holding out elsewhere! We're holding out in Norway. Don't you worry, we'll win in the end!" I said to Pierre, "He certainly is a Nazi. I should report him as a Nazi if I were you and have him taken prisoner." Pierre said, "Well, at least tonight we'll celebrate with his champagne!" So we requisitioned masses of French champagne, labelled *"für den Wehrmacht"*, and obviously stolen by them and hoarded in the hospital, and brought it back to the *popote* and had ourselves a ball. How we celebrated! We spent that night in a doctor's house which had been requisitioned by Pierre Langlais. The doctor was away at the war but Pierre had a lovely time with his grass widow.

The Ambulancières. That's me, the tall, dark girl, standing at the back on the right.

When peace was declared I found it a terrific let-down, anti-climax. I had been busy and in danger and suddenly my job had stopped and there was no Howard. After a few days all the *ambulancières* had to move to Trossingen where we requisitioned a hotel and led a more or less relaxed life. When I went back to Paris and was an interpreter in the French Army in General Leclerc's H.Q., my pay as an officer was only seven thousand francs a month. So to have money to dress on in Paris, I sold a beautiful piano acccordeon which Herr Hohner of the Hohner factory in Tuttlingen gave to me rather than have it requisitioned. I sold it for one hundred and fifty pounds.

Immediately after V.E. Day, Fafa de Langalleris and I drove to Dachau to collect all French P.O.W.s and transfer them to the Isle of Mainau on Lake

Constance where Prince Bernadotte's castle had been turned into a hospital for typhus quarantine. On the way, the French *Intendance* truck arrived to give us rations for the journey. Well, apart from *bidons* of petrol and wine, all they gave us were noodles and coffee which are no earthly good to you when you've no water and nothing to cook on. So, when we arrived at Dachau, I went to see the American Colonel. I said, "We haven't any food. Could we have some?" "You can have a sack of potatoes." was all he said.

We went into this ghastly camp. We saw the gas chambers, fitted out like showers. We saw dormitories where three or four men had to share a bed, hiding the death of a comrade so as to obtain his rations. We saw children's remains where they had sheltered under their mothers' skirts from the gas and, if not dead, were taken by their legs and bashed against walls. We saw pyramids of naked bodies. We saw an experiment room where, mad but still living, there was a man turned into a dog, growling and on all fours, and injected with special hormones. Terrible. Awful. Many of those brutal S.S. men were on the run then. Those the French found were shot without trial. I can understand it. I took back a German girl who told me she had worked for the Colonel of the S.S. in the military barracks as a secretary. One day she was going across the prison square and a prisoner fainted at her feet. She had a lump of sugar in her bag and she gave it to him but was seen by a watchman at the top of a tower. Within ten minutes she was in her boss's office and within a quarter of an hour she was in prison herself.

But we were mainly, of course, concerned with the French exprisoners. Fafa and I took four in our ambulance to Mainau. None of them weighed morc than thirty kilos and they were riddled with typhus and diarrhoea – poor things, we had to keep stopping and cleaning them up. They had all been in the Resistance. If they lived, they were to be repatriated to France after three weeks in quarantine. They longed to get back to France even if it was only to die there. I was so glad to be able to get them to within *sight* of France at least. I know that one of our four, Martin, a former jockey, survived because he wrote to me two years later to tell me he was riding professionally again.

Part 5

Peace

Chapter 14

PEACE

There were horses on Mainau – Prince Bernadotte's. And I mean really gorgeous horses. The groom was frightfully pleased when Fafa de Langallerie and I asked if we could ride them. I was English, you see, and apparently Lord Mountbatten had once been in the castle to stay. It was "How is Lord Louis?" and this and that. There were no saddles – they'd all been requisitioned by the Army – but there were some bridles, so we rode bareback round the island. We were all in quarantine and that three weeks was a marvellous holiday for Fafa and me. Not for all the *ambulancières*, though. One died and Desch got typhoid and all her hair fell out. I developed dysentery when we returned to Tuttlingen but I don't think I picked it up on Mainau: on Mainau, I was perfectly well and full of beans. It was the greatest fun: no work to do, riding, washing in the lake, eating in the hospital *popote* and sleeping on stretchers in an ambulance.

Back in Tuttlingen Pierre Langlais took me fishing and rock climbing. One day he drove me down with a friend of his to swim in the Danube. I didn't want to undress in front of these two men so, while they plunged naked into the river, I was changing behind a bush. Suddenly there was a shot from a Nazi sniper still at large the other side of the river and I screamed and Peter and his friend came rushing out of the water, thinking I was dead or wounded. As a matter of fact, at the identical moment of the shot, I'd been stung on the bottom by a bee!

Pierre later requisitioned an Adler and drove me for a long weekend to Paris. It was lovely seeing Monique and everybody again and going to Susy Solidor's and meeting people at the British Embassy. The Movements Officer was Carroll Fitzgerald. I was determined to visit my mother, however briefly, at Shepherd's Cottage, her new Domesday home near Winterborne Whitechurch on Aunt Vivian's estate. Little did I think, when I asked Carroll to procure a movement order for me to fly to England and back again, that one day we would be engaged.

I left Le Bourget on a French Air Force plane, a Dakota, expecting to land at Croydon. I was very tired and went to sleep. When I woke, I said to the *poilu* sitting next to me, "When do we arrive at Croydon?" "We aren't going to Croydon," he said. "We're going to Prestwick." "Oh gosh!" I said. "I've got on the wrong plane!" "You'd better make love to the captain," he said. We landed at Prestwick and went into the mess to have lunch. Of course I made huge eyes at the captain and fortunately, like most Frenchmen, he was very susceptible. On the return to Le Bourget he asked me to sit next to him in the cockpit, where he flirted with me like mad. I said, "You know, I really want to land at Croydon. I came over here to visit my mother and I can only get to her by landing there." He said "If you come out to dinner with me in Paris next week, I will land if they let me." So he radioed Valence to ask if he could come down in Croydon. They refused. "*Merde*!" they said. "We have only one Dakota flying! For the *Bon Dieu's* sake bring it back to Valence!" "I'm terribly sorry, *ma chère*," he said. Hardly had he spoken when there was a mechanical failure. The manifold pressure went down on one engine. "*Alors, je pose*," he said, going white as a sheet. He *had* to land at Croydon! There we were met by a furious senior French Air Force officer who shouted at him and I don't think believed about the manifold pressure. It took weeks to mend the plane, so I never had dinner with him in Paris – but I did get to see Mummy.

In Paris again, I was invited by Monique's mother to a very smart luncheon party with Lulu de Vilmorin and all sorts of duchesses and princesses. In the middle of lunch Monique said something I knew was rubbish and denigrating to my darling *6ième R.I.C.* – she hadn't actually been in the Front Line like me. So I said to her, "You are stupid, *ma petite conace*!" Madame de Nervo had to explain to the horrified guests how I'd picked up such language. In the Army, the phrase "you pretty little cunt" was virtually a term of endearment. I was often called it, especially when I did something stupid.

Pierre drove me back to Tuttlingen. Monique came with me. There were parties, that sort of thing. During this time, the French Army decided to give a parade for an American General who was coming to visit. We polished our ambulances and our uniforms. It was to be at Lindau and we rehearsed scrupulously with the Army. They decided to have a trial run for the Swiss War Minister. He was delighted to be invited and took the salute from the balcony with General de Lattre, which was to be repeated when the American General arrived. I said to Anne, "I am sure the old boy would be furious if he knew this was only a dummy run".

An American I'd met at the Peter's Finger pub in Lytchett Minster while on leave from Shenley, and who wrote to me throughout the war, hurled down in his jeep from Berlin to see me. Poor darling, he wanted to marry me, but I wasn't interested. So he went back to Berlin.

Soon after, I met a very attractive officer in the French Army called Jean de Villèyre. He was very insistent and I allowed myself to be seduced by him. As I was twenty-five and I didn't love anybody except Howard, I decided to get on with it. Jean has always been very sweet to me since. I might have married him if he hadn't a wife in the Pyrenées.

At the start of June I returned to Paris. I was invited to transfer to the French Army itself and was promoted to *sous-lieutenant* becoming liaison officer *à titre interprète* in the A.F.A.T. (Armée Féminine de I'Armée de Terre) on the Headquarters staff of General Leclerc in the Champs Elysées, liaising with the British and the Americans and organising Social Services for the French Expeditionary Force to Indo-China. Air Marshal Ackerman was very helpful – he showed me how the Social Services were run in the British Army. So was Lady Kemsley, the *Daily Sketch* Kemsley. As she was French and I knew her personally, I was sent over to see her in England and she raised an awful lot of money. Then I went to the N.A.A.F.I. and saw Sir Arthur Royle who gave me unlimited supplies of beer, footballs, chess sets, cigarettes, games, tennis rackets, tins of food, all the N.A.A.F.I. goodies. Except for obtaining a few battledresses, I didn't succeed with an American General I saw in Marseilles. I wanted tanks. "Everything's got to go back to America," he said. "If not, I've got to push it in the sea."

Jean de Villèyre

Leclerc had gone out in Indo-China. I was to join him later with the rest of his personal staff. He was coming back to fetch us when the news came through that his plane had crashed in North Africa. I believe it was a kamikaze operation and that an Indo-Chinese Communist on board blew the plane up. I saw the manifest and on it there were twelve names, yet thirteen bodies were discovered.

Well, though Anne volunteered to go to Indo-China as an ambulance driver, I was now a proper officer in the French Army and I didn't want to go to Indo-China with de Lattre de Tassigny who took Leclerc's place. Leclerc was a darling, one of the most marvellous men I've ever met and I adored him. I didn't like de Lattre much and, as he didn't like women, I thought being on his staff would be difficult. So I told Gaston Palewski who put me in touch with de la Tour du Pin, de Gaulle's Chef du Cabinet, and I asked him if instead I could do *Presse et Information* in the Quai d'Orsay, the French Foreign Office. This was arranged: I was transferred (still a *Sous-lieutenant* paid by the French Army) to the Quai d'Orsay under Etienne Dennery, *Ministre des Affaires en Amerique.*

I was living partly at Monique's and partly at Jean's and I was having a whale of a time, free as a bird. I was learning the job and had a certain amount of leave to spend with my mother in England. When I got back to Paris in 1946, I was working as an interpreter and liaison officer and, in the summer at the Embassy, I met a chap called Colonel Diggle whose daughter Susan asked me to go down with them in July or August for a couple of days to a hotel on the Croisette in Cannes. The hotel had been taken over by the Services and only cost about four shillings and sixpence a day. Four shillings and sixpence a day was something I could just afford on my seven pound a month and I had sold my Hohner accordion and bought some clothes. Because I couldn't be bothered to go to the *popote*, I lived on a dozen oysters and a fresh roll a day and a camembert which lasted for three days, and I've never felt so healthy in my life. I did, of course, get taken out at night.

Anyway, I shall never forget it. I'd never been to the South of France: I'd literally never seen it. We went by train and it was absolutely gorgeous to see those red rocks and that blue sea.

The Diggles left but I decided to stay on, and, the next day, I was sitting in the hall having a cigarette when a very good-looking young man called Gerald Paul in Naval uniform picked me up and took me out to dinner. A cricketer and a journalist, had been Flag Lieutenant to Admiral Sir John Cunningham. His sister, Rosemary, was married to Peter Townsend, Princess Margaret's former boyfriend, and he was at present on leave from the Naval Volunteer Reserve.

He told me a marvellous story about joining the Reserve. He was on the Isle of Wight doing manoeuvres, and a dear old lady came up to him in the street and invited him to tea. He was rather bored so he said, "Well, I'd simply adore that. Thank you very much." So they had tea together and then she asked him would he like to see her husband. He thought this rather odd as there was no sign of a pipe or any other husbandly things around, but he said, "I'd love to see your husband," whereupon she lifted the lid of the grand piano, and there was her husband embalmed inside! "I loved him so much," she said, "I decided to keep him with me always."

Gerald Paul

Gerald was the greatest fun. By the end of my holiday, we were engaged. I didn't really want to marry him. In fact I knew I wouldn't marry him. But, it was easier if we were engaged.

While we were talking about our lives that first night, I told Gerald about Howard and he said, "You realise the Coninghams are down here?" I didn't. I didn't know *where* they were. "Yes," he said. "The French Government has given them a villa in recognition of all that the Air Marshal has done for France." So, of course, he took me round there and then to see Nan and Mary and we had the most marvellous reunion and Nan said, "Both of you must dine with us tomorrow. Noël Coward is coming with Graham Payne. Noël will be on my right and, as you're practically family, Dodo, I'll put you next to him. But he'll only talk to me. He won't talk to you as he doesn't talk to girls of your age." She was wrong. At first he talked to Nan, then he turned to me politely as he would, being a polite man, and asked me what I did in the war, and when I told him I was a nurse, he spent the rest of dinner talking to me about all the operations I'd assisted at and the ones had got permission to watch himself – he'd always wanted to be a surgeon, you see. Afterwards, he played us all the songs from a new musical he was producing that autumn.

A few days later, Nan took Gerald and me to lunch with the Duke and Duchess of Windsor at their villa in Antibes. It was just after they'd been back to England where her jewellery had been stolen. Some of her personal jewels were found in a ditch, but it was the gossip of Paris and London that Crown Jewels he ought never to have given her weren't recovered.

Nan said, "I'm not going to curtsy to her, and you're not to, either." I said "I wouldn't dream of doing so!" When we arrived, we both curtsied to him and only shook her hand, and she looked absolute daggers. While we were on the terrace, I noticed through the window of the dining-room that she asked the waiter to move a place name to below the salt – I'm sure it was Nan's because Mary stayed above it.

After lunch she talked to Gerald and practically ignored me. She was saying how "that bloody old bitch back in England" arranged for her jewellery to be stolen. Well, I didn't think one should talk about Queen Mary like that, especially in front of Frenchmen. I never liked her. She behaved badly. She believed her letters were going to absolve her, but they really damn her. Quite frankly, I think everyone sighed with relief that they weren't our King and Queen. He was madly in love with her, but she was jolly fond of the idea of being Queen. But when one gets tied up with important people, royalty and people of power and that sort of thing – one *is* rather fascinated by the aura. The Duchess of Windsor took a fancy to Gerald, actually. At a dance we went to, he danced with her for ages.

Anyway, my Cannes holiday was the greatest fun with beach parties and I met all sorts of fun people, including Sholto Douglas. Gerald even had a friend who took us on a short cruise on a yacht had requisitioned when he took Ibiza. At Antibes we found ourselves sailing next to George Miller and his wife in their yacht. George had been in the same réseau as me, only over the other side of the mountain, and his book called *Maquis* was a great success. I had never met him before, although we had a lot of mutual friends, and knew each other afterwards, in Dorset.

After returning to Henriette' Vieilhomme's flat in Paris, I then spent the first of many weekends at Plessis Chênet, her *château* on the Seine, just outside Paris on the Fontainbleau Road. It had been occupied by the Germans during the war and, though it was very pretty, it was in very bad nick. The conservatory had been partly broken and we had one marvellous day throwing stones and completely demolishing it in the seizieme, the smart district of Paris

Round about this time, I often used to go and have tea in the Seizieme with Princesse Aliette de Croy, a great friend of Monique's mother. I liked the old girl enormously. She grew mustard and cress in her bidet and she hid the butter in her undies' cupboard because she thought the servants used too much. She had a lover, an old baron, who came to see her every evening at six o'clock, the habit of a lifetime. He'd have an apéritif, then return to his flat and have dinner on his own. She always made up like crazy before he came and, one evening, she wasn't quite ready so he went into the drawing-room and sat down, waiting for her. Noticing a rather pretty silver box on one of the sofa tables, he opened it and saw some white powder inside. "Good heavens," he thought, "she's taken to drugs!" He took a pinch in his fingers and sniffed it up both nostrils and felt absolutely marvellous, about thirty years younger. From then on, he came a little early every evening so as to have a good old sniff. This went on for weeks and months till she said to him one day, "*Mon cher ami*, I think that my late husband must have been a saint because I put his ashes in this silver box And they're gradually being assumed up to heaven!"

Chapter 15

WORKING FOR THE QUAI D'ORSAY

The head chap of *Presse et Information* in the *Relations Culturelles* in the Quai d'Orsay was a man called Jox. In 1946, "Aunt" Vivian Pleydell-Railston's sister, Aunt Daphne, wrote to me and said, "I hear you're had some extraordinary adventures. Would you come over and speak at our annual Red Gross function" – which, was at her manor house near Reading. Dennery sent me to Jox to discuss the idea. Jox was in favour of my going. He said, "If you do it well, the French Embassy in London will arrange an English lecture tour for you and, after that, we might send you on a similar tour of the United States."

So I went over to London, where I met Gerald again, and immediately contacted Ivor Lambe who by now had left the *Mirror* and started his own advertising agency, Lambe and Robinson. Ivor put me in touch with someone to advise me about speaking in public. Hitler may have said I ought to be a good orator, but I'd never yet tried it. This man really did help me a great deal, though. He told me you must say what you're going to say, then say it, then say what you've said. He told me to put headings on cards and to bring one out if ever I dried up, and I've always done this since, lecturing in the United States or standing for Parliament or whatever, though I have quite a good memory. Also, before making a speech, I've always learned the statistics by heart so, if anybody in the audience has asked, say, "How many thousand tractors do you want out of Marshall Aid?" I've been able to answer without hesitation.

At the Red Cross Jamboree I had a huge ovation. And Madame Dax, sent from the French Embassy to hear me, reported this back. I wore my strange French Colonial Army uniform with my medals. I spoke about the Résistance and the French Army and the Front Line and Dachau. Everybody was fascinated by a girl who'd experienced so much: they didn't have a lecture like that every day. So now the French Embassy and Jox and Dennery *knew* I could speak and Jox rang me up and said, "Remain in London. We're organising a lecture tour for you in England and, if it's a success, we'll definitely send you to the United States." I'd only be paid eight dollars a day, with expenses, in America, but I didn't care about the money. Like all young women, I was dying to go to the States, but what mattered most was doing an interesting job and helping the French cause. Otherwise I might, perhaps, have married a millionaire. I've always had the hope I could help to reform things.

I stayed in London with Evelyn Northcroft and with Moyna Chattey, Averell Harriman's former P.A., who later became my son's godmother. Sometimes I went down at weekends to see my mother at Shepherd's Cottage, where she was very happy gardening and watching birds. She had a daily to look after her as well as Aunt Vivian's butler – he used a path leading past Shepherd's Cottage from Aunt Vivian's and, if my mother wanted him to do anything for her, she put a flag out the bedroom window.

My lecture tour covered the whole of the South of England. I travelled to Tidworth, Sandhurst, Aldershot, H.M.S. *Daedalus*, Middle Wallop . . . mostly to Army, Navy and Air Force barracks, but sometimes to village halls and lots of schools and colleges. Of course, all the men, especially the young recruits, were absolutely riveted. I was still quite young and rather pretty and I could use these advantages to get my message across, namely that the French *had* done something during the war. People were thinking about Pétain and the collaborators and all that jazz and I was able to tell them from first hand that there was jolly well another side to the story.

Before I returned to Paris, my mother introduced me to a Catholic friend of hers called Frank Sheed of Sheed and Ward, the publishers – Frank was married to Maisie Ward, a cousin of ours. He said, "Look, I think I can fix up this American tour for you through Alma Savage, my agent in New York," and he got her to *tâter le terrain*. Everybody was very interested in this English girl who'd been in the *Maquis* and who wanted to put the French point of view, and I was booked up literally within a month. The Quai d'Orsay were delighted to have all their work done for them.

Meanwhile my social life continued unabated. Nora and Dick Lewis, a king-pin in U.N.N.R.A. which was providing butter and stuff for the deprived places in Europe, introduced me to Prince Marc de Beauvau-Craon, whose stepfather, Sir Richard Gale, was the head of U.N.N.R.A. and was married to Marc's mother, a very great friend of Gaston Palewski. People always said that Marc was Gaston's son, which I doubt, but he did look terribly like him, I must say. Actually, Marc and I became lovers miles later on, though he was hopeless in bed which is why I didn't marry him. He was a terribly nice person and very intelligent and interesting, and later I was fascinated by his gorgeous *château* in Haroué. We interested one another immediately. Though he happened to be on holiday in England, he was a flier in the French Air Force and had been in the Resistance so, naturally, we had much in common. But I was engaged to Gerald Paul who was now back in journalism and was my constant companion at cocktail parties and things.

At a London cocktail party with Gerald I again met Carroll Fitzgerald, my Movements Officer in Paris. He was now back in his old job, making French Letters, I think, for a firm called Revertex.

Carroll was madly attractive. He was very Irish and very naughty, and *every* woman was attracted to him because he was so elusive. A friend of his, Edward Robinson, said to me, "My dear Dodo, beware of Carroll. He's death to women." He was a huge friend of Margot Fonteyn's, though he always said they never had an *affaire*. One night I pretended to Gerald I'd tummy ache and I went with Carroll to the ballet at Covent Garden. Margot was the star and we went backstage to see her afterwards, then on to her flat nearby for coffee and biscuits. Of course I was being vetted – Carroll didn't take every girl he met behind the scenes to meet the lady with whom he had this "little thing". But Margot and I, though we hadn't seen one another since childhood, had plenty to talk about and made friends.

In fact in '47 I broke off my engagement with Gerald and became engaged to Carroll after my coming American tour and we spent Christmas Day that year with Margot and her mother, the Black Queen, at their home in Pelham Crescent. I'd intended to take Carroll down to spend Christmas with my mother, but we went to a party the night before Christmas Eve and Carroll and I woke up too late to catch the only train.

Meanwhile, after Christmas '46, I returned to Paris and was briefed by Etienne Dennery and Monsieur Jox. They gave me lots of statistics and promised to send them through the embassy to await me at each stop.

Chapter 16

AMERICA!

I left for New York on the S.S. *Washington* in February. I travelled in uniform but Monique de Nervo, who had gone ahead to promote gloves and scent for Christian Dior, said. "Look, Dodo. I'll talk to my chums in the *Chambre Syndicat de la Couture*, and see if they would like to dress you for the actual lectures. She wore *haute couture* herself, and knew designers such as Dior personally so I ended up being dressed by the top people. Madeleine Vramont made me a very pretty black silk top and skirt. Anyhow, it was absolutely next year's fashion. And Dior made me a beige suit. Lanvin made me two dresses – an evening dress and a day dress. Jacques Fath made me an absolutely lovely dress, a black velvet *basque*, shoulderless, all embroidered in jet, with a huge wide skirt and a crinoline. I was quite unused to so many fittings and so much fuss – you know, in *my* life one bought a dress in Harrod's or had one made by the local dressmaker.

What is so interesting, *they* chose what they thought would suit me, I had no say in the matter: they chose the dresses, the bags, the shoes, the lot. And everybody except Jacques Fath *gave* me everything. Jacques Fath made me sign a piece of paper saying I'd give his outfit back to him. He also expected me to have it insured. I said, "What must I pay?" He quoted a figure which was my salary for at least six months and agreed in the end to insure it himself.

Conditions on the *Washington* were horrendous. I had my Movement Order and "Government Official" stamped on my passport so I was allowed on board and allocated a bunk in a hold full of Jewish refugees, poor, terrible things, thousands of them, from camps. When we arrived at Southampton from France – my mother's very much the *grande dame*, took one look at where I was sleeping and asked to see the captain who moved me to a cabin, though the boat was absolutely crammed. We were eight in a four-berth cabin. One of the eight was the wife of the Head of Chancery in the French Embassy in Washington. A French Counsellor's wife in a four-berth cabin! But we made do with mattresses and things, and I was much happier, even when it was my turn to sleep on the floor. Sometimes, actually, I slept on a sofa in the bar. And I ate in the First Class and, as it was a liner, I could go there for a drink if I wanted one. Nobody stood on ceremony and I soon found it all the greatest fun. The officers, of course, chatted me up and, as I already adored the sea, I'd go and watch the wake and think of Howard.

On arrival in New York, I went straight to Monique's flat in Park Avenue, which she shared with Geneviève (The Duchesse de Noailles). The flat, which consisted of a big drawing-room with a divan (where I slept), and a double bedroom with twin beds, and a kitchen and bathroom, was very comfortable and not very expensive as it belonged to a friend of Monique's mother who let us have it at an unfurnished rent, which we split in three. Berthe David Weill, the wife of the banker, eventually bought the flat for her lover, Ted Rousseau, the Curator of the Metropolitan Museum . . . Anyway, Monique immediately introduced me to all her 'fun' New York friends, and took me to the Beach Club and that sort of thing. She knew all the Embassy people. Thanks to her, before I even started meeting people elsewhere, I was, as it were, a part of the social scenery. There was a gorgeous Russian of about ninety called Zizi Zwirski, a marvellous pianist. Zizi adored me and was frightfully flirtatious. I'd trot off some mornings and have coffee with him, and he used to play me Debussy – *La Cathédrale Engloutie* and things like that. He'd say, "My darling Dodo, I'm too old to make physical love to you so I'll I do it this way."

Well, I went to see Alma Savage, my agent at 37 Madison Avenue. My lecture was called "The Fighting Spirit of France" The Quai d'Orsay gave me my allowance of eight dollars a day and I got a percentage of the fees after Alma's cut and, of course, my seven thousand francs a month salary as an officer in the French A.F.A.T., which I received on my return. When I went out to lecture again the following year, I was allowed to keep all of the lecture fees – minus Alma's-cut, of course. Alma arranged for Dorothy Doan to come to the flat and interview me the very next day. Dorothy Doan wrote in *Woman's World*, was the International News Servicewomen's editor, and was syndicated in newspapers all over America – and abroad, too. As a result of that interview, the Lions Club of New York invited me to address them on April 1st, ahead of my other bookings. It was the first time a woman had ever addressed them, and I spoke after lunch for about twenty minutes:

" . . . The French, whether they were dukes or duchesses or dockers from Marseilles, whether they were Communists or Right Wing, they got together, forgot their differences and were incredibly brave because they were occupied and wanted to defeat the Germans. There was a feeling of 'we are all together and we mind about each other, but we mind most about our country'. It wasn't *my* country, but it was a *part* of my country because Free France was a part of Europe. You didn't mind if you slept in the snow. You didn't mind if you had nothing in eat. You had no money. You had no trains. It was a life you can't envisage, here in New York. I do think that, before you criticise the

French, you should listen to *my* story. Then I want you to help them financially. I want you to help them with your know-how. People say in America and all over the world that France was a complete collaborator and didn't resist and fell too easily like a pack of cards and so on and so forth. It is *not* true! I can tell you from my experiences in the *Maquis* and in the Front Line that many of the French were completely and absolutely devoted to fighting the Germans. It is quite true there were many collaborators. But amongst them were the Jewels, the people who fought and the people who protected them with no thought of their personal safety and with no thought of preserving any of their *biens*, at risk of being sent to concentration camps and of having their homes taken over. I wonder how many collaborators there would have been in New York if *you'd* been occupied! . . . It has been a great honour to be asked as a first woman to speak to you. I know women have a reputation of being illogical. But we can be *very* logical at times. There is a gravestone in Paris which says, 'This is to the memory of Michel Gobart, an excellent husband and father, whose inconsolable widow continues to carry on the grocery business at No. 135, rue de la Pompe . . . "

The audience roared its approval. There was terrific publicity in the press and on the radio. It was arranged that I be on the cover of *Town and Country*. As always commercialism got in on the act and they arranged for me to wear a mackintosh for the publicity. It didn't really go with my French dress but, of course, it was nationwide hype. Although the magnolias were out, I remember shivering with the cold. I was even interviewed with P. G. Wodehouse at Sardi's. I was at a table with him and his wife and their awful little dog. I loved his books but I wasn't in favour of him. I tried to be polite, I did try, but we started off badly. When he asked me over lunch what I did in the war, I said "I was a *Maquisade* and you were a collaborator!"

Ed Weidemann, after hearing me at the Lions Club, offered to do all my P.R. free. He had an enormous office in Fifth Avenue. I got half way across this vast expanse of flooring when he said, "Lie down on your back!" I thought, "Gosh! This is what Mummy has always warned me about! But my career is at stake. I'll do it." So I lay down on my back and he came over and put the heaviest book you can imagine on my tummy and said. "You're going to lie there until you breathe from the diaphragm and can throw your voice." He kept me on the floor for, oh, I should say an hour, and it's helped me all my life – I have spoken to two thousand plus without a microphone and they've all heard me. When I stood for Parliament his advice stood me in *very* good stead.

I spoke at about seventy different places in three months, and, unfortunately, Alma had accepted *any* engagement for me irrespective of the geographical convenience to where I was previously. I was sent down to Washington DC, across to Illinois, up to Vermont, down to Colorado, back to New York City, up to New York State. I had to spend an awful lot of time travelling, travelling on the cheap – mostly long train journeys – and arrive very tired. I couldn't afford porters so I took a minimum of luggage. I'd wash my undies and hang them up in the loo, and hope they weren't nicked. I *did* sometimes have sleepers if I was travelling overnight. If I didn't have a sleeper in the South, I went in the black section and sat next to an Old Black Momma who'd protect me – in the white section your bottom would be pinched all night. The ticket collectors used to be furious when they found me.

Of course I got an awful lot of lifts and, now and then, I took a plane. Once I flew to Springfield, Illinois, and I had to come back via Washington where Lewis Jaeger, a multi-millionaire bachelor with stores in the Middle West, boarded and sat next to me and started chatting me up. I gave him my telephone number in Park Avenue. When I told Monique that I'd met a man who was rolling in money and had chatted me up like crazy and taken my phone number, she said, "Oh, Dodo, you'll meet a lot of those in America." Then we went out to dinner and, when we got back at about one in the morning, the telephone was ringing. It was Lewis Jaeger. He said, "I've been ringing you every half hour for the last three hours. Come and have lunch with me tomorrow."

From then on, Lewis – I called him Lew – used to pick me up either in his car or his private plane and take me to my Middle West engagements – he could have been arrested for taking me from one State to another as there is a law against it. Very often he'd stay at my hotel, though we never slept together. He wanted to marry me, actually, and wherever I went, for every lecture, I always found a dozen red roses from Lew. He was very faithful. Ages later he was still sending me presents. During the Queen's Coronation I was staying with my mother in her Domesday cottage, and John Minors, the postman, – you could almost touch his head from my bedroom window – looked up and said, "You've got a present from America and you've got to pay two pounds and ten shillings on it." I said, "My God! Have you looked at it?" He said, "No. I'm not allowed to do that. You have to pay before you open it." "Oh gosh, John," I said. "I wonder is it worth it!" Anyway, I reached down and he reached up the parcel and I opened it to discover a hideously ugly handbag and a sort of silver coronet. So I gave the coronet to my mother's daily for her children and the bag to someone else. Poor old Lew, the bag had cost him eight hundred dollars.

In Paducah, Kentucky, where I was speaking to the Te Deum

International, I met Bea Baker, who asked me to stay in her charming house for a few days before I went on to Indianapolis. I had a gorgeous room with a four-poster bed, real Southern stuff, like Scarlet O'Hara. She was a great friend of Alban Barkley, the Vice President, who took me up into the Blue Ridge Mountains where the hill-billies are. We were stopped on a track by a man with a blunderbuss and wearing a rabbitskin hat. In this area they speak Elizabethan American and use words like "prithee". He said, "Thou shalt not pass!" Alban said, "I am your Vice President!" "Thou shalt not pass!" so we didn't get any further. Alban told me it was more than his life's worth to pass.

Bea Baker still writes to me all the time – I've got a letter from her on my desk. Last year she asked for a recent photo, and she says she's had it blown up and put it in a golden frame next to one sent by her friends Nancy and Ronald Reagan. She says in the letter, "Yours and Nancy and Ronald's are the only photographs in my living-room except family."

One of my lecture dates was at a university in Canyon City, Colorado, run by the Benedictine monks. They were absolutely horrified when they saw me. They had thought *Sous-Lieutenant* D. Lees was a man, so I was put in the Guest House with a chaperone, the Reverend Mother of the local Carmelite convent. The Abbot said to me "There's no reason why you should trek in buses and trains to any lectures you have around here (I had one a day and luckily Alma, for once, had fixed them in the same locality) "We will drive you, and Reverend Mother will go with you." I stayed at the monastery for one whole marvellous week. On our trips we saw marvellous rock formations, and my chaperone, who had been behind the bars of her convent ever since she came from Germany years before, said, "God has sent you to me in my old age as a consolation."

Most mornings I went out riding on the ranch – I borrowed trousers from one of the students and helped to bring in the steers. The monks – I called them "my dude monks" – lent me a Palomino stallion called Don Philipe. Oh, it was a marvellous creature! "But," I said, "I'll wreck his mouth with one of your Western bridles. I'm used to riding with a snaffle." The Abbot said, "Well, isn't that extraordinary? The Abbot of Ampleforth" (where my brother, Mike, went to school) "sent us a snaffle two years ago as a present and we've never used it." So, rather uncomfortably on a Western saddle with a high pommel, I rode with the Ampleforth snaffle all over the ranches of my dude monks in Colorado! There was one very painful episode. I asked a monk, could Phillipe jump? He said, "We never jump in the prairie." I said, "I'm going to try him over this cactus," and I did and he soared, and I came off into the cactus!

Back in New York, one evening, in Park Avenue, Monique and I decided to stay at home, as Geneviève was out with her fiancé, Jean Raindre. We'd sent the porter to get two of those take-away dinners that come on a tray and you just stick in the oven, and had washed our hair and were sitting in our dressing-gowns, reminiscing and gossiping, when Monique said, "Tell my fortune with your crystal ball." So I looked in my crystal ball and I saw quite clearly a tall, dark man with a white plaster on his nose. I also saw Monique in a white dress, indicating marriage. I said, "You're going to marry again" – her first marriage was over – "and fairly soon." She said, "Oh, how exciting! Can yon see any more?" "Yes," I said. "Sea and mountains which means a lot of travelling together." She said, "Do you know this man?" I said, "No. I've never seen him before."

Soon afterwards she took me to the Hotel Pierre to meet a man of whom her mother didn't approve because he was a Jew. When he opened the door of his suite, I recognised the man I'd seen in my crystal ball, and he was wearing a white plaster on his nose because of a recent sinus operation. This was François Louis Dreyfus, the grain monopolist and shipping magnate I've mentioned before, the second richest man in France; he was also one of the most charming men I have ever met. From the beginning we liked one another instinctively. The last letter he ever wrote was to me: he died when he was about to become Bruce, my younger son's godfather. I said to Monique that night, "He is the man you're going to marry." She said, "No, I'm not! I'm not!", but she married him during 1948, the following year.

In May, I returned to Europe on the liner *Marine Jumper*. I disembarked at Plymouth because I wanted to spend a few days with my mother. A journalist came on board and the following write-up appeared in the *Daily Mirror* the next day. 16th June, 1947:

> *"'6 ft Amazon' Dodges Party To See Mother*
>
> With the ribbon of the Croix de Guerre pinned to her tunic, Lieutenant Dodo Lees, 27, in the French Army, slipped ashore at Plymouth yesterday on her way back from a lecture tour in the U.S. Across the Channel, at Le Havre, an official welcome party awaited her arrival in the liner Marine Jumper from New York, but she landed at Plymouth – 'because I wanted to see Mummy so much'. Her home is at Whitechurch (Dorset). Dodo joined the French Army after aiding the Maquis in 1944. In France they called her 'the 6ft Amazon'."

I returned to Paris where I wrote a report on my tour. Jean de Villèyre helped me with my French. Jean always tells me he had to correct a hundred spelling mistakes a page. Collections had been made at each of my lectures for families of dead *Maquisards*. It was good to know that Roco, now in local government, was partly in charge of the money's distribution.

Monique and Carroll in Portofino.

During the summer, Monique and François and Carroll and I went on a holiday to Portofino. Monique was more or less engaged to François, and I was engaged to Carroll. We drove down to Portofino through Andermatt in François' car. Our tiny little hotel, the Splendido, then had only three double bedrooms. Now it's huge. Carroll and I were in one, Monique and François were in another, and the other was occupied by Jacques Fath and a boyfriend. Glancing at the boy, I said to Jacques, "My dress was such a success! I've got it here and I'll give it back to you, but can I please keep it for this holiday at least?" He said "Oh bother you, Dodo! Have it!" I've still got that dress. It's up in the roof. But I can't get into it any more. Alas, alas, alas.

Monique and François on holiday in Portofino, 1947.

Chapter 17

America Again

Because of the success of my '47 tour, the Quai d'Orsay sent me to lecture in the States again – from February to May, 1948. And again Alma Savage made the arrangements, this time more efficiently. The title of my lecture was "The French Revolution of 1948" and its object was to foster the idea of Marshall Aid.

This is the sort of thing I said:

> "I don't think that over here in America you can really imagine what France is going through. You, who have never been occupied, can have no idea of the chaos this can produce. Nor of the terrible psychological effects. Perhaps your brother was a collaborator and you were not. Perhaps your sister was taken away and raped. Perhaps she was taken to Dachau. If you'd seen Dachau, as I have, if you'd seen the terrible things the Nazis did, you would realise the horror of it all. But now the French have to get on their feet again, and I hope you will help them. General Marshall has this plan in train, this Marshall Aid Plan, and I want to tell you exactly what the French are going to do with it. To begin with, they are going to try to get their agriculture onto its feet again. Farmers who lost a leg, lost an arm, blown up by mines – I met them in Normandy bringing in their precious harvests though they had just been through a very bad battle, in fact a tremendous battle – you could smell dead people and dead cows – the farmers now want X number of tractors. Manufacturing industry, also, is at rock bottom. Factories that were taken over by the Germans and used for making planes and guns have been closed down by the Allies, including *you*, I may say, when you decided to come in. These have got to be put on their feet again. They need tools, machinery. . . . "

And I always ended with a statement of my own political ideal:

> "We, in Europe, don't just want to build our own Welfare States, we want your help to be able to build a truly Welfare World."

I'd obtained a movement order from Dennery to travel on the SS *Ernie Pyle*. Then Mary Coningham, who happened to be in Paris and had left the Air Force and was setting up an airline to South America, said, "Get your movement order changed and come with me by plane via South America and I'll get you back to New York in time for your first lecture."

So I went to the Quai d'Orsay to get my movement order changed so that I could travel with Mary. I waited and I waited at the Quai d'Orsay for clearance by Bidault, the Foreign Minister, who was in conference. At one o'clock in the morning I gave up, and went back to Henriette and Paul Veilhomme's to pack; otherwise I'd have missed the boat. Poor Paul. I always slept in his dressing-room. French apartements never have a spare room.

Anyhow, the extraordinary thing is that the journey took three days longer than usual because we got into a terrific gale, and, all the way across the Atlantic, we were receiving radio reports about the loss in the Bermuda Triangle of Mary's plane, the plane on which I'd hoped to be a passenger. Neither the plane nor the bodies of Mary and the others on board were ever found. I spent most of the time in the radio room biting my nails, but there was no news.

I travelled from January 23 to February 1. The *Ernie Pyle* had been a Liberty Boat, thrown together like a do-it-yourself kit by the Americans to take troops and cargo during the war. I used to play poker with a French captain who was going out with his officers to collect a ship in California and bring it back. We became great friends. We used to go up on deck and, when things got really hairy, he said to me, "Look, if the boat splits in two, I want you to be on *my* side of the split!" I spent as much time on deck with him as I did in the radio room seeking news of Mary.

By now, the French had used up all the wine they'd brought on board but, as this ship was "dry", I was a frequent guest of the ship's doctor, a Russian with a plentiful supply of bourbon in his cabin. We'd sing "*Nous avons soif*" to the tune of the Volga Boatsong every time he walked through the so-called saloon while we were playing poker. There was only one other woman on board. She was Dutch and became a very great friend of mine. We shared an enormous cabin with about ten bunks, empty except for ours. The ship got into this terrific gale and, in order to avoid it, we went right down as far as the Azores where it became a hurricane. A French seaman went berserk and started slashing the passengers' baggage with a knife. Then, when he was put in the ship's hospital, he started attacking officers and members of the crew, so he spent the rest of the voyage in a strait-jacket. One newspaper said the captain was stood on his head and got a black eye. Actually he was hurled off the bridge and broke his arm. His name was Stanley Thompson. We had on board a Catholic padre who was asked to say Mass and, as he hadn't got a proper chalice, he put the little *pinaud* or *cassis* remaining to one of the crew in a china cup. We tied him with ropes so he could stand to lift the Host and, by the end of Mass, the sea had become calm. But my prayers for Mary's safety were in vain and his disappearance has never been explained.

I was better known now, so when we arrived in New York, the Press came on board to interview me and take pictures. After refusing to lift the skirt of my uniform for the umpteenth time, I took a taxi to a hotel in 3rd Avenue, at eight dollars a day the cheapest I could find. I had to pay my own expenses but, after Alma's cut, I could keep the lecture fees which were sometimes fifty dollars, sometimes five hundred, so, in the end, thanks to Lew Jaeger taking me by plane or car to XYZ, I actually made some money.

I spoke with Dr. Kurt von Schuschnigg, the former Chancellor of Austria, to a crowd of at least three thousand. People were fascinated by the idea of this young woman, looking like a model, and they came to catch me out with questions, thinking I couldn't possibly know anything about politics. But the French Embassy kept me briefed with all the latest statistics which I memorised in advance. Statistics apart, one question I always got, at Rotary Clubs, High Schools, Universities, Te Deum Internationals, everywhere, was, "If we give this money to Europe, won't they hate us?" I answered, "Yes, they will. Everybody hates a giver. But I still think it's your *duty* to give." I said it quite squarely, and they took it.

Boston was very amusing because it was there I met my sister Bumble's husband's cousin, Lawrence Curtis, Governor of Massachusetts, a Senator and a very big knob indeed in the political hierarchy. General "Squeaker" Curtis, Bumble's father-in-law, wrote to him, asking him to get in touch with me. I was doing my face in the hotel before a lecture, when Reception rang to say that Senator Curtis was down below. I said, "Ask him to come up and have a drink." As he was Squeaker's age and Squeaker was terribly prim and proper – I mean, he was even shocked when "Atty" made a mildly naughty joke – I expected Lawrence, especially as he was a Senator and all that jazz, to be the same. Well, he got me onto the bed within ten minutes! I said, "Look, this is like being attacked by the Archbishop of Canterbury! Get *off* me!" He came to the lecture and, later, when I was in Washington DC, he took me out to dinner. I eventually introduced him to Bumble in London where he groped her in a taxi. We've called him Larry the Lover ever since. He'd only one leg but he was very well known and he tried.

I did seventy lectures on that tour, and probably the same on the first. Seventy lectures in three months is a hell of a lot, and one of the reasons I don't eat ice cream now is that practically every single night for three months, twice in a lifetime, I was fed ice cream. I should think the only State I didn't go to was California. Iowa gave me a slight surprise. I was sitting on a train, happily reading a novel over rather a nice lunch and a half bottle of white wine. When we crossed into Iowa, the waiter suddenly whisked away my bottle. I said, "Why are you doing this? I've only had one glass!" He said, "Unless I'm very much mistaken, you haven't got a licence." So, on reaching my destination in Iowa, I had to obtain a card giving me the right to buy a drink.

Truman at this time was up for re-election as President in November against Dewey, and the general opinion was that Dewey would win. I however, was convinced that Truman would win. You see, it's all very well. You talk to people in Washington, you talk in San Francisco, you talk in New York, but you're dealing with a different sort of person. The *heart* of America is the Middle West, and I knew its people and that they favoured Truman. On holiday in Cannes that summer I met Wynn Idris, the lemonade man, in a night club and we sat up talking politics until four o'clock in the morning. Inevitably the conversation got round to the Presidential Election. I told him Truman would win. He said, "I hope not! I've God knows how much money on Dewey. I'll give you 100-1 in any currency you like to name." I had 4 dollars in my New York bank and you had to have 25 cents a month to keep the account open. So I said, "I'll bet one dollar." "All right," he said. "I'll bet you 100-1 it's Dewey." "Taken!" I said. "I bet it's Truman," and, in November just before I went to Punta del Este in Uruguay, I received my hundred dollars.

I spent my Easter holiday – a ten day break from lecturing – in New Hampshire, under Ackerman's Gap in the White Mountains at the back of which are carved all those Presidents' faces. The hotel, the Dana Place, was specially for skiers. I chose it from a travel brochure because, ever since skiing at the age of seventeen with the Gräfin Rex in the mountains of Bavaria, I'd longed to learn properly. The trouble was that, when I arrived at the Dana, I found I was literally the only guest. Its owners, a charming couple, sold me a pair of skis at cost price and asked me to live with them as one of the family, and, every day, I spent two hours walking up to the Gap and the whole afternoon coming down. The American Olympic Team were practising there and I think each one of them had a turn at picking me out of snowdrifts. It was a marvellous holiday.

Carroll Fitzgerald rang me the first night to say he couldn't live without me. Before I left for America had said he wasn't ready for marriage, we must break off our engagement. Now, he said, we must definitely marry. So that made my marvellous holiday even more marvellous, though perhaps I wasn't in love with him any more, just terribly infatuated by his wickedness.

During that, I was made the only non-American Sheriff of Macoupin County, Illinois – I still have my star. They were going to make me a Kentucky Colonel if I came back again. Also in Illinois, I spoke in the State Capitol in Springfield. Quite an honour. They all rose when I came in, then clapped after I had said a few words about the importance of Marshall Aid. In Washington I stayed with Isobell Brookings, a friend of Gaga's and the widow of the professor who founded the Brookings' Institute. A very old lady by then, she lived in a gorgeous house with a heavenly garden and masses of servants. I also stayed with Peter Sollyflood who was working in the British Embassy. Peter had been in Yugoslavia with my brother, Mike, and was now engaged to Melinda Maclean's sister. Melinda was Donald Maclean's wife.

I travelled home Third Class. After paying for my ticket and buying some presents, I was almost down to the four dollars necessary to keep my New York bank account open against my intended return.

I was seen off by various friends including Mr. Rose, François Louis Dreyfus's New York manager. There I was surrounded by orchids in this Third Class cabin with a darling cockney called Mrs. Smith, who'd been out to see her daughter who'd married a G.I., and with two old German women from the Middle West who'd never been back to Germany since they'd emigrated after, I imagine, the *First* World War and couldn't even speak American. I was settling in before joining my friends for a farewell drink in the bar, when suddenly – I was informed that I was wanted in the Purser's Office. I went up to the Purser's Office and found Mr. Rose there with two tax men who wanted to know why I hadn't declared my income. I had no *idea* I had to declare my income, and, for at least an hour, I had to go through the dates of all my lectures, how much I was paid for each, my expenses, and Alma Savage's cut. I'd have had to leave the ship, but for Mr. Rose's influcncc. As it was, the sailing was delayed. *I* delayed the *Queen Mary*. That must be unique!

Despite being engaged to Carroll, I was determined to have myself a ball. Gilbert Yates, a civil servant with the United Nations who picked me up coming on board, was travelling First Class, and a friend of mine, Anne Leith, an Embassy wife with her little girl, were Second, so I had the run of the whole liner. Gilbert had at once invited me to dinner. I explained this to my steward. "That's all right, Miss," he said. "I expect you'll be going to the First Class often," and he showed me the stewards' way round. I had a marvellous evening with Gilbert. We ended dancing cheek to cheek. When I returned to my cabin at about three in the morning, darling Mrs. Smith was awake in the bunk under mine, reading. I said, "Mrs. Smith, can't you sleep?"

She said, "I thought I'd better wait, dear, to help you into your bunk if you'd had a little bit too much to drink." Actually, in those days I hardly drank at all. I said, "No, I'm quite O.K. You must go to sleep in future. I'll always be late, but I promise you I'll behave."

The next day I went up to Second, where I swam and sunbathed with Anne Leith and her little daughter. In the afternoon I swam in First. Johnny Weissmuller, who was training for a Tarzan film, was going backwards and forwards, using the first flippers I'd ever seen. We had a chat, of course, and I thought him awfully nice.

And so on till we reached Southampton where I received a lot of Press attention. I was mentioned in the *Star*, the *Daily Graphic*, the *Western Gazette* and the *Bournemouth Times*. Because Nigel Bruce, the Dr. Watson of Sherlock Holmes films, was on board, the *Star* ran a heading: DR. WATSON ARRIVES WITH SHERIFF – I was wearing my Sheriff's badge for fun. One photo showed me in a hat given me by Henriette – heart-shaped, stiff net on buckram. Because that photo was on file, I was often shown in that hat later when I entered politics.

After visiting my mother, I went up to London and stayed with Carroll Fitzgerald in Cranmer Court, a block of flats in Chelsea. Doric Bossom, my boyfriend of Watford and Shenley days, rang one morning to ask me out to dinner. I said, "Oh Doric, darling, I'm going to the ballet with Carroll!" He said, "You're so unkind! I don't know what makes you tick!" and proceeded to spend the day walking up and down in front of Cranmer Court with a poster on his back saying: DODO IS UNFAIR TO DORIC.

Carroll's mother then gave us a huge engagement party in her house in Henley, after which we went dancing at Phyllis Court. Flora Caley, one of the three McAlpine sisters, came dancing with us. So did a Swedish businessman. Carroll said to me, "Do dance with the Swede," which I did till I realised there was no sign of Carroll. Well, off I went to look for him and eventually found him in a hotel kipped up with Flora Caley!

We had a huge, huge row and henceforth the engagement was off and on, off and on until my mother wrote to him and said, "If you value your immortal soul, you will not marry Dodo," and we finally broke it off in January, the, following year. He eventually married a young American girl – they had three children. He's lived now in Gozo for ages with his second wife who is Polish. Stavros Niarchos once said: "When you're old, marry a nurse." Carroll's still got a roving eye. I don't think he's ever been a really *happy* man.

Photograph used during canvassing, 1950.

Soon after our engagement party and before I reported again to the Quai d'Orsay, Carroll and I stayed in Cannes with Monique and François who were now married. Then, after Carroll had returned to London, I spent a few days in St. Tropez with Henriette and Paul Vieilhomme, who had an absolutely heavenly little house by the church in the Place de l'Ormeau. For a lot of the time we ran around with Charles Cachin, the celebrated Communist doctor, and his wife, Ginette. Charles was the son of Marcel Cachin, the leader of the Communist Party in the Chambre. Ginette was the only daughter of Paul Signac, the father of *pointillisme* and the painter to whom Van Gogh willed a lorryload of his work, some of which Signac kept and some of which he gave to Russia. Charles was rather a strange Communist – he had three houses and three cars. La Lune, the Cachins' gorgeous house in St. Tropez, had belonged to Paul Signac and was full of the most marvellous paintings by Signac himself, Van Gogh, Modigliani, everbody. Back in Paris, they invited Henriette, Paul and me to a party in their house on the Ile St. Louis. Among the other guests was Picasso, a little man with enormous magnetism. I remember a rather philistine American woman pointing to a picture of his which belonged to our host. She asked "*Qu'est-ce gue ça représente*?" and he replied, *Ca représente cent mille balles, madame*!" . . . À propos Charles' Communism, he went to Russia in the Fifties to examine its medical services as part of a Communist delegation. He told me afterwards that he was very shocked. The doctors, he said, only did six hours work a day for the State: the rest of the time, they treated Party members and ballerinas and privileged people privately.

François had been married before and, by his first wife, he had two children – Alain and France. France eventually married Jacques Charnier, Brigitte Bardot's ex-husband, and she had two daughters. Monique, of course, was absolutely thrilled to have a ready-made family, and she naturally thought she was qoing to have children of her own, knowing that François could produce them and was very much in love with her. They tried and tried and, when nothing happened, she saw a specialist who did various tests and gave her hormones. She rang me up at last and said, "Darling, I'm having a baby! Isn't it marvellous? François has taken a sweet little bungalow-type house in Punta del Este in Uruguay to fly to at weekends while he's in Buenos Aires on business and negotiating with Peron the amount of Death Duties to be paid on his father's Argentinian estate. If I go to Punta del Este, too, will you look after me on the trip and stay with me there as a companion? We'll pay your fare."

As you can imagine, I immediately approached the Quai d'Orsay with the idea of doing a series of lectures in Argentina and Uruguay. No problem. In November 1948 I was given the necessary Movement Order and off I went. On the plane, Monique and I shared the same couchette, head to toe. As she was supposed to be two months gone, the dangerous time, she was allowed to stay in bed when the rest of us left the plane during refuelling.

François flew in his private plane from Buenos Aires to Montevideo to meet us, then drove us in his Buick to this lovely, comfortable bungalow in Punta del Este where we were greeted by a maid, a cook, a nanny and the two children – Alain who was five or six and France, a very pretty little girl, who was two or three. With the help of the maid and the city's gay social life and a book called Assimil, I was soon speaking Spanish fluently in readiness for my lectures, to be based on those I gave in the States. Obviously Monique couldn't come riding in the eucalyptus forest, but she did join gambling parties at the casino and bathing parties often on the Isla de los Lobos.

At first, on the nights we gambled, François gave me up to twenty thousand francs and I would just about break even. Then Truman was elected and Wynn Idris sent me my hundred dollars. I placed the lot on a 9 and won, and, all that night, I won and won and won, making me enough to buy new clothes and share the lifestyle of these expensive people independently. François and Monique *were* expensive people. François had more suits than any man I have ever met – hundreds and hundreds, literally – and, when we played Canasta, the stake was over ten pound.

On Christmas Eve we drove to Montevideo to meet François and, on the way back, I felt terribly ill. When we reached home again, I was covered in spots – chicken pox caught from France, the little girl, and had a temperature of a hundred and three. I'll always remember spending Christmas Day in bed and having to eat a Christmas pudding specially flown out for me while everyone else had a delicious *buche de Noël*. Christmas pudding is *not* very appetising when you're in bed with chicken pox and it's ninety in the shade.

Monique burned my blue bathing dress and gave me a white one instead. The extraordinary thing about *that* is that when I'd gone again to Daisy Carter, the fortune teller, immediately after the war, and she saw me in a white bathing dress, sitting on a seal-surrounded rock with two friends to whom something sad would happen. Well, the Isla de los Lobos is the Island of Seals, and Monique and François later separated during the week I married Chipps in 1953, and, five years later, François died. Daisy Carter was a wonder. She even told me I'd have trouble with my legs and that my life would be the Cook's Tour it became. "A Cook's Tour" – those were her words. And, quite apart from breaking the Achilles tendon of my right foot which I'm having treated now, I've broken my left *leg* once and my right leg three times!

In late January, François and Monique returned from Punta del Este to Paris for a fortnight or so, leaving me in charge of the house, the children, the nanny; everything. Monique said I could use the Buick, but François pointed out that, for insurance purposes, I needed a Uruguayan driving licence and so must do a test. I went off by bus with my British passport and international licence to see the Chief of Police in Maldonado. A great chap with all sorts of buttons and medals, he chatted me up, asked a few questions and said, "I'll take you for the test myself." We got into an old black Citroen parked outside and I said, "Would you remind me about the gears?" He looked rather surprised, but he showed me and we started off. Just as we started off a woman, her arms full of parcels, came running down the street shouting, "My car! My car! Stop thief!" The Chief of Police looked at me. He said. "I thought it was *your* car!" I said, "I thought it was *your* car." He explained the mistake to the irate woman, and gave me a licence without testing me.

While Monique and François were away, H.M.S. *Glasgow* came in to Punta del Este and, as I knew the Captain, I went on board and asked him could I bring France and Alain to the usual children's party. He said, "Yes, of course!" and they adored it. The following week, the ship was to be in Buenos Aires and the Captain asked me to bring along the Louis Dreyfuses as they'd then be back from Paris. This time Eva Peron was on board with her husband and, when I introduced her to François, she said, "I hear you're having trouble about Death Duties on your inheritance over here." Under French law, you see, François didn't expect to have to pay Death Duties outside France. The French Embassy in Buenos Aires was very much involved in the case.

Anyway, Eva Peron then hinted that if a diamond necklace were delivered to her home, the Villa Rosa, François' court case might go in his favour. François was horrified. "That isn't how I conduct my affairs," he said. In the end, he won his case by taking it to the International Court at The Hague.

As regards my lectures, I didn't, to be honest, take them frightfully seriously. But I *did* speak to the Rotary in Maldonado and to the Rotary and to the University in Montevideo. In Argentina, Nazis were said to be in hiding. Certainly an awful lot of people in my audiences were pro-German. On the ski-slopes at Bariloche, I thought I saw Martin Bormann. In fact, I was so sure I saw see him that I reported the fact to the French Embassy. They investigated but I believe that by then he'd gone on to Paraguay.

Meanwhile, it was discovered that Monique's pregnancy was all in her mind and there was nothing there. A false pregnancy, the result of longing for a baby. She never did have a baby. I find that so very sad, especially as I am so fond of her.

Part 6

Labour Politician

Chapter 18

FLEET STREET

I decided that five years working for the French was long enough: I wanted to build a real career in my own country. In summer, 1949, I returned to England where Ernie Bevin persuaded me not only to join the Labour Party but to make a career in politics.

Meanwhile I had to earn my living, so, through the Lambe and Robinson advertising agency, I started a car magazine called *Daily Delivery*, a sort of P.R. stunt of the Car Collection Company which devoted each monthly edition on one make of car. For a lump sum of about one one hundred and sixty pounds my job was to interview the Managing Directors, the Sales Managers, the shop stewards and the people on the factory floor. Jowett's and Rover's were very exciting. At Jowett's they made a gorgeous little sports car called the Jupiter, and at Rover's I saw the first Land Rovers being tested on huge ramps and walls that seemed practically sheer.

A friend of mine, Toni Palamountain, who'd moved with her husband up to Birmingham, let her lovely little house, 10, Burnsall Street in Chelsea, to Anne and me for eight pound a week – Anne, back from Indo-China was now working for the *Evening Standard* on the columns "In London Last Night" and "Londoner's Diary". Later, we let the top floor for three pound to a journalist called Jimmy, also on the *Standard*, so in the end we were only paying two pound and ten shillings each, which was really not too terrible, as by then I was a journalist on the same paper myself and earning twenty-five pound a week.

One weekend in summer, 1950, I was staying with my mother at Shepherd's Cottage when Chipps rang me. Just after the war, I'd received a scarf in the post and, with it, a note saying, "I do hope you're still alive. Thinking of you so much. Love, Chipps Bennett." Well, I didn't recognise the name because I thought of him as Chipps Pittar as his mother was Mrs. Kitty Pittar. In fact, every time he came back to England on leave from the Navy, he used to ring up my mother asking to see me, but I was always abroad.

This time, Mummy said, "Oh, she *is* here but I don't think she'll want to see you as she's just washed her hair." He said – typical Chipps – "I want to come over now!" She said, "I don't think she'll want that but I'll hand you over." I said, "Who is it?" He said, "Chipps Bennett." I said "Who's Chipps Bennett? Do I *know* Chipps Bennett?" He said, "I sent you a scarf." "Oh, yes," I said. "Thank you. But I didn't recognise the name and I don't recognise it now." "I'm Mrs. Pittar's son," he said. "We did the Concert Party together." "Oh, *now* I know who you are!" I said. "You must come over. But not tonight. I want a quiet evening, as I've just washed my hair." Round he came at once, though, in an open Morris 8, and, after shocking my mother with a story about pansy Spanish priests, he invited me out to dinner next evening at the Branksome Towers Hotel, and I accepted.

Chipps had been good-looking even as a schoolboy but now he was tall (six foot four), very fit and very physically attractive. He was staying with his mother at Slepe House.

Anyhow, at the Branksome Towers, we dined and danced cheek to cheek and he told me more about himself. He was twenty-four – six years younger than me, actually – and his Morris 8 was a birthday present from his mother. He had been in various ships all over the world since he joined the Navy in 1943 and ending up at the end of the war in Tokyo Bay. After the end of the war he'd joined the frigate *Alacrity*, based in Hong Kong, and had travelled throughout the Far East. In Hong Kong, he'd met a girl and he wasn't quite sure if he loved her. He was now a junior lieutenant. He'd just come back from Madrid where he'd been studying to be a naval interpreter in Spanish having previously spent some time in St. Jean de Luz, studying to be an interpreter in French.

On the way back, he stopped the car at Stag Lodge in the Drax's estate and put sentimental French records on a wind-up gramophone and started kissing me. It was all very romantic. As I was staying with my mother, I didn't let anything dramatic happen, but I wasn't not sleeping with any other man since I'd broken with Carroll – I'd had an affair with someone in Buenos Aires and also with Prince Marc de Beauvau-Craon at Haroué, his gorgeous *château* near Nancy – so, from then on, I let Chipps stay with me at 10, Burnsall Street whenever he was in London.

We went skiing together that Christmas at Kitzbuhel in Austria. Though I'd skied in Bavaria and in the White Mountains, I was very bad at it, I couldn't turn well. Chipps was excellent as he'd skied since he was two. His family had an awful lot to do with "inventing" skiing. His great uncle, Teddy Richardson, started the Ski Club of Great Britain, and the Richardson family and Bill Bracken and Arthur Lunn more or less brought skiing from Norway to Switzerland – I've got pictures of Kitty Pittar, my mother-in-law, in a long skirt with a long sort of stick, doing a telemark before the First World War.

Eddie Shackleton (Labour Parliamentary Candidate for Preston, later Lord Shackleton) and a friend had started a travel agency to make a bit of money to help things along and suggested we use his agent in Kitzbuhel called Admiral Ruck-Keene. The Admiral died only a few years ago, but he and his wife became such friends and very much a part of our lives. He had a gorgeous house in Kitzbuhel and a cottage in Devon, so he fished all summer on Dartmoor and skied all winter.

He met us at the station with a huge great sledge. He really was a fantastic person, a terrific extrovert, an enormous great figure with an earring in one ear. He'd go with his dog Smuggler in the lift, poking the Italians and Germans out of his way with his ski stick. Anyway, he eventually got us into a doctor's house where there was only a double room. I said to Chipps, "Look, this is simply frightful, all too embarrassing and it'll probably get back to my mother." so I explained to the doctor's daughter that we weren't married and needed *two* rooms, and Chipps officially slept in the surgery on the surgical bed.

It's just as well I had my own room, because I broke my leg, and the whole of Kitzbuhel came to see me. My left leg was Pott-fractured, and Chipps was absolutely sweet about it – I hadn't yet taken him very seriously, but now I began to fall in love. He said to the *Skilehrer*, "This is my fiancée! You must get her down in the blood-wagon!" and, on New Year's Eve, he hired a restaurant orchestra to come and play frightfully romantic Viennese music under my window.

I had to go back to England with my leg in an open plaster. At a station just before we reached Liechtenstein. Chipps said to someone, "Have I time to buy chocolate?" "Yes, lots" was the answer, so Chipps got off the train and suddenly heard chug-chug-chug, and there I was going off by myself into the wilderness with my leg in plaster! He had to chase the train all the way across Liechtenstein in a taxi and he only caught up when it arrived in Switzerland. I've never been so pleased to see anybody in my life.

That was our first holiday together and for years afterwards we returned to Kitzbuhel again and again to stay with the Ruck-Keenes themselves.

I'd only been with the *Daily Delivery* six weeks when Anne resigned from the *Evening Standard* and changed to ghosting books and running the Coal Board's magazine. She said to me, "Why don't you try for my job?", so I rang up the news editor, Ronnie Hyde, and went to see him and he said to me, "Can you type and do shorthand?" I said "I can type but not do shorthand." "What a nuisance," he said. "Otherwise I'd have taken you on as a secretary. As it is, I'll have to take you on as a journalist at much more pay." So he took me on for the "In London Last Night column".

I'd go in on the No. 11 bus every day and report at four o'clock to Ronnie Hyde for my assignments. Sometimes I finished early: sometimes I was still working at four in the morning. There were about seven reporters on the column, but no one else had my sort of background. Pam Hampshire's was the same, I suppose, but she was younger and hadn't been a deb., so she didn't know so many people. I was useful, you see, for Gossip and Social, and diplomatic and parliamentary receptions, that sort of thing. Later, of course, being actively involved in politics myself, I could cover political meetings.

My first assignment was to cover a big City dinner where I was placed next to J.B. Priestley. After we'd made friends, I told him I was a reporter for the *Evening Standard* and said, "I'm terrified! It's my first night on duty!" So he took a pen out of his pocket, asked me for my menu and wrote my story for me on the back.

My assignments were very varied. There might be a hairdressers' "do" in the East End – I met Raymond at one and we made such friends that he often did my hair for free and he made me a hairpiece for free, too. His wife, I remember, had sparkles in her hair, a new technique he'd just developed. This could be followed by a Royal Gala at Covent Garden.

In the summer of '50, I went to the birthday party that Beverley Nichols gave at Merry Hall for the French Ambassador's wife, Odette Massigli. I arrived early – Lord Foley, who was to play the piano, drove me – and discovered Beverley out in his gorgeous garden, specially floodlit for the evening, pinning flowers onto his gardenia plants. Beverley was frightfully proud of his home. "All this," he told me, "I've achieved from my own writing. Nobody's ever given me a penny." We got on like a house on fire. He wasn't affected and he didn't have unpleasant boyfriends hanging around. I wrote to him later to ask would he do a book for us when I was in charge of tourism in Malta, but he said he wouldn't because the Maltese were too cruel to cats.

Another party was at that Buchmanite place in Berkeley Square. A friend of mine, Peggy Williams-Wynn, invited Chipps and me, hoping, I suppose, we'd be inveigled into Moral Re-Armament and that I'd write about it favourably. We all had to sit round in a circle and, people confessed they'd stolen jam when they were ten, that sort of thing. Chipps was absolutely impossible. He dug me in the ribs and said, "If you're not careful, I'll confess *you*!" Neither of us was converted to Buchmanism. I think it was very very Right Wing, very fascist.

After the February election in '50, I met Etienne and Jacquie de Crouy-

Chanel at an embassy cocktail party – Etienne was No. 2 at the French Embassy. Chipps and I got on very well with them. They had small children and quite often, at weekends, we'd all go to Whipsnade Zoo and have a picnic.

Then, during the summer of '51, just after the Edinburgh Festival, Etienne, Conte de Crouy-Chanel, said: "Our Russian equivalents suddenly invited Jacquie and me to dinner *à quatre*, Dodo. We felt we must ask them back and, as they're now apparently allowed to visit people's houses, we've invited them to our home for lunch. Will you be our guest as well? It'll just be us and them and you." Why Etienne asked me, I didn't know, but of course I went.

We talked in English. The Russian wife was a very dowdy little person who, before lunch, spoke to me about boring things like how much better Russian nylons were than American – everything was *better* in Russia. At lunch, luckily, the conversation turned to world affairs and Trade Unionism which was altogether more interesting. Etienne had introduced me as the Labour candidate for Lancaster, we'll come to all that later – so the Russians, thinking I was politically O.K., talked quite openly. When I asked the husband what Trade Unions in Russia were *for*, he said, "To make the workers work. To keep them up to their target." "Well," I said, "it's quite different in England. Trade Unions here are on the side of the workers."

After lunch, when we were having coffee, Etienne, naughty Etienne, suddenly threw out, "Oh, I forgot to tell you Miss Lees is also a journalist on the *Evening Standard*. You'll probably see her around." The poor man, obviously terrified of what I might report, looked as white as a sheet: I thought he was going to faint. But, there were certain things, as a reporter, one did not do. One might invent the remarks of a V.I.P. arriving at Victoria Station. but one didn't relay conversations at a private lunch.

Dick Stokes – later Lord Stokes and Lord Privy Seal, Catholic, attractive, very rich, Labour and a bachelor, and a possible alternative to Chipps with whom I was still only flirting – invited me to lunch to meet Adlai Stevenson, the most fascinating man I've ever met. Really fascinating. An intelligent American with good political ideas. He'd have made a marvellous President. It's a tragedy he wasn't elected in the '52 election. During lunch, Dick asked me if I was coming to the cocktail party at the Russian Embassy that night, so when I went on duty at four, I said to Ronnie Hyde, "Are we going to the Russian Embassy tonight because, if so, you'd better send me, as my friend Dick Stokes is going and he'll introduce me to people." Ronnie said, "No, we aren't invited, but you can jolly well gatecrash!" So I went back to Burnsall Street to put on a smart dress and found Nicky Phipps, a friend of Anne's, on the doorstep, asking could he stay the night. I said, "On condition you come with me and gatecrash the Russian Embassy."

Off we went in our best clothes to the Russian Embassy where nobody bothered to ask us for our invitation when I said we were the Comte and Comtesse de Lees. Zarubin, the Russian Ambassador, saw me actually, once we were inside. He knew I was Press because he'd met me at other functions. He also knew that I hadn't an invitation, but he only grinned.

It was quite extraordinary because the party was divided up into three classes. There was one room for the hoi polloi who were being served beer and sandwiches. Darling old Manny Shinwell, the veteran Labour M.P., was there with his wife, saying, "We'd much rather 'ave a cup of tea." Then there was another room with a guard on the door, armed with a revolver. In there were all the Left Wing people like Tom Driberg who were being served cocktails and canapés. And, upstairs, was a V.I.P. room with caviar, champagne and vodka.

I don't know where Nicky was by this time, but, when I met Dick Stokes on the way upstairs, I said, "Oh Dick, please take me to the room with the VIPs." He said, "I'll take you to the door and, if they let you in, you're on your own." Well, we reached the door and I heard the voice inside of Odette Massigli, the French Ambassadress, who, of course, I knew, but there were two guards on this door, each armed with revolvers, and when they'd let Dick in, they stood in front of me and asked me what I wanted. I said, "Can you show me the way to the Ladies?" So they directed me down the corridor to the Ambassador's bathroom, a fascinating marble bathroom where, after locking the door, I sat on the loo and started writing some notes. Suddenly the door opened and in came a woman, using a master key, obviously to check what I was doing. Seeing me there, she quickly went out again.

Having made my notes, I went downstairs and found Nicky at eight o'clock, the very moment the lights went down for everyone to leave. Next day, the headline for my story about the three divisions and so on ran: IT WAS TIME GENTLEMEN PLEASE AT THE RUSSIAN EMBASSY LAST NIGHT.

I then met, at some do or other, the wife of the Polish Ambassador. She was absolutely charming and became a great friend. She told me a marvellous story. Though she was supposed to go for her hols to some frightfully cold beach in Poland, she adored gambling and she adored the sun, so, using their little bit of foreign currency, she went for four days with her husband to Deauville where she won so much money in the casino that she was able to buy lots of Dior dresses. On the last night of the holiday, before returning to London, she hid in the bathroom and took the Polish labels off her old clothes and put them on the new ones. I said, teasingly, "Oh, I'm going to put that in my paper! It's too good to waste!" She said, "Don't you dare! I'll be sent to Siberia!"

But she did tell me *one* thing which I tried to use. She said, "There are rumours that Zarubin is leaving England." I looked at him across the room. He had spots on his face and an expression of great anxiety. He obviously didn't know if he was being promoted or sacked. I went back to the office and informed the editor. He said, "It's a news story if Zarubin *is* leaving. You're the first to know. Who told you this?" I said, "I won't reveal my sources, but it's someone who knows." He sent a top journalist round to the Russian Embassy to check, and the story was denied and denied and denied. Three days later the news broke that Zarubin was going to Washington but the *Standard* didn't print it first. However, they gave me a cheque for my scoop.

Which brings me to the disappearance of Burgess and Maclean. During May, '51, I was invited to dinner at the Ritz by Fred Warner. I'd known Fred for years: we went to the same dances in Dorset, and "Aunt" Mamie Colfox, when she gave a dinner party or a dance, used to ask him to be my partner. He was now in the Foreign Office, stationed in Moscow but on leave. Anyway, Fred then suddenly rang me up at the office one evening at about five o'clock, "I'm awfully sorry I can't take you out to dinner tonight. I've a friend who's in dire straits. Come to lunch tomorrow instead." I said, "That'll be lovely. It'll be easier, actually, because I won't have to fit it in between assignments." So I went to have lunch with him the next day, and he told me he'd spent the whole of the previous night persuading a friend of his not to commit suicide. The friend was Burgess. Fred, of course, didn't know Burgess and Maclean had gone to Russia and didn't know anything about their being traitors – the Foreign Office were taken completely by surprise.

All of us on the *Evening Standard* knew Beaverbrook took a terrific interest in his newspapers. We were told he read them in the bath every morning with a telephone to hand so he could ring up and say, "Sack the cartoonist!" or whatever. We certainly knew he had a black-list. It wasn't written down: we just knew about it. We knew nothing nice about Mountbatten would be printed; we knew nothing nice about almost *every* member of the Royal Family would be printed. Not that Beaverbrook wasn't liberal in other ways. An awful lot of his journalists were Labour, and, never did I have a word altered of anything I wrote – my articles were subbed, if you like, but their point of view was never altered, and sometimes I wrote quite controversial things. In fact, when I stood for Lancaster, Beaverbrook not only gave me five weeks' paid leave instead of the obligatory three, he sent me a telegram on Eve of Poll wishing me luck . . .

I went to report on some official event where Mountbatten was speaking, and Wol Drax from Dorset, his Flag Lieutenant, said to me afterwards, "Are you going to write about the speech?" I said, "Yes, but it won't get in." Wol said, "Why not?" I said, "I know it won't" – I didn't actually say, "We've got a black-list." And I wrote up the speech and, of course, it didn't get in, though it was a good one.

The next night, I went to a dinner where Stormont Mancroft (Lord Mancroft) was the guest speaker. Stormont was an old boyfriend of mine – I'd known him since he was a "debs' delight". Anyway, he was another person you couldn't say anything about. He made a very witty, apposite speech. quite controversial, and I got some very good quotes and, when he saw me afterwards, he said, "Come and have a drink" and we went to the bar and had a drink. He said, "Are you going to write up my speech?" I said, "Yes, Stormont, but it won't get in because you're on the black-list." He said, "Am I really? How extraordinary! I wonder why." I then went back to the office. wrote my piece and went home to Burnsall Street.

Now, usually I wasn't woken in the morning because I never got to bed till about four, but on this occasion I was woken by Ronnie Hyde at half past *eight*. He said, "Come in at once! You're getting the sack!" I said, "Why?" He said, "You told Lord Mancroft there's a black-list. and Beaverbrook's been on the phone already." Stormont had gone back to the House of Lords for a late night-drink and had said to one of his cronies, "I hear I'm on the Beaver's black-list," and when the crony asked who told him, Stormont replied, "Oh, a girlfriend, a dancing partner of mine who's working for him."

Of course this got straight back to Beaverbrook who rang Ronnie Hyde. I thought, "Gosh! What will I do?" So I immediately took a taxi to Stormont's house in Montague Square where, thank God, he was still having breakfast. I said, "Stormont, you must deny it! You must say you made it up! I'm getting the sack and I can't afford it! What's more, I'm standing for Lancaster and I shall be dirt in Fleet Street!" I don't know how Stormont fixed it exactly but, when I got to the office that afternoon, I was hauled in front of Ronnie Hyde who said, "I gather Lord Mancroft denies you said he was on any black-list. That gives us a let-out. For God's sake be careful what you say in future."

There was another unwitting boob on my part. I was sent to cover a huge gala ballet performed at Covent Garden in connection with the Silk Conference. The women were wearing silk. Even the programmes were supposed to be made of silk. I got my photographer to take a photograph of a very nice girl in a very pretty silk dress, and did a piece on her. She was Mrs. Carole Louise who had a dress shop two doors away from Claridge's, next door to Claridge's House where Gaga used to have her flat. In my piece I said that, as far as I could see, the so-called silk programmes didn't look like silk at all: they were more like rayon. Well, the next day, Ronnie Hyde rang me up and said he'd been informed the programmes *were* silk and the paper was likely to be sued. I said. "Before we print an apology, let me check this out."

So I took my programme to Mrs. Louise and asked her to check whether it was silk or not. She was only too pleased to help me because I'd named her shop. Late that night, though, she rang me and said, "I've had the programme factory-checked and, I'm sorry, it *is* silk." So we had to print an apology. But, for quite some time, in return for the marvellous publicity I'd given her, Mrs. Louise let me have dresses at practically cost price. She even made my wedding dress.

Chapter 19

Parliamentary Candidate

It was Clifford Davies, actually, – the journalist who got me back into the swing of writing when I was on the *Daily Delivery* – who suggested I stand for Parliament. I rang up Ernie Bevin and said, "Do you think it would be a good idea?" He said, "I think it would be a *very* good idea. Go to Transport House. I'll ring the Secretary", the Secretary of the Labour Party, "and tell him you're coming." So I went to see the Secretary who talked to me for about an hour and put my name on the B list.

The first people to contact me were Bournemouth East and Christchurch and I went down for their Selection Conference and was adopted almost immediately – on Friday, September 30th, 1949, to be exact – and Transport House approved the appointment on October the 7th.

I'd already started on the *Daily Delivery* – I didn't join the *Evening Standard* until December – so I stayed the weekend of the Selection Conference with my mother. She, of course, disapproved madly of my being Labour, but she lent me her car not only to go to the Conference in Bournemouth but also, "for the sake of my health", as she put it, during the election. The Party paid for the petrol. I'd spoken, the same September, for Lady Drax at the Women's Institute, Lytchett Minster, about my experiences in France. Like my mother she was very high up in the local Conservative hierarchy and, when she asked, "Would you like to be our candidate for South Dorset at the next election?" and I replied, "I hope to be fighting as the Labour candidate for Bournemouth East and Christchurch." She was somewhat taken aback. But she wished me luck.

My job in Fleet Street left me free to campaign at weekends and, in addition to my mother's car, I was lent an enormous Rolls-Royce, complete with chauffeur, by three old ladies in Highcliffe. My agent agreed that I should go to thank them. They lived in a huge house with a maid in a starched apron and a white cap – you know, there were cucumber sandwiches and Dresden china and a silver teapot. I said, "I'm terribly grateful to you for lending me your car, but do tell me why you're Socialists." "Oh, my dear," they said, "if there'd been a Communist standing, we wouldn't be lending it to *you*. We thought you were the next best thing." Another of my supporters was a woman who walked about the Bournemouth promenade in a kilt with VOTE LABOUR written on her back and playing the bagpipes. You do meet the most extraordinary people in Bournemouth.

Throughout the campaign I said exactly what I thought and felt. I even said some controversial things from the point of view of the Labour Party. For instance, I wasn't opposed to fox-hunting. Foxes have to be kept down and hunting is the kindest way of doing it. Gassing is very cruel; with shooting you very often don't kill them cleanly; and snaring is even worse. I also approved of people having the choice to send their child to a Catholic school – in fact, the Party did in the end aid Catholic schools. And I was very pro-French, which many in the Party weren't. But no one tried to influence anything I said in any way – not that I would have allowed it.

Of course Bournemouth East and Christchurch was an impossible seat to win. I was fighting Churchill's great friend, Brendan Bracken – the Liberal was Mr. Holland who had a chicken farm near my old home in Lytchett Minster – and, though Labour had come in with such a swoop in '45, the swing was now against us. But I had terrific publicity and fantastic meetings. When Herbert Morrison, the deputy Labour leader, came down to speak for me in the Drill Hall, Bournemouth, I had an overspill audience of two thousand.

At that meeting, a boyfriend of mine, Major Norman Charrington, tried to climb in through a window, and fell and broke his leg.

Clifford Davies wrote a piece in the *Daily Mirror* headed "Why Deb Dodo Doesn't Talk Politics At Home". He quoted me as saying:

> "Most of my friends find it hard to believe that I have been chosen to fight Bournemouth East with Labour. They know that in doing so I have broken away from the traditional outlook of my family, for Toryism runs in our blood. The family motto is 'Without haste, without rest'. My grandfather, the late Sir Elliot Lees, was the Tory M.P. for Oldham, and my mother is a member of the North Dorset Conservative Committee. For the world into which I was born – hunting, holidays abroad and servants – has no place in Britain today so long as it remains the inheritance of the privileged few. But please don't imagine I'm basing my campaign on class hatred. I don't envy people who have privilege, but I believe it should be the inheritance of us all."

The people who were really upset by all this were the estate workers, in particular Polly Dance, the wife of the head gardener at Lytchett Manor. I had to go round to Polly and explain. And "Uncle" Philip and "Aunt" Mamie Colfox – they, too, thought the article a bit much. But I had so many letters of appreciation from people all over England. And several people wrote to Labour Headquarters in London saying it ought to be made into a pamphlet and distributed. They found it moving.

Because the constituency was so Conservative, there was a lot of heckling, sometimes by my own Tory friends but mostly by a big band of Young Conservatives. There were even a few scuffles. But my chaps were pretty tough and very protective. When canvassing in Christchurch I stayed with a darling old Salvation Army couple who fed me and spoiled me and looked after me like goodness knows what. Fortunately, I was very used to public speaking, having lectured in North and South America as well as England. I wasn't frightened of being on a platform: I could throw my voice to the back; and tackling difficult questions and being heckled were no trouble to me at all. I actually *liked* heckling: I got a lot of adrenaline from it.

One press cutting said:

> "More than 150 people were turned away from the Christchurch Town Hall on Wednesday night. Inside it was a case of standing room only. The attraction was the first public appearance of tall, dark, vivacious Miss Dodo Lees since her adoption as prospective Labour candidate. For more than three quarters of an hour Miss Dodo Lees expounded Socialist policy without interruption, but at Question Time she did not find it quite so easy going. She held her own, however, and only once did she show any signs of annoyance, and that was when a member of the audience made a remark which she felt savoured of personal insult. There were shouts of 'Withdraw!' but Miss Lees restored the calm with a snappy answer. This was the remark which caused the incident. 'We've heard a lot about France and America and the burning of coffee in Brazil. I suggest it's time Miss Lees found out something about this country.' When the cries of 'Insult!' and 'Withdraw!' had died down, Miss Lees with complete composure replied, 'I venture to suggest that the remark comes from one who is as ill-mannered as Americans who keep their hats on in the house."

One point I always underlined was that an awful lot of our manufacturing industry had gone over to the war effort, to making Spitfires and things. Everybody had agreed with Churchill at the time that this was necessary to win the war, but it did mean that we had imported too much and were living on tick, if you like, and without assets. It was a long job for the Socialists, when they came to power, to get industry up and going again and, of course, people were grumbling. They were objecting, for instance, to the fact that the country was still on rations. Well, as Socialists, we thought rationing was fairer, because otherwise there wouldn't have been enough food to go to the poor as well as to the rich. I produced statistics to show all this wasn't the Socialists' fault: it was the fact, as I say, that we'd put ourselves in hock by the war effort.

I spoke on many, many subjects. I spoke about the fisheries, I spoke about agriculture. I spoke about having markets where we would cut out the middleman and the farmer would sell to State-run or Local Government-run markets without the need for places like Billingsgate or Covent Garden which only raised prices. I spoke about the need for nationalisation . . . Look at privatisation now! Do you think British Telecom's any better since privatisation? I think it's a worse service and more expensive . . . I also said more could be done to attract tourists. I suggested that extra food rations should be given to caterers and, if only for a few weeks, to visitors from overseas. Of course. that went down well in a tourist centre like Bournemouth!

Another article said:

> "Miss Dodo Lees Answers Queuetopia Charge. Answering Mr. Churchill's Queuetopia speech, Miss Dodo Lees made queues her theme."

I said that there were hardly any queues for necessities, though, due to the neglect of the past, many people who were nearly blind couldn't afford glasses so there were still queues for glasses as well as for false teeth and wigs. "There are also queues," I had said, "for houses" but we are building as many houses as we can (our target is 350,000 a year) and as quickly as private enterprise did, the only difference being that they are going to different people. There is one queue that we *have* done away with and we are the only country to do it – and that is the queue for the dole." That was the punch line. I'd learned through experience to have a punch line at the end.

Anyway, I was beaten and, though I didn't reduce Brendan Bracken's majority – on the contrary – I did get an awful lot of new Labour votes. I remember a steward waving a pound note at a meeting in Boscombe and shouting, "Here is a contribution for our election fund from a Tory who says he's been converted."

The election was on February 23rd, and Labour won. The trouble was we had such a small majority that it was virtually a hung parliament and Attlee had to call another election on October 25th the following year when the Conservatives got in. In that election, Maggie Thatcher, Margaret Roberts as she was then, stood for Dartford. She didn't win her seat. I stood for Lancaster and didn't win my seat, either. I was standing then against Fitzroy Maclean, and I was one of the very few Labour candidates who brought their opposing Conservative majority down. Of course, one or two, like Barbara Castle and Bessie Braddock. actually increased their majorities.

After my 1950 defeat, I was sent orchids by the *Sunday Pictorial*, who wrote in their paper:

> "Orchids for a lady. Orchids for our admiration for a young lady who revels in fighting against odds. The twenty-eight year old daughter of a wealthy squire took on the Germans by joining up with the French Red Cross in Normandy and then won a Croix de Guerre fighting with the Underground. Although her mother is on the North Dorset Conservative Committee, Dodo took on Brendan Bracken in Bournemouth East. Yes, of course she lost. She has our congratulations and our orchids for another courageous fight."

I was so tired. I mean, after a campaign, you're whacked, and so are all the chaps who have been working for you. Above all I was disappointed in the general result, which interested me more than my own little pad. Bob Salisbury, Lord Salisbury, Bob Cecil as he was then – retained Bournemouth West for the Conservatives – he, also, was standing for the first time. During the campaign we'd met once or twice and pulled each other's legs – we knew each other very well, because he'd been a debs' delight and was in the Grenadiers with Ian Farquhar and Howard.

Brendan Bracken I only met on polling night. I hardly saw him during the election because he was speaking all over the country – he knew he was going to win so he didn't have to come down and campaign. He did, though, have Eve of Poll meetings as I did. We had a long talk about this and that, and, when I told him how, at the time of Munich, I'd heard Jimmie Maxton make his very dramatic speech in the House of Commons, he said. "Oh, Maxton was a great friend of mine. I've an interest in a well known public school in Scotland and I offered to send his son there free but he refused me because the public school system was against his principles."

Later in the year, as I'd had so much publicity and so many votes, I was sent to an international Labour Party seminar, financed by a well known

Scandinavian socialist, at a *château* near Compiègne. Denis Healey – he was accompanied by his wife, Edna – represented the British Labour Party in general and I was representing its women. Edna and I were the only women there. Very high powered people were taking part, including Guy Mollet and Willy Brandt, and the seminar lasted a week. I got to know Denis well, and I've met him several times since over the years. In fact, he was Chipps' boss as Minister of Defence when Chipps was a Naval, Military and Air Attaché in South America in the Sixties.

International Seminar, Compiègne, 1950.

At Compiègne he was rather a schoolmaster. He was always putting me down. He'd say – everyone spoke in English – "That's enough of that! Don't be so emotional!" and the others would say, "Let her speak! Let her speak! We're interested, even if you aren't!" It was my task, you see, to put the woman's point of view. I don't say that women are more caring, but they have a different way of looking at things. A man will often think in terms of Trades Union practice or statistics or economics, whereas a woman thinks more in terms of the human angle, of the actual welfare of children and the plight of the old and the unemployed: she looks at things in a *personal* sort of way. I very much emphasised the woman's point of view later in my Lancaster campaign. I even did so in my printed address.

I was getting fonder and fonder of Chipps. There was terrific sexual magnetism between us, and he was the greatest fun – full of anecdotes – and very intelligent and we looked rather alike, tall and dark, and people often thought we were brother and sister. In 1950, still a Naval lieutenant, he had been selected to take the Long Course at H.M.S. *Mercury*, the Naval Signal School near Petersfield, Hampshire. It was an old house that once belonged to Lady Peel, where Naval Officers train in communications, often also to become A.D.C.s and Flag Lieutenants. Now he was Signals Officer to the Captain of "Bramble", who commanded several squadrons of minesweepers in the North Sea.

During his summer leave, I agreed to drive with him down to Dorrea, the lovely old house of his maternal grandparents at Ciboure, part of the old Basque town of Saint-Jean-de-Luz, near the Spanish frontier. His grandmother had died there before the war and his grandfather died there soon after the war, but his grandfather's second wife, Betty, was still living there. During the war, his grandfather, Colonel Selby Ormond, came over to England on the last boat from France and stayed for a time with my mother-in-law, Mrs. Geoffrey Pittar, at Slepe House, before taking a house in Cornwall where he met Betty. They were both artists and they met when out painting and married shortly afterwards. He was then seventy-five and she was twenty years younger.

Betty was absolutely sweet. We became huge friends. She was brought up first in Tasmania where, as you know, my great-grandfather was Governor, and then in Mexico where my great-grandmother, Bernada Maria Elisa Turnbull's family lived in Puebla . . .

Just before the Germans arrived during the war, Chipps' grandfather said to Anna, his Basque cook-housekeeper, and Andrée, his parlour maid from the Landes, "Look. I've five hundred pound in my bank in Biarritz. Use that, then sell the silver. Then after that sell the furniture, sell the pictures. Sell everything you have to keep alive, but try to keep the house from being ruined by the Germans." And these two marvellous women didn't sell anything – they didn't even touch the money in the bank. Instead, they got themselves work in the local canning factory which belonged to Chipps' friend, Comte Yves de St. Angèle, and they took all the silver and they hid it in the church tower. Anna and her brother carried all the good bits of furniture up into the Pyrénées on their backs and hid them in a haystack on his farm. They also used water from a secret well and turned off Dorrea's stopcock which was hidden under a carpet under the billiard table in the billiard room so that, when the Germans came and occupied the place, they had to walk quite a long way to a standpipe to get their water. Of course the Germans only stayed for about three days – they weren't going to stay in a house where they couldn't have a bath when they could go and stay in a luxury hotel!

Those two women were simply wonderful. They showed marvellous loyalty to the Colonel. They even covered his two cars in the garage with logs, although they risked the death penalty for hiding cars. And when Chipps went back to Dorea in 1946, everything was again in place, including the magazines which had been laid out on one of the tables in 1940.

There's rather a nice story in this connection. When Chipps and I were married, we had a cocktail party once at the house while Betty was away. We had the party on the balcony, a gorgeous balcony overlooking Saint-Jean-de-Luz bay. Thinking it was awfully wasted, I took a Ming vase off the top of a cupboard in the billiard room and put it in a corner of the balcony, and filled it with some heavenly flowers from the garden. Just before the party was due to begin, Anna and Andrée came to me in a delegation. They said, "Madame Dodo, *ce n'est pas juste*. Nothing in this house has ever been changed. Even after the war Monsieur found everything in its place. That Ming vase must go back on top of the cupboard in the billiard room." So I had to put the flowers in a bucket!

They were a fascinating couple. Anna died this Christmas, actually. Till then, she sent us a Christmas card every year and I used to send her a little money. She must have been nearly a hundred. A family doctor's got Dorrea now. My mother-in-law sold it for peanuts whilst Chipps was away at sea. We went over to see it in '66 while in Fuenterrabia to brush up our Spanish before going to South America.

Anyway Chipps suddenly came to see me one day at 10, Burnsall Street. He said his Hong Kong girlfriend had turned up unexpectedly in London and wanted to marry him – I hadn't realised there was anything so serious between them – and he was supposed to be taking *her* on holiday with him, not me. Naughty Chipps in his wily way had written to her at the last moment to try to put her off, saying it was rather inconvenient for her to come to Saint-Jean-de-Luz as he was taking someone else, so, as you can imagine, she was on the next plane. I was absolutely horrified by all this: it was a frightful shock. I was absolutely miserable. I said, "You go off on your holiday with *her*! *I'm* not going!" and I broke everything off.

He came over to plead with me one morning and I chucked his dressing-gown and his shaving things out of the window onto the pavement, shouting, "You're not coming back into this house ever again! Bugger off!" It was only because of Anne, who acted as a mediator, that we ever got together again. We had a tearful reunion in the Unity Restaurant in King's Road, and Chipps said, "I love you best" and all that sort of jazz.

Unknown to me, Chipps had discussed what to do with his Captain, who said: "Take 'em both, my boy!"

So there I was going off on holiday with Chipps, and it wasn't until I was getting into his tiny car – an open Morris 8 that I saw a very attractive blonde, sitting in the back seat. When Chipps said she was coming along "as a friend", I made another scene and remained in a stinking mood the whole way across the Channel and all the way down to Saint-Jean-de-Luz, with poor Kay trying to be polite.

When we stopped at Biarritz to go to see the Statue of the Virgin on those dangerous rocks, I said to Chipps, "Whose bed will you be sleeping in? If you're sleeping in *hers*, I'm leaving now to stay with Monique!" He said, "As I love you the best, darling, of *course* I'm sleeping in yours." And he did sleep in mine but, as Betty didn't want this row going on in her house, she borrowed a nearby flat. It only had two bedrooms for the three of us, so we spent the nights there in a state of terrific rivalry. Every time Chipps took Kay to a night club, I went out with his friend, Yves de St. Angele, and made him jealous. The whole of Saint-Jean-de-Luz was watching this battle between the blonde and the brunette. It was a marvellous topic of conversation. Nobody talked of anything else. Betty was on my side and the Parisienne who had initiated Chipps in sex – she had a house in Saint-Jean-de-Luz and was on holiday there – was very much on Kay's side.

When Chipps' leave was over, I went to stay with Monique for a week in a lovely farmhouse François had given her outside Paris, and Chipps returned to England to see Kay again. This gave him a chance to make up his mind, and he made it up in my favour. After that, our relationship was rather different and we began thinking in terms of permanence. Though I still wanted a career in politics and was then the parliamentary Labour candidate for Lancaster.

Kay married a charming Army officer. They live quite near us in Hampshire, and we are all friends again.

Meanwhile at Le Bourget, when she was seeing me off, Monique introduced me to Sita Devi, the Maharani of Baroda, an awfully attractive little woman who was travelling on the same plane. We made great friends. She invited me to dinner with the Indian cricket team at her marvellous flat in Grosvenor Square, and my editor agreed I should go. It was all frightfully interesting because, in the big dining-room, the Maharajah had his own separate table, the Maharani and her sister, the Maharani of Cooch Behar, sat with me at another, and each member of the cricket team had a table to himself – because of the Hindu Caste System. Before dinner, some of us had champagne in another room and, when I went to powder my nose, a woman, followed me and said, "A certain Maharajah is very interested in you. Would you like to go to India? Would you like me to arrange something?" I said, "Oh, I'm afraid I'm engaged to be married," which I was, almost, though still thinking about my career. I gathered this woman arranged all this Maharajah's girlfriends for him.

Chapter 20

FIGHTING LANCASTER

I still have to tell you about the election of October. '51. First I was up for Kemptown (Brighton) and lost it to a man called Cohen, the head of a local building society. Then I was up for Hendon and lost that to another prominent local. But, in February, I was selected for the marginal seat of Lancaster.

I received an enormous amount of pre-election publicity. Even the *Australian Evening Standard* wrote:

> "There will be more than seventy-seven women candidates standing for the British election, and there will be not too much of that little housewife background. The majority of them have qualifications that any male candidate would be proud to claim."

The article went on to describe the present Maggie Thatcher as "Miss Margaret Roberts, the belle of the Tories, the youngest candidate, the daughter of a grocer, reading for the Bar." I was "Labour's glamour girl, holding the Croix de Guerre." With the article were photos of me, Jennie Lee, Margaret Roberts and Lady Tweedsmuir. As a result, a Dodo Lees Fan Club was started in Melbourne and, for several years, they wrote and sent me clothes and food parcels. I met the Secretary, an Irishman called Peter Moran, when I was in Melbourne in 1959.

Here's a cutting from an English paper with photos of me and Maggie. The caption runs:

> "There may be more glamour in the House. One of the features of the General Election is the large number of women candidates. Complete results may show a substantial increase in good looks among our administrators."

The accompanying article says:

> "Dodo Lees. Labour. Lancaster. Born 1920. Lecturer, journalist and artist. As a Red Cross nurse she took special training in 1944, was demobbed from the V.A.D. to join the French Red Cross, landed in Normandy, crossed enemy lines and nursed the *Maquis*."

Then it says:

> "Miss Margaret Roberts temporarily gave up reading for the Bar in her spare time to fight Dartford. Kent. for the Conservatives. Born in 1925, she won a bursary to Somerville College, Oxford, and has since worked in the plastics, catering and iron and steel trades."

Here's another cutting with photos of both of us . . . The *News Chronicle* of September 28th, 1951, said:

> "The palm of Conservative youth, beauty and brilliance probably goes to twenty-six year old Miss Margaret Roberts."

At least I was *Labour's* glamour girl! My cousin Shimmy Lovat, Lord Lovat, when he came up and made a speech for his brother-in-law, Fitzroy Maclean, said something like; "She's not a *bad* filly. Her legs are all right." This made my people absolutely furious, really got their goat.

There was also a lot of publicity along the lines of "guerilla girl fights guerilla man" because I'd been in the *Maquis* and Fitzroy Maclean, my Conservative opponent, had been parachuted into Yugoslavia. You remember that Fitzroy was parachuted to Tito and my brother, Mike, to Mihailovich. Then they were both in the Maclean Mission where my sister, Bumble, was Fitzroy's PA. Fitzroy and I had often met at the French Embassy in London, but we had to be rather distant in Lancaster. We both came from Conservative backgrounds yet saw things from a different point of view, in my case an international point of view. His wife, Veronica, was my cousin, Shimmy Lovat being her elder brother.

Chipps lent me his new car, a beautiful long low Triumph sports car, for the duration of my campaign. My appointed driver was in the Salvation Army. He said he had to wrestle with his conscience because, although he was a lifelong Socialist, he was very anti Catholic. But Socialism won and we ended up the greatest of friends. He'd drive ahead of me with a loudspeaker in the gorgeous Triumph, announcing the venues, and I'd follow in the agent's old banger.

Chipps, of course, thought it very odd that I dressed in *haute couture* and wore a family diamond brooch, but the Labour people wanted me to look nice and were proud of the fact I was much smarter than Veronica – actually the factory girls were just as smartly dressed as many debs, and on much less money. The Labour people were completely on my side, they really were, I was called the Red Rose of Lancaster and children used to run through the streets shouting, "Vote for Dodo! Vote for Dodo!"

My agent, Pat Deegan, a marvellous agent, was an Irish Catholic, and we went very often to morning Communion together. I stayed in two houses, one belonging to an old couple whose name escapes me and the other belonging to a darling old girl called Mrs. Shuttleworth. My hosts' lifestyle was very different from mine but they were very spoiling, and made me *so* comfortable. Frightfully civilised people. I was brought breakfast in bed and we had delicious high tea, usually lovely Morecombe shrimps. Tea would be at about six, then I'd go to a meeting and, when I got back, have a hot drink before going to bed. I was treated like family. I loved them all. Mrs. Shuttleworth bought a bottle of wine when she was paid on Friday and we had a glass with our high tea every evening. When I spoke in Working Men's Clubs, though, I only accepted lemonade.

Well, as I say, a driver went ahead of me with a loudspeaker while I was speaking somewhere else – I devised the idea, actually, and it's now the norm. He'd say, "In ten minutes time Miss Leas will be at X street corner or Y street corner" or "Miss Lees is coming in ten minutes time to such and such a shopping area or such and such a factory." As a result, I was heard by an enormous amount of people. I was the only failed candidate of the whole election who got more publicity than the successful ones. I went to speak at a mill where I met a Polish refugee who'd been in Dachau – there was a tattoo on her arm. The Welfare Officer told me she worked far harder than everyone else, so they had rebelled. He eventually persuaded her to do much less if they would do a little more. As I wasn't allowed to speak inside most of the mills and factories, because the owners wanted Fitzroy to win, I had meetings outside the gates and everyone just downed tools and came outside to hear me.

I also went to a "Loony Bin" and gave a speech. It was in the Lake District, part of my constituency. Actually I lost the election *because* of the rural areas which were still very Conservative. Lancaster voted for me solidly . . . I went to this Loony Bin and gave a speech to the loonies in their main room, and I was asked the most intelligent questions of my whole campaign. One man had been a professor; another had been head of an engineering firm. I said afterwards to the Superintendent, who was allowed to choose the voters, "Well, who are you going to choose? *How* can you choose? I hope you're not going to be political about it." Twelve votes were allowed. All my friends, including Fitzroy, said, "If you win by twelve votes, we'll know who voted for you!" It became a sort of joke in the Party.

I fought a long, hard, five-week campaign. In the morning I'd make ten or twelve speeches at street corners and so on. In the afternoon I generally spoke to ladies' groups. At night I'd travel long distances to make three or four speeches in the rural areas. Barbara Castle. Eddie Shackleton, Bessie Braddock, Denis Healey, Dick Stokes, all came and spoke for me. Dick Stokes spoke for me at a ladies' group one afternoon. That's when he made his famous "Mossadegh couldn't run a sweetshop" speech – Mossadegh had become Prime Minister of Iran and was nationalising the oil industry, causing problems for the Anglo-Iranian oil Company. He was to speak that evening for Eddie Shackleton at Preston but, of course, Attlee was on the telephone within half an hour, saying, "You can't speak for Eddie! Come back to London at once! You've made the most awful gaffe!" The gaffe was marvellous publicity for me. It was in all the papers that he was speaking from my platform. I was news and could get coverage, for example, for my idea of turning a TB sanatorium, no longer in use because of penicillin, into workers' flats.

I'll always remember an old girl coming up to me after a meeting and saying, "I worked for your grandfather when he stood as a Conservative for Oldham. I'm sure, if he was alive now, he'd have come round to the same way of thinking as you."

I had a terrific Eve of Poll Meeting in the Town Hall – hundreds were turned away. I spoke about Socialism and the dangers of Fascism. I even brought in Dachau and, when I did, you could have heard a pin drop. I ended up with "The strength of the pack is the wolf, and the strength of the wolf is the pack" and "I don't only want a Welfare State, I want a truly Welfare World." The whole place rose to their feet and there were people in tears.

The next day I went round to all the polling stations. There were notices everywhere saying "VOTE FOR DODO, THE RED ROSE OF LANCASTER", that sort of thing. My Labour supporters were terribly chuffed: they really thought I was going to win – and I would have, of course, if the swing had been with us. In fact, when the counting began, I saw from Fitzroy's face that *he* thought he was going to lose. My piles went up and up, until the rural votes came in . . .

Here we are: "Brigadier Maclean. Conservative. 20,555. Miss D. Lees. Labour. 18.099. Majority 2.456." I reduced his previous majority from 3,096 to 2,456. "Both candidates increased their polls from the last election when, however. there was a three-cornered fight with a Liberal taking part. It was the fourth election which Brigadier Maclean has successfully contested in Lancaster since he was first returned in '41, but this was his first straight fight. The counting started before nine a.m." – this would have been on October the 26th – "and, although there was a slight delay because one of the ballot boxes had been so firmly secured that a crowbar had to be used to prize it open, it was completed at about ten minutes past ten . . . The counting was watched by supporters of both parties from the gallery of the Ashton Hall . . . Miss Dodo Lees, who was presented by supporters with a bouquet of red roses, congratulated Brigadier Maclean and told those inside and outside the Town Hall, 'I know he will represent you to the best of his ability.' When they compared the Lancaster result with what was happening in the rest of the country, she said her supporters would realise that their efforts had been well worthwhile. 'When you are fighting for something in which you believe, the effort is never wasted, even if you are not victorious,' she observed. Miss Lees, who promised that she would not desert Lancaster, expressed her intention of continuing her fight for Labour in that constituency."

When in '53, just before I got married to Chipps. I was asked to go to the Selection Conference for Loughborough – the candidate there was retiring – I wrote to the Lancaster Labour Party to tell them I hated the idea of letting them down, of leaving a marginal seat for a safe one. But they wrote me back the most charming letter saying, "We want you to be in Parliament. Take the Loughborough seat and we won't have any hard feelings."

So. you see, they really did love me. I gave up Loughborough because Chipps was seconded to the Foreign Office and thought he was going to Beirut as Second Secretary in the Embassy there. As I was hopelessly in love, I decided I couldn't live without him and I left politics. So John Cronin was selected for Loughborough. It's ironic that, in the end, Chipps *didn't* go to Beirut and remained temporarily in London instead . . .

To go back to '51. Your work, doesn't stop because you haven't been elected as M.P.; you have to think in terms of the *next* election and try to get things done for your constituents through your friends in Parliament – Bessie Braddock, for instance, helped me a lot. So I travelled up to Lancaster at least twice a month to run a sort of unofficial surgery, assuming I was going to stand for the next election and also get in. In fact, a relation of Attlee's stood for Lancaster and *didn't* get in, though Humphrey Berkeley did, the election after that . . .

Anyway, I went up to Lancaster one weekend in '52 and, when I got back to 10, Burnsall Street. I found a note from Mrs. Bliss, my daily help, which said, "I've tidied up but you've been burgled." I was absolutely shattered and called the police at once. Jimmy was PG-ing on the top floor and Anne was away, and the burglars had been very picky and choosy. All the silver had gone, even the cigar case Nan gave me after Howard died, and they'd taken my typewriter, a little Hermes with a French keyboard given to me by François. From the fridge they'd taken a long sausage, which Chipps had brought me back from Amsterdam, as well as the butter, but they'd left the margarine. They'd also left my furs, which weren't very grand.

The police noted everything down but had no clues because Mrs. Bliss had tidied up and cleaned off all the fingerprints. The extraordinary thing was that, six months later, they rang me and said, "We've caught your burglars. We know it's them because we've got your typewriter." They'd found a man with a younger one climbing through a window in Golders Green and gone back to their room in Notting Hill. It was full of loot, including my typewriter. So I went to Golders Green Police Station and looked through all this loot, but nothing else of mine was there – I suppose they sold the silver but couldn't sell the typewriter because it had a French keyboard. They got four years. Mine was one of the the burglaries taken into consideration. In court, one of the men said, "Oh yes, I remember that house in Burnsall Street. There was a note on the table saying, "Chipps, the key is under the mat. Dodo." We'd have taken it and come back and done her again, but we thought we'd everything we wanted."

There was a funny sequel to all this because, about six months later, the police arrested Jimmy, the PG. I'd got very bored with the police fining me ten bob every three months or so for parking Chipps' car in Burnsall Street, and I said to them very crossly, "Instead of fining me for leaving the car outside my *own* front door, will you watch the house when I'm away!" So, one weekend when I was in Lancaster, they saw a light on the top floor and rang the bell and, when Jimmy went down to answer it, they hauled him off. He said, "But I sleep here! Look! I'm in my pyjamas!" They said, "Oh, yes? You put the pyjamas on when you heard us coming. That's an *old* dodge!" And, of course, he couldn't get in touch with me because I was staying with working-class people in Lancaster who hadn't got a telephone. Finally, he managed to get hold of the night editor of the *Evening Standard* who said, "Yes, he *is* a journalist and he *does* work for us and he *does* live with Miss Lees." Poor Jimmy! He refused to pay the rent that week!

Part 7

A START IN MARRIED LIFE – MALTA

Chapter 21

Marriage

Chipps and I became officially engaged in February, 1953, and were married two months later, on April 18th. By then I'd left the *Evening Standard*, abandoned my career in politics and moved out of 10, Burnsall Street to live with my mother at Shepherd's Cottage, Winterborne Whitechurch.

Andy Bennett, Mr. Justice Bennett Q.C., Chipps' father, gave an engagement party for us at the Mirabelle.

I loved him and he loved me. A darling man. Among those he invited to were Betty, Chipps' grandfather's second wife, and a friend of Chipps', John Templeton-Cotill. Chipps met John, also seconded from the Navy, on his very first day at the Foreign Office. He was one of the few naval officers at that time to have a university degree and was already a Lieutenant Commander. We just fell for one another immediately, and, ever since, we've been great, great friends. He said to me *en passant* at the Mirabelle, "You're the girl I'm going to marry." I said, "This is supposed to be an engagement dinner for Chipps and me!" John makes me laugh more than anybody I know – he's witty and he's abrasive.

François sent me a hundred pound as a wedding present so I went to stay with Henriette and Paul Vielhomme in Paris to buy my *trousseau* – at Prestige you could have Dior models made in four days for as little as twelve pounds. My going-away outfit was a dream: blue linen very tight fitting, with a blue organdie collar in a very pretty shape, and a blue and white coat and a blue hat with a tiny veil.

I went to have dinner with François and thank him. Monique was in the Swiss mountains with her current boyfriend. He said, "Monique's leaving me. I'm so unhappy." I rang her up from François' flat. I said, "Oh, Monique, *don't* leave him! He's *so* unhappy! This isn't a good thing for you!" But she wouldn't come back. She said the marriage was over.

Chipps and I were married by Father Pedrick, the Catholic priest at our Blandford Catholic Church. We were married in Poole in the Catholic Church, my great-grandmother, Kitty Doughty Tichborne, subsequently

Lady Radcliffe, built with the money left to her by Roger Tichborne. The whole thing went down terribly well, even though I was marrying a Protestant.

Leaving the Church.

The only thing about a Catholic marrying a Protestant is that in those days you had to have a special dispensation, you were not allowed flowers on the altar and you couldn't have a marriage mass. The children, of course, have to be brought up Catholics. You're also supposed to try and convert your husband, but I'd hate Chipps to be a Catholic. I'd be made to go to church every morning – he never does things by halves – and I don't even go to church every Sunday. I'm like the French, "born, marry and die in the church"! Anyway, my children *were* brought up Catholics: I've .done the right things in *that* way. Father Pedrick said to Chipps, "My dear chap, I'm not going to try to convert you. If you're going to be a convert, you'll most likely discover Catholicism one morning when you're shaving." He's a very, very human man, Father Pedrick, and a great friend of ours.

Wedding Reception, Whatcombe House. 18th April, 1953.

At the wedding were all Chipps' Naval friends and all my relations and friends, including Monique and Paul and Henriette from France, and the Mayor of Lancaster, my friend Reg Butler who was Chairman of the Constituency Labour Party up there, and my agent and various other Labour people. Sid Osborne, a North Thames Gas Board foreman, came. He once fixed a leak for me at Burnsall Street and wc started talking politics and he turned out to be a Trades Unionist and a shop steward, very Labour. We made such friends that he snow-cemmed and whitewashed the area at the back of the house and made me a lovely little patio garden where we planted creepers and trees. I invited him to the wedding and told him my Labour people were coming down from Lancaster, and he met their train in London and drove them down in The North Thames Gas Board van. This enormous van was parked outside the church when I arrived, and I thought, "How marvellous! Sid and the Labour Party are here!"

John Templeton-Cotill was best man – he and Chipps were both in uniform with their swords – and my brother gave me away and Monique was my matron of honour. During the ceremony, Father Pedrick read out a telegram, blessing our marriage, from Pope Pius XII who can't have realised Chipps was Protestant.

There was one horror I didn't know about, thank God, till later. As soon as Chipps and John arrived, Father Pedrick asked Chipps to go immediately to the Sacristy to see the Registrar who said, "You can't be married! I haven't received the bride's papers!" – I'd forgotten to pick them up from the Blandford Register Office and deliver them to Poole. Chipps said, "Listen, I can guarantee you one thing, I have a lot of Naval friends in the congregation and they're only here for the champagne. I very much doubt if I go out and tell them the wedding's off that they'll let you get away from here with your trousers on!" The Registrar was absolutely furious. He said, "You can't talk to me like this! I'm an Officer of the Crown!".

However, he pulled back the curtain, saw my relatives in the front row and said, "Yes, they are a rough-looking lot. Alright, I will allow you to get married if your mother-in-law promises to bring the papers round on Monday. But on no account must you tell this to anybody! Your marriage isn't legal." We've dined out on it, of course, ever since, and when he's angry, Chipps says we aren't even properly married.

We had a lovely reception at Whatcombe House which belonged to "Aunt" Vivian Pleydell-Railston – it's a Georgian house, quite big enough for our five hundred guests. Maggie, our old nanny cum cook who'd semi-retired, did all the eats and the wedding cake. Sid Osbourne was a marvellous help – he opened bottles of champagne for us the whole time. He said to me, "I say, Dodo, a lot of toffs at your wedding!" I said, "Oh no, Sid. They're all just ordinary people like you and me." "Oh no, they aren't!" he said. "When oi went into the church, a toffee-nosed little squirt in a morning coat, 'e says to me, 'Broide or broidegroom?' I says to him, 'Oi don't mind, Chipps or Dodo's the same to me!' So they put me in at the back. Oi wasn't going to sit at the back, Dodo. Oi was going to see you was married proper! So Oi moved up and sat in the front!" Actually he sat in the place reserved for my "uncle", Sir Philip Colfox, and I was delighted to see this tall man with his cheerful face as I walked down the aisle.

We spent our wedding night at Claridge's before going on honeymoon for a fortnight in Corsica. Monique spent the night at the Branksome Towers in Bournemouth – François hadn't come over due to their pending divorce. She rang me up the next morning – we were in bed having breakfast – and said, "You do know, don't you, that the clocks have been changed because it's Summer Time?" We didn't know, and we had exactly half an hour to dress, pack and get to Heathrow. Claridge's rang up Air France and, being Air France, they were sentimental enough to hold the plane for us. We were given the only three-seated place – the seat next to us was empty – so we could be on our own, and, of course, there was champagne all round and everyone pulled our leg and drank to "the honeymooners who couldn't get out of bed" and that sort of thing.

Dodo on her Wedding Day.

When we reached Paris, François got into the seat beside us, the empty seat, the only empty seat on the plane. He was going to the Hotel Splendido in

Portofino, where he and Monique and Carroll and I had had such a happy holiday before they got married. So I saw him on my honeymoon though he wasn't at my wedding.

Chipps and I spent the night in Nice before flying on to Corsica. As we absolutely adore snails, we had two dozen snails each for dinner. An English couple, obviously honeymooners too, were sitting at the next table and they stared at us in horror. When we got on the plane next morning, there they were again, still staring at us and disapproving madly.

We landed in Bastia and Chipps said, "At last I've got you away from politics. Now we can talk about something else." Then, after hiring a car for the fortnight, a present from Paul, and spending two days in Bastia, we drove all the way round the island, to Calvi and everywhere. When we got to Porto, a lovely place with red rocks which Signac liked to paint, we stayed for the weekend in a hotel owned by the Mayor. He was a Socialist, so we got on very well, but, to Chipps' dismay, there was a mayoral election in progress so we talked nothing but politics for the entire weekend!

The Mayor had hired a plane to bring all his voters in North Africa over to vote for him and his opponent had done the same thing for his supporters in Marseilles. They arrived in separate buses, firing revolvers out of the windows. The Mayor went to church on the Sunday morning, came back, parked his missal in the downstairs loo, picked up a revolver, went out again, and, all day long, it was bang, bang, bang, a real Corsican election. In the evening, I was sitting on the terrace having a pastis when he finally returned. I said to him, "Monsieur, what happens after all this excitement and shooting and bringing people over by aeroplane if you lose?" "Oh, I shan't lose," he said. "If there's any doubt, I've got the *urnes*" – the ballot boxes – "from last time!"

Last time he had won by seventy-one votes. This time he won by seventy-one votes!

After Porto, we went down to Bonifacio and crossed over to Sardinia in the ferry. We didn't go far in Sardinia: we just stayed one night in Maddalena where there wasn't a hotel. All I remember about Sardinia is that the people who put us up didn't have a loo – there was a communal loo for the whole of one little street. When I said, "Where's the loo?" they said, "Use the garden."

My sister, Bumble was swanning around in Germany so we spent our first year of married life in her flat, the top floor of the headquarters of the Family Planning Association in Sloane Street opposite those lovely Cadogan Gardens – on the stairs you kept meeting the toads and things they used for their experiments. Sid Osborne made us some lovely kitchen furniture in his spare time, and he used to pop in for a cuppa whenever he was my end of London.

Funny coincidences happen in life. The house once belonged to the Reverend Austen-Leigh, Jane Austen's brother. My grandfather, Sir Elliot Lees' sister, Gracia, read Jane Austen to me when, as a child, I stayed at her house near Blandford. But, as I said before, I think my love for Jane Austin really grew from the fact that my father read her to my mother when she was expecting me – *she* used to fall asleep in the middle, but *I* was listening. The Reverend Austen-Leigh haunted this old house of his in Sloane Street. Once we were all sitting round in the living-room and the door opened and a voice said, "What are you doing here?" *Everybody* heard it.

It was a gorgeous hot summer that year – 1953, Coronation Year (from our Foreign Office seats in Carlton House we saw everything in the Mall). I wrote up the Corsican election story for the newspapers and continued, in fact, freelancing for twelve years – and I started a novel. We had the key to Cadogan Gardens where I sunbathed endlessly, listening to the Test Matches, often with only one other occupant, a film star trying to get a tan. Chipps and John and Etienne de Crouy-Chanel from the French Embassy and various friends from the City would come to sunbathe and picnic with me at lunch-time. We'd have bottles of wine, sandwiches from a sandwich bar and mulberries which I picked in the Gardens.

One day the gardener saw me picking mulberries and said, "Can you eat them things?" I said, "Yes. They're absolutely delicious." A pity I said this. The next day there weren't any left on the trees. I suppose he picked them all and sold them. Still, it was a most marvellous summer and we were blissfully happy.

Though Chipps played the euphonium at Marlborough and there was a lot of theatre on his father's side – his great-great-grandfather was an actor, his grandfather owned several theatres and his grandmother was an opera singer – Chipps wasn't really what I call cultured: as far as I could make out he knew little about the arts. I like to think I added another dimension to his life because, in those days, we went to thc ballet quite often. Sometimes Margot Fonteyn got us tickets and sometimes we got them through Mr. Martin, the head commissionaire at Covent Garden, to whom she introduced us. Mr. Martin was in Howard's regiment, a Grenadier guardsman, very tall and vary impressive. I'd just ring him up and ask for tickets and he always got them for me.

We dined a lot with friends, for instance, with the Bossoms (Doric was now married) and with the Hopwoods (Moyna Chattey had married Michael Hopwood who later became the 3rd Lord Southborough).

Moyna was terribly pretty with lovely soft fair hair and blue eyes and a marvellous English rose complexion. She was very intelligent and read a lot and, though she was the greatest fun, she was, without exception, the *goodest* person I have ever met. She was Jamie's Godmother and, for the three years we were in South America, she got all his school clothes, took him down to Eton, visited him on Speech Days, put him on the plane to come to visit us. In other words, she was his guardian as well as his Godmother. In fact, she and Michael agreed that, if Chipps and I were killed in a plane smash or something, she'd look after our two boys. She always longed to have children and she wasn't able to, so she adopted a daughter. But, in a way, she *did* have a son: she had Jamie for those three years.

One day, Chipps said, "I must ask my boss to lunch" so – I've always loathed cooking – I rang up my mother and asked what to give him. She said, "Oh, give him a cheese soufflé." I said, "How do you make a cheese soufflé?" She said, "Put it in a hot oven for twenty minutes and, as soon as you can smell the cheese, take it out and serve it. It's absolutely essential that it's in for exactly the right amount of time and that you serve it immediately. You mustn't let it drop." I thought this was very difficult, so I said to Chipps a week before this famous lunch party, "Please time exactly how long it takes you to get down from your office, into a taxi, and back here, up the stairs" – four flights – "have a dry martini and go in to lunch. Then you can ring me up as you leave the F.O. and I'll put the soufflé in the oven for the right number of minutes after that." Well, they didn't get stuck in traffic, they arrived at exactly the right time, we took exactly the right time to drink our martinis. I smelt the cheese, sat them both down at table, and served my soufflé. It looked like a little flat sort of yellow cowpat on each of our plates. But we ate it, and the boss went to hospital with a gastric ulcer and Chipps had indigestion all over the weekend. I said to my mother, "Mummy, my soufflé was a *disaster*! What did I do wrong? I did this and I did that and I did the other, and it was in exactly the right time and I smelt the cheese!" She said, "Did you beat the eggs properly?" I said, "But Mummy, you never *told* me to beat the eggs!"

We took our hols in September at Paul and Henriette's Vieilhomme's in St. Tropez. Chipps could only have a fortnight so I went ahead by train to have a few days rest without him and to be relaxed and tanned and smart when he arrived. Before this, we hadn't spent a day apart since our marriage, and Chipps was so keen to see me that, once he was off the ferry, he took a Benzedrine and drove to St. Tropez non-stop through the night. In fact, he arrived just after breakfast – I wasn't expecting him till evening so we went straight off and swam and made love in the sea.

That, I think, is when Jamie was conceived. I said, "Oh my God! Perhaps in nine months' time there'll be a little mermaid!" and there was, but it was a little merman. Actually, I thought I was going to lose him at four months, but a marvellous gynaecologist in Queen Charlotte's did a progesterone implant and I kept him. In June the following year – looking like a vegetable marrow, I was hardly a good advertisement for the Family Planning Association, coming out the door! – I went down to stay with my mother so that I could have my baby at the Cornelia, now Nye Bevan's Poole General, where I'd worked at the beginning of the war. But the maternity ward, in the charge of Sister Godwin who remembered me, had been moved to the old workhouse nearby. I can't, however, say I *enjoyed* my pregnancy. I felt terribly, terribly sick for the whole nine months.

Chipps came down to see me on the weekend of the 12th June and, on Sunday 13th, we went over to Slepe House to have lunch with Kitty Pittar, my mother-in-law, who gave us gooseberries. That night I started having what I thought was indigestion. My mother said, "You must go into hospital." I said, "Rubbish! It's Kitty's gooseberries!" At four in the morning, she insisted on Chipps taking me to the hospital as the "indigestion" was happening every twenty minutes. I had a suitcase packed and a layette and everything, but I refused to take them. I said, "They're only going to throw me out, for goodness sake!"

The hospital, of course, put me in a bed at once. When Sister Godwin came on duty and asked me how I was, I said, "Perfectly O.K. I just have indigestion. But I'll continue to do my Dr. Grantly Dick Reid relaxing exercises just in case." Back at Kitty's, Chipps had to be woken because he was screaming and yelling, "Get it out! Get it out!" as though *he* was having the baby! Anyway, due to my exercises, I had Jamie in five minutes with no pain at all, and Dick Norman, my obstetrician and a great personal friend – his father was our doctor when we were children – delivered him on the 14th on the dot of twelve, midday, which didn't inconvenience him as it was the time he did his rounds. When I was shown this little baby with blue eyes and fair hair, twenty-two inches long and ten and a half pounds, I said, "That's not mine! You've mixed him up!" Sister Godwin said, "I can tell you it is yours, Dodo. It's the only baby that's ever been born stark naked in this hospital!" You could imagine them all appearing in a top hat. She meant, of course, that they'd nothing yet to wrap him in but a blanket. Actually, though I hated the nine months before, I adored the birth. My next baby was the same.

I was terribly spoiled. I had a cubicle to myself and Sister Godwin used to feed him because I wasn't very maternal; then my mother insisted on my having a nurse for him – Nurse Rock – at Slepe House. He was christened at Lulworth Castle chapel. Monique and Moyna were Godmothers, and Ian Farquhar, at whose wedding I met Howard, and Paul Vieilhomme, Henriette's husband, and Etienne de Crouy-Chanel were Godfathers. All French, except Moyna and Ian, and all great friends and very good Godparents.

Jamie's Christening, Lulworth Castle, 1954.

Left to right: Conte Etienne de Crouy-Chanel, Moyna Hopwood, Chipps, Father Pedrick, me and Jamie, Ian Farquhar, Monique de Nervo, and Paul Vieilhomme.

We went down to Saint-Jean-de-Luz for our hols, leaving Jamie with Kitty. Maggie had always told me she'd be nanny to my children and, if I'd married Howard, she probably would have. But I married Chipps too late, you see, and she was too old. So at every party I mentioned I was looking for an *au pair* till somebody said to me, "I know an awfully nice girl. Her name is Maite. She's sixteen and she's the daughter of a Spanish hotelier and she wants to go to England to learn English. She can get a passport because she's done her Social Service."

So we went to San Sebastian with Betty, and Maite came down from Pamplona with her mother and met us in a bar, and Betty convinced her mother that I was a proper person to look after her. So Maite came to me and she stayed with me for four years. She was a bit homesick to begin with, as she'd never been outside Spain, but she was terribly efficient and absolutely marvellous. She'd done her Social Service in a children's *crêche*, so she was much better at coping with the baby than I was.

I'm very like my mother in that way. Neither of us were good with babies. I mean, we couldn't even change a nappy. I adored Jamie, absolutely *adored* him and used to cuddle him all the time, but I didn't particularly want to change his nappies. Maite's day out was a nightmare.

Dodo with Jamie, 1954.

Chipps had now gone back to the Navy and so had John Templeton-Cotill. I was delighted: I *adored* being a Naval wife. Because Chipps was doing a teaching job back at the Signal School, H.M.S. *Mercury*, we were given Naval quarters in a little row, rather like Council houses, in Petersfield. The house was very comfortable. I put a few things in to make it look more like home, like pictures, cushions and lampshades – but it was completely furnished. Unfortunately it had one of those awful solid fuel boilers which I never could understand. The day Maite arrived it went wrong. It started spurting steam and she put her finger in the hole while I rushed next door to get help.

I went shopping one day in Petersfield – on Maite's day out, my murderous day – in the Triumph roadster Chipps bought just before the Lancaster election. It was the most glamorous car you've ever seen, a sports car, a *décapotable* with a sort of dickie where Maite used to sit with Jamie. Anyway, I was parked by a pavement with Jamie playing with his toes and happy as a sandpiper in a wooden drawer on the back seat when I overheard a woman saying to another, "Isn't it *disgusting*? She can afford a sports car like that and she can't afford a carrycot!"

That winter, we rented a furnished house at Milland. I wanted something nicer than the Naval quarter. I'd seen lots of houses, but none were suitable. Then, one day I was sitting in the corner of a pub in Liphook with a retired Naval officer and his wife, and they said they wanted to let their cottage, Mill Cottage, in Milland because they also had a home in London and it cost rather too much to heat two places. Chipps and I went and looked at it, and it was the most lovely sort of old beamy little place you can imagine. We took it until April the following year and, while we were there, Chipps became a Lieutenant Commander and was appointed Signals Officer to Captain "Baldy" Heslett, afterwards an admiral, in *Battleaxe*, a Weapons-class destroyer, which was the leader of the 6th Destroyer Squadron. We celebrated with a "half-bottle" party, because a lieutenant commander only has a extra half stripe. The party was greatest fun. Carroll Fitzgerald came with his newly acquired American wife and I introduced him to Paddy Hampshire. He and Paddy then had a terrific affair, which upset his wife terribly. He had three children with his wife but, in the end, she committed suicide. My mother was quite right to stop me marrying him. He was too much of a *coureur*.

Chapter 22

H.M.S. *BATTLEAXE* – MALTA, EGYPT AND CYPRUS

In April, 1955, I followed Chipps and *Battleaxe* to Malta. Maite was coming later with Jamie, and I drove down to Sicily through France and Italy with Kitty, my mother-in-law, in a Ford Anglia bought cheaply on export in place of the Triumph. I knew I'd be taking a furnished house in Malta, as we'd be there for a good seven months, so the back of the car was absolutely full of things to doll it up, not to mention all our cases and a huge Dunlopillo mattress strapped to the roof. In Milan, we booked into an enormous hotel with a huge great sort of marble entrance hall. The hotel keeper took one look at the car and said, "You can't leave that in the street. All your stuff will be pinched." I said, "Well, have you a garage?" "No," he said. "You'll have to drive the car into the hotel." So we drove it into the hall and left it there all night.

When we got to Siena, Cardinal Petrelli showed us round and gave us lunch. Cardinal Petrelli, the Vicar of Siena, was a friend of my mother's. During Coronation Year I had taken him round Regent Street and Oxford Street to show him the decorations, and I remember him saying, "But they treat this woman as though she's a saint! This is blasphemy!"

We then went on to Rome where David Mansel-Pleydell was working for BP. David was the nephew of "Aunt" Vivian Pleydell-Railston and, if there hadn't been Salic Law, he would have inherited her properties which went instead to her two girls. Anyway, he had a lovely house in the gardens of the Villa Borghese and we had dinner with him and he introduced us to all his friends.

After an amusing couple of days in Rome, we went down through Calabria and over to Syracuse in Sicily from where I was catching the ferry to Malta. It was quite fascinating going through Calabria. For long stretches there was nothing there. There was absolutely no motorway then, and you had to motor along very narrow roads for two hundred miles without petrol. No garages. No cafés. Nothing. Finally we arrived one evening at the Jolly Hotel in Nicastro which is in the heart of Calabria – Jolly Hotels were subsidised government hotels put in places where there were no ordinary hotels *en route*. This one was very well run by Germans.

As we arrived, we saw a procession led by a very sturdy girl. She had a cupboard on her head and there was a man beside her and an older-looking woman behind. Some of the women had different coloured frills and bands on their skirts, and everyone was fair with blue eyes. After dinner, I said to a priest, "Do tell me about the fascinating procession!" and he explained that this part of Calabria was once a Greek colony – that's why everyone was fair with blue eyes. A man would marry a girl not because she was pretty but because she had a strong neck and could do the work and bring the harvest back from the fields on her head. Before her wedding, a girl walked in procession to her future home with an item of furniture on her head, with her husband beside her and her mother-in-law walking behind. As for the colours on the girl's and women's skirts, they allowed the boys and men to tell who was already married, who wanted to get married and who was a widow who wanted to get married again. "This," said the priest, "helps my job a lot." He told me that an American visitor thought the whole thing so disgraceful that she'd tried to get up a petition to have it banned. However, a delegation of the women of Nicastro had come to him, saying, "Father, for goodness sake, stop this foreign woman interfering in our lives! If the men have to work all day, they're not going to be any good at night."

At last we got down to Syracuse, stopping at Taormina and all those lovely places in Sicily on the way. Kitty remained in Syracuse – her husband, Geoff, flew out to join her for a holiday there – and I took the ferry, the *Star of Malta*, over to Malta where Chipps was waiting for me. We were joined by Maite and Jamie who came out by air, and we all stayed in a hotel in Sliema while I house-hunted. Married life was great fun then.

Clare, the wife of my cousin, Lord Clifford of Chudleigh, had given me an introduction to Mabel Strickland and Desmond MacCarthy's wife, Agatha, whose bridesmaid I was at the age of five, had given me an introduction to Mabel's sister, Cecilia de Trafford. *All* Catholics in a certain upper *échelon* are related. After the Reformation, we couldn't marry Protestants till the Catholic Emancipation Act, so we married our cousins over and over again. My friend in Gozo, Anne Monserrat, the widow of Nicolas Monserrat the writer, met Hugh – Lord Clifford of Chudleigh – once and asked him, "Do you know Dodo Lees?" He said, "Yes. She's a cousin of mine." "Oh," she said, "then you must be connected with the Welds." "Yes," he said. "Five times!"

Mabel and Cecilia were the daughters of Lord Strickland, Prime Minister of Malta from 1927 to '32, a terrific figure in Maltese politics and the first person to really publicise Maltese as a written language. His mother, Donna Maria Aloysia Paula Bonici-Monpalao, Countess Della Catena, was Maltese.

Mabel ran the *Times of Malta* and was the founder and king pin of the Progressive Constitutional Party and much opposed to the Prime Minister, Dom Mintoff, whose Labour Party had just come into power. Cecilia de Trafford, was terrifically pro-Labour. Both of them invited me to lunch, but it was Cecilia and I who fell for one another and she and her children became *very* great friends of mine.

She was a great swimmer but hated going on a boat – she'd had polio and it affected her balance so when we invited her to cocktail parties on *Battleaxe* in Sliema Creek, she wouldn't come. In fact, rather than go by boat, say, over to Gozo, Malta's sister island, she swam there. Once – and this will give you an idea how primitive Malta was in those days – she landed in Mgarr in a perfectly respectable bathing dress, and a policeman came up and said, "You can't walk about the streets of Gozo in a bathing dress," and, there and then, she had to swim the four or five miles back again to Malta.

Anyway, Cecilia suggested I look at a house in St. Paul's Bay because she thought I might persuade its owner, Henry St. Cassia, to let it to me, as he was now living elsewhere. St. Paul's Bay, with St. Paul's Island where St. Paul was shipwrecked, is rather spoilt by tourism now, but then it was the most gorgeous fishing village. So I went there and Henry St. Cassia – very English army and married to Anna, a barrister, who became another very great friend – happened to be painting the boathouse. I introduced myself and told him I wanted to rent somewhere furnished with the bare essentials, and he agreed to my having the house, including the boathouse, on the spot.

It was on the Vecchia Wharf and it was too pretty for any words. You went up to it from some steps on the wharf, and the boathouse was down below. Nothing anywhere but fishermen's houses and boats and sea. Enchanting. Beyond the drawing-room there was a wide terrace, literally looking over the sea – you could dive from below the terrace into the sea. And, beside the rocks, was a sweet semi-circular *plage* where Jamie learned to swim like a fish at ten months old. My bedroom looked onto the wharf. Jamie and Maite were in a room actually looking *over* the sea to Xemxia. The dining-room led to another bedroom which led to the kitchen. It isn't high luxury to have people walking through your bedroom to the kitchen, but the lots of people I had to stay didn't mind.

John Templeton-Cotill, now a Commander, turned up in command of a squadron of minesweepers and based himself in my house. John was a super chap, the sort of person who, when he gave a cocktail party on board, arranged gorgeous flowers in the spouts of the guns. I remember him doing just this for a party to which Grannie Grantham, Admiral Sir Guy Grantham, then the Commander-in-chief and later to be the Governor of Malta, was invited. Grannie Grantham took one look at all the flowers and went white as a sheet. A very serious minded man, he thought this was *not* behaviour proper for an officer and a gentleman of the Royal Navy.

He can't have approved of me, either. I wasn't the sort of Naval wife who went on board and said, "Hello, No. 1!": I was the sort who went on board and said, "Hello, darling!"

Whilst we were in Malta, several scenes for the film *The Baby and the Battleship* were shot onboard another ship, and when Grantham come on board for a cocktail party their officers had the marvellous idea of dressing up John Mills and Richard Attenborough as ratings to serve the drinks. Grannie Grantham looked very surprised when they didn't serve them in a properly respectful way, and, when Richard Attenborough leant against a bulwark and actually had a drink himself, his face had to be seen to be believed . . .

One of the perks of being a Naval officer was you could borrow ponies to play polo and you could hire boats to sail and water-ski. Chipps hired a little sailing boat so, in the evenings when he was off duty, we could go off for an hour's sail round St. Paul's Island. Henry St. Cassia leased St. Paul's Island from the Government to breed rabbits to shoot. In Malta you have to have a licence to shoot, and there are certain places where you can shoot and certain places where you can't. The Maltese, unfortunately, enjoy shooting small birds such as larks. But anyway, Henry liked his rabbit pie.

Chipps and I, the de Traffords, Peter and Sheena Bence-Trower and Reggie Fitzgerald, *Battleaxe's* 1st Lieutenant, and his wife, Di, were all very much in each other's pockets, and Maite ran the house, cooked and looked after Jamie and, within two minutes, had so many Naval rating followers that she always had somebody to do the washing-up.

When Chipps went off on *Battleaxe* to visit Suez and Cyprus I couldn't bear it. As I waved him off from Sliema, there were tears in my eyes at the thought of his not being with me that night. So I went down to the dockyard and said to the Movements Officer, "Is there any way I can hitch-hike to Port Said? My husband is Signals Officer on *Battleaxe*, and I can't bear to be without him!" This was then practically unheard of! Certainly none of my friends had ever followed their husbands by hitchhiking! He said, "Well, there's an R.F.A." – a Royal Fleet Auxiliary – "coming in this afternoon, and she's going to Port Said. The captain's Captain Shacklock and he had a French girlfriend in the war and, because of your war experiences in France, he'll probably like you. Come back at twelve and I'll introduce you to him."

So, at twelve o'clock, I met Captain Shacklock who was charming. I said,

"Any hope?" He said, "Yes. I can put you in my cabin. I'll sleep in the storm cabin. But," he said "it would be better for my reputation and my future career if a girlfriend came with you."

I went back to find Sheena Bence-Trower – she'd no children then and her husband was, of course, on *Battleaxe* too. I met her on the road. I said, "Sheena, you're going with me to Port Said!" She said, "No, I'm going on a picnic!" I said, "You're going to Port Said!" She said, "Well, all right I *am*, but I've a Naval widow staying called Eve and she'll have to come with us."

So, I went back to Maite and I said, "Darling Maite, can you cope with Jamie? I don't know how long I'm going to be – I might be a week, a month, a year – but I'm going to Port Said. How much money shall I leave you?" She said, "Thirty pounds" I cashed a cheque and left her thirty pounds, and then I rang up Cecilia and I said, "I'm going to Port Said. Will you keep an eye on Jamie and Maite?" And Cecilia came over every day and always found they were perfectly all right. She and the whole village looked after them. Cecilia gave fruit and meat and Mario gave vegetables and Joe gave bread and fishermen left fish on their doorstep every morning . . . When I came back, Maite had eaten like a queen and I've never seen Jamie look healthier. I said to Maite, "How much money have you left?" She said "twenty-eight pounds. All I'd to pay for was the milk and a few shillings for cinema outings."

The R.F.A. was called *Wave Ruler* – usually R.F.A.s refuel ships at sea but, on this particular trip, *Wave Ruler* was refuelling the fleet at Port Said. That evening Sheena and Eve and I were ushered into Captain Shacklock's cabin, where they'd rigged up three bunks and there was a sort of sofa. We sailed in the early morning and we had a gorgeous trip, if you don't count being eaten alive by sandflies the first night. Food cost us about four shillings and sixpence a day and, as you had to sign on for insurance purposes as a crew member for something like a shilling a day's pay, the trip only cost us a couple of quid each. We had to have salt water baths and special soap, but who cares! And, though Captain Shacklock was always peering at Sheena and me from the bridge with his flybuttons undone, and saying, "Not bad for a couple of old battleaxes" when we sunbathed on deck, we loved him dearly. There was a cinema every other night, and you played things like Liar Dice and Bridge. Liar Dice was another R.F.A. captain's *great* thing. Captain Warrington was his name. Whenever I came on board one of *his* R.F.A.s his First Officer used to say to me, "Thank God you've come aboard, Dodo! Now *you* can play Liar Dice all night with the Captain!" One way and another after marriage I was hardly ever parted from Chipps for more than three weeks while he was at sea.

The Movements Officer sent a signal to Chipps and Peter, saying

"Baggage Arriving By Wave Ruler." and of course they knew what it meant! Captain Shacklock had a bit of a reputation as a lecher and, when they came on board to collect us, Peter was rather worried about his Sheena. Looking very anxious, he said, "Was it all right, the trip?" We said "Marvellous." And they *are* marvellous in the Merchant Navy. The captains, even if they're as high as kites, manoeuvre their boats divinely. They never have prangs like the Royal Navy does. Practically never. Anyhow, *I* have great faith in them. We said, "We've enjoyed ourselves *so* much and what fun it is to see *you* again." And then, to Peter's horror, Sheena said, "Oh my God! I've left my nightdress in the Captain's cabin!"

At a cocktail party, Chipps had met Miles Fitzalan-Howard (the present Duke of Norfolk). Miles was commanding the Grenadiers out there and Chipps told him he was married to Dodo Lees. "Oh," said Miles, "she's my cousin!" This cousin business was always rather a joke between Chipps and me. Once, at a wedding reception in Claridge's, practically everyone in the room came up to him and said "I'm your Cousin May" and "I'm your Cousin Edward" and "I'm your Cousin Something Else," and, in the corner there was King Freddie of Buganda from Uganda and Chipps thought, "Any moment he's going to come up and say, "I'm your Cousin Freddie"! . . .

Anyway, Miles and his wife, Anne, put us up and we had a lovely time with cocktail parties everywhere. Even the Egyptian Navy, gave us one – this was before Suez – though they're dry and had orange juice themselves. Oh, we had lots of fun. We went sailing, and, with Peter Vernon, the doctor on *Battleaxe*, we hired a car and went to Cairo for the night, stopping to see Farouk's yacht. Farouk had been kicked out and Nasser was in charge, and we were allowed to go round his cabins and look at the terribly pornographic paintings – to show how corrupt he was, I suppose.

All the way to Cairo, Chipps was saying, "I'll show you the naughtiest night-clubs. You'll be so shocked you won't want to come here again. You'll even see people doing things with donkeys . . . " I thought it was going to be frightfully exciting. We booked into a hotel somewhere and went round the museum and the mosque, saw the pyramids by moonlight, and dined in a gorgeous hotel. I also had my fortune done – "Cook's Tour and three loves in your life" – the same old thing, and I bought a camel stool off the merchant, Jim Cairo.

Then Vernon went to bed, and Chipps and I went out again to a night-club. Well, I've *never* been so bored! No eroticism, just this belly dancer, quite pretty to look at, revolving her tummy button, and no other women in the room except me. Afterwards we took a taxi back to our hotel and we were just holding hands, not doing anything else, just holding hands, and the taxi driver stopped – this is to show you how moral Cairo was under Nasser – and he said he couldn't take us any further as we were behaving so badly, and we had to walk the rest of the way.

Chipps went off to Cyprus where E.O.K.A. was starting its revolt against British Rule – the job of the squadron was to intercept the *caiques*, the Greek fishing boats smuggling in arms for Colonel Grivas who was leading the guerillas in the mountains. I think Sheena and Eve returned to Malta but, as I was determined to follow Chipps, Miles Fitzalan-Howard arranged for me to go up to the Bitter Lakes army camp to see if I could get on an R.A.F. plane. There I met a great friend of mine, David Martin, who was younger than me but had fancied me even as a little boy. A Grenadier, he had come from the Middle East H.Q. and was taking part in a parade in Cairo the next day. After dinner in the mess, he told me he'd brought his uniform but he'd forgotten those things you clip behind to keep the buttons on. I said, "Perhaps Kirby grips will do," and I put all the buttons onto his uniform with my Kirby grips. Years later when I met him in Barbados, where he lived, I said, "Did all your buttons pop off?" He said, "No. They stayed." He's such fun.

I've found, following the Fleet around the world, that the thing to do is not to bully anyone, but just go to an airport and say, "I *do* want to go to Cyprus," or wherever, and hang about all day, and they say, "I'm afraid we can't take you today." Then you go back the next day and they say, "I'm afraid we can't take you today", and the third day they say, "Well, if you wait, we'll put you on when we've done the manifest." Then they weigh you, if they're sending supplies and ammunition and stuff, so that the manifest shows the correct weight. They know you're determined, you see, and that you can't afford to pay the civilian fare. They know you're prepared to put up with things so they don't mind putting themselves out for you. If you go saying whose wife you are and so on, then *no way* will they take you because they don't have to. Apart from being weighed, all I then had to do was pay about seven shillings and sixpence and sign a paper saying that if I was damaged I wouldn't sue the Royal Air Force.

Whenever I followed him like this, Chipps was always glad to see me. We were madly, madly in love. We're still in love, though we fight occasionally. I think, when you're old, you love in a different way. I mean, you're so used to each other. You still care *awfully* about each other if the other one's ill or something but, if they're away for a bit, it's rather a relief; you can put your feet up and not do your face. You couldn't keep that pace up for ever. Now, when Chipps goes to London, I watch the television.

Anyway, an R.A.F. Dakota, with canvas seating all the way round and crates of guns in the middle, took me to Famagusia, Chipps told me a bomb had been thrown over a wall into the middle of a cocktail party he was attending the evening before. We stayed in a gorgeous hotel on the beach, with its miles and miles of silver sand – we swam near that marvellous temple where the heads have been chopped off the statues. It was frightfully hot: I don't think I've ever been so hot. Chipps always goes sightseeing and he always takes me up some ghastly monument or something at midday when the sun is absolutely boiling. He hired a car and we went to see Kyrenia, and then he made me climb up to St. Hilerion Castle, which I must say *is* worth seeing. But, on the way down, I very nearly had heat-stroke. At the bottom, we drank twenty-eight Coca Colas between us and, from the next day, I carried salt pills in case of dehydration.

Chapter 23

DOM MINTOFF

A few days later, Cecilia de Trafford invited me to lunch at the Villa Bologna. She said, "Look, I've been talking about you to Moyra Mintoff." Moyra was the English wife of Dom Mintoff, the Prime Minister of Malta. "She's very impressed and she wants you to meet Dom with a view to starting Tourism here in a big way." So I went and had lunch with Dom, Moyra and Cecilia, and Dom asked me if I thought I was capable of taking charge of Tourism. I said, "Well, I'm certain I'd be more capable than the people you've got at the moment!" And I certainly was. I mean, I'd been in Fleet Street and I'd spent several years in *Presse et Information* at the American Desk in the Quai d'Orsay, and I could write to my great friend, Jamie's Godfather, Etienne de Crouy-Chanel, for all the gen on how the *Syndicats d'Initiative* ran Tourism in France.

So Dom decided to appoint me Tourist Advisory Expert to the Maltese Government. "But," he said, "I can't pay you more than the head civil servant in your office." I said, "I won't bother about being paid. Just give me five pound a week while I'm here so that I can have a maid to help Maite in the house." So I really did Tourism for nothing and, ever since, whenever I've been in Malta, I've done it for nothing it's my big charity. I've always been idealistic. I've always wanted to do some good, something that helps people, and, in Malta, there are 350,000 people. That's why I became a Socialist from the moment I went down that mine as a child. That's why I became a politician. And that's why I've been a sort of unofficial Ombudsman for the people of Gozo.

Dom retired in 1985 and he was out of office, when Borg Olivier was Prime Minister, from '62 to '71, and from '55 to '61, when Bob Laycock ran things as Governor, as relations between Malta and Britain were so bad that the Constitution had to be suspended. But, whenever possible since 1955, I've written annual reports and I shall continue to write them. Dom always gets things done when I tell him what is needed, whether he's in power or not.

Actually, I was able to help him in another way in the winter of '58. Cecilia rang me up at a flat Chipps and I had taken temporarily in Sandbanks and said, "Dodo, it's absolutely awful. Dom's been staying in a grotty little hotel in Notting Hill Gate for ten days. He wants to negotiate with Alan Lennox-Boyd, the Colonial Secretary, and Lennox-Boyd won't even *see* him!" I said, "Well, Cecilia, I've just had another baby and my new *au pair* is very inexperienced, so I must spend the nights at Sandbanks, but I'll come up to London by day." So I went up to Westminster three days running and lobbied all my friends there and, finally, Nye Bevan tackled Lennox-Boyd in front of me and said he must pull his finger out and see Dom. And, because of my intervention, he did see him. Dom, though, was never to forget how badly the Conservative Party had treated him.

My budget in 1955 was a thousand pounds. One thousand pounds was not very much to start Tourism, but I managed it. Charles Bone, the commercial artist – he was staying with the de Traffords – designed a brochure for nothing (I did the wording) and Chipps' uncle, Uncle Dudley, was a printer, and he had the brochure printed cheaply through a friend in the Isle of Wight. It said, "Come to Malta, the English Riviera, the Island in the Sun!" I mentioned the history, the monuments, the sea bathing, the rock bathing, the friendly people. I hardly mentioned the food because it wasn't frightfully good unless you ate in a Maltese house. You see, all the English service-men and their wives said, "We don't want foreign muck!" so the few restaurants there were gave them what they wanted – steak and chips.

Anyway, I duly wrote to Etienne who was frightfully helpful and sent me an enormous amount of literature about how they organised things in France, and I did exactly the same for Malta. For instance, I set the precedent in Malta of taking statistics, you know, getting people to write on cards their address and why they were coming, to discover who were genuine tourists and who were just relations of those in the services. This was the time Dom's Labour Government (and the British Labour Party) were very keen for Malta to integrate with Britain and have three M.P.'s sitting at Westminster. Alan Lennox-Boyd, Macmillan's Minister for the Colonies, was then taking the idea quite seriously and people such as Nye Bevan, Attlee, Lord Kilmuir, David Maxwell-Fyfe, Lord Perth, Julian Amory and Dick Crossland were soon to come out for a Round Table Conference on the subject. I realised that Malta would be headline news in Britain and, as part of a P.R. campaign linking this event to Tourism in Malta, I went over to London and arranged for posters, designed by Charles Bone, to be on the buses and the Tube. Meanwhile I was getting free publicity on my own behalf "Dodo Sells Isle", locally and in the English nationals.

The Tourist Bureau in St. John's Square, Valetta, which, till now had been the responsibility of a Minister, who wasn't much interested as he wore several other hats, was at last fully professional: I was given a full-time civil servant to assist me. My usual routine was to arrive at half past seven in the morning, stop work at two, have a swim, eat a tortilla prepared by Maite, and then sunbathe until it was time to get dressed and go out to parties in the evening. I had a Press Conference every week and members of the Tourist Board (mostly hoteliers and restauranteurs) held regular meetings with me when people could put forward propositions.

Tony Cassar, an estate agent, travel agent and property developer, and now a great friend, said, "I can get you a charter flight from London to Luqa for nineteen pounds return." I said, "We'll have to get it agreed by I.A.T.A." – the International Air Travel Association. I.A.T.A. are absolute murder so I said to Dom, "I know Hartley Shawcross (the former Labour Attorney General) through politics. He'll do it cheap for me. I can get him to handle this for a thousand pound." Dom said, "A thousand pound! You must be joking. I can get a Maltese lawyer to do it for ten pounds!" Well, unfortunately he *got* a Maltese lawyer to do it for ten pound so we lost our case.

Dom and his Ministers would very often meet me for discussions and a swim at Peter's Pool while they were relaxing in the afternoon. It was almost like a Cabinet Meeting. I'd pull their legs and say things like "Whoever dives off the highest rock fastest will get the best Ministry!" and Moyra would feed us cups of tea from a thermos. Dom, then, was a great water-polo chap. Later he took to water-skiing.

When the Round Table Conference came out, Dom asked me to entertain Nye Bevan because I knew him. He said, "Show Nye Bevan and Dick Crossman around, will you, before we dine with the Governor tonight." The Governor was Bob Laycock, the guerilla hero who was with the S.A.S. during the war. Angie, his wife, was very nice, and they'd a daughter called Tilly who was then engaged to Mark Agnew, Bob's A.D.C. Mark is now married to Tessa, Lord Ilchester's daughter, and is the British Field Sports Society chap for Dorset, so I see him still . . . Anyway, in the morning, I took Nye and Dick all round the Tarxien Temples and the Necropolis. In the Necropolis there's a hole from behind which the High Priest used to terrify his flock by talking to them as if he was God. There's a Malta story that you can only be heard through the hole if you're a man: if you're a woman, it doesn't sound, unless you're Mabel Strickland!

After seeing the Necropolis, we came back to St. Paul's Bay for lunch. Now, Dom had told me at all costs to keep Nye sober as he would be sitting next to the Archbishop at dinner, and it was frightfully important that Nye was on his best behaviour. It was Dom Mintoff and his Labour Party who were pro-integration. The Nationlists and the Church were not only anti-British, they were anti Tourism. The Church, of course, believed that links with Britain would bring birth control and divorce and modern manners into this medieval country which they ruled with a rod of iron. But I didn't think dry martinis before lunch would do Nye any harm and I'd told a sailor friend of Maite's how to serve them – ice, plenty of gin, and Noilly Prat just waved over the top. Well, we all had a dry martini and we had another dry martini, and Nye said, "I don't think your dry martinis have much kick in them, Dodo!" We always boiled our water and put it in gin bottles in the fridge, and so what we were drinking was ice and water with Noilly Prat waved over the top! But at least Nye was still sober and I'd promised Dom I'd keep him sober.

After lunch we did more sightseeing, ending up at Medina, the medieval fortress city, the old capital. I was showing Nye and Dick the marvellous view when suddenly Nye said he'd like to visit the Norman house of a chap called Mr. Golcher. I said, "I'm sure he's a Nationalist, but I'll go and ask him." So I banged on the door and Mr. Golcher opened it. I said, "Mr. Aneurin Bevan would like to see your house." "Mr. Aneurin Bevan!" he said. "All my life I've wanted to meet him! Come in!" So we went in, and he took us all over his lovely old house and showed us his collection of chastity belts – the eyes of the Maltese civil servant accompanying us were out on sticks. Then Mr. Golcher said, "I've got a bottle of Napoleon brandy I've been waiting to crack on my eightieth birthday. We're going to crack it now!" Nye got merrier and merrier and I couldn't get him away. I said, "Nye, we've *got* to go. You've got to be at the Palace at eight-thirty and you won't have time for a bath." He said, "There's a water shortage in Malta, Dodo!"

That was another of my problems in Tourism – keeping the water and the drains up. Every year I had to keep bullying Dom. He said to me finally one year, "If you talk to me once more about drains, I won't have you to breakfast!" I'd say, "Darling, if you have a country of three hundred and fifty thousand people with drains made by the English sixty years ago, it's not going to be adequate for more than a million, including the tourists, washing and spending pennies!" When I started we had two thousand tourists a year and in 1985 we had eight-hundred thousand. It was the achievement of my life . . .

Anyway, I finally got Nye away, and we all drove to the Phoenicia Hotel where the visiting members of the Round Table Conference were staying. But there we came across my friend Henriette Vieilhomme, who was in Malta to see me, and Nye insisted on standing her a few martinis in the bar. So by the time I got him to the Palace to meet the Governor and the Archbishop, he was in good form, and he turned to the Archbishop over dinner and said, "The trouble with you Maltese is that you breed like rabbits. If you're to integrate with the United Kingdom, you'll have to do something about that first, won't you?" The Archbishop was furious. There were processions because of "the insults to our beloved Archbishop", and the Nationalists really went to town. Needless to say, the press cuttings poured in!

Visiting Gozo, we crossed by boat with Lord Perth and Julian Amory while Nye and Dick and David Kilmuir went by helicopter. The world press covered that. I then got Nye and David to go to the Blue Grotto on Malta itself, by boat. It was rather rough and they were both frightfully seasick and looked like nothing on earth, poor darlings, when they got back. The world press covered that, too. Tourism was well and truly started, and only for a thousand pound.

What I wanted, especially, were lots of good hotels and restaurants all over Malta – the only decent hotel then was the Phoenicia. Gradually, now that I'd achieved all this publicity, people stepped forward with projects and ideas – Cecilia eventually opened a restaurant in the Villa Trafford called The Griffin (which is the de Trafford-Strickland crest) and another up at Rabat and they were both a roaring success. But unfortunately I said at a press conference, "We must have more night life. We need nightclubs and a casino." This was headlined and, the next day, the Archbiship's secretary rang up mine and said, "His Grace wishes to see Miss Lees" – I've always been called Miss Lees in Malta though, in Gozo, where I've a house now, I'm also known as "The Lady with the Parrot", because I arrived back with him there from South America in 1969. Anyway, I went round to the Archbishop's Palace and, being a good Catholic, I kissed his ring and he said I could sit down and I sat down, and he talked for an hour before I realised that his idea of a casino was quite different to what mine was, and that "casino" in Maltese could mean "brothel". So there was Miss Dodo Lees saying "We must have a brothel in the Dragonara Palace." So it had to be called a Kursaal.

I wanted it at the Dragonara Palace because it was empty and it belonged to the Marquis Scicluna whom I knew well. So I asked him could we have it. "Only," he said, "if the Archbishop agrees," and it wasn't opened for seven years, though the idea was in my original report. The Nationalists and the Archbishop, I'm afraid, never took to me because I was a Mintoff supporter. It was I who invented the slogan "Dynamic Dom". A newspaper cartoonist depicted me in a most unflattering light wearing a big hat with a cigarette hanging out of my mouth, and holding a palette while I painted Dom. The caption read: "Greatest Tourist Attraction Dynamic Dom"!

The only person who really put his hand in his pocket for a hotel at this early stage was Moses Fennick, a hotelier with a small hotel in St. Paul's Bay which his brother, Tony, still runs. He said, "I've some land at Golden Bay.

Will I lose all my money if I build a hotel there?" I said, "Moses, you won't. But it will take you a few years to make a profit. Take my advice, though, and get an English manager." Well, he built a small hotel at Golden Bay and he got an English manager who taught him and his family how to run it, and he's enlarged and enlarged it and made a fortune, and his family now run hotels like they've been Mr. Ritz all their lives. He's built an enormous one at Paradise Bay and made a fortune out of that, too. I'm awfully glad for him, especially as he was the first to take my word that tourism would succeed.

Joe Scicluna, the Marquis's son, rang me up before I left. He said, "There's a shipwreck. I'm having a barbecue at the Dragonara Palace to watch the rescue." This was the *Star of Malta*, the ship on which I'd first come over. We didn't realise there was a casualty and that a passenger was trapped in his cabin.

Joe was the greatest fun and a little crazy. He'd challenged someone to a duel in Hyde Park for pouring yellow paint on his car. He was very much on my side over tourism, though, and he started a restaurant for me, making the bar out of an old fishing-boat. He ran a pop group and he played his guitar at my parties. He once arrived too early for one of the big lunch parties I often gave on my return from the office. So Maite lent him a pair of Chipps' bathing trunks so he could have a quick swim beforehand, below the terrace. When we sat down to eat at about three-thirty, I said "Where's Joe?" Joe had lost his trunks about an hour and a half earlier and was still treading water.

In November, I travelled back to England with Jamie and Maite on an ammunition ship, the *Amhurst*. The ship was supposed to leave at half past seven in the morning. I said to the Movements Officer, "Will it really leave then?" and he said "No". I said, "Have we time to go to Mass?" and he said, "Yes". He was wrong. Cecilia and I went to Mass, then we picked up Jamie and Maite and took them to the customs' steps in Valletta, and the *Amhurst* had left. We had to go out in a launch and climb up rope-ladders, carrying our luggage and the baby. The mattress of Jamie's cot floated away in the sea.

We stopped off for a few days in Gibraltar. Chipps was there with *Battleaxe* and the rest of the fleet. A cousin of mine, Anne de Zuluetta, had married a Gibraltarian called Jaime Russo and he had a hotel in Gibraltar called the Queen's Hotel where we all stayed. I remember we went for a drive to Algeciras in Spain and I suddenly said to myself, "All these marvellous trees! In Malta I miss trees!" I put "We must grow more trees" into my next report and Dom was very much in favour. Australia gave us an awful lot. It's extraordinary how Malta has changed over the thirty-one years I've known it. Among other things, it's greener and cooler because there are so many more trees.

Part 8

Naval Life

Chapter 24

More Following The Fleet

In February '56 I flew to Gibraltar to be with Chipps – some army people put us up – before the Home Fleet went off on its spring cruise. Sheena Bence-Trower went out too and, of course, all our friends in *Battleaxe* were there and we also saw a lot of my cousin, Anne and her husband, Jaime Russo, so we had a very amusing time. The car had been shipped by aircraft carrier from Malta, and Chipps and I drove to Marbella and all over Spain. I saw a lot of bullfights. I do love a good bullfight. It's beautiful, a sort of pageant, and very exciting. Not particularly kind, but then nor is two bulls fighting one another on the prairie to the death – it's natural for them. The bull is so infuriated by the whole thing, he doesn't seem to feel much pain.

One night, in a Gibraltar nightclub, I did a dance with Reggie Fitzgerald, *Battleaxe's* First Lieutenant, and everyone sat down to watch us and we were made to go on and on and on. I went there almost every night from then on and did my own turn after the main cabaret. When Chipps left on *Battleaxe*, I went over to Tangiers several times with Anne and Jamie. Barbara Hutton and her current guitar-playing boyfriend were polo friends of theirs. One evening, Barbara gave a terrific party with a buffet and music and dancing. She and her boyfriend sat like royalty on sort of thrones to receive the guests.

During the spring cruise, our fleet was visiting the Spanish fleet in Cadiz. England and Spain hadn't really been on speaking terms since the Civil War and Chipps, because he spoke Spanish, was in charge of the arrangements for this historic meeting of the two navies. Sheena and I drove up to attend the big cocktail party that was to be given on H.M.S. *Maidstone*, in Cadiz harbour. We stayed in an *arctic* hotel, all glass and made for the summer. It was so cold, I had to go out and buy an electric fire. C & A had given me a rabbit fur coat for fifteen pounds for writing up some annual bunfight of theirs when I was in Fleet Street. It still passes for mink. In '57 I was offered a thousand pound for it, actually, but I didn't sell, and I'm very thankful I didn't because I couldn't have lived without it: I've worn it all over the world – in gales at sea, on mountains . . . Anyway, in this hotel in Cadiz, Chipps and I had to sleep with the electric fire on the bed and with one arm each through the sleeves of my fur coat buttoned down the front. We were *frozen*.

This terrific cocktail party took place on H.M.S. *Maidstone*, all very dicey politically, with no one knowing whether the Spanish Admiral was coming or not. But he did arrive, and suddenly, as Sheena and I were chatting up two Spanish officers, Peter, Sheena's husband, came and said, "You two keep the Admiral happy, will you? There's something going on." There certainly was.

Chipps and Peter rushed back to *Battleaxe* with the Yeoman of Signals who had come to fetch them. She was berthed alongside, opposite the main square of the town, which was packed with a huge crowd admiring the searchlight display that *Battleaxe* and her squadron of destroyers was apparently putting on for their amusement, with the powerful beams playing over the waters of the harbour.

Appalled, they rushed onboard to be told that a frogman had been seen in the water. The Navy had been warned that the Russians might use frogmen from their merchant ships to provoke international incidents by attaching mines to the hulls of N.A.T.O. warships visiting foreign ports. A Russian merchant hip was in Cadiz . . .

The ships were at Action Stations, and urgent signals had been sent to Whitehall and to the Embassy in Madrid saying that a frogman had been seen trying to approach the British warships, and that a major diplomatic incident was inevitable.

Suddenly caught in the beam of a searchlight, only fifty yards away was the helmeted head of a frogman. The Captain's Secretary, a Russian interpreter, challenged him. There was no reply. Chipps tried in French and then in Spanish. Then the Coxswain, who was responsible for discipline onboard, smelt a rat.

"Who are you?" he called out in English.

"Joseph bloody Stalin!" came the very drunken reply.

It was one of the ship's cooks, a keen skin diver, who, not being allowed ashore following a drunken brawl in Gibraltar, had used his equipment to slip ashore unseen to taste the delights of Cadiz. He was now desperately trying to slip quietly back onboard again.

After Cadiz, my plan was to drive from Gibraltar to pick up Maite who was on holiday in Pamplona, stay at Saint-Jean-de-Luz with Betty Ormond, then drive on to Paris and stay with Henriette and Paul Vieilhomme. After picking up Sheena Bence-Trower who was flying to Paris, we would drive to Le Havre, *Battleaxe's* next stop. You see what fun it was, following the fleet! Especially as there were gorgeous parties at every port and you met all the amusing local people. Anyway, just about two days before I was due to leave,

I met a Commander's wife – Deidre – who was flying back to England. I said, "Why not drive back with me as far as Paris. You'll only have to pay your share of the petrol." She said, "I'd love to. I've never been over Spain and I've never been to France." She was a typical Naval wife who hadn't a clue about the Continent.

All the way to Madrid, where I was to stay with Alan Seymour-Hayden, the Naval Attaché, the car kept breaking down – something wrong with the fan belt. We arrived frightfully late at night and I couldn't suddenly impose Deidre on Sally, Alan's wife, because I didn't yet know her – she's now a very great friend of mine and lives in Malta – so Deidre agreed to stay in a hotel. I stopped in pouring rain at a crossroads and asked a man if he knew of a hotel nearby. He said he'd take us to one if we parked the car. We parked the car and he took us to the back of a cinema where we went up in a lift and were welcomed by a very bosomy lady in a long red velvet dress.

Of course I realised at once we were in a brothel, but Deidre didn't. However she had to sleep somewhere, so I just went with her to see that her room had a lock *and* a bolt, and I said to her, "Oh, you'll be all right here, and I don't suppose it will be very expensive. If somebody rattles your door, don't pay any attention. On the Continent they do rather try it on." And, in a very loud voice, I added in Spanish, "If you want anything or anything goes wrong, ring me at the British Embassy."

I then left to stay the night with Alan and Sally. The next day, when I came back to pick up Deidre, she said, "Frightfully comfortable, Dodo. Marvellous breakfast, too. And it only cost a pound." I suppose they didn't know how to deal with non-executive guests. Not even when I dropped her and Maite off in Paris to fly back to England did I dare tell her where she'd stayed in Madrid. She was far too shockable.

Battleaxe then went on an extensive tour of Scotland, including Invergordon and Loch Eriboll (which the sailors always call Loch 'Orrible). Sheena and I, with Maite and Jamie, drove up for a fortnight in Invergordon and, after one day in a hotel, which we found too expensive, decided to look for a guesthouse as Henriette was joining us later and we needed a room for her, a room for Sheena and Peter, a room for Chipps and me, and a room for Maite and Jamie. Well, we found a Miss Macleod, a real Scottish spinster, an ex-schoolmistress who ran a strictly teetotal hotel. It so happened, she had four spare bedrooms and a living-room so we took over the whole hotel! I said to her, "Maite will cook if you like, and we can have salmon kedgeree for breakfast because Sheena's stepfather fishes on the Spey." "Oh," she said, "I wouldn't let another woman in my kitchen!" And when Chipps and Peter brought back whisky and gin from *Battleaxe* and made a bar, she said,

"Never before in this house has a drop passed anybody's lips!" But she soon succumbed under the spell of two attractive men and there was no further trouble with Miss Macleod. Sometimes she even looked after Jamie while Maite did lovely cooking, and she also took Henriette for drives in our car. She hadn't driven for years and Henriette said it was absolutely sweet: every time a bird hopped across the road, Miss Macleod stopped in case she'd hurt it.

Henriette invited her afterwards to stay in St. Tropez. She was lying naked on the beach one day when suddenly she saw this tartan-skirted figure with a suitcase trudging across the sands. She said to her, "Miss Macleod, you're frightfully hot. You must undress!" "Och sure," said Miss. Macleod, "I can't undress!" But eventually Henriette persuaded her.

That's the end of Scotland, except to mention the usual cocktail parties on board ship. At one of them we met Eric Linklater, the author of *Private Angelo*. We went back to his home afterwards for dinner. There were eight of us altogether. Next morning, when he came on board *Battleaxe* for lunch, he said he'd counted twenty-eight champagne corks on his lawn!

Before leaving *Battleaxe* to study Italian for four months as an interpreter in Rome – to be a Naval interpreter in French, Spanish and Italian must be pretty unique – Chipp's last official visit was to Ostend. Again I followed the fleet with Jamie and Maite, and I remember Jamie had his second birthday – June 14th, 1956 – on the ferry. I also remember crossing over the frontier to Lille to have lunch with Nanou Masurel, a friend I'd met with Monique in the Argentine. They hardly even glanced at my passport going over and, when I showed it to Nanou over lunch, she said, "But this is the face of a little baby!" I'd taken Jamie's passport by mistake! I was terrified crossing back again, but again they didn't notice.

We stayed in Brussels with the Renkins and, when Chipps had gone off again on manoeuvres, Jamie, Maite and I went to stay with Andy, his father, in Herford, Germany, where he was an international judge. A happy memory is the final big cocktail party on board *Battleaxe* in Ostend. There was such a varied collection of fleet followers in attendance, it was so *international*. All my Belgian friends came and so did Monique from Paris with her sister and brother-in-law, Claudie and Gilbert Cahen D'Anvers. At these parties, the entertaining is done by the officers – they don't get an allowance for it. I doubt if that's generally known. And when they invite guests to a buffet dinner and a film, that, too, is at their own expense.

Chapter 25

ROME

Chipps left *Battleaxe* in July, and we spent part of August in St. Tropez before going on to Rome. My portrait was done in St. Tropez that August by a young artist we met through Signac's daughter, Ginette Cachin. It's an oil, and the varnish, I remember, stained the back of the car. As a little boy, Jamie used to say, "There's Mummy in a bubble bath!"

On our way to Rome, we thought we'd look at Florence to find out if it would be cheaper to live there. Naval interpreters are sent abroad at the Navy's expense, but "at the Navy's expense" meant only about three pound a day allowance on top of Chipps' Naval pay which wasn't very much for a family of three plus an *au pair*. The other interpreters went to Italy on their own and stayed with an Italian family, but Chipps was determined to keep me and Jamie and Maite with him. He also knew that I had a great gift for languages, and, in fact, I was as fluent in Italian after three weeks as he was at the end of three months. Of course, he learned all the grammar and the Naval terms and could read a newspaper, but I was the better *talker*, And, in March the following year – 1957 – Chipps, the only officer not to leave his wife behind, was the only one to pass the exam!

Anyway, we stayed in a hotel in a Fiesoli, up above Florence, and went sightseeing. We had one introduction – to a girl who owned a gorgeous castle with a pool – but, as we knew nobody else, we decided, though we loved the place, to press on to Rome after touring Siena with Cardinal Petrelli. At lunch, Cardinal Petrelli said he was arranging for us to see the Pope, Pope Pius XII. Perhaps being a relation of the former Cardinal Weld had something to do with the Pope seeing us. As I mentioned earlier, he was the only Cardinal to have had a legitimate family!

I remember I had a ghastly cold when we suddenly received the summons to an audience at the Vatican. Chipps went in uniform, and luckily I had a black, long-sleeved dress and a veil. There were half a dozen of us – the rest were Ambassadors from South America. Chipps, of course, kept taking the mickey. He said, "Gosh, this is positively prehistoric!" when we got into the ancient lift that would take us up to the Pope's private apartments. In Rome everything is marked with the name of the Pope in whose reign it was made.

"This lift must have been made for Pope Pius I," Chipps added in a loud voice. Whereupon, the lift attendant stopped the lift and in a strong Irish brogue said, "Yer may be a British Naval officer, but Oi can see ye're not yet in a fit state of respect to see his Holiness. Yer'd better get out and walk up!"

So poor Chipps, dragging his clanking sword, had to climb up two hundred and fifty steps.

We sat in silence on small stiff upright chairs in dimly lit antéroom. After what seemed hours, there was a sudden swish of robes. But it was only a Cardinal coming out from seeing the Pope. We all got up and bowed to him and he bowed back to us.

Another half hour passed. A wizened old man, dressed like a fifteenth century lackey, with a curley point to his shoes, silently beckoned us into another room. We were going to see the Pope!

But it was just another dark antéroom – and with one chair less. After another long wait in silence, we were again beckoned into another room – again with one chair less. And so it went on with Chipps brushing aside the Latin American Ambassadors so as to get a seat. It was just like musical chairs.

Finally we were shown into what we assumed was yet another ante-room – and there was the Pope standing up to greet us.

With the Pope.

I had whispered to Chipps that he had to kiss the Pope's ring, and he had replied in a loud voice, "I won't kiss anybody's ring! I won't even bow my head!" But when the Pope, ignoring the Ambassadors, came straight up to him in his Naval uniform, he practically fell flat on his face. I thought he was going to lick the Pope's boots.

That Pope wasn't my favourite. He'd been pro-Hitler *and* a friend of Mussolini's until he wanted to abolish Christmas, which was too much even for *him*. But he was a very charming person to meet. He spoke perfect English and had even stayed at Lulworth Castle, and talked about Dorset.

When we first arrived in Rome, we went straight to dinner with "Aunt" Vivian's cousin, David Mansel-Pleydell, then on to the flat of Olga Fersen – a Russian friend of his, descended from Marie Antoinette's boyfriend – who had agreed to put us up as *PGs* till we found a flat of our own. A friend of Olga's, Assia Busiri-Vici, the interior decorator and wife of the famous architect, then agreed to let us her absolutely charming flat near the Nomentana. We agreed to pay the rent immediately, but as it was September and still very hot in Rome, she said we could use the room over the garage at the back of her summer villa at Fregene, near Ostia, an easy drive, till the end of the month.

So, for the rest of the month, we stayed there beside a gorgeous beach and Chipps started Italian lessons with the local priest. It was on the beach at Fregene that I met Cecilia Foley and Princess Irina Vasiltchikoff. Cecilia was to be another great influence on my life and became Bruce's Godmother. Tall, dark, good-looking, terrific fun, she knew *all* the amusing people in Rome. A divorcée, she had her own flat in Rome. Her current boyfriend, Luciano Zingone, ran the Rinoscento, a sort of Italian Marks and Spencers and, at his weekend Drag Hunts in the country, she was hostess. In October, when we returned to Rome and Jamie flew out with Maite to join us, she helped greatly by finding me a maid to cope with the washing and the housework.

Apart from a maid, we were also looking for an Italian girl to live with us during the day and teach Chipps Italian, so we put an advertisement in the *Messagiero*. The day the advertisement appeared, the phone started ringing at six o'clock in the morning. Cooks and chars, very working-class voices, said, "I can teach you. I can speak Italian." Then, from eight o'clock all the schoolmistresses and professionals who had been reading the *Messagiero* rang. Then, from about half past nine, all the duchesses and countesses started ringing: "Would you like my daughter?" "Would you like my granddaughter?"

We arranged some interviews that morning and decided to interview together and that, if we liked a girl, we'd say, "The sun's coming out" and if we didn't we'd say, "I think the sun's going in." I was in the bath when the doorbell rang. Chipps answered it and came and told me that a completely uneducated woman, who couldn't possibly teach him Italian, had come to the door. This was my maid whom Cecilia had got for me, whom Maite and I desperately needed to help with the washing and ironing, and Chipps had said to her "I am very sorry the post is filled," and sent her away. I couldn't leave the flat because of all the other people coming so I rang Cecilia who had to chase all over Rome to find her, and she didn't come back till about two in the afternoon.

Well, the real prospective "tutors" started arriving. A frightfully tarty one batted her eyes at Chipps and wore a dress split to the *nombril* so I said, "Chipps, the sun is going in! The sun is going in!" But, Francesca, the daughter of a Baron, was absolutely sweet. Chipps and I took to her at once and, from then on, she lived with us on weekdays, as one of the family, from nine in the morning till seven, eight, nine at nights. I still see her whenever I go to Rome now. She's a darling.

One day she mentioned that her brother, a student at the University, was on strike so as to get more time to prepare for the exams. She laughingly told Chipps that as he was also a student, he ought to take part in the big student demonstration that afternoon. Well, Chipps shot out and had a huge poster made on which was written "Assassini!"

The Romans are quite small, and the students made way when this giant of a man, carrying his provocative poster, arrived at the Piazza Venezia – the main square where Mussolini used to make his speeches from a balcony. So there he was in the front rank of the large crowd, facing the hated *Celeri* – the Fast Ones – as the Riot Police were called.

The *Celeri* were sitting in a line of pink-painted jeeps, under a barrage of stones from the students, talking to each other on their radios and pointing to Chipps and his banner. Suddenly, they all drove straight into the crowd and, still in their jeeps, chased the students up the steps of the huge memorial to Vittorio Emmanuel, the first King of Italy, before being driven back by more salvoes of bricks and stones.

Finally, the battered *Celeri* withdrew and two *Carabinieri* appeared immaculate in their feathered hats, with swords and white leather gloves. Politely they told the students that it was time to go home – which, with a great cheer for the *Carabinieri*, they did. How to break up a riot!

Chipps went on to the Embassy to pick up our mail. He was looking pretty dishevelled after the riot. I think he'd lost a shoe, and the sleeve of his coat. "My God!" said Colin Madden, the Naval Attaché. "Have you been run over?" "Oh-no," Chipps replied. "As a language student, I just thought I ought to take part in the student demonstration."

"You, a Lieutenant Commander in the Royal Navy, taking part in a student riot! Who saw you?" wailed poor Colin, reaching for the telephone. "I must speak to Dodo about this!"

Which is how I heard about it all!

At the end of October, the Suez affair blew up. Chipps, who in the event of trouble had been nominated as Liaison and Signals Officer to Admiral Launcelot who commanded the French aircraft carriers during the operation, went rushing round at once to Colin Madden, the Naval Attaché. But finally Colin advised him to get on with his studies and pretend he hadn't heard anything, as he thought the whole matter would shortly end in tears. How right he was!

Nella Gavronska, an old half Polish–half Italian friend of mine in London used to bring round her powerful radio so we could listen to the debates at the United Nations. At the time of Suez, Hungary tried to free itself and the Russians sent in tanks. Bonde Esterhazy, Prince Esterhazy, who ran the Hungarian Refugee Organisation in Rome, used to come to listen to Nella's radio, too. He asked me to help him with publicity, which I did. He desperately needed volunteer nurses in Austria on the border and I offered to go if Chipps went to Suez. I've always felt very strongly that England let the Hungarians down due to Eden getting us involved in all the Suez nonsense.

Nella Gavronska lived in No. 1, Piazza Leonina, just opposite the Vatican. We saw a lot of her there and at her lovely house in Cortona, one of the prettiest towns in Italy. Nella's mother was a poet. Through her and Cecilia and Assia and David and Colin, we soon knew the whole of Rome society, including the British Ambassador, and, despite our small income, we gave innumerable lunch parties in return for the hospitality we received. At the very first party we went to it was given by Cecilia – I met an unmarried playboy called Mario Giusti, who fell very much in love with me, though nobody could quite believe it. I wasn't in love with him, though I must admit I did enjoy the flirting.

But, when I met Lulu de Guerra (Count Lulu de Guerra de Boeckstyns), a former army officer, at another party about a week later, we fell for each other completely. He was divine, and I simply adored him and he me. I saw him practically every day: he'd even come and sit on the end of my bed and talk to me at breakfast. He was the only real danger to Chipps in any of my flirtations since I've married and Chipps had to put his foot down.

Funnily enough, Lulu had been in Yugoslavia during the war like my brother Mike. But Lulu had been in Croatia which was occupied by the Italians, whereas Mike had been in German occupied Serbia. In our discussions, I, of course, was prejudiced in favour of Mihailovich. He, on the contrary, had taken Chetniks as prisoners of war, and, when I expressed my horror, said, "Dodo, you don't understand the Italian point of view. We Italians don't like war and we don't like killing, and we certainly didn't want the Chetniks to be handed over to the Germans to be shot. So, as the Catholic Church was on our side, I'd just go to see the local priest or bishop and ask for the names of those in the Resistance and then arrest them – knowing that as Italian prisoners of war they would be completely safe."

Lulu often took us to the opera – we saw *Aida* at the old Baths of Caligula as well as other operas at the Opera House where his regiment had a box. But, what we used to do with him a lot, which was great fun and also very good for our Italian, was to go on picnics to see lovely places in the countryside, marvellous places with castles and Etruscan remains, which we would never have found on our own. While Lulu and I were sightseeing, Maite and Jamie would sit in the sun and play, and Chipps and Francesca would do Italian verbs and *conversazione*.

I didn't sleep with Lulu because Chipps had put his foot down, but, he was very attractive to me – we had the same sense of humour and the same ideas, except about Yugoslavia. His wife lived in Paris and they weren't separated. She's still alive and I very often hear from her.

Very often on Sundays, Chipps and I went to drag hunts at Luciano Zingone's lodge in the country where Cecilia received the guests and Mario Giusti did the whipping in. You were served on arrival with drinks by men in green hats and peasant shirts and, if, like me, you were only following the hunt, you were driven in horse-traps by coachmen. I didn't hunt because I had Jamie and Maite with me. Anyhow, I thought the whole thing was rather cruel because Luciano bought foxes from local peasants and, at the end of the drag, a fox was let out of the bag to be hunted by hounds.

Half way round, hounds always checked and drinks were handed round again. One day, after one of these sort of half-way parties, I was sitting on a hill with Jamie and Maite near the end of the drag, when I saw a man shooting larks, something which I *hate* the Italians (and the Maltese) doing. I went over to him and I said, "Look, in a minute, there'll appear a brown animal that's delicious to eat with a little bit of onion and some garlic and some wine." Whereupon he shot the fox! It was the only fox that died painlessly during all the drags we went to. I got absolute stick from Luciano later. He said, "I bet you arranged it!" I said, "You're telling me!" After the hunt, everyone sat down to an enormous Italian dinner and sang Italian hunting songs or recited poetry about the glories of the chase. It was all a far cry from fox hunting in Dorset.

One evening Chipps and I gave a small cocktail party after which we were all going on to "Georgio's" for supper and then a nightclub. When I came down, Mario and Lulu were waiting outside, quarrelling as to who should drive me. I chose to go with Lulu so Mario challenged him to a duel. It's quite fun to have a duel fought over you. Chipps was frightfully amused: he took it as a great joke. I think he was rather proud of a wife who was having such a whale of a time.

For Christmas we went up to Kitzbuhel to stay with the Ruck-Keenes. Christmas day was always such fun with them. We'd go to Midnight Mass the night before, ski all day, stopping somewhere to have goulash and a glass of wine, ski down right into the garden and then have Christmas dinner. That year, we bought the turkey from Rome because they couldn't get fat turkeys in Austria. From then on, when we went from England, we usually brought the turkey and some port and beef sausages and kippers.

During this holiday Maite learned to ski, and Jamie, though he was only two, paddled around on tiny skis and enjoyed himself thoroughly. The last day but one, I broke a bone in my right leg. They bound it up, but it swelled and swelled. So, when we got back to Rome, Chipps took me to a clinic, which the Embassy recommended, to get a walking-plaster. But they'd never heard of a walking-plaster! The nurse said to me, "In Rome, if somebody breaks their leg, they go to bed for two months." I said, "Well, I don't lead that sort of life. Anyway, if I went to bed for two months, all my muscles would weaken." So they found an old walking plaster in the roof somewhere and put it on – Maite had to wait on me hand and foot for twenty-four hours until it dried. But they were so unused to putting one on that, as soon as I put my foot to the ground, it broke, and this happened three times!

In the end I said to Lulu, "Lulu, for God's sake take me to a working-class hospital where they know how to put on a plaster!" so he took me to a working-class hospital where they put on a walking-plaster which was perfectly all right when it dried.

As I didn't particularly want the long drive to England with a sore leg, Chipps decided to drive back alone and to send me by air while Jamie and Maite went by train. I had one night, therefore, by myself in Rome, the one night in my married life when I might easily have deceived my husband. But Lulu took me for dinner to the ghetto where we ate bad *gefülter fisch* and I had the most ghastly tummy upset. No way could I even kiss the poor darling goodnight! The next morning he took me to a restaurant on the way to the airport and gave me some chicken soup, which settled me a little bit. When he saw all the baskets and cases I was taking, he said, "I doubt if we could ever marry, darling. I don't think I could bear travelling with you!"

Actually, the following summer, I suffered from an even worse food poisoning. Chipps and I went to stay with Betty Ormond at Saint-Jean-de-Luz before going on to Paul and Henriette Vieilhomme in St. Tropez. We went to a bullfight in San Sebastian and afterwards, on our last evening, Betty took us to dinner at a very smart restaurant. Sitting at the next table was the Marquesa do Villaverde, Franco's daughter, with her party. Betty had quails, and Chipps and I had *chiperones en su tinta* – octopus in its ink and a wine sauce, a most delicious dish.

That night, Chipps was sick fourteen times. Luckily for him, he managed to get rid of the poison, but I became very ill indeed and, the next day, as we drove across the Pyrenees to St. Tropez, we had to keep stopping because I was so ill. I really was sick, I looked absolutely like death. When we arrived, Henriette took one look at my face sent me straight to bed and rang Charles Cachin, the son of Marcel Cachin, Leader of the Communist party in the French Government and a doctor with me in the Resistance. Charles at once sent round a friend of his, Pierre Klotz, the famous Parisian specialist, who diagnosed paratyphoid and gave me a very strong antibiotic. I am convinced that Chipps and I were poisoned by mistake for the Marquesa de Villaverde. In San Sebastian, she had been eating *chiperones en su tinta* too . . .

London, 1957.

Chapter 26

Back In England

From March '57 to August '58 Chipps was back again at H.M.S. *Mercury* as Head of the Electronic Warfare Department. This time we all moved in to a Naval quarter on the edge of Haydon Wood. *Mercury* is surrounded by beech trees and lovely rhododendrons of all colours, and we were in a row of six redbrick modern houses close by. My mother came and helped me make a garden, and my next door neighbour helped me and Maite with the solid fuel boiler, very difficult as usual! The garden sloped down to a fence and, beyond that, was the wood, and all the birds of the world were there, as well as five tame squirrels. These squirrels used to climb up the drainpipe and come in through my bedroom window and share my breakfast. Jamie and I once watched all five of them get hold of a coconut I'd hung up for the tits. It was like a military operation. They gnawed the string and, when the coconut fell, they rolled it till they got it over the fence into the wood.

In June, Mario Giusti (rang up out of the blue). He invited me out to lunch in Petersfield where he was staying in a hotel, and, when he came over to collect me, we were suddenly struck by lightning. I was upstairs doing my nails and Mario was impatiently waiting downstairs having a drink. Maite was also downstairs, on a stool feeding Jamie at his tiny table and armchair in the pram-room. Just as Maite was holding out the spoon, a blue flame ran between her and Jamie right to the telephone in the hall where it earthed, splitting open the front door – I found fragments of it round the corner in the drawing-room where Mario was standing. Mario was absolutely as white as a sheet. He said, "I long for you and, for this mortal sin, I've been struck by lightning!" He came with us that night to *Mercury's* Summer Ball. I had to teach him the eightsome reel, and he was frightfully good at it. I suppose it relates to some peasant dance in Italy.

Bruce was born (we called him Amanda for nine months) on July 13th, 1958. Apart from feeling sick – I couldn't smoke a cigarette for nine months with both my sons because I felt so sick! – being pregnant had its advantages. In Kitzbuhel, old boyfriends who didn't know I was pregnant, still took me to nightclubs and made passes and in Paris where I went to stay with Monique, Jean de Villèyre, my wartime seducer, brought me a dozen roses, and Prince Marc de Beauvau Craon brought me a dozen roses. And then each of them kept bringing more and more, sort of vying with one another – all with no response. One day Monique announced that she was taking me to dinner at the Petit Club des Cent. I wasn't awfully sure if I could digest the terrifically rich food it's so famous for, but she said it was the *petit dîner maigre du Mi-Carême* (the little meagre dinner of the middle of Lent). Actually it wasn't so very meagre. We started off with oysters. Then we had caviare and delicious white asparagus. Then we had lobster and then the most gorgeous *merluche*, flown up from St. Tropez, with herbs and delicious vegetables. Then we had lovely cheeses and ended with a marvellous *bombe glacée*. And the wines were out of this world. You see, because there was no meat, it counted as a *petit dîner maigre*.

There was now the matter of Bruce's Godparents to settle. I'd chosen Nella Gavronska and Cecilia Foley as Godmothers, and Joe Weld and Lulu de Guerra de Boechstyns as Godfathers.

For the third Godfather, I was very anxious to have François Louis Dreyfus, Monique's estranged husband, because I loved him so dearly. I went to see him and he was delighted to accept the responsibility, subject to Monique's approval. He returned with me to talk to her. It was a dramatic meeting but alas she had no wish to save the marriage, though she had no objection to his being Bruce's Godfather. Still, I'm glad they met again, because he died on Monday, July 12th, less than a week before Bruce was born. On that date he wrote me the last letter he wrote to anyone. He said, "I'm thinking about you so much. My bag is packed ready for the christening at Lulworth and I wish you all the luck in the world. Don't worry about the baby's education. I will take care of that." The same day, he rang his doctor because of a pain in his chest. He had staked this doctor with a fortune to start his clinic. The doctor said, "I can't come. I'm going to Deauville. Take an aspirin." François then rang Alain, his son, who drove to see him straight away but, by the time he arrived, François was dead. A heart attack. A young man in his forties who could easily have been saved.

At the last minute, I invited a very great friend of ours, Jack Abrahams, to be Bruce's Godfather. Jack is a terribly nice person and in de Beers, diamonds. He was single then. Eventually, rather late in life, he married a Frenchwoman called Dora and they had a boy and a girl. The little girl went to that school where Lady Diana, now the Princess of Wales, was a teacher. The first day she took her in, Dora was a little bit upset because she thought the girl mightn't be happy. So Dora went out and bit her fingers in the car for ten minutes and came back, and there was her little girl sitting on Lady Diana's knee, happy as a sandpiper.

Then, when she married the Prince of Wales, the only children at that school to be invited to the Wedding were this child and the Hambro child who was a bridesmaid. And Lady Diana only had a certain number of guests she was allowed and, of those guests, she asked Dora and Jack Abrahams who she scarcely knew. She did it just for the sake of the child, and I thought that was terribly sweet. She even asked them to the dance. Very touching.

Talking of kindness, towards the end of my pregnancy we went over from *Mercury* to see my friend, Bun Kitson, at Sutton Place which she was decorating for Paul Getty, supposedly the richest man in the world. This particular day, Paul showed a side of his character which isn't generally known. It was quite obvious I was having Bruce and, after lunch, he said, "I expect you'd like to lie down," and took me upstairs himself and got me a hot-water bottle from his kitchenette. I was terribly amused by this. I said, "Paul, why do you have a kitchenette in your bedroom?" He said, "I work most of the night and sometimes I like to make myself a hamburger. I can't rouse the cook, just for that, can I?"

It was quite late and rather cold when I came down again. I tried to go out to the car for my cardigan, but the front door was locked. I found the butler and I said, "Will you open the door? I want to get my cardigan." "Oh no," he said. "Mr. Getty locks all the doors in the evening and he keeps the keys on his person." Finally Paul, who was still having tea with everyone in the library, went to get the cardigan himself. I asked him was he afraid. He said, "Yes. All the time." He was frightened of being bumped off, you see, and had enormous dogs to guard him. But I thought it was interesting how frightfully kind he was.

The story about him installing a pay phone for his guests at Sutton Place is quite ridiculous. Bun had it put in specifically for the workmen when they were doing the place up, and it was removed as soon as the work was finished. The story was started by journalists who didn't know him.

Bruce's birth in July presented no problems except for my feeling sick and except for Chipps' being flirtatious with a rather boring Welshwoman. I was looking like a vegetable marrow beforehand and not feeling very sexy afterwards, I couldn't really compete. I spent my confinement in a little house in Shillingstone, not far from my mother. Miss Lambert, who was matron of the Cornelia when I was a V.A.D., and Miss Alday, home sister at the same time, had both retired and bought this house where there was room for one mother. Dick Norman was again my obstetrician and I asked him not to go sailing on the 13th as I knew that's when the baby, already ten days late, would be born. When Bruce actually started, he was so quick that I literally had to hang on to him till Dick arrived. The next thing I remembered was

Dick smacking him and saying, "*Breathe*, you little bastard! *Breathe*, you little bastard!

I often wonder if having to make him cry like that was the cause of his dyslexia. Despite this illness – I treated it as an illness as soon as I discovered it – Bruce got everywhere he wanted. At the moment he's not only a reinsurance broker at Lloyds, he's also the youngest director the London Co-op has ever had.

Of my two sons, Jamie is the one who has always wanted a base. Even when he was four – Bruce was on the way – he said to me at Haydon Wood, "I must have a home where I can unpack my toys." And he got what he wanted almost immediately because of an awful tragedy. Geoff Pittar, Chipp's stepfather, was found dead in Wareham Forest in June and this made it possible for me to ask Kitty to give us Slepe Green, then only a cottage-cum-barn on Geoff's farm. When Kitty died in '76, Chipps sold Slepe House, keeping the farm and farmhouse which are now Jamie's. It was an ideal outcome as darling Geoff was so fond of Jamie and Jamie has been able to preserve his roots. Actually, Geoff and Kitty's ashes are buried in the same church, Lytchett Minster, as are my Lees relatives.

When Geoff died, Kitty moved the farm labourer living there to another cottage and we immediately called in the architect who'd renovated Post Green for my cousin, Tom, but he gave us such a dotty design that I decided to plan everything myself. After spells at a flat in Sandbanks, and at Slepe House with Kitty, we were able to move in during April, 1960, when Bruce was nearly two and Jamie was nearly six. For the first time we could actually be together as a family in our own home!

Chipps left the Electronic Warfare Section of *Mercury* in August 1958. He'd been appointed as First Lieutenant to the destroyer H.M.S. *Lagos* which was to be commissioned in Chatham in November before sailing off to the Cod War after only ten days working up in Portland.

There is a marvellous story about Portland. It was much later and John Templeton-Cotill had been out to Russia as Naval Attaché and had been married for two years and was now divorced.

He was captain of the frigate *Rhyll* and he gave a party on board specially for me. Of course, John, who had put flowers into the barrels of his guns in Malta, was bound to have a marvellous cabin. It was beautifully furnished. All over the place were lovely icons from Russia and everything in the loo was decorated with transfer roses. At dinner, I was on John's right and, on his left, was the captain of the German destroyer alongside. The meal consisted of the most *recherché* dishes and was served by a bevy of Maltese stewards, who adored me and were all great friends of mine because I'd done so much for Malta – in their white gloves they looked divine. Finally, as a compliment to me, they brought in a strawberry ice-cream meringue in the shape of a Maltese *fregatina*.

The German couldn't get over all these stewards and all this luxury. In a thick German accent he asked John, "How many sailors do you hoff?" John said, "Two hundred and fifty. How many do *you* have?" "I mean," said the German, "how many men do you have to look after you?" "I have these Maltese stewards," said John. "Who wakes *you* in the morning?" "I hoff only a clock," said the German rather wistfully! Actually, he and I got on very well together on account of my speaking German, and I invited him here the next day to a simple picnic on the lawn to show him how the other half lived . . .

Chapter 27

H.M.S. *Lagos*

The commissioning of Lagos in Chatham involved two ceremonies – one for the Protestants in the fo'c'sle and one, in the aft of the ship, for Catholics who were called "left footers" by some of the Navy. As a Catholic, I felt I ought to attend the Catholic ceremony but, as the First Lieutenant's wife, I was expected to go to the other. I talked to the priest and he very kindly held his ceremony a little earlier so I could go to both. You'd never think such ridiculous things could ever have happened, would you? They don't now because everything's ecumenical, but, in those days, at church parades and so on, Catholics fell out.

Chipps had asked me to type out some good recipes for Sunday parties and this I did – *paella*, *coq au vin*, *pasta*, *chiperones en su tinta*, *pizza*, etc. He also had some special benches made out of teak so they could be used by the crew when relaxing on deck. When *Lagos* was paid off in the summer of 1960, Chipps bought them back for very little and they're in the garden now.

Anyway, *Lagos* went off to the Cod War until January, '59. Chipps told me, during his leave, that cocking a snook at the Icelandic Government had been one of the most unpleasant experiences of his life – the seas were rough and the temperature was so cold that, to avoid frostbite on the open bridge, the officer of the watch had to be relieved every twenty minutes. Chipps, luckily, had a good woollen balaclava helmet.

In February, he rang me from Gibraltar to say he'd put my name down for a charter flight of officer's wives to Lisbon where there was to be a Home Fleet visit. So I flew to Lisbon and stayed with Baroness Ditty Beck, a friend I'd made in Kitzbuhel, at her house in Malvera. Ditty was so considerate. Not only did she meet me at the airport and lend me a Land-Rover for the duration of my stay, on the eve of the fleet's arrival, she took me to dinner to meet a group of exiled kings and queens. I sat next to Don Juan of Spain, which was fun. He was *charming* – mad about sailing and, like me, rather Left Wing. I was tactful and didn't talk about the situation in Spain. The Queen, also charming, was very statuesque and magnificent. She had with her the Duquesa de Luna, her lady-in-waiting at the time, whose husband had been Naval Attaché in England and started Spanish tourism. Don Juan told me that the Spanish nobility came to Portugal for a month or so to be In Waiting. He said it was a sort of holiday for them and that, in this way, he could split his court up evenly throughout the year.

The fleet was due to arrive the next day, and all the Naval wives went out onto the promontory near the fortress to wave like mad when we saw H.M.S. *Lagos* appearing. An enormous Union Jack had been hung up in front of the Catholic Seminary. This was made by Father Pedrick who had married us and baptised our sons – he was our family priest. And guess who was behind me as I tore up the gangway of *Lagos* to greet Chipps? Father Pedrick! As it was his twenty-fifth anniversary of being a priest, my mother and the rest of the congregation in Blandford, unknown to me, had collected enough money to send him out to Lisbon to stay for a fortnight in the Catholic Seminary where he had originally trained.

Chipps went hunting with Fritz Beck and the Infanta, Don Juan's daughter, who whipped in and gave a marvellous picnic lunch in a forest hut. Fritz lent him one of his horses and the Infanta was enchanting.

I was able to join Captain Norrington's tanker, R.F.A. *Tidereach* as far as Gibraltar and fly home from there. Felicity Ogilvy came to Gibraltar with me. I didn't meet her till the engines had started and I'd gone into my cabin and put my nightdress on the bottom bunk. Suddenly, Felicity, much younger than me, bounced in and said, "Oh, *I* want the bottom bunk!" I said, "Too bad! I'm there already!" Not a promising start but, in fact, we made the greatest of friends.

What Felicity and I didn't yet realise was that we were part of a big scale N.A.T.O. exercise called Dawn Breeze. British, French and Portugese ships were having an exercise while the R.A.F. looked out for them. I, of course, was only interested in *Tidereach* refuelling *Lagos* and Felicity in its refuelling *Apollo* where David, her husband, was on board – they were newly wed – and we were sending messages over the jackstay to our beloveds. Well, the first thing that happened was our anchor snagged up and we got away, heartbroken, a day late. Then, when we *did* start refuelling, it was a Portugese destroyer. An awful shambles was going on. I don't think the Portugese Navy had ever been fuelled at sea before. They didn't even know where to put the hosepipe in! So Captain Norrington said to me, "You speak Spanish. You tell them what to do!" and there was I, not knowing the technical words, trying to tell them over the radio in Spanish what to do: "Look, you must take that long curly thing and put it into the hole on the left. Do you see the hole? *Al izquierda! Al izquierda!* The hole on the left! That's it. You've got it. *Bueno! Bueno!*" Chipps says he and all the other warships heard the whole thing loud and clear on the bridge at five o'clock in the morning. I'm sure, thanks to me, the Portugese were sunk by the R.A.F., but, nevertheless, their admiral was very pleased and he sent a bottle of brandy over on the jackstay and we all went into Captain Norrington's cabin and celebrated.

A bit later that day, we refuelled *Apollo*. Felicity, of course just couldn't bear to have David waving so close to her, yet so unattainable. Refueling at sea is quite a difficult thing to do as both ships have to go at exactly the same speed – what they call "station keep". Suddenly the First Officer noticed that we were shooting ahead of *Apollo*, which was extremely dangerous. He said, "My God, Dodo! Get off that!" I was leaning against the Engine Room Telegraphs, making *Tidereach* move away like billy-oh. Anyway, that was put to rights and we all waved again, and off went *Apollo*, while Felicity, with her arms flung around me, said she longed for a helicopter to fly her to David.

We went on South, all the way past Portugal, then past Gibraltar and into the Mediterranean. By then it was night and we were in our bunks, but we said to the Officer of the Watch, "Please wake us up if the fleet comes into sight." He woke us at about four, saying, "They'll be in sight within half an hour." It was frightfully exciting and most romantic to see *Lagos* with two other destroyers coming into view in the dim early light of morning . . .

During Chipps' Easter leave, we took Jamie with us to visit Andy, his grandfather, in Berlin. Then, on the 12th May, 1959, *Lagos* sailed from Chatham to the Far East, via Lisbon and Karachi, on exercise.

Part 9

An Eastern Odyssey

Chapter 28

Singapore And Hong Kong

In the summer of '59, I flew to see Chipps in Lisbon again at the time of the British Trade Fair. It was a great occasion – Princess Margaret came out and there were terrific parties everywhere and marine bands playing concerts on the quay and the Coldstreams did a military tattoo.

Then, after travelling by R.F.A. to Malta to work on tourism, I flew back to England to complete the decorating and furnishing of Slepe Green. My intention was to meet up with Chipps again in Singapore during September when *Lagos* was refitting. I asked Jamie, who was now five, "Do you want to stay with Granny Kitty or do you want to come with me? I assure you it won't always be comfortable," and he said he wanted to come with me. Bruce, of course, I couldn't take because he was only one. As Kitty felt she couldn't cope with a baby at Slepe House, even with the help of Marie Luz, my present *au pair* – she considered her too young and inexperienced. So Marie Luz went back to Spain and I sent Bruce to a house at Broadstone where Dr. Norman's old nanny ran a boarding nursery for children whose parents were abroad. Mummy and Kitty could visit him there and take him on outings whenever they wished.

My problem was to get Jamie cheaply to Singapore – alone I could get there in an R.A.F. Dakota from Lyneham for fifiteen shillings. I asked my friend Air Marshal Sir Sholto Douglas, head of B.O.A.C. at the time, if Jamie could fly by himself on a British plane, but even he couldn't fix it. He said it was an absolute rule that a child under seven must be accompanied: he could travel at half price but he *must* be accompanied by a special air hostess. I might just as well accompany him myself and I couldn't afford the fare. So I tried other airlines, and the only one that would take him unaccompanied at half price – fifity pounds – was Air India, so he went Air India. I went out from Lyneham in September and my mother put Jamie on an Air India flight from Heathrow in October. Air India is a marvellous airline. Jamie adored it. They were absolutely sweet to him.

I arrived in Singapore, terribly excited to see Chipps again. The journey was very comfortable and we had to stop for a night in a sort of hostel en route in India. Anyway, we stayed in Singapore with Mr. Hutchinson, manager of the Hong Kong-Shanghai Bank, whom Chipps had met at a cocktail party on board *Lagos*. Hutch, as we called him, lived alone in a lovely house with a gorgeous garden and three divine servants and a chauffeur in the Tanglin Road, and had said Jamie and I could remain there, even when Chipps went away manoeuvering, in return for a small contribution towards household expenses.

This, of course, was much better than staying in a hotel as Tanglin Road is one of the nicest roads in Singapore and the garden really was lovely, with two fascinating, friendly cobras for Jamie to watch, not to mention the Tanglin Club nearby where we could play tennis and swim. And Cookie, who was Chinese, provided the most delicious Chinese and Malayan food. And Hutch used to send back his long, air-conditioned car for us to use while he was at work.

Unfortunately, when Jamie arrived at the airport in October, he was seven hours late. I was in a terrible state. His plane had crashed on take off after refuelling in Madras. It had taken them several hours to repair. The Indian air hostess was absolutely marvellous and gave him lots of work to do, like taking round magazines and sweets to everybody, so he was very busy and not in the least worried. Eventually, when he *did* land in Singapore, it was in the middle of a terrific thunderstorm and he'd been very airsick. But he seemed quite happy from then on.

As we hadn't had a sort of honeymoon weekend for a bit, Chipps and I, before Jamie came out, hired a car and went up to Port Dickson to stay in a Government Rest House – wooden huts on stilts against the ants and things. We went for a swim, the first morning, before breakfast. The water was like a hot bath, and crabs of different sizes seethed on the hot sand, the little ones scurrying away from you like a cloud as you walked along. We then came back to have a shower, and Chipps slipped in the shower room and, as I guessed, broke his back. That night there was a hurricane and all the telephone lines were down but, by the grace of God, Sir Robert Thompson, the Secretary for Defence for Malaya, happened to be staying in the same Rest House. Because he was in touch with the police on his private radio, he arranged for an ambulance to take Chipps to the Military Hospital in Kuala Lumpur where he had to stay for two weeks on his back before re-joining *Lagos*. At the hospital – beds in the open and grass all round and just a shelter above – he caught *dengue* fever. Lucky it wasn't malaria which had similar symptoms, because, if he'd caught that, he could have been courtmartialled for not taking proper precautions.

Anyway, these divine people, the Thompsons, who were at Port Dickson, let me stay in their house in Kuala Lumpur with their daughter, and the nanny and their maids to look after me. My bed was a sort of four poster with a mosquito net over it and, the first night, I was reading a book by lamplight when, looking up, I saw on the ceiling an *enormous*, absolutely enormous spider. As I have a phobia about spiders and cats, I just looked at its blue, bulging eyes staring at me and I screamed and yelled. Their little Jack Russell heard me, and when the spider, taking fright from my screams, skimmed along the celling, sailed down to the floor and rushed towards my bed, it went for it and killed it. Frightfully brave.

At the Tanglin Club in Singapore, I made friends with a very amusing Irish couple, Mike and Mary Henegan, who ran the racing in Singapore and had a lot to do with the polo, too. They invited me to a big dinner party in honour of the Sultan of Johore. I was introduced to him – we all called him Your Highness – and was able to tell him that, while working in Fleet Street, I'd met his father when he gave a party at Grosvenor House for his daughter, Princess Miriam, by Lady Marcella, his fourth wife. Anyway, we went to sit down to dinner and, as I was only a First Lieutenant's wife and not as important as most of the other guests (which included Paddy Bandon, the "abandoned earl", the Air Marshal at Changi, and Lady Bandon, I was right down the table below the salt. But, suddenly in the middle of dinner, the Sultan called to me, "Where do you live in England?" I said, "Dorset." He said, "Do you know Bingham's Melcombe?" I said, "Yes. Very well indeed." Moyna Hopwood's father-in-law, the 2nd Lord Southborough, had just bought it and, in fact, I'd often been to tea there with Lady Grogan, the previous owner. He said, "Have you ever seen the ghost?" I said, "No, I haven't, but I know someone who has – a friend of my mother's, an old Colonel, who used to stay with Lady Grogan quite often." He said, "Well, I stayed with Lady Grogan when I was up at Cambridge and I was thrown out of bed by it!" So, after dinner, he came and talked to me for the rest of the evening about ghosts and Bingham's Melcombe, and we made great friends.

In November, Chipps went off in *Lagos* to Hong Kong, and Jamie and I managed to get onto a troop-ship to follow him. This time I wasn't travelling unofficially as a crew member, so it cost me a couple of bob more. The first night, when I went up from our cabin to dine and dance with the various unattached officers, Jamie got a bit frightened as he'd never been alone before at sea. He called a steward and said, "Will you go and get my mummy!" and, when the steward asked what I looked like, he said, "She's dark and tall and she's got a dress with green buns all the way down the front and she's got a black bun on the back of her head." I had a dress with green roses all the way down the front. A good description! Anyway, I went down and saw him and he went to sleep quite happily.

We had a very good time throughout the trip. There was a round sort of swimming-pool, like the one I've got now, as well as a place where children were looked after, and, apart from swimming and dancing, I could sunbathe and play deck tennis. I'm so glad I didn't go to Hong Kong by air. Not only because of the fun we had, but because to come into Hong Kong by ship is quite extraordinary. With mountains reaching down to the sea, it's too pretty for any words, much prettier than Rio de Janeiro. The Isle of Skye is the only other place that has affected me so much by its beauty.

Remember I told you about Kay, Chipp's ex-girlfriend? Well, we stayed with her mother, Betty, in her gorgeous house up on the hill, not the Peak, the other one – in complete luxury. Kay was now married to an officer in the Tank Corps, and living in England. Betty, a very good-looking and very, very clever and well known business woman, owned and ran a big advertising bureau in Hong Kong. We were so awfully alike; we took to each other immediately, and she adored Jamie. I got to know her very well because, when Chipps was at sea, I ate with her alone. She said to me, "You know, if I'd been twenty years younger, *you* wouldn't have married Chipps: *I* would have!" She took us to lots of parties and to the races where she had a box.

Once, when *Lagos* was preparing for battle – there was an awful scare a, British ship being fired at by the Chinese off Amoy – Betty took me to dinner with Chinese friends in Repulse Bay. She explained to me beforehand that, for a balanced Chinese meal, you need twenty-one dishes, which is why, it you eat out, there should be eight of you at least. She said, "You will sit on our host's left, because you are the guest of honour, and he will give you on your chopsticks exactly the correct helpings. Even if you particularly like something, you mustn't ask for more. And, at the end of twenty-one dishes," she said, "they will bring in the coolie chow which you must reject with a gesture. All these awfully bad-mannered English people, they come to a Chinese dinner and they *eat* the coolie chow and then, of course, there's nothing for the coolies to eat in the kitchen." Can't you see the poor English stuffing themselves to be polite, not knowing there are going to be twenty-one dishes, and then doing the same with the coolie chow? "But to eat the coolie chow," said Betty, "is a terrible insult to your host because it implies he hasn't given you enough."

I told her that all this reminded me very much of my Uncle Alan (Lord Alanbrooke) going to a dinner in Moscow where, because it was so delicious, he had a second helping of the first course, not knowing there were going to be endless courses afterwards, and couldn't get any further than the fifth.

There's another lovely story about when the Fleet went to Leningrad for the first time in the early Sixties – I think John Templeton-Cothill was Naval

Attaché at the time. There was an official lunch party given by the Communist Party and local Naval officers and their wives. Our Admiral's wife went ashore in an ordinary suit with her pearls and hat and gloves. But, to her embarrassment, all the Russian ladies were in long, full evening dress in her honour. Then, in the evening when they all came to dinner on board the Flagship, she, of course, put on a long evening dress, but all the Russian women not wanting to embarrass her again arrived in tweed coats and skirts! That was the sort of thing that Chipps, later, as Flag Lieutenant to the Admiral on various aircraft carriers, had to prevent . . .

While I think of it, it *was* rather fun to see on sale in Hong Kong – as I did later in Australia – Moore's Dorset Knobs. The butler of my great-grandmother, Lady Weld of Chideoak Manor, used to collect her scones from Moore, the local baker. One day he came back with some that had gone wrong, but which she liked better. She said, "From now on I'd like these instead" and, when she died, she left him money to start a special factory to make them in. Moore's Dorset Knobs are still in the Moore family and I've bought them all over the world. The exact way they're made is a secret. We used to joke that it was to do with lime or something falling from the ceiling!

A particular feature of Hong Kong was the Side Party. A Side Party in the Navy paints the ship's side. But in Hong Kong a Side Party of pretty girls take over. They all live in a small Chinese sampan, paint the ship's side, do non-mechanical repairs, and serve at cocktail parties and so on, all in return for the *gash*, or what the sailors leave on their plates and would normally be thrown away. But the Side Party puts it carefully into bags to sell to the poor. They make a fortune. If a ship goes back to Hong Kong again, it generally has the same Side Party, or, if the First Lieutenant goes back on another ship, he'll probably take on the same one.

Our Side Party on *Lagos* was a woman called Ah Moy and her six daughters. Ah Moy still sends me Christmas cards. She sent me once the most beautiful linen table cloth and twelve napkins, hand embroidered by her daughters – I use then very often for dinner parties. Sometimes she says, "If you have a friend coming here, recommend me." It's the sort of thing which brings home to you how valuable food is. Later, in South America, I saw children scavenging in rubbish dumps, hoping to find leftovers in tins. Do you wonder so many have amoebic dysentery?

Hong Kong was a paradise, not nearly as crowded as it is now, I believe. One day, when the Amoy thing died down, I obtained a pass, crossed in the ferry to Kowloon and took a train through the New Territories into China to have lunch with an ex-Naval officer friend. Compared with China, Hong Kong seemed far more prosperous. I often went over to Kowloon on my own.

There's a Hilton Hotel there. When Cecilia de Trafford opened the Griffin Restaurant in Malta to boost my tourism, she had a very good English girl to run it for her. The restaurant became a great success and the girl said to her, "You must pay me more. Five pounds a week is really ludicrous." I said to Cecilia, "For God's sake, pay her more!" But Cecilia refused and got a Gozotan to do the job for three pounds instead. The Griffin from then on went down very much and, in the end, it failed, but the girl she'd sacked went out to the Hilton in Kowloon where she ran the coffee shop-cum-buffet.

In November, '59, *Lagos* went with the Task Force to Sydney for Christmas. Unfortunately the admiral in charge, Admiral Varyl Begg, didn't approve of Naval wives following the fleet. He hadn't brought his wife and nor had anybody else. He said he wasn't going to have me following in a tanker to Australia during fleet manoeuvres. Later, in 1969, when Chipps was Naval Attaché in Caracas, Varyl Begg, by now First Sea Lord, came out and, for the first time, Lady Begg was with him. Chipps took him to see the Commander-in-Chief of the Venezuelan Navy, while I looked after Lady Begg, showing her a bit of the jungle, that sort of thing. Afterwards we all had tea together at our house and, when it was time for them to be chauffeured to the airport in Chipp's official car, Varyl Begg said, "Goodbye and thank you very much" and started to leave as if he were on his own. I said, "But Admiral, you know Lady Begg's with you?" He looked quite surprised. He was so used to not taking her round the world with him, you see.

In Hong Kong I went down to the docks, and in sailed darling Captain Norrington, this time in an ammunition ship. I said, "Are you going to Singapore?" He said, "Yes." I said, "Will you take me and my son, Jamie?" He said, "Of course I will! I'd love to meet Jamie!" And the First Officer said, "Oh, thank God you're coming on board, Dodo! Now you'll be able to play Liar Dice with the Captain all night instead of us!" Then, of course, there was the thing of getting some girl to go with me and, at a cocktail party that night, I met a girl who wanted to get back to South Africa from her hols, and she signed on as crew like me – she wasn't actually Naval, but the Movement Officer managed to fiddle it somehow. So I was on my first leg to Sydney.

Then, when we got to Singapore, Chipps had gone on with the fleet to Sydney via Brisbane where they were celebrating Captain Cook's discovery. I couldn't go with him because Varyl Begg had refused to allow me to, so I went to see darling Admiral Gladstone, the admiral in charge of the entire fleet, who was flying to Brisbane via Darwin in his private plane. He said he'd take me there, but without Jamie as he was under-age (they have to be 21). I then went to Air India and asked how much it would cost for Jamie to fly to Brisbane. Well, at half-price, it wasn't *very* deadly, so I said to him, "Do you want to stay for Christmas in Singapore with Hutch or do you want to be in Sydney with Daddy and Mummy? I thought he might be a bit frightened of flying on his own after his last experience but, he said, no, no, he wanted to spend Christmas with Daddy and Mummy. So Hutch put him on an Air India flight to Brisbane, and I went off with Admiral Gladstone.

Chapter 29

AUSTRALIA

We arrived in Darwin. Admiral Gladstone was staying with the Governor. I was staying with the Naval Advisor, who came to meet me. I said to his wife during dinner, "I'm terrified. My child's arriving at the airport tonight, refuelling for Brisbane. I must find out if he's all right, but if he's not and he has to be taken off, how will he get to Brisbane?" She said, "Don't worry. We'll all go along to the airport and my husband will go on board to take a look at him." So the three of us drove to the airport, and she held my hand while he went up into the plane. He came back and said, "You're allowed to go on board, Dodo. Jamie's happy as a sandpiper. At the moment, he's sitting upstairs, having dinner with the captain and one of the stewardesses." So I went up to see him and he said, "Oh, Mummy! I didn't expect to see you till Brisbane! I'm having a lovely flight. I'm in charge of all the drinks and newspapers." Aged five! He learned young, didn't he?

The next day, Admiral Gladstone's plane took off for Brisbane. When we arrived, I thought *he* would get all the publicity. But I did because of my Fan Club in Melbourne – the one that had started when I stood for Lancaster. Another reason for the publicity was that Chipps met me in his Aunt Pat's ancient Rolls-Royce. She lent it to us for the whole visit – traffic used to be specially delayed to let us pass. It was one of those marvellous high Rolls-Royces you climb up into, with millions of dials and gadgets and things, a gorgeous car which, of course, *had* to be photographed.

Aunt Pat lived in Beenleigh. She was Andy's youngest sister and she married in England a doctor called Kilvert and they had six children. On a doctor's pay in England, he couldn't afford to educate them, so they emigrated to Australia where doctors are paid better. He told me there was a Nazi Party in Australia during the war, ready to take over if we lost. A lot of them, he said, were still living in Beenleigh, When they needed an injection, they always asked for it in the bottom, but, one day, he said to one of them, "No, I'm jolly well giving it to you in the arm," and when the man pulled up his sleeve, he saw his Nazi tattoo.

Anyway, Jamie arrived in Brisbane half an hour after I did, and Chipps and I booked into a hotel. At nights, because of the number of official "do's", we put Jamie in Chipps' cabin on *Lagos* where Lyte, a sailor, babysat and gave him supper.

Lady May Abel Smith was there, as wife of Sir Henry, the Governor of Queensland, and so was Patsy Tuffnell, the wife of Captain Mike Tuffnell, the Naval Advisor to Peter Carrington, the British High Commissioner – I knew Peter Carrington because he was in the same regiment as Howard – but, as the only Naval wife, *I* was more or less "receiving" a lot of the time, especially on the aircraft carrier *Centaur*, where at parties I showed people where the loo was and listened to any complaints.

The first day, we went to a cocktail party given by the Australian Army. I said to Chipps, "I haven't got a hat." I practically never wear a hat and I certainly didn't have one in Brisbane because I was travelling light. He said, "Oh, I don't suppose it matters," so I just piled my hair on top and put a flower in it so it would appear sort of "done". Well, the Colonel met us at the barracks and he looked at me in *horror*. I thought, "Oh my God! It's because I haven't got a hat!" So I immediately said, "I'm awfully sorry, but I didn't bring a hat to Brisbane with me." "That's all right," he said. "Do come in," and, it sounds as if I'm awfully vain, but it took me twenty minutes before I realised that I was the only woman in the room! I mean, I was used to being surrounded by men at Naval parties. Anyway, I suddenly looked round and realised that this was a stag party. Could anything have been more silly? A stag party for Naval officers who have been at sea for weeks! Meanwhile, the poor Colonel had rung up his wife, who arrived with half a dozen girlfriends and they all had to entertain me in another room, segregated.

Lady May Abel Smith gave us a marvellous dance at Government House. She said to me beforehand, "Have you a ball dress with you?" I said "No, I didn't think I'd need one" – I only had a cocktail dress and my dress with "buns" down the front, and silk trousers for nightclubs. She said, "In that case, I Ill say that long dresses will not be worn." So everybody came in party dresses and I wore my one with "buns" down the front. But I thought it was sweet of Lady May. After all, though I was strictly the only Naval wife, I wasn't very important as Chipps was merely a Lieutenant Commander.

The next day we went to the races. To begin with, Lady May hostessed a lovely sort of champagne buffet in the main building. We all ate together, Lady May, Patsy and me and the High Commission people and the Naval officers. Then, when we went to powder our noses, Lady May said to me, "I hope your husband's got some money. I forgot to tell you that from now on we're segregated." I said, "No. He doesn't carry money. *I'm* always moneybags." She said, "Oh dear! He won't be able to buy a beer, will he?" Anyway, we went upstairs to the stand where we were, in effect, segregated, and the men were in another stand behind a sort of grille, taking their coats off and getting round the keg. Too funny. Chipps had to borrow so as to bet or have a drink or anything.

Well, then there was a big cocktail party on the flightdeck of the aircraft carrier, *Centaur*. Later on, several women came up and talked to me and one of them said, "Ain't much food at this party, is there?!" I said, "Oh, do have a canape! Do have a little caviare! Do have some smoked salmon!" She said, "That's not what I call food! This time of night we have a steak!" Six o'clock was the time they usually ate, you see. I remembered this when we went North to Gladstone, before turning back again to Sydney for Christmas. Jamie went on *Lagos* with Chipps and Lyte, his cabin hand, as it wasn't on manoeuvres and I took a train. Everybody said, "Don't go by train. Only sheep go by train," but it was cheaper. Actually, it was rather a fascinating train because, at well as being full of sheep, it kept stopping to drop off mailbags . . .

Anyway, in Gladstone, it was *our* cocktail party on board *our* destroyer, *Lagos*, and I said to Chipps who, as First Lieutenant, was arranging such things, "Darling, don't give them expensive caviare and smoked salmon and so on. Give them sausage rolls and jolly good hamburgers and thick ham sandwiches, and lots of them. And I know it'll be expensive, but don't give them your duty free gin and whisky. Buy them local beer instead." Beer is far more expensive in the Navy because it has to be bought locally, whereas spirits are duty free.

I arrived on board from my hotel at half past five, thank God – our guests hadn't been asked till six but they all turned up at a quarter to, when the officers were still in their baths. So I received them and handed out enormous doorstep sandwiches and hamburgers and sausage rolls, and they absolutely adored it. They'd finished all the food by half past six, but they said it was the best Naval party they'd been to in their lives: they said, "You've given us a proper meal *and* we've had some beer!"

One evening we went out to dinner with the richest man in Gladstone and probably in Queensland. He owned all the meat-packing stations and must have been a multi-*multi* millionaire. We expected him to live in a palace but it was a house like an English council house, with a drawing-room not as big as mine and no dining-room, just a kitchen, and three or four bedrooms and one bathroom and a downstairs loo. We'd been asked to dinner so we arrived at a quarter past eight. But we'd forgotten, you see, that Australians eat at six.

We found, when we arrived, that the drawing-room furniture had been cleared except for chairs all the way round the walls and some tables in the middle. All the women were sitting there together eating the odd nut, just like at a Women's Institute party in England, and all the men were in the kitchen round the keg with their coats off! Every now and then, a man would come into the drawing-room and tell us a joke or do a little dance and then go out again. The usual segregation. Extraordinary! Actually, I didn't really mind. I had always known that you can learn an awful lot about a country by talking to the women. But, whatever I do, I never learn as much as Chipps. He has this extraordinary faculty for knowing exactly what makes a country tick – its interests, history, politics. You go with him to any country you like to name and, even if he's never been there and only seen it on the map, within two days of being there, he knows it all. It's an absolute gift. He ought to write travel books.

Chipps couldn't take Jamie with him down to Sydney because *Lagos* was on manoeuvres. So I decided to take him by air. Now Jamie had a toy poodle called Bobby and he had to have Bobby wherever he went. Funnily enough, it was given to him by Andy's second wife, the one I didn't like at all. Poor little boy, having gone all the way to Singapore by himself from England and having a crash in the aeroplane, he *had* to have Bobby! Anyway, we set off from Gladstone and, half way to Sydney, we discovered Bobby wasn't on board. The pilot had to come back and talk to us and then send a signal to Gladstone where the sweet hotel man put Bobby on the next plane so Bobby could catch up with us.

We booked in to a hotel near the docks, very expensive at seven pounds a day, and terribly dirty. There was only one bathroom for an entire corridor, and our room was really grotty. I literally went out and bought a scrubbing brush and some Vim and a bit of rag and cleaned the bathroom and the bedroom before I could bear to unpack. Also, the food was indescribable, but luckily we ate on board and in other people's houses for most of our stay.

Then Horace Law, the captain of *Centaur* whose crew adored him and used to pull his leg about his poor ship handling, rang me up to say awfully few of the ratings on leave had been asked out for Christmas Day. So I went to the local Radio Station and just sort of announced that it would be marvellous if people asked them to their homes. Within an hour, they had to broadcast that they didn't want any more invitations. It just needed a word and they were asked. Literally, in an hour, the couple of thousand ratings from the whole fleet were fixed up.

Christmas Day for Chipps was a terrific contrast to the previous year when *Lagos* was rolling in the freezing Arctic Ocean off Iceland. Here, in Sydney, it was hot and summery and, before lunch, we went swimming with Jamie at Bondi Beach. At lunch on board *Lagos* I was hostess for the officers on duty. I went down first, of course, to wish the ratings on duty a happy Christmas. Then I handed round presents in the wardroom where we had our Christmas pudding and so on. We gave Jamie half a glass of champagne which he didn't like and didn't even finish. Whether this went to his head or not I don't know, but he fell all the way down a companionway afterwards and cut his mouth on the brass edges – he's still got the scar. We drove him to hospital immediately in the car we'd hired and, thank God, a very good young doctor was on duty and he stitched him up. Poor little Jamie he was so brave. But it was a horrible way to end Christmas. We didn't go out that night. We went back to the grotty hotel and had dinner at half past six or some terrible hour. On one or two nights *after* that, though, Chipps and I went to some amusing nightclubs. Nightclubs were terribly cheap in Sydney. You just paid ten bob for a beer and you could stay as long as you wanted.

We spent New Year with Clough Ellis-Flint and his wife at their gorgeous house in Sydney Bay. Clough was a rich business man who ran a surfing club and had a boat at Palm Beach where we swam and he gave me a lesson in surfing. The Ellis-Flints are awfully nice people and great fun. Since then, I've given their address to anybody I know who's going to Australia.

Lagos then went off to Portland which is in Victoria beyond Melbourne. According to Chipps, the fleet was dogged from port to port right across Australia by hordes of girls and women putting pressure on the crews to desert and marry them. Apparently the police were completely unco-operative and only too delighted to have more British immigrants – *Centaur* lost as many as thirty men! Anyway, I intended to save money by following Chipps with Jamie as far as Portland on a train which left in the evening. So we went and spent the day on Bondi Beach where we had a sandwich lunch and, thank God, I gave Jamie tea, because, after I'd put Jamie to bed in our sleeper, I said to the attendant, "Where's the dining car?" and he said, "You bloody Pommies! You think this is Yurrup!" Then, when we reached Victoria at four o'clock the next morning, we had to get out of the train into another – they hated each other so much, these States, they had different gauges – and I had to shift all our luggage. I said to a young man who was humping mailbags, "Would you mind helping me with my luggage?" He said, "Why lady? Are you paralysed?"

At Melbourne we had to change our tickets to go to Portland via Hamilton, and I realised that, if I didn't buy some food somewhere, my poor little boy would starve to death. So I said to Jamie, "You stand in that queue and change our tickets while I go to buy some food." When I got back, Jamie was still at the end of the queue. I said, "Darling, why haven't you changed our tickets? The train's leaving in five minutes!" He said, "Every time I moved up, one of the Australians pushed me out of the way. Mummy, what does 'little bastard' mean?"

Alas, we arrived in Hamilton after half past six so I knew we wouldn't get anything to eat. I said to the station master, "When's the next train to Portland?" He said, "Tomorrow afternoon at four thirty." I said, "Where's the nearest hotel?" He said, "We don't have a hotel in Hamilton." I said, "Listen, I am Winston Churchill's daughter and this is Winston Churchill's grandson and, unless you tell me where I can stay the night and get him a hot meal, I'm going to lie down on the track and a train will go over me and it will be in all the papers all over the world!" He said, "Try Joe's Bar."

We went to Joe's Bar and there were no women and there was no conversation. Every now and again you'd hear, "Your shout now!" and that was all. I went up to Joe in trepidation and said, "Can you put us up for the night?" and he did, in his own bungalow. There was a white cockatoo outside in a sort of patio and it was terribly hot, a hundred and something in the shade, and there were no fans. Anyway, Joe gave us scrambled eggs, the first meal I'd had for two days, and we went to bed. Then, at midnight, Joe crept in with two whiskies on a tray. Luckily Jamie was a good chaperone. He woke up and said, "Mummy, there *are* nice Australians! Joe's brought you a whisky!"

So, in this terrific heat, we had to sleep with the door shut. Then, at two o'clock in the morning, the cockatoo woke Jamie up as Joe came in through the window! He said, "Oh Mummy, the nice Australian's brought you *another* whisky!" So now we had to sleep with the door *and* the window shut!

Well, at last, after this horrendous journey, we reached Chipps in Portland where we made friends with lots of locals who took us for drives to see kangaroos and flowers and things, and then Chipps went on with the fleet to Perth. This time I *didn't* follow him but went back with Jamie by train to Melbourne and we lunched with the manager of my Fan Club before taking the train to Canberra to stay with Patsy and Mike Tuffnell. They lived in a *tiny* house, again like a council house. There were eight of us and only three bedrooms, but we all mucked in and did the housework and helped with the cooking and made canapes for parties. Mike, the Naval Advisor to the British High Commission, would be hoovering the floor while I dusted. Very Australian.

Canberra was very pretty. It was modern but they'd planted lots of gorgeous trees. Much of Australia is terribly bleak and bare and horrible because they ring their trees to kill them, so it's a landscape covered with dead trees and, therefore, with very few birds. But Canberra's different.

It's high up and it's got lovely, lovely trees and it's got wide, enormous rivers that you swim in.

We stayed with Patsy and Mike till they could get me back to Singapore. I couldn't afford to fly with Jamie from Sydney by civil aircraft. The Australian Air Force refused to fly us – they just wouldn't do it – but, one day, Mike came back and said, "I've fixed it with the New Zealand Air Force." You can see why I adore New Zealanders!

My sister, Bumble, who has lived very happily in Australia for many years, says I'm terribly anti-Australian. Well, probably I am. I said to Chipps when he left the Navy, "Darling, I'll follow you anywhere in the world except Australia. Never, ever, will I go there again!"

Chapter 30

Journeying Back To England: Johore, Trinco, Iran And Malta

Back in Hutch's house in the Tanglin Road, Singapore, I was lonely without Chipps, who I *thought* was on his way to Trincomalee in Ceylon. I decided to take Jamie with me up to Kuala Lumpur for a short stay with a Gurkha major and his wife – *Lagos* was affiliated to a Gurkha regiment and again there was an incident with a tree spider. We went out to dinner one night leaving Jamie with their Gurkha servant. When we got back, I went in to Jamie's bedroom and saw a huge tree spider, the size of a plate, just above his head. I called the Gurkha who took one look at it and threw his Kris right into its heart, pinning it to the wall.

We returned to Hutch in time for Chinese New Year. He said to me, "I'm going away to Malaya, Dodo, for the four days of Chinese New Year because my servants pack up and I don't think I could stand your cooking!" "O.K. Hutch," I said. "I'll run the house for you." All my English friends were saying, "Oh, Chinese New Year is simply terrible! Four days without servants in this heat! We'll be eating out of tins and we've brought paper plates so that we won't have to wash up!" It didn't worry *me* and I invited them all to lunch for the second day. The first day, I took Jamie swimming at the Tanglin Club and we had lunch there and, when we came back, I gave him milk and biscuits for tea.

Now the cook had prepared the usual marvellous duck dish as a present for Hutch who had gone away – duck taken out of its skin and made into a marvellous pâté and put back in the shape of a duck. When I found this, I thought, "That will do for my lunch party tomorrow if I also make a salad, so I won't worry about that tonight, I'll take Jamie to the Happy World" – the Happy World (there were three of them) was an enormous fairground with swings and roundabouts, the lot, including Chinese Opera. So off we went to the Happy World where everyone else was Chinese and no one would charge us a penny and we were always sent to the top of the queue, *un*like Australia. We spent several happy hours there. I even took Jamie into the Chinese Opera. We didn't stay for very long because, if you don't speak Chinese, it's just awe, awe, awe, awe, for ever and ever. But it's fun to see their costumes and their gestures. Anyway, we got back at about eleven, jolly late for Jamie aged five, and went to bed.

The next day I got up to make Jamie's breakfast. I went down to the dining-room and there was breakfast on the table with hot coffee. Yet the house was empty, completely empty! Then we went off and swam at the Club for a while till I said to Jamie, "We'd better go back early because I've ten people coming to lunch and I've to prepare a salad." And, when we got back, I found the table was laid, the wine was cooled, the duck was on the table, the salad was made, everything was ready including the cheese and the fruit. So we all had lunch and, afterwards, when we went out into the garden, the coffee was waiting. Yet we hadn't heard anybody else in the house! Then, when we'd had our coffee and cigarettes, I went in to the kitchen to wash up, and everything had been washed up and cleared away! And this went on for two more days!

Jamie and I were fed and I never lifted a finger. Even our clothes were taken in the morning and washed and ironed. Extraordinary. I think it's because they loved Jamie and because I wasn't afraid of doing some work over Chinese New Year, and because Hutch had pushed off, I wasn't their employer, I was a guest. Anyway, whatever the reason, the only time I heard any of the servants during those four days was when Cookie let off fireworks with Jamie in the yard. *He* allowed Jamie to see him, but I never saw any of them.

The Sultan of Johore's Coronation was on the 11th February, and Chipps and I had duly received an invitation. As Chipps was at sea, I went on my own. A few days beforehand, the Sultan invited me to dinner at his palace. Over dinner he told me that Princess Miriam had "nicked" the crown and the Foreign Office had had to send an air force plane to get it back, but the diamond was missing. So they had to vote a special vote through the Johore parliament to replace it. He took me round Bukit Serene, which is a huge, modern, baroque-style house full of lovely and hideous things and with no taste about it whatsoever. While he was showing me round, I asked to see his bedroom. He said, "You'll understand this, Dodo, because you believe in ghosts. I don't sleep in my father's room as is expected of me: I sleep in Princess Miriam's. I'm afraid that, if I sleep where my father died, he'll come back and say, 'You should not be sultan!'"

You see, his father had rather cut him off and left everything to Lady Marcella, his fourth wife, and their daughter, Princess Miriam, but, as he was the eldest son, he had to be Sultan. He really was twitched about the possibility of his father's ghost coming back to haunt him and he slept in this old room, a children's room with bunny rabbits on the walls, where he kept his clothes in packing cases!

He then took me to see the Coronation car, a Mercedes, all beautifully dolled up with the Malayan colours. It subsequently happened that the poor man was in such a state of stress about the Coronation and his father haunting him that he got an awful attack of gout and couldn't get into this lovely car and had to go round in an old Cadillac which broke down and had to be drawn by his umbrella bearers. His father's third wife's daughter had married a British Army officer and, with rather a lack of tact, they had sent him out to be stationed in Singapore so, of course, the Sultan had to invite her to the Coronation. He told me to go before eight because he was going to shut the causeway, as he had arranged for the Post Office to deliver her invitation too late for her to get there in time.

It was the most fascinating Coronation. I took my place in the grounds outside the palace at about eight o'clock in the morning and, sitting next to me for about five hours, was Somerset Maugham, a great friend of the new Sultan. When ever somebody new came into the V.I.P. seats, he would say, "That's the girl in *The Boot Bag*", "That's the man in . . . " one of his other stories. He knew, you see, all the English who'd been in Malaya for any length of time.

He told me he wrote five hundred words a day. Sometimes he spent an hour pondering over one sentence but, once he'd put anything on paper, he very rarely altered it. He was very interested in my war experiences in France and the fact I'd been a journalist. He knew Jack Garbutt and Ronnie Hyde and a lot of my other Fleet Street contacts. He also knew Monique's mother and Berthe David Weill and several of my friends in the South of France. Like me, he loved France.

Anyway, the Coronation began and, as all the Sultans in their marvellous robes arrived from all over Malaya with their umbrella bearers, the national anthems of their particular states were played. Then the Sultan and the Sultana were crowned on a dais. It was like a Gilbert and Sullivan opera, it really was. Then they all went into the palace for some other ceremony and when they came out again, the Sultan, chubby and charming and covered in millions of decorations, was drawn around the whole of Jahore to wave to the crowds from his brokendown car.

Then he came into the grounds and wandered amongst us and invited me to sit after the buffet lunch, on his left for the Procession of Dragons, long dragons with six or more people inside and fire coming out of their nostrils and eyes rolling. The Sultana sat on his right. She said to me, "I'm so very glad you're here, Dodo, because I know you smoke and I'm not allowed to carry a bag." So, during the procession which went on for hours, I sometimes passed her my cigarette behind the Sultan's back so she could have a quick draw.

At the end, there was a lovely supper party under the trees. Everybody was there – Lois and Paddy Bandon, Mary and Mike Henegan, and Geordie Selkirk, the High Commissioner who was a brother of Douglo Hamilton . . . Singapore was very gay that night and there were many more parties to go to. I didn't get to bed till four in the morning.

Soon afterwards, the Sultan gave a lunch party for Edwina Mountbatten. She was on one of her tours. She looked awfully tired and she had to attend a Red Cross function in the afternoon and I said, "Couldn't I do that for you? They won't mind. I'm a Naval officer's wife and I was in the Red Cross during the war." She said, "No, no, no. I must keep my engagements." I never saw her again because, that evening, she got on an R.A.F. plane to Borneo where there was a dinner in her honour and for the first time ever she missed an official engagement. She said she really *was* too tired and went to bed and died in her sleep.

I wrote to Lord Louis and he wrote me back a sweet letter saying how conscientious she was. I adored her. It was she who got me into the Front Line after Howard was killed. People write rude books about her, yet all I saw of that woman was good. John Templeton-Cotill always tells the story that she wanted her ashes to be scattered at Portland because she was so fond of the Navy, and he had the task of doing it, and he got the wind direction wrong . . .

I now went to see Paddy Bandon at the R.A.F. air station in Singapore – he was Air Marshal there – and I said, "Please can you get me onto a Dakota to Ceylon because I can stay with Peter and Venetia Troubridge in Colombo, and Peter will then get me onto a tanker as far as Malta."

Sir Peter Troubridge and his wife, Venetia, who's the sister of Pam Drax, our neighbour in Dorset, were both great friends of ours. Peter was commanding the Naval Wireless Station in Colombo and Chipps had taught him on his Long Course at *Mercury*. His brother Tom, by the way, was, married to Princess Michael of Kent. After he retired Peter was with the firm of stockbrokers, Brewin Dolphin, in the City, and Chipps actually deals with them every day about Portfolio Management from his office in Wareham.

I also said, "I don't want to pay Air India to take Jamie. Can he come with me, too?" Paddy said, "I can get *you* officially to Colombo, but I'll have to fix Jamie sideways." He did just that, by having Jamie hidden in a jeep. The jeep was driven onto the plane and he came out from under the blankets as soon as the plane was airborne . . .

Peter Troubridge met us at the airport in Colombo where, as a publicity gesture, I suppose, we were given simply disgusting cups of tea – I never *did* like Indian or Ceylonese tea. He then drove us to his house. The children, Tom and Amanda, were about Jamie's age, so they could play together. There were about ten servants. A nanny, of course looked after the children but, because of the caste system, one servant did the bath, another the bathroom floor, another the loo, another the beds, another the dusting, another the washing, another the ironing, another the cooking . . . Yet it seemed to me that it was Venetia who did all the work. I was always finding her ironing a dress or cleaning the silver or dusting.

After four days, Peter drove Venetia, Jamie and me to Trincomalee for the Naval visit. Admiral Varyl Begg had sent *Lagos* to Gan, a remote R.A.F. staging post in the Indian Ocean, as Guardship, but I had to go to Trincomalee to board *Wave Ruler*, the tanker which was to take Jamie and me to Malta. Peter was a very able and interesting guide. He's like Chipps in that way. As we drove along he told me the history of the country and all about tea planting. I remember we passed some jungle wild life and things, including some sweet elephants bathing their children in a river – a lovely sight.

At Trincomalee, we all stayed in the same hotel, and I shared a room with Jamie. As the only naval wives, Venetia and I had a whale of a time: we simply didn't stop sailing and swimming and going out to dinners and, when we actually left the hotel *without* Jamie, a sailor was always posted to keep an eye on him.

But, one particular night, something rather frightening happened which I would never have expected – I suppose I'm frightfully naive even now. I was making up my face and, as the room was sort of L-shaped, you couldn't see the dressing-table from the door. Jamie was asleep in bed, and I was about to go downstairs to dinner with Venetia and Peter and various other Naval officers. Suddenly the door opened a crack and I heard somebody stealthily creeping in, and, as he came to the bend in the L-shape, I saw it was a sailor and he was making for Jamie. I jumped to my feet and I seized his hat – I'm a tall woman – and he turned and ran. But I kept his hat and it had the name of his ship on it. I told everyone what had happened and it turned out that he was a submariner and that one of the officers I was dining with was his commanding officer.

The Ceylonese manager of the hotel heard about this at once – in those countries everybody knows everything before it happens – and, even before I went down to dinner, he came up and said, "It's all right, madam. I'm having a guard put on your door all night," and from then on, there was a guard on our door for the remainder of the fleet visit. That was a great shock. Jamie was a very pretty little boy with lovely blue eyes and curly yellow hair, but such a possibility had never dawned on me.

The next day we all went sailing with a Wing Commander of the Ceylonese Air Force. During all our travels, Jamie and I had an imaginary friend called Fred who was a parrot, and I used to make up stories for Jamie about Fred. While we were sailing this day, we saw in the water what I thought was a toy parrot. I said to Jamie, "Oh look! There's a toy parrot just like Fred!" and we tacked the boat and turned round and picked it up to give to him. Suddenly it winked an eye, and we realised it was alive. Later the Wing Commander sent a signal from Air Force Headquarters, as an inter-service joke, saying, "We have found a parrot which, by the fluency and frequency of its language, must belong to the Navy." Almost immediately, it was claimed by one of the sailors on *Wave Prince*, the tanker we were going to Malta on! So, for our whole journey to Malta, Jamie was able to go aft every morning to the crew's quarters and say hello to Fred!

We were a week in Trincomalee and, the night before we left, we dined with Admiral Varyl Begg aboard his flagship, H.M.S. *Belfast*. He put me on his left and he said to me, "Now look! You're a very naughty girl and, as you know, I don't approve of you following your husband and the fleet at *all,* and now I hear you're going to Malta on *Wave Prince* tomorrow! I, personally, will make sure that *Wave Prince* doesn't refuel our fleet or any other fleet. I will make sure it doesn't even go *near* our fleet or any other fleet. You will go on *Wave Prince*, you will stay on *Wave Prince* and *Wave Prince* will go straight to Malta. I wish you a good journey!" I said, "Admiral, I promise you I will not go on any other boat. I'm absolutely too grateful for words that darling Peter has got me onto this one. I gather that *Wave Prince* will be stopping at Abadan to pick up some oil, but the captain will be delighted not to have to do any refuelling."

Wave Prince was small and old-fashioned, the same sort of class as *Wave Ruler*, the tanker on which I went to Port Said with Captain Shacklock. We were going to be in the worst cabin, the cabin of two apprentices who'd have to sleep in hammocks instead; but still, I *was* grateful. I was grateful to get anything for four shillings and sixpence a day. I didn't even mind having to share with the usual chaperone – a daughter of an Air Force Sergeant in Colombo who I think had been getting on a bit too well with the chaps and was being sent back to England.

So we moved on to *Wave Prince* with all our luggage, I got to know the crew. The First officer, Brian Bowyer, was sweet – he became a *great* friend. The Captain was sweet, too – a Scotsman, rather quiet, who didn't play Liar Dice like Captain Norrington – but Brian, even after he left *Wave Prince* and became a Trinity House Pilot, guiding ships like the *Queen Mary* Into Southampton, used to take me out.

After we arrived on board *Wave Prince* I soon discovered there was no fresh fruit onboard, only tins. So I went to the Captain and I said, "Could I possibly have a Liberty Boat to go ashore as we'll be a month at sea and there isn't any fresh fruit here for Jamie?" He said, "I suggest you ask one of your officer friends who are refuelling on either side."

Well, Jack, a great friend of mine, was refuelling his frigate on one side, so Jamie and I – I couldn't do it now but, having been used, as a child, to climbing the parapets of Lytchett Manor and also, perhaps, because of my ballet training – crossed the plank from the tanker to the frigate. Jack was having drinks in his cabin with Edward, the captain of a submarine on the other side of *him*. When I asked if he could lend me a boat to go ashore and buy some fruit, he said to Edward, "Will *you* do it?" and Edward said, "Of course! I've never actually used my submarine for a shopping trip before, but I'd love to do it for you, Dodo!"

So we crossed over onto the submarine and started off towards the shore to shop. Frightfully exciting. I'd never *been* on a submarine at sea before. I've been on many since – in South America, but Chipps has never been at sea in one *ever*!

We were halfway there when, to my horror, I suddenly saw H.M.S. *Belfast* coming towards us, and I knew that Varyl Begg would be on the bridge with his binoculars glued on us, and I knew that crossing his mind would be, "My God! She's going back to Malta in a submarine!" I said to Edward, "Dive!" but he thought it would be quicker if we hid down below. So Jamie and I rushed down below to hide!

Anyway, when returned in the submarine from shopping, Jamie and I went down with Joan, my flighty chaperone, to our apprentices' cabin, which was very small, hot and airless – the porthole was partly obscured by a sort of chimney – and with only two bunks and a lilo on the floor for Jamie. Actually, after we got going, my friend the First Officer, gave us his fan so we wouldn't be so hot. But we were still very crushed and the Captain said at dinner, "Look, this is very unofficial but, when we're not in port at Abadan, Joan can sleep in the sick bay which is air-conditioned." Joan then had a marvellous time, though I gathered from Jamie's Fred-owning friend that the sailors objected to her concentrating on the officers. What she did was of no interest to me. At least Jamie and I had the cabin free to ourselves and we both had bunks.

The Captain then said to me, "I hear you nursed in the war. Would you take the medical round with the First Officer?" You see, when the crew is under a hundred in the Merchant Navy, they don't have a doctor on board and the First officer takes the medical round and just reads it up in a book. So I agreed to help the First officer, and, as I was infinitely better qualified, he let me do the penicillin injections, which the sailors said they were very grateful for, as I didn't hurt them – apparently *he* was murder. As you can imagine, there are always injections to be given on board after sailors have been in port, but we didn't really have many other problems. One man had ear trouble. Another had a bit of sinus which I was able to cure: I gave him some penicillin but I cured him mainly through Vick inhalers which the First Officer hadn't thought of – I always take Vick with me when I go abroad. When I eventually left *Wave Prince*, I was presented with a marvellous cartoon of a terrified-looking sailor and the First Officer with an enormous syringe and me saying, "No darling! Just squeeze *gently*!"

It was a very happy ship. There was a little swimming pool on board and cinemas every other night and the odd game of bingo or a card game. There was also watching the sun set . . . oh, it's lovely being at sea! I adore it. I'm never happier than when I'm on the ocean wave. I ought to have been a man – I'd have been a sailor for sure.

In the Indian Ocean we saw dolphins and flying fish. They're so sweet the dolphins when they follow you and play. We also saw a spouting whale. I'm very short sighted, and at first I thought it was a submarine. We were on deck for hours on end and, after swimming, when we were sunbathing, I taught Jamie to read. When we began, he didn't know the alphabet, but every day we read his *Chicken Lickin* book and by the end of the trip, he could read Kipling.

We sailed up the Persian Gulf to Abadan. Entering the Gulf was great fun. There's an island there just off the coast and you're not supposed to go through that way because it's such a narrow channel, but the Captain said Yah-boo and did it. Very adventurous of him but then all R.F.A. captains are marvellous navigators. Land was practically touching us on either side. Anyway, we arrived at Abadan and, as I'd never been to Persia, I thought I must get out and see it a bit. But I didn't have any Persian money. So, when the ship's agent came on board, I said to him, "Can I possibly change some money somewhere, because I'd like to go ashore and hire a taxi and see around?" He said, "Impossible. There are terrific regulations, but I've got ten quid in Persian money if that will do you." I said, "Thank you *very* much" and gave him a cheque for ten quid, the equivalent of which he handed over. So I went with Jamie and found a taxi in the dockyard which was very heavily guarded at the gates. I said to the taxi-driver, who spoke English, "I've only got ten pound. Will you take me as far as you can for one pound? I'd love to see some carpets."

This taxi-driver took us out into the desert where there was an isolated carpet shop, and, hanging on poles outside and marked "one thousand pounds", "two thousand pounds", that sort of thing, were some very gaudy modern Persian rugs which I don't particularly like, but I went inside and said to the merchant, "Have you any cheap rugs?"

The custom in those countries is that you sit down and they give you coffee and you talk and then you bargain. I sat down and we were offered coffee and he complimented me on my son and that sort of thing – though he was Iranian, he spoke perfect English – and, after about a quarter of an hour of this, he said, "I haven't got anything under one thousand pounds" and so I started to leave. But, as I was leaving, I suddenly saw a very nice old blue Persian carpet which I knew would go very well in the drawing-room of Slepe Green. I said, "How much is that?" "Oh," he said, "That's not for sale. It's in for repair. It's, got a hole in it." I said, "I can't see the hole. It must be very small. Would you let me have it cheap?" "Well," he said, "I expect the owner would be delighted. Nobody wants an old . . . " "Listen!" I said, "I'll make a bargain with you!" So we sat down again and, over another cup of coffee, I said, "I will give you all the money in my bag except for one pound in return for that carpet. Is it a deal?" He said, "Yes." It was a pig in a poke, you see, because he didn't know how much money I'd got. So I opened my bag and put all my money on the table and, in exchange for nine pounds, he gave me the carpet. I expect nine pounds was quite a lot to a chap in the desert, because he seemed happy and he took the money. We then shook hands and back I went in the taxi with Jamie.

With the carpet in full view on the back seat, I showed my pass at the dockyard gates, we were let through, and, when we got onto the quay, we found an officer and two soldiers waiting to arrest me. I said to the taxi-driver, "What's this all about? Why am I being arrested?" He said, "It's because you have to have an export licence to take a Persian carpet abroad and you didn't show it to the guards at the gate."

Jamie was terrified. He was white as a sheet. I mean, he thought his mother was going to remain in a Persian jail for the rest of her life. So I said to him, "Jamie, go on board and get the First Officer." Brian Bowyer, came down, with a tin of fifty cigarettes and sort of supported me while I explained to the Persian officer that the carpet was an old one and had a hole in it. Finally, after being given the tin of cigarettes, he said, "I don't know what the exact regulations are for *old* carpets and it will take me too long to get through to the Ministry to find out. You can take it." Quite dramatic!

Next, a huge gale blew up and it hailed! We were in the Persian Gulf in February and it *hailed*! I had to wear my fur coat it was so cold, and the hailstones were as big as golfballs: they really hurt when they hit you. Absolutely extraordinary. The gale was so strong that we couldn't get the pilot off outside the harbour. We had to spend the night rolling from side to side. How I loved it. I'm never seasick. It sends me to sleep, actually. I adore that movement. But little Jamie, he was very green in the morning.

I said to him, "Listen, Jamie! Why are you talking about feeling sick? Sailors' sons are *never* sick!" It was quite untrue. Chipps was always being sick on his destroyer. Still, I said it because I think seasickness is physchological, up to a point. I said, "Jamie, I'm absolutely ashamed of you! Go up on the bridge and get some fresh air!" So he went up on the bridge and the Captain, who adored him, said, "Young man, you look very green about the gills." I heard this from below, you see. And Jamie said, "No I'm not! Sailors' sons are *never* sick." And the Captain said, "Well, I'll take you aft now and show you a lot of sailors' bastards who are being very sick at this moment!" and he gave him some ship's biscuits and Jamie was all right, and he wasn't ever sick in all our travels from then on.

The storm calmed and we got the pilot off and we went on to Suez. We anchored off Suez itself at the bottom end of the canal, and Jim Cairo, the merchant, came aboard to sell his wares. He remembered me and brought me the most enormous bouquet of asters for my cabin. I thought it was so touching that he still loved England enough to do this after the war over Suez in between. Then all the bumboats came alongside to sell *their* wares, and Jamie who'd been given a pound by the Wing Commander's wife in Trincomalee, leant over and called, "I have a pound, and I want that camel for me and I want the bracelet for Mummy and I want those earrings for Georgina." This was Georgina Weld, my cousin Joe's youngest daughter, who was a year older than him. The man said, "Yes. This camel – he twenty-five pounds. This bracelet – he thirty-five pounds. These earrings – they ten pounds." Jamie said, "Well, I have a pound, and I want that camel for me and that bracelet for Mummy and I want those earrings for Georgina!" This went on for half an hour and, at the end of the half hour, the man gave him everything for a pound!

We then went up the Canal and into the Med and on to Malta where we stayed with Cecilia de Trafford until I could get an R.A.F. plane back to England. Before leaving Malta, of course, I did some work on Tourism and wrote a report. The number of tourists were now increasing substantially, but there was still the old-fashioned rule that you couldn't wear a bikini, and men were even arrested in the street for not wearing a shirt. Well, I do agree that in a very Catholic country like Malta the street is *not* the right place to walk around half naked. Nor the bars. But I thought women should be allowed to wear bikinis on the beach and I was irritated that notices I'd arranged to be put on the beaches in '55 saying "PLEASE KEEP THE BEACH CLEAN" were changed to "DON'T WEAR BIKINIS ON THE BEACH". George de Trafford, Cecilia's youngest son, had a girlfriend, who was very pretty. I persuaded her to lie on St. George's Bay beach in full view of the road, and I then told somebody to report her to the police and informed the newspapers of her pending arrest so they could take photographs. We employed a good lawyer at the hearing and she got off, and, since 1960, bikinis have been allowed on the beaches. In fact, that was the thin edge of the wedge because now you see topless girls. That *does* shock the Maltese very much. Last year I rebuked a woman myself for lying topless on the fishermen's jetty in Xlendi. I mean, the jetty is part of the life of the village; that's where the Gozitan fishermen earn their living. So I'm on their side up to a point. Men are still frowned on for going into a bar, say, wearing only shorts and sandals, but I doubt if they'd be arrested . . .

At the start of April, 1960, I came back to Lyneham with the R.A.F., and Cecilia put Jamie on a civil aircraft to Heathrow the same day. Jamie was supposed to arrive after me. In fact, he arrived first. Then I had the most awful roundabout journey to meet him at Cromwell Road Air Terminal, arriving there three hours later than him. But he was quite happy. He was sitting on a counter, being fed drinks and sweets by thousands of adoring women.

One thing, though, did give me rather an unpleasant surprise. A few days later, I went over to collect Bruce from Broadstone, the boarding nursery, and he took one look at me and burst into tears and wouldn't come near me. It wasn't that Bruce had been unhappy without me: the nanny was a darling old thing and he was very happy with her, and very healthy; but I had to go over about six times before he'd come into my arms and I could bring him with me to Slepe Green to join me and Jamie and the new *au pair*. You do choose between your children and your husband, and I had chosen my husband.

Part 10

Family Life in Dorset and the Med

Chapter 31

A Home Of My Own

After Gan, *Lagos* visited Cochin and Mombasa before being paid off into reserve at Portsmouth in May, 1960. Chipps was then sent as Signal Officer to the Amphibious Warfare Centre at Poole, only a few miles from our new home on Slepe Farm. Incidently, it was when he was at Poole that Chipps wrote a Communications book that formed the basis for the Combined Ops in the Falklands War over twenty years later.

Everything was ready for him. I'd furnished the house during the spring of the previous year – with some second hand stuff bought in junk shops, and my mother gave me some antiques and there were items I'd had at Burnsall Street which I could take out of store. A chaise longue and the pretty Victorian matching chair only cost me 10 shillings each, and I re-upholstered them myself. And a marvellous seamstress in Blandford called Mrs. Hizzy ran up curtains from designs I made on old sheets. Almost everything here was done to my design.

I acquired quite a reputation because of Slepe, and, as I've always had to make money to boost up Chipps' income, I took up designing and decorating in quite a big way during the next five years. Everybody kept saying to me, "Your house is so beautiful, will you come and do mine?" And, though I'm a terrific social butterfly and not a workaholic like Chipps, I can work – and doing up houses is bloody hard work.

First of all I helped Cecilia de Trafford decorate flats in the Villa Bologna in Malta and also in the Villa Trafford. Then I did a house for Trifene Freeman, a Weld cousin near Shaftesbury. Then Sheena Bence-Trower's mother asked me to do her house in Sandbanks. Now, if you're a decorator, you do not charge a fee for your skill, you make your profit by buying your materials wholesale and charging retail like a shop. And Sue Priestley, a friend I'd made in Kitzbuhel, was able to give me a leg up by introducing me to all her wholesalers. She did up the Spanish Embassy in London and the Post Office Tower and the Hotel Georges V in Paris. Well, with the help of Mr. Cuff in Morden, a marvellous man with a wooden leg who did my painting and carpentry, and a marvellous woman in Wareham who did my loose-covers and curtains, I set up business. The trouble was that, not being very good at accounts and having to mark up carpets by fifty percent, and fabrics by thirty percent and wallpaper by twenty percent, 1 had to employ a secretary and, by the time I'd paid the secretary, I wasn't making an awful lot of money. This, combined with the fact I didn't like working for people who hadn't exactly the same taste as me, made me realise in the end it would be far more fun just to buy an empty house and do it up and sell it at a profit.

So, with half of the money Chipps gave me when we married, I bought an empty three up and three downer behind the Post Office at Organford. It was almost a shell, though its tiled roof was intact. Sid Chappell, my gardener for many years, Sid's brother who was a bricklayer, a chum of Sid's brother, and Cyril Hill, the heating engineer from Blandford who had done the heating for Slepe Green, all helped me to rebuild and decorate this house on the cheap. The place was terribly damp but I soon found the well and we drained it with land drains and made it dry as a bone.

Then I took Chipps' Land-Rover and horse-trailer and went round scrapyards and so on, collecting seasoned wood. In Bournemouth they were demolishing a hotel and I bought the most gorgeous radiators for ten bob each. Somewhere else I got doors for ten bob each – their copper handles and locks were worth more than that! In the kitchen I made a corner seat with ratan and bamboo. Everything on the cheap. In the living-room was a modern fireplace and I was sure there was an old one behind with an inglenook. I chipped away like mad and found to my horror that the middle of the beam above was missing. Sid's brother said, "The house will now fall down!" So he and Sid and I jumped into the Land-Rover and scoured the farm here till we found a Concrete lintel thrown over a ditch, and we fixed that in to last the night.

I then rang up Wol Drax at Charborough and said, "This house I'm rebuilding. I've suddenly discovered a beam's been cut in the middle where a new fireplace was put in. The two ends are there but the middle isn't! What do you suggest?" "Oh," he said, "go to Botany Bay" – a barn where some of the Tolpuddle Martyrs congregated before leaving for Australia – "There's an old beam lying across the midden. You can take that." So we measured how much we wanted, cut that amount off, took it back and put it in place. But that house could have fallen down! I eventually sold it for five thousand, five hundred pounds at a profit of about a thousand pound, money hard earned over a period of nine months . . .

Chipps has been hunting seriously since Geoff, my step-father-in-law, died and he could use his grey horse, Jungle. He started whipping-in for Simon Clarke, the Master of the South Dorset in 1963, and he's been whipping-in, whenever possible, ever since. Whipping-in involves going on for a view and hollering the fox away so that the Master knows where he's gone and you are, of course, responsible for keeping the hounds together. In the late summer he goes off every Saturday morning and exercises the hounds and learns to recognise them by name. There was once a hound which Simon and he decided to call Dodo. They both hugely enjoyed shouting, "Come here, Dodo, you little bitch!" Cubbing begins in September and the last meet is in April. Once the winter wheat is coming up in the spring, the farmers don't let you hunt over their land, but we can hunt in Wareham Forest and on other heaths . . .

That summer and autumn, we had a real family life until, in November, 1961, Chipps flew to join the aircraft carrier Victorious in Capetown – the start of a two year stint on aircraft carriers as Flag Lieutenant and Signals Officer to two successive Flag officer Aircraft Carriers.

Meanwhile my cousin, Tom Lees, lent us a boat and Chipps and I would go sailing in Poole Harbour or riding on Gerald and Jungle for miles and miles across Wareham Forest. We didn't actually buy Jamie a pony till '62 when he was eight and at prep school. His name was Lucky and he was exactly Jamie's age. He was a skewbald, half Welsh and half Exmoor, an absolutely gorgeous pony, a darling. Jamie would go with him in his summer holidays to Pony Camp.

The Bence-Trowers gave us our first dog, a golden retriever, on Jamie's seventh birthday in '61. The previous February I'd stayed a night with them at their house in West Meon as there was to be a big cocktail party followed by a dinner on board the carrier *Hermes* at Portsmouth the next day. Peter said to me, "Our bitch has just had puppies. They're absolutely adorable. Come and help me feed them." So, just before leaving for *Hermes*, I helped him feed these puppies, and one of them jumped on me and split my nylons (I only had one pair) from top to bottom. I said, "I must have that puppy!" Peter said, "You can have him when he's weaned" and he nicked a little bit of fur on one of his ears so he'd know which one it was.

That summer, when Sheena brought her son to Jamie's party, she gave him the puppy as a present. Jamie was thrilled. He rushed at it and hugged it and said, 'Oh, Mummy, isn't it bliss!" so we called him Bliss, and Bliss became a great figure in our lives. I considered Bliss my dog. When I went away I always left him with my mother-in-law, Kitty, at Slepe House and that dog always knew the day I was returning. Sid Chappell, who was also Kitty's gardener, told me it was quite extraordinary. He said, "The night before you come back, Bliss goes over and sits waiting at your front door."

Meanwhile, in '60, we'd sent Jamie to "Mrs. B's", a little private school for about twelve infants – an old cottage with a shed for lessons – run by a marvellous teacher called Mrs. Belcher up the road from Slepe in Morden. Once a week, with a group of other mothers in the neighbourhood, I took my turn ferrying children to and from the school. Then, after looking at almost all the Catholic prep schools in England, we decided, when he was eight, to send Jamie to Avisford – its headmaster, Michael Jennings, had been there with my brother, Mike, under Michael's father, so I'd known him since he was a boy.

Sending Jamie to Avisford was not, I'm afraid, a good idea. Though he wasn't very good at cricket; he won quite a lot of things such as hurdling on Sports Days and he was very good at his work, very bright, and he seemed to have a lot of friends. But he always wept when he went back at the beginning of term and, whenever I drove over to Speech Days or to take him out, he didn't seem happy either. In the summer of '65 when he was eleven, I took him to the beach at West Wittering in Sussex for a swim, and I noticed weals on his bottom. "Oh, Jamie! Why have you been beaten? What did you do?" He said, "Mummy, I've been beaten this year about sixty times! And some of the boys have been putting my head down the loo and pulling the plug!"

Jamie was a very sensitive and nervous child then. I said, "Darling, do you want to leave Avisford? Because, if you do, I'll take you home today." He said, "Does it mean going to another school or staying at home?" I said, "It means going to another school," "Well," he said, "I think the devil I know would be better than the devil I don't." So he stayed at Avisford, though he hated it so much that he took all his Common Entrance papers when he was only just twelve. I went, of course, to see Michael Jennings about the beatings and the bullying, and all he'd say was that Jamie was a liar. I certainly hope my grandsons are not so unhappy at their prep school.

For their public school we'd put Jamie and Bruce down for Eton and Ampleforth. In fact, because we were so hard up, we paid insurance for each of our boys from the time they were born. Ampleforth is Catholic and my mother thought they should go to Ampleforth and I thought they should go to Eton because my father had been there. Of course, as a Socialist, I really thought they should go to comprehensives, but I'd made a pact with Chipps that, if our children were brought up as Catholics, he could send them to public schools if Labour didn't manage to get rid of them first.

In 1964, actually, I was able to express my views on public schools at Weymouth Town Hall when Labour organised a Conference to decide education policy in the South West. Amongst others, Wedgie Benn and Tom Dalyell were there. Tom Dalyell had been to Eton, and I represented the South Dorset Labour Constituency Party. One of our theories was that we would make Eton into a Sixth Form, open to everyone. I was terribly interested in this because, though I knew very little about education, I did know an awful lot about internationalism. Nowhere else in the world is there this ridiculous two class system. The boys are picked more carefully for Eton now, but so many idiots used to go there, relations of mine among them. In France, the duke's son and the butcher's son go to the same *Lycée*. The duke's son has the advantage of having books by Proust and Colette at home, but if the butcher's son is clever and has determination . . . Look where Nye Bevan got in spite of his drawbacks.

Anyway, it was on the cards that Harrow would be a comprehensive for London, that Marlborough would be for boarding children of soldiers, sailors and airmen who had to go abroad, and so on and so on. The only reason Labour didn't abolish the public schools, when it was in power, was money. Most of Eton's houses were slums, with coal fires instead of central heating. And there weren't enough loos, there weren't enough bathrooms, the ceilings were too low and there weren't enough windows. The cost of satisfying planning requirements would have been prohibitive. Also, of course, the tutors were paid much more.

A photograph taken of the family before leaving for Caracus in 1966.

We didn't actually know Jamie had passed into Eton until we were on the *Flandres* at the end of '66 going out with Bruce to Caracas for Chipps to take up the post of Naval and Military Attaché to Venezuela and Defence Attaché to Colombia, Panama and the Dominican Republic. Mike and Moyna Hopwood were standing in loco parentis with full responsibility for Jamie while we were away. Moyna was marvellous. She coped with everything and got him all his clothes. Her brother had been at Eton and she said this was like having her own son at the same school (she hadn't any children of her own, but an adopted daughter). It was she who put Jamie on the plane to come out to Caracas for our first Christmas there. Oh, it was so exciting going to the airport to meet him! I don't think anyone who isn't a mother can know the thrill you experience when you see your son coming back from school. Jamie stayed at Eton till he was just seventeen. He passed all his "A" levels, but he didn't want to go to university because he wanted to marry 'Scilla and become a solicitor.

At first Bruce went to Mrs. B's like Jamie. Then one day she said to me, "I can't teach him. There's something wrong. You must send him to a Special School." So he went by bus every morning to a private Special School in Poole where they couldn't teach him either. I couldn't understand this as he was obviously a very intelligent child.

The situation was getting very serious by the time he was seven, and down to go to Avisford in the autumn term when Chipps and I were leaving for Caracas. The plan was that he would come out to us in the holidays from Avisford as Jamie would do during his holidays from public school. Then, one morning, as I was sitting upstairs doing my face and reading the newspaper, Bruce read a headline in the looking glass. As he could hardly read, I thought this was extraordinary. So I rang up a great friend of mine, a psychiatrist called Dr. Bill Whiles. Bill and I had always worked closely together in local politics, and he was a paediatrician dealing with children needing special help. He said, "Don't frighten him. Bring him round to tea and I'll cope with this."

Bruce liked going to tea with Bill because he had some lovely toy soldiers and Bill's wife, Marjorie, always baked us a cake, so, after tea, when Bruce was playing with the toy soldiers, Bill said to him, "Bruce, I hear you're having difficulty learning to read. Come into my study and I'll give you a lesson." Then, when Bill had done all the tests on him, he explained the whole problem. He said, "Bruce is dyslexic and crossed-lateral." He said that, instead of seeing the word "book" as a picture like you and I do, he reads it from right to left and mixes up "b" with "d" and reads "Kood". He added, "He's got an intelligence of 133" – which is higher than Chipps' – and he's university material, but you must treat this as a disability as he'll probably fail all his exams first go. You must cancel him going to prep school and keep him with you all the time as he needs very much to be in the family setting.

Also, you must constantly bolster up his ego and stop Chipps pressurising him. He won't learn to read until he's ten and then you've got to send him to a crammer."

Bill also told me to try at every opportunity to make Bruce look at things from left to right, and he listed all letters and numbers such as S and Z; p, d and b; 5, S, and 3; which cross-laterals confuse and suggested I write these out large, cut them out in emery paper and stick them on cards so Bruce and I could blindfold ourselves and play a game tracing the letters and numbers with our fingers. Years later, Bruce told me that, when he was taking his degree, there was one word he couldn't read, so he shut his eyes and traced the reversal letter it contained with his finger, opened his eyes and found he could read the word!

So I knew exactly what to do. Whenever, for instance, we went for a drive, I made Bruce look at things taking his eyes from left to right. I taught him personally from the age of seven, though, when he was eight, he also went to the Shell school in Caracas. The school was mixed and about half of the children attending it were Spanish and about half English. It wasn't, of course, the standard of a good English school, but it had a headmistress who herself was an intelligent dyslexic so she very much understood Bruce's problem. She said to me, "Oh, he'll be all right. Among other things, he'll learn how to speak Spanish. We'll give him extra reading lessons and, don't worry, his reading will come when he's ten."

Well, in 1968, when he was nine, about a year before we were due to return from Caracas, Bruce said that, if he was to get into Eton he'd got to learn Latin and they didn't teach Latin in this school. So I looked into this and the headmistress of the Shell school told me she'd met a young man called Andrew who'd just got a degree at Oxford and was bumming his way round South America and wanted to earn some cash. So I asked her would she let Bruce off in the afternoons if this young man came to our house and coached him – diplomats are not paid allowances for anything like educational expenses – and Andrew came in the afternoons and Bruce liked him very much. He wasn't a trained teacher, but he was very good, and he not only taught Bruce Latin, but also took him for reading and writing. He did him so much good, in fact, that at Easter Bruce suddenly said he wanted to go to the crammer. So we wrote to Millbrook House School, the Crammer's in Berkshire and they agreed to take him at once. The school usually took boys from the age of eleven till they were thirteen, but it was prepared to make an exception in Bruce's case.

Bruce was very happy there: he liked the school and he liked Mr. Glazebrook, the newly appointed Headmaster. But eventually Mr.

Glazebrook rang me up and said, "Look, we can't believe what you told us about Bruce's IQ being 133 because we're finding him very difficult to teach and I doubt if he'll get into Eton. Do you mind if I have the Public Schools' psychiatrist test him?" I said, "No, not at all. I'd like to have another opinion." So the public schools' man tested him and found that his IQ was 133, probably a little higher.

Anyway, Bruce failed Eton and he was terribly upset. But one day, when Chipps and I were lunching at Charborough with the Draxes, Pam, who had just sent her son, a bit older than Bruce, to Harrow because he couldn't get into Eton, said, "Why don't you send him to Harrow?" Chipps' elder half brother, John Walker, and several other relations had been there. So we wrote to the headmaster of Harrow who accepted him. He told me afterwards that he was going to say no because they were absolutely booked up, but he went fishing with Tim Warr, the house master of Rendels house, the house where John Walker had been, and Tim Warr said, "I'm getting more and more interested in dyslexics. I think we've a lot of them at Harrow. I'd like to fit this boy in. I'll turn a single room into a double." So that's how Bruce got to Harrow. Bill Whiles had been absolutely right, too, in predicting he would fail his exams the first time. He failed Eton, got Harrow. He failed his "O"s the first time, got them the second. He failed his "A"s first time, got them the second. He failed his degree the first time, got it the second . . .

In 1961 I was back in politics again, working for the South Dorset Constituency Labour Party and on the Selection Committee'. When we had a by-election in November '62, not only was I on the Selection Conference that selected Guy Barnett to fight Angus Maude, I canvassed very hard for him with Eddie Shackleton (Lord Shackleton). I remember so well going to an old brigadier in Wareham. He said to me, "Who are you canvassing for?" I said, "Mr. Barnett." He said, "Oh, that's who I'll be voting for. I don't want that Agnes Maude. I don't approve of women in politics!" It was all terribly exciting because we got Guy in, the only Labour M.P. ever elected for a southern rural constituency, though it was a one-off as in the General Election of '64 he deserted us for a safe seat which, incidentally, he didn't get.

By-elections are always a bit different, but I think my P.R. helped Guy a lot in South Dorset. For instance, I arranged for the press to photograph him at Slepe Farm interviewing the dairyman in the bullpen and I got Southern and B.B.C. Television to film both of us riding across the ford my father built down on the Sherford River. He was very amenable to my suggestions and agreed to do what I had done in Lancaster: visit all the rural areas which no

Labour candidates had bothered to do before. Up till then, they'd concentrated on towns like Weymouth but I arranged for a loudspeaker to go ahead of him to the smallest villages like Morden and Bloxworth.

Dodo and family, 1961

At most meetings I was his assistant speaker or else I chaired the platform. I was with him for his Eve of Poll meeting in Weymouth. A Labour member was speaking first and Guy, knowing he could be delayed at Portland, said to me, "Look, he'll speak for twenty minutes and, if I'm late, you take the second speech." So I took the second speech, thinking I'd have to talk for about a quarter of an hour. But Guy's car broke down and, having talked about housing and unemployment and fair shares, not equal shares, for all, and all our normal Labour policy, I found after three quarters of an hour that I was rather running out of steam. So I said to the audience, "I don't think I can go on much longer. What about you asking me some questions?" Well, the whole hall were on my side because I'd done my stint and, by the time Guy arrived, we were all in cracking form and we weren't talking about Socialism at all: we were talking about Hitler and bombs and my experiences in the *maquis*! A very joky platform for Eve of Poll!

Guy won the next day and in the New Year, I was able to get him some very good publicity because it snowed and snowed and snowed. I was going round on skis with milk and drugs and things for people in outlying places that were cut off. I said to him, "Can you ski?" He said, "No, but I've done a lot of mountain climbing." So I told him to put on his mountain boots, lent him a pair of Chipps' skis and showed him how to ski! I arranged for a T.V. crew to film us skiing down to "Tanky" Burbridge at Foxhill Farm, Higher Lytchett. "Tanky" was a terrific Labour man. He got his name because he drove the first tank, in the First World War.

That winter really was a terrific, marvellous winter – there was no need to go to Austria to ski with the Ruck-Keenes: we could ski here in Dorset for six weeks. Chipps was home from sea for Christmas and was about to join the Joint Signals Staff West in Salisbury for a year, but the roads were closed by snow so neither the Army or Navy were able to get to their work and he was able to ski with us.

He then became a Commander and, for two years, commuted between here and the Ministry of Defence in Whitehall before becoming a Naval Attaché . . .

Anyway, on Boxing Day '62, we went to the usual meet of the South Dorset Hunt, and it started snowing, and, when we woke up next morning, the snow was two feet deep. And afterwards it went on snowing. Most days we and our friends dropped everything, got into our Land-Rovers and drove to the lodge above Milton Abbas School. Peter Addeley of Delcombe Manor had cut the wires of his fences so we could ski down a wood path and through three jolly good fields with a Schuss at the bottom. Boys from Milton Abbas were there with walkie-talkies, and we ran races, or we took it in turns so that people could hang on to a rope at the back of a LandRover to go up again. Then, for *après ski*, we'd go to Wendy Hodgkinson's – her husband, Hughie, was the headmaster of Milton Abbas – and have huge thermoses of goulash and lots of Glühwein. I think it was the most amusing winter I've ever had in England.

Chapter 32

Back To The Med – Beirut And Gozo

In 1962, I took the children out to Malta with Maggie, our old nanny and cook at Trokes, and Cecilia lent them a flat in the Villa Bologna while I went off in the tanker, *Tidesurge*, to join Chipps in Beirut which, as Flag Lieutenant and Staff Communications Officer to the Flag Officer Aircraft Carriers, he was visiting in the aircraft carrier Victorious.

I found a Naval wife as "chaperone" and set off for Beirut on *Tidesurge*. Then, halfway between Cyprus and Beirut, because we were ahead of schedule, the captain stopped so we could climb down a rope ladder and have a swim. The Med was choppy and the Captain forgot to put the tanker into reverse, so he travelled on quite a distance without us and a boat had to be lowered to come back and rescue us. But it's a most gorgeous feeling, swimming with so many fathoms below you. The water is buoyant and frightfully invigorating. You feel like a mermaid.

We arrived at Beirut in quite a lot of publicity. All the journalists were there to see these two Naval wives getting off the tanker, and also the admiral arriving with the fleet. But, when I went ashore, I found to my horror that the Naval Attaché's wife had booked me in to a suite at the most expensive hotel which cost twenty pounds a day. I said to the manager, "I can't possibly afford twenty pounds a day. I'm going instead to the St. George's," – the St. George's Club was only a pound. "Oh, but madam," he said, "you can't go to the St. George's! It's been in all the papers that you're staying here and, if you leave, everyone will think there is something wrong with our plumbing! We will only charge you one pound a day if you agree to stay with us. So Chipps and I stayed for about five days in this frightfully expensive hotel with a lovely swimming pool for one pound a day!

Anyway, in Beirut there was delicious French food and we met lots of amusing people and, of course, there were lots of parties including one on board the flagship. Officially it was for the Lebanese but I well remember the sight of twenty gorgeous English Bluebelle dancing girls from the Casino coming up suddenly on the aircraft lift to the flight deck where the party was being held – and the effect on all the pilots who had been at sea for a month. The next night there was a party with the dancing girls which the Lebanese

Government gave for us at their beautiful Casino.

Chipps hired a car and we drove with another Naval officer to Baalbek with its gorgeous temples. Chipps, of course, insisted on arriving at twelve o'clock when it's boiling hot. While the other two were looking at something somewhere, I went among the ruins of the Temple of Bacchus to find some shade, and there I saw some little Lebanese girls doing a dance. They looked so Bacchanalian you could practically see the gods beaming down at them and having wicked thoughts. It was too pretty for any words.

The last day of the visit, Chipps flew off with his admiral who was shifting his flag to *Bulwark* in Singapore and I decided to spend the night on *Tidesurge* so that, at five the next morning, I could get up in my dressing gown, put my face out of the porthole and watch *Victorious* going to sea. In the afternoon, though, I was sunbathing by the hotel's swimming-pool, when a sheik arrived with his all-male retinue and sat down and absolutely stared at me. And when I went into the pool he stared at me. And when I came out of the pool he stared at me. Finally, this made me so uncomfortable that I decided to go up to my room early, have a bath, change, pack my luggage, take it down to *Tidesurge* and have dinner with an officer on board *Victorious* instead of in the hotel. Well, at about six, when I was paying my bill, the manager, after talking mysteriously with one of the sheik's retinue standing in the lobby, approached me and said, "Madam, you may stay another night at our expense. Someone is very anxious to meet you." I said, "I'm awfully sorry, but I've arranged to leave and I'm dining elsewhere." "You won't," he said, "regret staying. There'll be a diamond in it for you." I declined again and said goodbye. Inwardly, I was giggling like mad. Being propositioned by a sheik was rather fun.

I sailed the long way back to Malta, stopping at Majorca where Chipps' arrived this time in the aircraft carrier *Hermes*, and where my old boyfriend, Ian Farquhar, had taken a house for the summer with his wife and son on a very pretty hill near a beach, and we joined his house party for a weekend. Robert Graves was in the party. He told me all about windmills and, in my report that year for Dom, I suggested windmills for Malta's water problem.

I was able to help start Malta's Middle Sea Yacht Race, too. It's rather an interesting race because you go from Malta and back again round the islands of Sicily, and the conditions are very varied so you've got everything from flat calm to high winds. I wrote to Theo Rossie and Stavros Niarchos and Ari Onassis, another friend of mine who I'd met in the South of France, and asked if the idea interested them. Theo, actually, was the only one who bit. He came to look at Malta and so much fell in love with it when

Dom showed him round that he agreed to be the sponsor. So that was yet another boost to tourism.

My friend, Prince Yurka Galitzine, was a particular help to me when Dom Mintoff was back in power in 1971, he came out and suggested – and I had suggested it in my reports – that we have more P.R. in Scandinavia, France, Germany, Italy. After Independence, actually, the English weren't deterred from still having holidays in Malta. In fact, the Maltese continue to like English tourists best: it's just they didn't all like our Navy virtually occupying their country.

Do you know, how important Malta is to our history? I mean, the Siege of Malta was when the whole of Western civilisation was defended from the Turks. I can't begin to tell you how steeped in history it all is with its Roman catacombes and its Knight's castles and its old towers and palaces. Valletta, itself, is baroque. People are inclined to think of Malta as one island but it's an archipelago there's Malta, Gozo, Comino, Fifla and Cominetto. Five islands, though Fifla is really only a rock full of birds.

It was about now that John Templeton-Cotill arrived in his frigate, H.M.S. Rhyl. I did a certain amount of receiving for him on board, and we went to a fancy dress dance together on H.M.S. Bermuda. John corked himself all over to look like an Indian, and I dressed as a siren in very slinky green sparkly trousers and a very slinky green sparkly top. After this super dance in Bermuda, with masses of rum punches were served and the wardroom dolled up with palms, I was dropping John back at Rhyl in the car I'd hired, when two policemen questioned us as we came into the dockyard. John, of course, wasn't carrying his papers so they got into the back of the car – a machine gun was actually resting on my shoulder – and they accompanied us to Rhyl where the Quartermaster, who lets you up the companionway, did nothing but giggle while John kept asking him to explain he was captain of the ship. All the poor man could do was go, "Heh, heh, heh. Yes, Captain. Heh, heh, heh" for a full five minutes. I was making the situation even funnier by insisting John was a Russian spy. By now lots of John's sailors were watching from the rail, and they and I were helpless with laughter. Finally the police did accept that John was a naval Captain. Is it any wonder that sailors adored John so! Is it any wonder that admirals and, later the Foreign Office, didn't always adore him quite so much! . . .

In May, '65, Cecilia wrote to me from Xlendi, the fishing village in Gozo where she had a little house, informing me that, because of all I'd done for Malta, Fidel, a fisherman – he's dead now – was willing to sell me his house for a thousand pounds, the price he would ask from another fisherman.

You see, I hadn't just helped Malta itself, I'd helped Gozo, too, and the whole of the archipelago. When I'd taken Nye Bevan and so on to Gozo by helicopter back in the Fifties, the place was terribly primitive. It was all donkeys and dirt roads and dung, with, of course, an awful lot of Malta fever and tetanus and polio – Cecilia had caught polio electioneering there.

I'd stayed a night once at the "Duke of Edinburgh", then the only hotel, and the light flex in the middle of the bedroom had been crawling with flies. It was two inches thick with them. Well already, through tourism, all that was beginning to change with fly-screens and fans, and mini tractors taking the place of donkeys in the fields. So Gozo was becoming a much healthier place.

Anyway, Fidel offered me this house in Xlendi and Cecilia said, "You must come out and look at it. I'm sure you'll want it." So I went out immediately because Xlendi is very, very pretty. It's in a bay which is like a little fjord, and it's down a sort of gorge with rocks on either side and enormous, spectacular cliffs, very high and very steep that go sheer down to the sea.

It was only a boat house with the foundations for an intended flat beside it. Inside, there was only a tap. There wasn't even any electricity – Fidel had cooked on a portable stove. I decided to buy it though, so we would have somewhere of our own for holidays when we got back from being diplomats in South America. The new foundations were just a trench really, but they were foundations, because Fidel had originally intended to build a place to sell on the open market. He then decided that my thousand pounds, together with his old age pension, would be quite enough to keep him in his council flat in Victoria until he died – in Xlendi, the fishermen always have a second place to live as their caves and boathouses are too damp in winter.

So, in '66, following Fidel's foundations, I built a lovely flat at ground level, adding an upstairs later. I did it from just nothing and furnished it and made a terrace and garden and let it, all within three weeks! The whole village helped me. The schoolmaster did the electricity. The priest did some of the painting. I had two carpenters. A local furniture hop made furniture to my design. I had to be up at four every morning for the mason. And Gerald de Trafford, Cecilia's eldest son, lent me a plumber and a drains chap from the Villa Bologna. They would arrive on the first ferry at six and leave on the last ferry at five. They wouldn't sleep in Gozo. They were poles apart in those days. the Maltese and the Gozotans. For a Maltese peasant to go to Gozo, and for a Gozotan peasant to go to Malta, was much more difficult than going to Australia . . .

The garden, of course, I could make by myself with Gerald's help. There was a well just outside, so everything I planted grew like mad. When I got back three years after, there were peaches, nectarines, lemons, oranges, pomegranates, palm trees, a jacaranda, poinsettias, all waiting for me.

I didn't have time to install the indoor wall lights – these were completed a few days after I'd left, before the tenant moved in. For these I just did a squiggle on the back of an envelope, and the wrought iron-worker interpreted them as snakes. I'm sure a lot of the villagers thought at first, "She's the devil, this woman," because I'm the only person I know in Gozo who's got snakes in their garden. I suppose it's because of the well and the damp and the luxurious undergrowth. But they're grass snakes: they're not venemous. The Maltese always say that St. Paul took the venom out of the snakes in Malta and put it into the tongues of the Maltese women. I've never actually seen one in the house, but I lent Dorrea once to Barbara and Hilary Young – Hilary was our ambassador in Bogota – and she found one in the dining-room.

Anyway, wages, materials, the lot, only came to about five-hundred pounds so, altogether, my house in Gozo cost me fifteen hundred pounds, the profit I'd made from the house I rebuilt at Organford.

My three-year tenant was an Englishman called Julian Nixon, a former cook in a restaurant in London. He had a very rich mother who gave him an adequate allowance to live in Gozo, enough then to have jolly good parties in my garden. I was doing an inventory for him on my last day, just before I caught the ferry to fly home, when Josephine Micaleff, who is still my maid over twenty years later, suddenly said, "You haven't got any plates for him to eat off." I'd got cups and saucers and knives and forks and spoons and glasses, but I'd forgotten plates. So I rang the ferry and asked them to wait for me – you could do that in those days. Then I went to Victoria where there were only three shops. The first one said, "We've enamel plates and we've paper plates for picnics." I said, "No, I mean china." The second one was the same. The third shop, Grech, was run by the priest who owned it. He said, "Wait a minute, there's a crate which has just come in from Yugoslavia along with a lot of bags of cement. There may be some plates in that." So we opened the crate and, in it, were the most lovely white china plates with a gold rim round them and, underneath, the words "Made in USSR". I said, "You had better not tell the Archbishop or you'll de-frocked and I'll be booted out of the island!" Anyway, I got the plates, then caught the ferry and flew back to England.

Next day, I flew with Chipps, the children and a new *au pair* to Spain where Chipps was being sent by the Navy for two months to requalify as a Naval Interpreter in preparation for South America. The previous *au pair* had gone back to New Zealand and I'd found this one through The Lady, an awfully nice girl called Carol, who was used to cooking for five hundred people at Leeds University. We'd be needing somebody in Caracas to cook for us and look after Bruce – Jamie, except in his school holidays, would be at Eton or with the Hopwoods in England.

She was absolutely invaluable to me because, if ever we gave a party – we had to have enormous parties with up to three hundred and fifty people, dining and dancing – Carol did the catering. She said, "I won't cook for you every day, so get a Spanish cook. But, if you give a party, I'll do that." And she always did it marvellously, knowing how to get things cheaply so we could live within our allowance without calling in the caterers.

In Spain, we rented a house at Fuenterrabia on the French fronter. Fuenterrabia was great fun because we already had lots of friends there, such as the Lunas (the Duke and Duchess de Luna) whom I had met in Lisbon with the exiled King Juan. Henry Cabot Lodge's brother, John, the U.S. Ambassador, was there with his daughter who'd just married a Spanish diplomat. John and I swam together. He was very right wing so we were always treading water and arguing politics. I am a political animal and I would still be in politics if I hadn't fallen in love with Chipps.

Part 11

SOUTH AMERICA

Chapter 33

OFF TO CARACUS!

November, 1966 – November 13th: my lucky number – we left for Caracas which was-to be our base for three years. Chipps was now a diplomat and I was a diplomat's wife. Funnily enough, we were under my old friend, Denis Healey, the Minister of Defence. I must say he was very helpful – he sent out all sorts of tanks and guns for Chipps to sell.

Actually, Chipps being also accredited to the Dominican Republic was very amusing. He'd always dined out on the story that he was once offered the job of Commander-in-Chief of the Dominican Navy. As a young man in Madrid, he ran around with a girl who had connections with the Trujillo family, then the Republic's dictators. Later, she turned up in some important capacity at their Embassy in London, and they went out together again. She invited him to a big cocktail party at the Embassy in London one night and he was approached by their Naval Attaché who said, "Now that you're marrying into our presidential family, we must think very seriously about your future. What about being the Commander-in-Chief of our Navy? We've just bought two British destroyers. We're determined to dominate the Caribbean." Chipps, at the time, was only a young lieutenant! The girl, though, had other fish to fry, and the man who became commander-in-Chief of their Navy was a former sergeant of the American Marine Corps, who married Trujillo's sister . . .

We were absolutely dying for this adventure, and had no idea what to expect – we hadn't got a house waiting for us or anything! My predecessor had written, saying, "Bring poppadoms and bring lampshades and things to doll your house up," and she told us more or less what quantity of drink to order, and so on. Well, I didn't bother about poppadoms, but I took cushion covers, silver, cutlery, our large mattress . . . Twenty four crates, which were taken by removal van to the boat at Southampton, the *Flandres*, the "Queen Elizabeth" of France.

I'd received a book from the Foreign office, telling me how to behave as a diplomat's wife. I knew about *placement* and things already. I mean, you behave like you do normally. But there were certain details I didn't know. For instance, you mustn't give a party where foreign ambassadors are present, unless your own ambassador presides at your table. Actually, none of my ambassadors bothered about that, except Sir Anthony Lincoln, the one in Caracas, who took life rather seriously. During my first summer in Caracas, I gave a *despedida* – a farewell party – for Monsieur de Vaucelles, the French Ambassador, who, perhaps as a result of French experience, had become a great friend of mine, and who was being transferred to Teheran. As he and his wife were so popular, they'd been invited to an awful lot of *despedidas* so he said to me, "Do you know what I'd like, Dodo? I'd like an informal lunch round your pool, and then I can relax and then go and play golf in the afternoon. He then told me all the people he'd like me to ask, without including Anthony Lincoln. But Anthony Lincoln heard about this and said to me, "You can't possibly have the French Ambassador to lunch without me being there and presiding!" So the poor ambassador, instead of having a nice informal lunch round the pool, had to have a pompous lunch party with Sir Anthony at the top of the table.

John Cronin came to that lunch, too. Chipps had come back from the office and said, "There's a director of Racal" – the electronics firm – "coming out. Because of your politics, I've been asked to look after him. His name is John Cronin and he's M.P. for Loughborough." Loughborough was the constituency I was offered after Lancaster, so I said, "I want him to lunch!" so John came to my *despedida* for the French Ambassador and we made great friends. After that, he stayed with us whenever he came to Caracas . . .

Anyway, we piled our hand luggage into my mother-in-laws car – our Ford Consul was shipped ahead of us – and she drove Chipps, Bruce, our dog, Bliss and me to Southampton where we went on board the *Flandres*. Chipps and I had an outside cabin. Bruce had a bigger inside one so we put a lot of our luggage in there and Chipps used it as a dressing-room. Bliss had to go into a big cage on the top deck. Our neighbours in Dorset, Pam and Wol Drax, had sent us a bottle of Champagne. Carol, our gardener Sid Chappell, and John and Madeleine Sherbrooke came to see us off. We entertained them to dinner – delicious French food, of course, as it was a French liner. We then set sail for Vigo, which was to be our only stop before a Caribbean cruise from Martinique to Guadeloupe, and on to St. Martin, Puerto Rico, Jamaica and Curacao, ending, for us, at La Guaira. There weren't many other passengers till the cruise began. Chipps and I ate sometimes at the captain's table, sometimes on our own. Bruce, who was only eight, usually had lunch without us at the first sitting and then went off to play in the crèche.

The Mayor of Vigo, after a signal from Chipps, who'd recently been to Vigo in *Victorious*, entertained us to lunch and gave me a key-ring with a silver tag depicting Sant' Iago. But, back on board, the most terrific storm blew up. I mean, it wasn't just a storm: it was an enormous tempest, a hurricane. I said to a steward, "I must go up to see my dog, Bliss!" He said, "I'm sorry, Madam. The only way to reach him is through the bridge. Nobody's allowed up there, anyway. The waves are coming right over the ship." Hanging on like grim death to every rail I could find, I sneaked past the captain on the bridge as far as Bliss's cage, and got inside and stayed with him for an hour. The waves were coming right up but, luckily, not into the cage itself. Bliss was so happy to see me and to know that I was still around.

During the hurricane, the dining-room almost emptied. I'm never seasick, and Chipps and Bruce took Avomine pills and weren't sick either. Actually, apart from one other couple, we were the only three in the dining-room for at least two meals. We sat and sort of looked at each other until finally the female half of the other couple came over and said, "Look, as we're the only good sailors on this ship, do let's have lunch together!" and, from then on, Chipps and I always lunched with them – Antonio and Marisa Posse de Rivas. He was a Venezuelan Ambassador and she was a well-known figure in Caracas. Marisa is still a very great friend of mine, and it was really she who launched us into Caracas' *grande monde* who were small in number and very snobbish about their friends. I'd been warned before I went: "Oh, Venezuela, like everywhere in South America, is a terrible place. They never ask you to their houses and, if you have to be asked for some official reason, they take you to a restaurant, or you have an official party at the Ministry or somewhere." Well, thanks to Marisa Posse de Rivas, that certainly didn't happen to us. On our very first evening in Caracas, she invited us to supper and, from then on, we were sort of "accepted" by Venezuelan Society.

The weather for the Caribbean cruise was divine. Though we weren't really crossing the Equator, we had a "crossing the line" ceremony between two of the Islands. Chipps was made King Neptune and I was Queen Aphrodite. Chipps and I carried tridents and I wore a white sheet and a crown and all my Jewels. We processed around the deck and then the others paid us homage while we sat on thrones. Chipps made everyone do Naval forfeits – handstands, somersaults, juggling, kissing my toes . . . The Purser, was thrown into the pool at my request. He was furious. He said to me afterwards, "I didn't mind the uniform – the company supplies that. But I paid for my shoes myself!" At the end, I was thrown in. By then the pool was full of washing powder, Ajax and God knows what.

Other memories are of coconut trees, coral sands, blue lagoons and marvellous coloured fish when we stopped at the islands. Bliss adored the beaches. In St. Martin, it was extraordinary to see Dutch and French blacks playing cricket in white flannels as if they were on an English village green.

"How's zat?" in a French accent sounded very odd, and I was tempted to send a telegram to General de Gaulle warning him that the French Empire was being undermined by strange Anglo-Saxon sports.

On board the French Liner* Flandres*, 1966.
"King Neptune (Chipps) and Queen Aphrodite (Dodo)" on the far right

We arrived at La Guaira towards the end of November. We were met by Anthony Redman, the Military Attaché whom Chipps was taking over from in Caracas – he was in the Scots Guards and had also fought for Franco in the Spanish Civil War. Anthony had been sent over to teach the Venezuelans how to fight the Cuban guerillas but, in fact, the Venezuelans weren't the least bit interested in his suggestions.

Chipps, was going to be both the Naval and the Military Attachés, so one moment he'd have to be in Naval uniform, the next in military uniform. Chipps, being Chipps, more or less invented his own Naval-cum-military uniform of naval shoulder straps, khaki tunic, riding breeches, and brown polo boots.

Anthony Redman drove us through a series of tunnels in the mountains to Caracas which is three thousand feet up. He pointed out the Shell Building, which was where our Embassy was. Shell and Esso, of course, made Venezuela what it is. Oil is the reason why it was the richest place in South

America and why, combined with a Socialist government, the standard of living was higher for all the people – the money hadn't all gone to the upper classes like in Colombia.

Anthony said "There is supposed to be an earthquake every sixty years. There was one at the beginning of the century and so logically there should be one next year." How right he was!

We hadn't a house yet so we were staying at the Tamanaco, a big hotel named after an Indian chief. Our room was full of flowers from the various embassies to welcome me, including a huge bouquet from Marisa and Antonio Posse de Rivas with a letter saying, "Come to dinner tonight." So there, we were, arriving in Caracas, having been told we'd never be invited into a Venezuelan house, already being asked to a private dinner. Caracas is a terrifically social town. Sometimes you'd have three or four parties in a night drinking and eating an endless procession of *passapalos* – very filling and complicated *canapés* in fig or banana leaves, including shellfish such as oysters, prawns and *langostinos*.

The following evening Anthony Redman took us to dinner with Mike Pocock, the head of Shell in Caracas at the time, and his wife Nina. Mike was later succeeded by his deputy Joost de Liefde, a Dutchman, whose wife was an Austrian called Mel, who'd been imprisoned as a child by the Nazis. I had introductions to both the Pococks and the de Liefdes from Frank Southborough, Lord Southborough, Moyna Hopwood's father-in-law. Lord Southborough was head of Shell International, and he and his wife, Audrey, knew Caracas frightfully well.

Anyway, Anthony Redman took us to dinner with Mike and Nina Pocock. Anthony's wife, Patricia, had recently died very suddenly while washing her hair in the river by Angel Falls near Canaima – her last letter was to me, the one telling me to bring out poppadoms – and, as I walked through the door, Nina went white as a sheet. She thought I was Patricia's ghost, because Patricia was tall and dark like me!

We made great friends, Nina, Mike and I. Nina and I are still great friends. Mike died of a heart attack and, a couple of years ago, she married Peter Samuel, a widower, now Lord Bearsted whose family started Shell. Having the Pococks and the de Liefdes as friends was a great asset because they had the Shell plane which could take you to lovely places in the Jungle.

I then started house-hunting. Chipps' secretary came with me once or twice, but, generally I was just driven by his chauffeur, Ortez. I must have gone to forty houses altogether. There was one absolutely gorgeous one belonging to a Senora de Nunes, which had the most lovely garden. It was a really lovely colonial house, one of the few old Venezuelan houses. I could have had it very cheap, but I wasn't allowed to have it because the Lincolns thought it was too grand – it was grander, you see, than their own residence.

Finally, the wife of one of the embassy people, said, "We're leaving. Why not come and look at our house? It's let to us by a chap in the Venezuelan Army." So I went round to look at it and I fell in love with it. Though it was modern, it was built round a swimming-pool and, all the way round the swimming-pool, were terraces on two levels with a small garden – I calculated at once that I could fit at least a dozen tables of six on those terraces, which would help me enormously with entertaining. It had a nice big drawing-room, unfurnished save for the bare essentials, so I was glad I'd brought out the stuff still sitting in the docks. But the dining-room had an enormous table, which would be quite enough for indoor entertaining, and there was a little room off it for Chipps' office and where Carol and I could do the invitations and things. The upstairs consisted of four bedrooms and two bathrooms – Chipps and I had a big double room with, next door, a large bathroom-cum-dressing-room with masses of fitted cupboards.

It was in Avenida Central, Alta Florida, a very short walk from the edge of the jungle rain forest that towered up to 9,000 feet and where you could pick wild orchids off the trees. All along the Avenida Central, were mango trees – they're planted in all the avenues of Venezuela. In Venezuela, anybody has the right to pick mangoes, wherever they are. Because they contain all the vitamins necessary to life, they belong to the people.

As regards entertaining, this was a dream house. My predecessor's house was terribly dull and without a swimming-pool and she spent five thousand pounds of her own money because she always used caterers. Without using caterers, I entertained far more than she did and, thanks to Carol, and later Mel de Liefde who lent me tables and chairs from Shell to put on my terraces, I managed to keep well within my budget of four thousand pounds a year. Mel even used to lend me her servants. Then, when she had a party, I lent her my servants. In Venezuela servants adored being lent for parties.

Apart from Ortez the chauffeur, I inherited Patricia's black cook and maid and, unfortunately, her husband's secretary, a Chilean who was rather a pain and wouldn't do anything for me whatsoever. Indeed, she did little for Chipps who couldn't get rid of her because the Embassy would have had to pay her too much redundancy.

The cook was called Pearl and the maid was called Angelita. From the moment I met her, I didn't like Angelita, but I did like Pearl. Carol was coming out as soon as I moved into the house, so I knew Bruce would be all right and that Carol could cope when I was away on trips to Chipps' other "parishes". I gave Pearl and Angelita alternative Sundays off and, one Sunday, I came back with Bruce from the Camuri Grande – a lovely beach club, with sand and tropical fish and gorgeous trees and iguanas, where you could have langostinos and whatever you wanted to eat – and found the fridge empty. Well, my Venezuelan neighbours told me that Angelita's family had been literally turning up with baskets to collect things and take them off. So I sacked Angelita. Then, because Chipps was finding Ortez a bit boring he decided to make a change. I decided to ask Pearl if she'd like a job with the Swiss Ambassadress. I said, "Look, Pearl, I've got Carol to do the housework. What we need is a married couple – a chauffeur/butler with a wife to do the breakfast, lunch and dinner." Pearl was with the Ambassadress till a short time before we left in '69.

So, in place of Ortez and Angelita and Pearl, we employed Juan and Teresa. This is a sad story because they were from Galicia in Spain, and the Galicians love money, and they're always trying to be bigger than their station: they're intelligent peasants. He was a very good chauffeur and she was a jolly good cook, but his ambition was to save enough money to go back to Galicia and be a taxi-driver and to re-join their children who were being brought up by her mother. What a life for a mother, never seeing her children being brought up! Anyway, they went back to Galicia and found they hadn't enough money due to inflation. So they returned to Caracas the following year, '68, and Teresa rang me up and said she'd like to come back to me. But by then we had a marvellous couple, Franklin and Maria, who were with us till we left. When Carol went to look up an old boyfriend in Canada, Pearl came back to cook for me and Maria did the housework.

Franklin and Maria were absolutely sweet. He came from the Islas Galapagos, and was a real Indian, and she was Venezuelan. He'd never been a butler in his life so I had to teach him how to "buttle". I was never stung in the jungle by anything ever because I always whistled my little tune but I was stung by a scorpion in my own house, and it was Franklin who rushed me to hospital for an injection, then went and found the nest and killed all the scorpions. To this day, I've the two little puncture marks made by the scorpion on my left thumb . . . I've always taken Christmas decorations with me all over the world so that the children have some sort of continuity and, to add to these, Betty Rhigi, – she was married to the owner of the bank that served the Tamanaco – made me a lovely Father Christams After Christmas, Franklin threw it and all my other decorations in the bin. I said to him, "Where are the Christmas decorations?" He said, "Oh I've thrown them away. Christmas is over." I said, "But, Franklin, I take them all over the world!" So he went through all the rubbish, darling little man, and retrieved them and washed them. I adored Franklin and Maria.

One night I went to a dinner party with Peter Muller, the Austrian Ambassador, and, in the middle of dinner, the butler came up and whispered in my ear; "Franklin wants to see you." So I waited till the next course, then said to Peter, "I've just got to go outside for a minute." I went outside and Franklin said to me, "Senora, my baby is ill at the ranchito." Ranchitos are the shacks you see all over South America. They're made of tin and cardboard. They've no plumbing, no loos, no water, nothing. People from the jungle and the interior come and live in them, and they're rife with disease. I've seen children, with vultures overhead, picking around in the empty tins on the rubbish dumps to find something to eat. The Socialist Government had built blocks of flats, but many people who had come to Caracus from the interior didn't want to live in them them because they couldn't keep their goats and chickens there . . .

So I excused myself from the party and went in our car with Franklin to this ranchito. I could see at once that the baby would die if I didn't do something quickly. It was completely dehydrated and had diarrhoea. Luckily I had a great paediatrician friend who I'd met socially with Marisa Posse de Rivas. He'd treated Bruce for amoebic dysentry, and, though he was very expensive, he was very good. I rang him up and said, "My chauffeur's child is dehydrated. He's going to die." He said, "Look, I can't get him into the hospital itself because it's absolutely full. Take him and his mother to my private office. They both can stay there as long as necessary. I'll come at once."

Franklin and Maria and I drove with the child to the hospital, and Maria stayed in that office, which had a surgical bed and a chair, for three weeks with her child in her arms till it was saved, and Pearl, who till then had been bloody to her about which were and which were not her duties, did all her duties for her.

Maria had started another baby before we left, and my successor got rid of her as soon as she saw that she was pregnant. But Franklin and Maria never forgot what I had done for their son. Their next child was a girl and she was named Dolores after me, and I'm her Godmother. If Franklin hadn't been my chauffeur, his firstborn, his only son, would have died for sure. Venezuela is that sort of country. It's tough.

But to go back to 1966. We settled in to our new home and then it was Christmas. On Christmas Eve I had everybody from our Embassy, including the black Trinidadian porters and their families to swim in our pool and have sandwiches and drinks in the garden – Jamie and I toasted the ham and cheese sandwiches ourselves. Christmas Day was a family day at home and, on Boxing Day, the children went to a party somewhere, and Chipps and I went off with the chauffeur in the Land-Rover, an official perk, to see the Llanos, the low lying country, which in the dry season is cacti and sandy soil and in the wet season seems like a vast swamp. Later we were to go there often in the rainy season to shoot duck with Blancie and Hupi van Nispen.

Hupi was Head of Chancery in the Dutch Embassy and Blancie, his wife, was one of my great friends. Every month there was a *Damas Diplomaticas*, a tea party at which an ambassador's wife would usually give a lecture. The lectures were frightfully boring so some of us would bring a pack of cards to play bridge. I met Blancie through playing cards at a *Damas Diplomaticas* when we should have been listening to a lecture! She was a Hungarian countess who'd been smuggled out of Hungary in a laundry basket when the Communists came in after the war. She'd lived on practically nothing, working as a chamber maid in a hotel in Brussels, though her Godfather was King Leopold of the Belgians. Then she'd met Hupi and married him.

Shooting duck with Blancie and Hupi was an extraordinary experience. You'd go out to the swamps at about six in the morning and the duck would come over in clouds. The whole sky was full of them, and the noise their wings made was quite beautiful. You had to be very careful in the swamps, though, to avoid caribes and bilharzia. Caribes are small fierce man-eating fish, known elsewhere as piranhas. Bilharzia are those parasites which go through your toenails and all the way up to your brain and kill you; they say the only way you can get rid of them is to catch them as they pass through your eye. So you are careful what rivers you step into in Venezuela! Generally, though, when there is a danger of bilharzia, there are skull and crossbone signs on the bridges.

Anyway, Boxing Day, Chipps and I wanted to see the Llanos. Unlike so many diplomats and their wives, we wanted, from the word go, to discover the country, and not just stick to the Caracas social round. First we passed through lovely rolling mountains and green rainforests full of parrots and other exotic birds to Maracay, The little towns we went through were rather like the ones you see in American Wild Westerns, just two rows of houses facing each other down a main street. Eventually we came to the Llanos themselves, terribly hot and sandy, and stopped at a bar-cum-garage called El Sombrero. While Chipps and Ortez were filling the Land-Rover up with petrol, I went inside and ordered three beers. The man behind the counter was wearing a sombrero and he was completely drunk. He took a revolver out of his pocket, pointed it straight at me and said, "You have a beer on me, Juanita!" I said, "Thank you very much" – I wasn't going to argue with a gun.

So he gave me a free beer. "Who's this?" he said, when Chipps came in. I said, "That's my husband." "Oh, he can have a beer on me, too." "I'll pay for it!" said Chipps rather crossly, as he often does. "Is he English?" asked the man suspiciously. "I've always longed to kill an Englishman." "Of course not" I replied quickly and turned to Chipps. I said, "For God's sake don't argue, darling! He's got a gun!" So Chipps accepted his beer. Then Ortez came in. "Who's the black one?" said the barman. Ortez was Venezuelan, but he had Negro and Indian blood so he was quite dark. I said, "That's our chauffeur." "Well then, he can have a beer on me, too." "I pay for my own beer!" said Ortez, whereupon the man pulled his gun again! Then Ortez started haranguing him and saying it was illegal to carry a gun when drunk, which made the man more angry than ever. I said, "Ortez, leave your beer and get out quickly! Go at once!" I really did think he was going to be shot.

We went many times to the Llanos afterwards, duck shooting and on official visits to the Army on business. Chipps was very anxious to promote British arms sales to the Venezuelans. To sell Naval and military arms is part of a Naval or Military or Defence Attaché's job.

In '68, Chipps wanted to sell little armoured cars called Ferrets to fight the Cuban guerillas who were landing on the coast, and going to live in the mountains. The demonstration took place on the army range down towards Maracaibo. Unfortunately a Shorland, an armoured Land-Rover, widely used in Ulster, was also sent out and Chipps assumed the armour plating was as bullet-proof as the manufacturers claimed. It wasn't. He persuaded the Venezuelan General to sit with him to be shot at in the Shorland and they would both have been killed if I hadn't phoned Chipps just at the moment about a tarpaulin. I thought it was going to rain and, as I was giving a big dinner dance for that night at the house and was worried that the balcony at the back, which held about forty people, would be open to the elements. I got the embassy to ring Chipps to ask if he could get the Venezuelan Army or Navy to lend me a tarpaulin. Thank God, he got out of the Shorland, with the general at his heels, to go to the field telephone, whereupon the tank was shot at by the Venezuelan Army and the bullets went straight through and smashed into the dashboard.

That was an awful mistake by London and, of course, we didn't sell any Shorlands or any Ferrets either, because the Venezuelans were so horrified by the incident. In fact, virtually no British armoured vehicles have been sold anywhere in Latin America since.

Chapter 34

THE HOVERCRAFT AND THE EARTHQUAKE

Also in '68, the same year as the Shorland fiasco, Chipps, through no fault of his own, failed to sell the Hovercraft. The Hovercraft was then a completely new thing to South America, though it had been ferrying passengers between Cowes and Portsmouth for about five years, and Chipps hoped to sell it to Colombia and Venezuela. He had to check the various fuels for when a Hovercraft, sponsored by the National Geographic, the "People" newspaper and the B.B.C., made its '68 expedition up the Amazon and across to the Rio Negro through the extraordinary natural Canal in the jungle that links the huge Amazon and Orinoco rivers, and then on down the Orinoco and over the Falls of Ayacucho, those absolutely fantastic falls which even an Indian canoe couldn't navigate because of the rocks and the thirty foot drop. Needless to say, everybody was agog to see if the Hovercraft could really get through the jungle and over these falls.

At the time Chipps was making arrangements with the Colombian Navy and Shell for putting fuel up the Orinoco, I was with him at a cocktail party at the Presidential Palace in Bogota and I happened to meet the French Military Attaché, Philippe, I said to him, "Look, I'm sure you've been here for years and years and, like most of the other diplomats, hardly know the country at all. My husband is helping to fix up this forthcoming Hovercraft expedition. Why don't you come with us to Leticia tomorrow and explore?" – Leticia is in a sort of corner right down at the bottom of Colombia on the Amazon between Brazil and Peru. He said, "Oh, what a good idea!" and decided there and then to join us.

Next day, we got into this old Colombian Airforce Dakota with just the usual canvas seating round the edge and crates in the middle. It was frightfully cold because there were holes in the fuselage, and we hadn't got any thick clothes. Chipps, as always, had half a dozen newspapers with him so he wrapped himself in those. Philippe had a mackintosh so he put his left arm through one sleeve and I put my right arm through the other and we rhumba-ed and tango-ed together most of the journey.

We arrived in Leticia in steaming heat and were put up in the local Naval barracks, basic but quite comfortable. Leticia had a Spanish bishop, called

Bishop Canez, and, next day, Philippe had the brilliant idea of paying him a call. So he and Chipps put on their uniforms and their gold *aiguillettes*, and off we went to call on the bishop. The door was opened by this charming man who had no robes or soutane, just white shirt and trousers, and a cross around his neck. He didn't look like a bishop at all, but I saw the ring and immediately kissed his hand. Chipps said loudly in English, "Don't be an ass! It's the butler!" But it was the bishop and he asked us to lunch and told us his story.

He'd been a bishop in Barcelona during the Spanish Civil War when, of course, the Communists were killing all the priests, especially the bishops, so he got on the first ship he could and it happened to be going to Cartagena in Colombia where he announced to the Church authorities, "I'm the Bishop of Barcelona." The church authorities said, "Bishops here are two a penny but, if you'd like to go and convert the Indians along the Amazon, we'll give you some money to set you up." So he went down to Leticia and started a series of convent and monastic schools up the Colombian side of the Amazon – from Leticia it then took six weeks by canoe to reach the furthest one. He was already now teaching the second generation of his pupils because the Indians married so young.

We were at Leticia for about a week. The Colombian Navy had river gunboats, but the bishop lent us his launch and driver, and his secretary as guide, and they took the three of us up the Amazon to visit some of his schools. Bishop Canez taught his Indians not only to speak Spanish but to read and write it, using basic bible stories. He taught them to wear clothes and to be monogamous. He taught them to grow lime trees and drink lime juice which is full of vitamins. Whenever they caught a fish, killed a wild animal with poisoned arrows, he gave them a bottle of whisky or some cigarettes in exchange so his nuns and monks could feed their children with protein instead of just the maize they were accustomed to. As a result of all this, his Indians were very much healthier and much more intelligent and alive than the Indians on the Brazil side. On another day we went across to see the Indians there, and they were like an absolute different race. They didn't speak Spanish or Portuguese. They were impoverished and obviously riddled with amoebic dysentry. They were unhealthy looking and pot-bellied, and the women were just working like slaves while the men lay in hammocks chewing coca – cocaine. And yet they were only separated by the Amazon.

On our first trip, we became rather thirsty so, when I saw on the Colombian side an Indian hut with a lime tree growing beside it, I said to everyone, "Oh, do let's go and have a lime juice!" So the driver stopped the launch and the bishop's secretary went ahead and talked to the Indian woman in the doorway and she welcomed us inside to give us lime juice. In a corner I saw a blanket. I said to the woman in Spanish, "What's behind there?" She whispered, "Get rid of the others and I'll show you." So I said to Chipps and Philippe in English, "Will you go outside with the bishop's secretary and flirt with her or talk to her about parakeets or something, darlings. This woman has something interesting to show me."

While they were outside, the woman took me behind the blanket where I saw a girl of about thirteen lying naked in a hammock. I asked if she was ill, but her mother explained that she was in puberty and had to lie there for six months before the ceremony of marriage and that, every day during the six months, her father pulled one hair out of her head. She said that, for the marriage ceremony, all her relations in the tribe would come from both ends of the Amazon and congregate on a nearby island and that her father, after pulling all the remaining hairs out of her head, would throw her into the water. Because there were no sharks or piranhas, she could refuse to marry the first man to catch her and could go on being thrown back into the water till she was caught by the man she wanted to marry, after which she went with him straight into the jungle and did what you think.

After explaining all this, the mother showed me a little cap she was making for her daughter out of jungle leaves. This would be put on her head to hide her baldness when she went down later to Leticia to be married in church by the bishop. I said in confidence to the bishop that evening, when we went to have a drink with him and to thank him for the loan of his launch, "Do you know that *peliada* still goes on in your parish?" He said, "Yes, but I would only admit to you that I know!"

Later, when I went to Panama, I saw a very similar incident. Jungle Jim, whom I met there, had a private aeroplane and spoke the Indian language and had cleared up malaria in the St. Blas Islands where he used to fly every week and give treatment – he made a lot of money out of rich Americans and spent it on the Indians, who adored him as a result. He took me in his plane once to the islands and we went into a hut and there in a corner was the same sort of blanket that I had seen in the Amazon. I said to him "Do find out what is behind there" and he asked the head man. The mother drew back the blanket and there was a girl lying naked in a canoe. She had to lie there for six months and then she was thrown into the water, but this time had to marry the first man to catch her because here there were too many sharks. It is extraordinary that these two Indian tribes, who were two-thousand miles away from each other with different languages and different upbringing had the same sort of tradition . . .

While we were in Leticia, I saw a lot of an American who was importing wild animals for zoos in America. He had a huge snake, a tragavenado, literally a "deer swallower" – in a cage with two poor little iguanas waiting to be eaten. Tragavenados only eat occasionally when they are hungry and then swallow their victims and gradually absorb them. I thought it was terrible, these poor little victims waiting to be eaten, so I let them out. The tragavenado went too. Luckily, no-one knew who had done it.

At this time I discovered there was a lot of American interest in Leticia, particularly because a Brazilian doctor had discovered that one of the tribes never got cancer. If their women had trouble with their breasts, they gave them the bark of the *palo* to drink in water. There are four types of *palo de arco*, but the one with the black bark is the one that was supposed to be a cure for cancer. The American pharmaceutical companies were there buying up tracts of jungle where they could find these trees. The Brazilian doctor had sent his findings to the Pasteur Institute for study . . .

Anyway, back to the Hovercraft. In the end, Chipps couldn't watch it negotiate the Falls of Ayacucho because he had to be in Panama sorting out what was happening as President Arias had just been ousted; so he rang me up and said, "For God's sake, you go down, Dodo, to see it go over the Falls and make sure it gets full Press and Television coverage."

Dr. Egon Herbiq was our embassy doctor and had his own little Cessna. So I went down in Herbig's plane, with Bruce to chaperone me – whenever I flew anywhere with Herbig I always took Bruce so people wouldn't talk. The bloody B.B.C., so they could hog the story for the piddling little film they were making, had made sure the Hovercraft crossed the Falls the day before they said they would, i.e. the day before we and the Press and Television people arrived. They behaved like s-h-i-t-s, they really did, and stopped Chipps from selling God knows how many Hovercrafts! Country should come first! As it was, the story went round Latin America that the Hovercraft had sunk – and the British were hushing it up.

Well, there wasn't a room to be had as they'd all been reserved by Press and T.V. people expecting to see something which, in fact, had already happened. So Herbig looked in his little book and found the name of a patient he though might put us up for the night. The patient was a furniture dealer, an Indian who lived with his numerous family in a little shack behind his shop, and, in his shop window, were two beds for sale, which Bruce and I slept in while Herbig used a hammock in the outside courtyard where we ate. I remember waking next morning to find a T.V. cameraman looking at Bruce and me through the shop window in absolute astonishment.

The captain of the Hovercraft stayed with me later in Caracas and told me that, though there was no media coverage at the time – which was why most people thought the craft had sunk – the event was actually a huge success: some windows were smashed, as the craft disappeared under the water, and the engines stopped temporarily, after dropping down thirty feet over the Falls. But he'd managed to get the engines going again almost immediately. What was more frightening, he said, was when a tribe came out of the jungle, their bodies painted and absolutely starkers, waving spears. He was so scared that he and everyone with him were going to be killed that he lit a cigarette, whereupon the head man held out a hand for his lighter, took it delightedly, and offered them a feast. As part of the feast, a baby was barbecued on a spit, But it wasn't killed to barbecue: it had already died of natural causes . . .

The Hovercraft expedition was in '68. The Caracas earthquake was in August '67. One Saturday evening we were going out to drinks with the Musgroves, the Air Attaché and his wife, Joanne, who were doing their last year of duty before being replaced by Peter and Heidi Thompson.

Anyway, the night of the earthquake we were going out to drinks with them, and then on to dinner with Mohammed, the Saudi Arabian Ambassador, who was a royal prince, a nephew of the King, and unmarried and a great friend of mine. I was ready before Chipps – I very often am ready before Chipps, though he always says I keep him waiting – and I went and sat in the car in the garage. Then Chipps came out into the road and, at that moment, there was a terrific rattling like machine guns. I thought, "Oh, it's another of those battles the students are always having with the police. When it's over, I may have to go and help pick up the pieces" – always thinking as a nurse, you see. So I sat there quite happily. The car was sprung so I'd no idea there was an earthquake, I didn't feel the tremor.

The next thing I knew, Chipps was shouting at me in the road to come out at once as the garage was caving in. The rattling had been the shudder of our Venetian blinds and he'd heard the roar of an almighty earthquake, which had lasted about a minute. It was seven on the Richter Scale. We went quickly into the house. Carol was in the kitchen where she'd been just about to give support to Bruce and Jamie, back from Eton for his summer holidays. Juan and Teresa were huddled terrified somewhere, but Bruce and Jamie had jumped into the swimming-pool which was very wise as, if the house had collapsed, they would have been all right.

I said to Carol, "You'd better come with us to the Musgroves and bring the children so we're all together." "No, no, no," she said. "There's nothing to worry about" and, practical Northern girl that she was, began sweeping up in the store cupboard where a whisky bottle had fallen off the shelf and broken – Juan and Teresa, of course, were so frightened that they wouldn't stay at night in the house for a week and slept in the Land-Rover, instead. So Chipps and I went on our own to the Musgroves.

We were sitting on the lawn having drinks when there was another tremor. I said, "I must get the children to have them with me," but Chipps – he's so pompous sometimes – said, "Don't be absurd. We're going on to the Saudi Ambassador and we don't know him well enough to have the children!" I said, "I'm sure Mohammed won't mind!" and I turned to Mike Pocock, who was coming to Mohammed's too, and asked him to drive me to collect them. Of course Mohammed didn't mind at all and put them in his own enormous, sextuple bed. They were terribly excited to be sleeping in the Saudi Arabian Embassy. They'd never seen a bed like it and the bathroom was all marble and obelisks and statues and mirrors.

Downstairs, we had drinks and we waited, and then we had taped music and more drinks and we waited and waited and waited, until Mohammed finally said, "Oh dear, something must have happened to the cook!" So he sent the chauffeur to look for the cook and he never came back – he'd obviously gone to see if his family were all right. Then he sent his First Secretary to look for the cook and he never came back – he was obviously doing the same thing. Then he sent his Counseller off and he returned with a terribly underdone sheep which he barbecued himself.

By now the *pasapalos* had been passed round till there were none left and we were starving. It wasn't till about four o'clock in the morning that we got our barbecued sheep. Later, Chipps and I went to see our Embassy in the Shell Building. The building was a skyscraper, but luckily it was on chains. Three other skyscrapers though, two in Caracas and one on the coast, had been reduced to rubble. All told, I think there were five hundred deaths.

The earthquake, of course, was all over the *Sunday Express* but it wasn't ever delivered to my mother's till about ten o'clock in the morning. Meanwhile, Frank Southborough had got straight through on the Shell line to Mike Pocock who'd just gone to bed, and asked, "How are Dodo and Chipps?" He said, "They were fine at four o'clock when we were eating barbecued sheep!" So Frank was able to ring up my mother before she got her *Sunday Express* and say that we were all right.

The *damas diplomaticas*, the tea parties for diplomats' wives in Caracas, were held in different embassies every month, and, during the rather boring speech or lecture, some of the younger women, like Blancie Van Nispen and I, used to play bridge in the garden or an adjoining room; whispering our "two no trumps" so as not to interrupt things. One afternoon I was playing bridge with Blancie Van Nippen and Susan Beckhoff and Dorothy Smith –

Susie, a Hungarian like Blancie, was the wife of a very well known architect in Caracas who'd built a lot of its skyscrapers and I said, "I think it's awfully silly. Here we are playing bridge for ten bolivars. I'm jolly well going to run charity bridge parties for sending deprived children on an annual holiday."

So I got in touch with an organisation that looked after the poor children in the ranchitos and I said to the woman in charge, "Look, if my friends and I all raise money by giving bridge parties, can we send some children for a fortnight to one of your Holiday Homes on the sea or in the mountains? That way, we can feel our bridge parties are doing some good." She agreed to the idea and, from then on, instead of playing for money, we each put one hundred bolivars into a kitty and, by the time I left Caracas, we'd sent sixty children for a fortnight's holiday. Susie then continued the arrangement.

The first of the bridge parties was held in my house. There were about thirty of us, including several Venezuelans and Elizabeth Muller and some other ambassadors' wives, By then I'd acquired my parrot, Porfirio, and, in the middle of this all-female event, he shouted "Casa de putas!" – Brothel – from the top of a palm tree!

At the outset, Nina Pocock had advised me to watch my belongings whenever Venezuelans were my guests. She said, "They will take things as souvenirs like Americans take ashtrays and coathangers from hotels." She told me she'd some old English pennies, one of which went missing at a big dinner patty when her guests included the Minister of Justice. Some time later, when she was dining with President Leone, he said to her, "I wish you'd give me an old English penny like the one you gave the Minister of Justice!" As she predicted, I was always losing things at parties – lipsticks were even taken off my dressing-table. At my party for officers and diplomats after the Shorland fiasco, I had vases like little silver sauce-pans on the tables with a single carnation in them, and one of those disappeared.

Apart from our monthly tea parties, the *Damas Diplomaticas* had an annual fair at the Military club. Each embassy had a stall where the ambassador's wife was the king pin. I, of course, helped Lady Lincoln at the English one. We sold English this and English that such as honey and Christmas crackers. To make the crackers, Betty Rhigi was able to give me the inside of used loo rolls from the Tamanaco Hotel.

The most important annual event in Caracas, of course, is Venezuelan National Day, when there's a parade in which the soldiers goose-step like the Germans. The Military Attachés and their wives sit behind the ambassadors to watch. In '67, seated just in front of me, was the Guyanan Ambassador, E.R. Braithwaite, who'd written the best selling novel *To Sir With Love*. He was frightfully good-looking, terribly attractive, great fun and very intelligent. We'd met at various cocktail parties and dinners and used to talk a lot about the East End.

Being a Socialist was a great advantage to me in Venezuela. President Leone was a Socialist so I got on terribly well with him and most of his ministers. And, unlike other embassy wives who said, "Oh, it's such a bore," when at parties the women went by themselves into a corner, I didn't mind at all. I spoke Spanish of course, which helped . . . I found out so many things by talking to Venezuelan women: I didn't talk to them about how many of their children had measles: I asked them about their country. One Venezuelan wife, the head Admiral's actually, told me there were two special tribes of ants in Venezuela – the soldier ants who have scythe-like teeth and cut leaves and leave them like confetti on the floor, and the other ants who come along afterwards and take the confetti away. This explained how the leaves disappeared off the lime tree in my garden – heartbreaking because we used to put its marvellous limes into our gin and tonics. Also she told me that the best way to make an orchid flower was to get your husband to pee over it and all sorts or things.

Anyway, Braithwaite was sitting just in front of me at the parade. I was wearing a blue dress made by Prestige in Paris, and Chipps had bought me a blue pillbox hat with a large daisy on the top, and Braithwaite kept looking back at me and making eyes at me and, while the President was making his speech, he pretended to take the petals off a daisy and mouthed, "She loves me, she loves me not, she loves ME . . . " oh, and sitting beside Bill Vale, the American Military Attaché, was a chap in British style army uniform. Chipps, though he should have known everybody, didn't know who he was so we sent a message down to Betty-Fox, Bill's wife, and she sent one back to say he was an Israeli. This was just after the six-day war that Israel had won against the Arabs, and Chipps was able to buttonhole him. He said that the Israeli victory was due the type of tanks that they had used in their British-made Centurion tanks. I was talking to darling Mohammed at the time and, as you can imagine, he wasn't listening to me: he was trying frightfully hard to hear what Chipps was learning from this Israeli!

Chapter 35

SNOWY

Shortly after our first trip to the Llanos on Boxing Day, Commodore John Townley, Senior Naval Officer West Indies, or S.N.O.W.I., always known as "Snowy", appeared on a Naval visit with his Flag Lieutenant, Michael ("Mick") Saunders Watson, the nephew of Sir Michael Culme-Seymour who, that same year, gave him Rockingham Castle to avoid potentially heavy death duties.

Rockingham is where they made that T.V. film *By the Sword Divided*. It was built by William the Conqueror. King John, after staying there, was supposed to have lost the Crown Jewels in the Wash, but the iron chest where they were kept was later dug up, empty, somewhere in the castle. The chest is now on view to visitors. Chipps and I went up to the ball Mick and his wife, Georgina, gave to celebrate their twenty-fifth wedding anniversary in 1983. Mick and I always sign our Christmas cards "Ting-a-ling". This is because we were once at a cocktail party in Panama and the American Admiral came up to me and drawled, "I see you smoke Pall Mall," pronouncing it Paul Maul I said, "Yes, but actually we pronounce them Pell Mell." "Then," he replied, "I suppose I must say to you 'bells'!" Mick's been sending me cowbells from all over the place ever since! He's now frightfully involved in English Heritage.

Snowy and Mick were staying with the very conventional Lincolns. Chipps met them with the chauffeur at the airport, brought them up for a drink with me, then returned them to the embassy to unpack and change for a dinner-dance in Snowy's honour at the house of the Head of Chancery. Snowy was a highly intelligent but hippy Commodore and a great character, not at all the type who would be *persona grata* with the Lincolns – his hair was nearly down to his shoulders and he liked to walk about with no shoes on – and I'd invited him to come with me before the dinner-dance, to a drinks party given by Venezuelan Society friend of Marisa Posse de Rivas where I knew he'd meet an awful lot of amusing people. And, at this 'do', he fell madly for a woman he always referred to from then on as Elizabeth Taylor – she'd only had a baby about two weeks before, but that didn't matter to Snowy, and he kept saying, "Elizabeth Taylor, will you dance with me later tonight at a night club?"

On the way back in our car to the embassy after this dinner dance, Snowy could talk of nothing but finding Elizabeth Taylor and taking her to a night club, and he was talking very loudly indeed. I said to Mick, "How can we get him in this state into the embassy without waking the Lincolns?" He said, "Tell him it's a night club. He won't know the difference until he gets inside." So, when we reached the embassy, I said, "Here we are Snowy. Here's the night club. You and Mick go in while I go and fetch Elizabeth Taylor." Mick opened the door, and the last thing I heard was Snowy shouting, "This isn't a fucking night club! This is the bloody embassy!" As you can imagine, Snowy wasn't asked to stay with the Lincolns again, so, whenever he and Mick were in Caracas, they stayed with me. I was considered the only person who could keep Snowy in order. Even in our other parishes, the ambassadresses would say to me, "If Snowy comes, you've got to come too, Dodo!"

A day or two later, our fleet was supposed to be chasing a Venezuelan submarine as part of a series of joint Naval exercises. It was the first time the British and the Venezuelans had ever exercised together, and Chipps had arranged the whole thing. Snowy said to me, "Dodo, I must have some girls on board my ship!" Well, this is never done during an exercise at sea but, as it was Snowy and Snowy was unique, Chipps thought it would be O.K., so I invited Elizabeth Taylor and Nina Pocock and another girl and the four of us joined Snowy on board to go chasing this old submarine sold to Venezuela by the Americans, which, as far as I can remember, "sank" us. The manoeuvres took place and we had a very good lunch. Then Mick suddenly announced that the Venezuelan Flagship was coming alongside for a *Jackstay* transfer, and instructed Snowy to dress up at once to take the salute. Snowy, who had his arm around Elizabeth Taylor on the bridge and was dressed simply in a sarong and wearing no shoes, said, "Don't bother me now! I'm having a good time!" I said, "Listen, Snowy! if you don't dress up as your Flag Lieutenant has asked you to, I'll withdraw my invitation to stay with me whenever you're in Caracas. You can jolly well stay with thc Lincolns. That's if they'll have you!" So he put on his hat and his shirt with his Naval shoulder straps, but insisted keeping on the sarong since it couldn't be seen below the guard rail, and took the salute.

I really was the only person who had any authority over Snowy whatsoever. He never flirted with me – that's one of the reasons we could remain great friends.

The next time I met Snowy was before Easter in Panama. Chipps visited his three other parishes, Panama, Columbia, and the Dominican Republic, three or four times a year and, often as not, I used to go with him. Snowy and Mick were staying on this occasion at the Intercontinental, and Snowy and I would sometimes have lunch by the pool and swim together. For fun one evening, Mick and I went the rounds of about six brothels. Absolutely fascinating. They were all on stilts, and most of them were red plush inside. In one of them we met Snowy's son. At another called The Blue Goose, the Madame at the door said to Mick, "You can't bring your tart in here. You've got to have one of ours," so I had to sit by myself in the car.

Chipps and I often stayed in Panama with the British Ambassador, Henry Hankey, and his wife Vronny. The Hankeys were an absolutely charming family. They all played musical instruments and sang and danced and they had a lovely tennis court. It was the greatest fun staying with them, and they're still great friends of ours. Margot (Fonteyn) had given me an introduction to her sister-in-law who ran all the Arias family's newspapers – Arias, who was later the President of Panama, was Margot's husband's uncle. Chipps got to know the National Guard and, on his suggestion, two senior officers were invited by Henry and Snowy to lunch on Snowy's flagship, H.M.S. *Zest*, because he thought one of them was likely to be the future President.

Chipps proved to be right. The following year, he wrote in a report to the Ministry of Defence that he believed Arias would be elected, then kicked out in three weeks. But Henry Hankey didn't believe him. Well, actually it was eleven days. Arias was ousted in October '68 – by José M. Pinilla, one of the two men who lunched with Henry and Snowy, on *Zest* the previous year. We were ten at that lunch – Pinilla and the other National Guard officer, the American Governor of the Panama Canal zone and his wife, Henry and Vronny, Chipps and me, Snowy and Mick. I was put between the two from the National Guard because I spoke Spanish. There we were in, the Pacific, yet we had salmon, deep frozen, followed by pheasant and then delicious shaped ice-cream. Lunch parties are always frightfully well done in the Navy, with lovely silver and that sort of thing.

Arias fell, Henry rang up Chipps in Caracas and said, "For God's sake come over and sort this out! We don't even know who's President! Every time we try and present our credentials, we're told he's in the Interior," which is the polite South American way of saying, "Fuck off."

So Chipps, as I said before, asked me to get Egon Herbig, the embassy doctor, to fly me down to the Falls of Ayacucho in his Cessna to witness that the Hovercraft got over the Falls safely. He himself then flew to Panama where he was met at the airport by Henry Hankey, which was unusual as he was generally met by somebody lower down. Henry said, "I think, Chipps, you might as well go back to see your Hovercraft crossing the Falls, because, even though I've rung the National Guard to say you're coming to visit the

President, they're still saying he's in the Interior." But Chipps said, "Give me a dime," and he went over and rang up the National Guard on an airport telephone. He thought he recognised the voice which answered so he said, "Oh, how are you, comrade! I'm here and I'd love to see you," and he got to see him in twenty minutes, and this was Pinilla, the new dictator, who even the American Ambassador didn't know! Not only that, during their half hour conversation, Chipps flogged him a couple of Vosper patrol boats to start a Panamanian Navy. Rather marvellous, especially in view of his prophecy, nine months before, to the Foreign Office!

I'll always remember, shortly after this, going down to the transit lounge at La Guaira, the airport for Caracus that's down to the sea, to have a talk and a drink with Margot Fonteyn. I said, "Would you like to come and stay with me for a week or two?" But she said she just had to go back to London for a dancing engagement. She really did have to work terribly hard to keep her husband – he had been shot, and even had to have people to lift him in and out of their swimming-pool.

We went from Panama to Santo Domingo where Snowy and his ships were now on manoeuvres. Santo Domingo, which is Spanish speaking, is one half of a large island next to Cuba, and Haiti which is French speaking, is the other half. It was Easter. I remember it was Easter because Jamie, who'd been at Eton for a term, joined us there two days later for his Easter holidays. The First Secretary met us at the airport and dropped us at the Embassy. Despite the heat I was specially wearing gloves and a hat and my best dress to meet Ian Bell, the ambassador, but he opened the door with two large buckets in each hand, and naked save for a sarong round his middle. He was going to flush the loo. He and his wife, Ruth, were terribly nice – they now live in Scotland – but, whenever we went to stay with them, there was a complete water shortage, and the only way to flush the loo was to use water from the indoor swimming-pool. Our room, interestingly, was the one in which Graham Greene wrote *The Comedians* about the Tonton Macoutes and Papa Doc in Haiti.

When Jamie arrived, I gave him a bottle of soda water and said to him, "Darling, you've got to wash with this. We haven't got water in any of the taps."

That weekend I took Jamie to stay with one of the generals who shot Trujillo, the then dictator, in an ambush in 1961. The first evening, we were having drinks on the terrace of his home overlooking the sea, and Jamie said, "Please, sir, may I see the gun what did the deadly deed?" and the general said, "Yes. Come into my study and I'll show you." Well, you can imagine how Jamie dined out on that at Eton!

Next morning, Jamie and I went swimming. Leaving Jamie closer to shore – he wasn't yet quite thirteen – I swam further out to sea for an hour and a half with a gorgeous barracuda in front of me. I talked to him, just like I talk now to Porfirio, and I knew that I was perfectly safe: we had a relationship, a long flirtation. Everyone said I was mad as barracudas are as vicious as sharks.

When Jamie and I got back to the man what did the deadly deed, he told us how Trujillo used to throw his enemies alive into these shark infested waters. That very afternoon, in fact, a child's hand was taken off by a barracuda – not by my friend, I hope. While the general was talking, we heard footsteps approaching from the beach. The guard immediately cocked his gun, the general froze and his wife looked terrified. I thought, "Gosh! Now he's going to be assassinated!" It was only a fisherman returning with his rod, but it shows the jittery state they lived in. The "other side" had once tried to assassinate him outside the British Embassy when Ruth was having a bath, and they nearly killed his chauffeur.

We returned to our waterless embassy and, before going to bed, I opened the window as I hate air-conditioning. When I woke, I saw a tarantula just by the bed. Thank God, Chipps killed it by throwing a shoe. I'm not crazy about vampire bats either. There were an awful lot of them in Caracas where they were inclined to go for the horses and suck the blood from their necks. It you're not careful, they can give you tetanus. Chipps came back from riding one morning – he used to ride early while it was cool before going to the embassy and as I went in to have my bath at about eight o'clock, there clinging to his riding boots, was a vampire bat – attracted by the smell of horse sweat. The stables had to have special nets to protect the horses from vampire bats.

Chipps rode a lot in Caracas. His predecessor, Anthony Redman, had brought out a horse, Baby, and he sold it to Chipps as he didn't want the trouble of shipping it back to England. We couldn't, of course, hunt – it was all too uneven and mountainous – but Chipps rode with the Presidential Mounted Guard and I rode when I was up in the Venezuelan mountains or in Bogota . . .

Back in Santo Domingo, Jamie and I were finishing breakfast one morning – Ian and Chipps had gone to see the President or something and Ruth was at the hairdresser because she and Ian were having a cocktail party that evening for the President and Snowy and so on – when suddenly two little black boys appeared at the table to say they'd found a cave. Ian Bell was an archaeologist and, when he came to Santo Domingo, he said, "While I'm here en poste, I want to enrich your Government Museum so you can really study your archaeology. In your caves you've got the most marvellous artefacts carved from stalactites made by water that had passed through coral. They're very, very old, pre-Columbian, and all you do with them, when you find them, is sell them to the American tourists."

From then on, everybody who found a cave immediately came to tell him, and, when these little boys announced that they'd found a cave, I said, "Wait a minute" and tracked down Ian on the phone. He said, "Take the Land-Rover. Take the chauffeur. Take a picnic. Take lots to drink. Give me half what you find. If you don't get back by tonight's party, I will tell the President you've got flu."

So off we went with the chauffeur, Jamie and I and the two little black boys, in search of artifacts. We went miles and miles until the road petered out completely and we found ourselves in scrub, dry scrub built on coral where we could drive no longer. I asked the boys, "How far is the cave?" They said, "*Tres kilometros*." I thought, "That'll take me about twenty minutes to walk. We won't want a picnic." So Jamie and I and the two little boys ate a biscuit each and took one thermos of water, and we started walking. The chauffeur – clever chauffeur! – stayed in the Land-Rover, which he said it was his duty to guard, with the picnic including our main drinks. We walked for three hours! "*Tres kilometros*" was certainly more than three kilometres. we became really dehydrated. I was saying to Jamie, "Darling, we've only got the one thermos. You must swill the water round your mouth before you swallow it, and make it last for ages." Anyway, we found the cave, a virgin cave save for one set of little footprints.

We went in. We hadn't the strength to dig for more than an hour and a half but, during that time we found ten pieces, of which I still have half. They've been dated by the British Museum at 2,900 B.C. I'm sure Thor Heyerdahl is right when he says these cave dwellers came from the Middle East and travelled down to Easter Islands. One of the pieces depicts a sheep. But then there were no sheep then in Santo Domingo though there were plenty in the Middle Eest. Ian told Commodore Jimenez, the head of the Navy, about the cave, and it was excavated for the Government Museum Jimenez was very attractive. We were great friends.

We were back in time for the Embassy party that evening. In Santo Domingo you dance – slow, sultry merenges – at all parties, and, while I was dancing with Jimenez, I asked could I take my artefacts out of the country – being a diplomat, I couldn't possibly smuggle them – and he said he would have them cleared.

Then, at about one o'clock Ruth came up to me and said, "Dodo, for God's sake, make Snowy behave! He's taken his shoes off and he's nibbling the American Ambassadress's ear. The Ambassador is getting very upset!" So I went up to Snowy and I said, "Snowy, you've to dance with me now!" He said, "Oh, Dodo, must I?" I said, "Yes, and with your shoes on! otherwise you'll have to stay with the Lincolns next time you're in Caracas!"

The next day, Chipps, Jamie and I were supposed to be going back to Caracas together, but the visit had been so successful that Jimenez asked Chipps to stay behind to talk about naval sales and what have you. We swapped tickets therefore with Bill and Betty-Fox Vale who'd planned to leave on an earlier flight. I was sorry about that because their plane was hijacked and taken to Cuba! I'd have enjoyed the experience. Betty-Fox told me that when they arrived in Cuba, the hijacker was arrested at once and put in handcuffs. Bill and she then pretended to be ordinary tourists, but it didn't work. They were ushered into a V.I.P. room and given marvellous cigars before being put on another plane.

Something dreadful happened on Good Friday. We got back from Santo Domingo to Caracas on Maundy Thursday. Next morning, Chipps went out riding with Bliss at six o'clock – even though Bliss had a heart problem and we were living at three thousand feet in the heat, he adored following Chipps out riding. Later that morning, while Carol and I were packing for a ten day holiday in the Mesa de Esnujaque, a gorgeous plateau eight thousand feet up in the Andes, Pearl came to me suddenly and said, "There's something wrong with Bliss – in the garden." So I went into the garden and there he was, obviously very ill.

I don't want to go into details: I don't want to think about it even. Ortez, who was still our chauffeur, put him in the Land-Rover and we drove straight to the vet. The vet said, "I don't know if I can save him, but you must leave him here." So I left him – I had to go back: I was giving a lunch party and there was more packing to be done. But I rang the vet every five minutes and finally, at about six o'clock, he said to me, "I've given him another Coramine injection, but he won't live long." So I drove in at once and I stayed with him until he died.

He died in my arms and it broke my heart. He was nearly seven and most retrievers live till they are nine. The climate and the altitude had been too much for his poor heart. Everybody in Caracas said, "You must get another dog immediately," but I couldn't. They were thinking of murder and burglary and God knows what. They knew my habit of leaving doors unlocked. Peter Muller, the Austrian Ambassador, was really cross with me one night when Chipps was away. He drove me back from a party and, when he found the front door open and all the silver on the table, he said, "You're absolutely awful the way you do this! You're a very bad example!"

Anyway, we drove to the Mesa de Esnujaque, going through Barquisimeto, then over the Llanos and up into the Andes. The place was very, very wild, not developed at all save for our small hotel. The extraordinary thing about the Andes is that they've a different climate at different heights, so at one height you grow wheat, at another you grow avocados, at another you grow pineapples, at another you grow bananas and at another you grow something else. Right at the top is the Paramo or desert where there's just what they call *Frailiejon*, a velvety kind of flower that looks like a monk's hood.

At our level of eight thousand feet there was nothing but lovely grass growing everywhere and wild lupins. I thought to myself, "Here's this grass which grows in the blazing sun for six months of the year. It ought to grow in Gozo." So I took some seed – it was spring, you see – and I put it in an envelope and I sent it to Johnnie de Brincat, the Director of Agriculture in Gozo and a friend of mine, and I said to him, "Will you sow it in my garden in Gozo so I've a lawn when I get back?" and, when I got back, I found I had a lawn and, apart from the de Traffords' lawn at the Villa Bologna, it's the only decent lawn in Malta. I arrived there once at the Customs with a simple push lawnmower." They said, "What is this machine? Is it a bomb?" I said, "It's a lawnmower." They said, "What's a lawn?"

If I'd been a businessmen like Nelson Rockerfeller, who I got to know very well in Venezuela, I'd have made golf courses all over the Mediterranean with that grass. But I've never been a businesswoman, thank God. I said to my great friend, President Leone, "Can I have the concession for all the grass in the Mesa de Esnujaque if ever I got somebody to make golf courses all over the Sahara?" He said, "Yes. You have my word on it."

I met Nelson Rockerfeller a great deal socially in Caracas. We'd talk about my lectures in the U.S.A. on Marshall Aid and that sort of thing. I know he died, poor darling, "in the act" with his mistress, and I know that he was eventually *persona non grata* in Venezuela when he came there as Nixon's envoy, but I liked him very much, and he did an enormous amount of good. The Cada chain of supermarkets was his. By the time I left Caracas he'd changed the face of the Mesa. He hired trucks to go there with masses of fertiliser and he paid people, who spoke Indian and who understood the locals, to show them how to use it. The same trucks picked up the produce of the area for selling in his supermarkets.

Chipps and I considered the Mesa absolute heaven. On that first holiday we hired ponies and went riding. We also went skiing on Pico Bolivar which is fourteen-thousand feet high and where there's snow all the year round. Chipps panted like crazy up there, and Jamie and Bruce both had height sickness. But height doesn't worry me: I love heights. Once, on the road to Buenaventura in Colombia, Chipps and I came to a rope bridge, slung over a wide gorge with nothing to hold on to. Chipps was terrified but I walked over it like a tightrope. Ballet and those parapets at Lytchett Manor in my youth had taught me balance.

We went back to the same hotel on the Mesa several times after that, without the children. Chipps had decided to leave the Navy and go into the City on our return to England and he found the hotel ideal for studying for his Chartered Secretary's exam – he sat it eventually at the British Embassy in Bogota, invigilated by a man from the British Council. In fact, all the time we were in South America he'd studied on a Sunday unless we were doing something official, and I'd hear and correct his lessons in bed. In '67, on our second trip to the Mesa, Chipps literally studied from seven in the morning till twelve at night. One day, a sweet little boy called Jesus came to the hotel – he was a friend of one of the cooks – and I asked him would he like to go for walks with me. Jesus was an Indian child, the son of a farmer. He was a very pretty little boy, about nine years old, and I adored him. We climbed all over the mountain together, collecting orchids. By now I had a marvellous collection of orchids in my garden. I took them from the jungle and places most other diplomats' wives, who stuck to the Caracus round, never went. Anyway, Jesus and I climbed all over the mountain and one day I saw a gorgeous scarlet orchid under a sort of hanging cliff. I braced myself on a tree and I held Jesus' feet and he got it for me. I said to him, "Jesus, I must give you a Bolivar for that." To such a child, a Bolivar was a fortune: they were ten to a Pound. To give him more would have been wrong. He said, "Can I have a tin?" So I gave him an empty cigarette tin saying, "Yes, Jesus. But explain to me why." He said, "Come to my home tomorrow and I'll explain to you why."

So he took me up to his home the next day – a great honour – to meet his father and his mother and his grandmother. His father had had about seventy children by various women and most of them were away robbing or bumming around in Caracas. But those who had actually earned some money were allowed to stay and farm. They kept their money in tins and, on a shelf above the mud where they cooked their maize, I saw eight tins including the one I'd given Jesus. Jesus, at his small age, had made a bolivar and his father was going to allow him to stay on the farm.

Chapter 36

More Caribbean Excitement

It was summer, the wet season, and the Navy were coming to Cartagena, the Colombian naval base. Bogotá, the capital, is very high up, and the airport is entirely surrounded by mountains – quite hairy coming in to land, especially if there's a thunderstorm, which there often is.

Bogotás quite different to Caracas. The Colombian upper classes are very Spanish, much more so than in Venezuela, and they have white skins as in Mexico. Caracas is a sort of international, bustling, rather Americanised town full of rich people and, despite the *ranchitos* and some appalling conditions, with a mostly happy, well-off working class. Bogotá I found cold – it's eight-thousand feet up – and dark – because of the thunder clouds – and the Indians in their woollen *ruanas* and round black hats looked miserable.

Bogatá is terrible for muggings and robbings. We were told by the chauffeur who met us that, whenever he stopped at a red light, he wound the window up even if it was hot because otherwise muggers put their hand through the window and seized your watch and money, if they could get at them, while holding a gun to your head.

We were staying with Hilary Young, the Ambassador, and his wife Barbara – they became great friends of ours. A week before we arrived, the wife of Philip Ziegler, who was Counsillor at the Embassy, was murdered by burglars who broke into their flat at night. The burglars had taken his diplomatic uniform and when she ran after them, they turned round and shot her dead. We didn't actually see Philip in Bogotá because he'd been sent home after the tragedy with the nanny and the children – that's when he went to work for his father-in-law, William Collins, the publisher.

During another of our visits, a secretary at the Embassy had her handbag seized whilst queueing outside the main cinema and, when she tried to hang on to it, the mugger shot her in the foot.

All this happened in the small circle of the Embassy so you can imagine what Bogotá was like as a whole. Actually, I'm never twitched by that sort of thing and I can't say it worried me frightfully. But the fact is Bogotá struck me as sad and not gay and busy like Caracas. Even the huge Salt Mine

Cathedral was eerie. But at least I could ride. Clive Russell, an ex-Naval chap we knew, gave us an introduction to some awfully nice people who had a lovely ranch just outside the town, and we could gallop over grass, unlike in Caracas which was either all rocks and mountains, or rainforest.

After our trip to Leticia to make preparations for the Hovercraft's expedition up the Amazon – I had an official party paid for by the Queen, at the embassy. A Defence Attaché, you see, gives an annual party for the local Army, Navy and Airforce officers. In Caracas I gave such parties in my own home but because, in Bogota, I was staying with Barbara and Hilary, they were kind and generous and let me give it in theirs. They even did all the invitations through the embassy and arranged the food.

All I had to do was receive the guests, with Barbara introducing them to me. And, that morning, she gave me breakfast in bed and came up with a list of those that were coming and described them to me in perfect detail. She said, for instance, that General de Brigadá Franz Risquez was fat and very dark, that his wife had blue eyes and a long nose and reddish hair, that they had X number of children and they liked doing this, that or the other, so that, when I actually met them, I'd remember them from her description and have something to talk about.

Barbara was a frightfully organised ambassadress. For instance, when Chipps ran into Christopher Dilke, my cousin Alice Dilke's husband who ran the Education Department of the B.B.C., she didn't hesitate to say "Yes" when he asked could he invite them to the Embassy for lunch.

Next we went up to Cartagena for the British Fleet Visit. The Colombian Navy, of course, was at Cartagena, and, as Chipps was the first Naval officer to be Defence Attaché, he interested them greatly. In fact, when we left South America, they awarded him a Naval medal which he had to refuse as a British diplomat isn't allowed to accept such things.

The Colombian Navy had, in effect, been founded just before the war by a British Royal Navy Commander called Bell-Salter who'd retired after a row with his captain. Colombia, at the time, was having a dispute with Peru and they recruited him to found a Navy and do a Pearl Harbour on the Peruvian Navy, using a couple of destroyers and some torpedo aircraft. Eventually the row with Peru quietened down so he just concentrated on getting the Navy into shape, buying British Naval uniforms from Gieves and starting a Naval College where he instilled everyone with our lingo and traditions. Then the war broke out in 1939 and he was called back to serve as Commander Bell-Salter, RN, and was no longer Admiral Bell-Salter, Commander-in-Chief of the Colombian Navy.

When Chipps was told all this, he immediately contacted the Admiralty and was informed that Bell-Salter was still alive. The Colombians said, "This is extraordinary! What Nelson is to you, he is to us! He must come out to celebrate the founding of our Navy and be the hero of the whole thing!" So Chipps wrote to him, but his letter back said that, at the age of eighty-five, he didn't fancy the idea of the height of Bogotá. So Chipps helped instead to form a Bell-Salter Society for Colombian Naval officers who'd been trained in England.

We went to Cartagena in a Colombian Air Force Dakota, and sitting opposite me was a general's wife who'd never been in an aeroplane like this in her life and was absolutely thrilled. In military Dakotas you don't have airline seats – just canvas benches round the walls. During the flight, we hit an air pocket and went down with a bump, and the canvas seat on which she was sitting broke and she ended up on the floor. I leapt to pick her up, saying in Spanish, "Are you all right, Señora?" and she just looked at me with a seraphic smile on her face and said, "Oh, *you're* here! I thought we'd crashed and I'd gone up to heaven!" I've never seen anyone look happier. Too funny. Sweet little woman she was.

Waiting for us at Cartagena among the fleet was H.M.S. *Rhyl*, John Templeton-Cotill's old frigate on which I'd often been his hostess in Malta! So now I was Mrs. Rhyl again with a different captain but as a Defence Attaché's wife! When I arrived on board, I said, "This is the *fourth* time I've been Mrs. Rhyl!" And, tied up alongside, was a submarine whose First Lieutenant was Rupert, the son of my Dorset cousin, Tommy Best, the Admiral. His mother was a Lees. So I spent an awful lot of time on Rupert's submarine. I'm frightened in a lift but not in a subarine, I don't know why.

At the end of the Naval visit, which lasted about a week and included various joint exercises arranged by Chipps, the Colombian Air Force flew us up to San Andres for two days leave. San Andres is fascinating. It's an island belonging to Colombia, but is off the coast of Nicaragua, with gorgeous palm trees and sand and coral – the coral is the most beautiful I've seen anywhere except in Boca Seca in Venezuela. On San Andres, which used to be English – it was Captain Morgan's base for his attack on Panama, and his treasure is supposed to be buried there. We found that almost everyone was negro and English speaking, being the descendants of the English plantation owners' slaves. They didn't particularly like the Colombians, who took the island over after the English left.

We stayed in a terribly tumble-down ropy hotel, the only one in those days. Awfully nice people, but, the first morning, Chipps went into our bathroom *en suite* to shave and, within minutes, the washbasin had disintegrated and our suitcases were floating about our room in two feet of water. We were given another room and, the next morning, the same thing happened. We didn't really mind. There was a little island we swam to where its only inhabitant cooked fish for us over a wood fire, and we'd swim around there for hours and hours, looking at forests and palaces of coral inhabited by brilliant aquamarine and cobalt spotted fishes, all the most colourful fishes in the world.

On the beach at San Andres, 1967.

Chipps decided that San Andres would be ideal for a Naval visit. There were plenty of girls and the sailors could also enjoy the bathing. So the following year, '68, he arranged for H.M.S. *Caprice* to stop off there, and returned, on this official occasion, with Hilary and Barbara Young. Because San Andres was Captain Morgan's Island, some of the crew did a landing dressed as pirates in a longboat – you know, one of them hobbled on one leg, some had blacked-out teeth or had patches over their eyes, and they let off *Very* lights. Of course, the natives adored all of this as they'd much rather have still been English, and the sailors were lent scooters and didn't have to pay for a drink the whole time they were on the island. At the end of the visit, when the Governor and his wife gave an official dinner for Hilary and Barbara and Chipps and me, the Governor's wife said to me, "Your husband had done us a favour. Let's hope there will be some real English blood in this island now!"

In Leticia, my friends, the *peliado* Indians had given me two little parakeets in a box, and when we were leaving Bogotá after our first trip, I said to Barbara, "Will it be difficult to get these birds *out*?" She said, "You'll have to go through the Ministry. It'll take weeks. If I were you, I'd not say anything about them." So, to avoid officialdom, I hid them under my fur coat till we were actually on board our Dakota. I adored those two sweet little birds, Jungle and Jim, and I bought a cage for them, and I let them out loose on the trees by day and got them in at night. Although they'd never been in captivity before, they were frightfully tame.

But I was doing the tables on the terraces for the party after the Shorland fiasco, when there was a terrific gust of wind and rain and one of my darling birds fell into the swimming-pool and was caught in the filter and drowned, and the other one flew away looking for him. Though a huge crowd were coming to dinner and to dance to a Venezuelan Navy Band, I just stayed by my swimming-pool and wept and wept.

Geza Payachevich was a great friend of Blancie van Nispen's; he was a Yugoslavian Count who had escaped from Tito's Yugoslavia without much money because all his properties had been confiscated. Well, Geza arrived early with some loose orchids for me to put in a vase. Usually in Caracas you were sent flowers in advance, all done up in beautiful ways in baskets. Half the time I'd take them out of their baskets and arrange them myself, but I couldn't do this with all of them for a party this size. I mean, I probably had a hundred baskets: the whole of the staircase was lined with them! Anyway, Geza brought me *loose* flowers and, finding me in tears by the side of the pool, he said, "Don't worry, Dodo. I'll ask my Indians in Yutaje to find you a parrot to replace your parakeets. It will be waiting for you when you come with me there, which I hope you will be one day soon."

In Venezuala, if you sit on a piece of land for twenty years and improve it, it's yours, and Geza had sat on a piece of land called Yutaje in the Amazon jungle where he'd made great friends with the Indians and taught their head man Spanish so he could communicate with them. These Indians used to cut him Heart of Palm which the Venezualan Air Force flew up to Caracas for canning – it's the most delicious delicacy.

He was also planning to turn the place into a safari camp for American tourists which he'd fly down in the Shell plane or in Dr. Herbig's Cessna. Anyway in '68 Geza took me down to Yutaje in a party and fulfilled his promise to give me a parrot, my darling Porfirio. Joost and Mel de Liefde were now Lord and Lady Shell as Mike and Nina Pocock had departed and we went down with them in the Shell plane. Also in the party were the Austrians Peter and Elizabeth Muller, the Dutch Hupi and Blancie van

Nispen, a Hungarian couple called Dolanyi and the Lebanese Ambassador and his wife.

We arrived at Yutaje, this absolutely divine place in the Amazonas surrounded by rain forests with a waterfall and a clean pool underneath where we could swim free of danger from the river's piranhas. We slept in mosquito nets on hammocks under roofs of jungle leaves, and Geza's partner, an Italian, cooked us Italian food from the store-house. We landed on this airstrip cut by Geza's Indians in the jungle, and, at once, the head man came up to Geza and told him one of the Indians had been struck and infected by a branch while climbing a tree for Heart of Palm, could he please be taken to Caracas to be seen by Dr. Herbiq in his clinic?

So Joost's pilot took him to Caracas and returned with him after five days when he came to fetch us. I'll always remember his tribe coming up the river in their canoes to greet him. Many of them were naked and they stood by the airstrip, with his wife and relations at the front, looking at their feet while they waited for the plane to arrive. When he got out of the plane, he stood quite still and, after about five minutes; his wife went forward and felt him all over, literally all over, before talking to him. Then everyone went forward. I asked the head man later what the Indian had thought of Caracas this was the first time in his life he'd been away from the jungle. He said, "There are a lot of Jeeps!" (the only car he'd ever seen was Geza's jeep) and, "Oh, that river is big!" – this was the Caribbean.

I was shown Porfirio the very first evening. After we'd had a swim and looked at jaguar prints and the bird life and the *chiguirris* and snakes and then had some supper on tiny little deck chairs, rather uncomfortable, round the camp fire, Geza said to me, "Your parrot is now six months old and the Indians have called him Porfirio. Do you want to come and see him?" "Yes," I said, "I long to." Actually, I think Geza probably called him Porfirio, and also taught him his rude words – Geza was always pulling my leg. Anyway, he took me into the Indian part of the encampment and the head man showed me Porfirio and told me he'd live to be a hundred and relate to me completely and never leave me, thinking I was another bird.

So I returned to Caracas with Porfirio who was free by day but lived in the parakeets' cage on the terrace at night. I also brought back two red-spotted tortoises I found in the jungle. And I brought back some gorgeous orchids which Peter Muller helped me to collect during a canoe excursion we made together down river. Geza put a mattress for us in a canoe and we lay back in complete comfort and travelled for miles and miles and hours and hours. With one Indian paddling and one in front fishing and using a machete to cut away the branches, we went through waters boiling with caribes to places few English people had ever been before.

Among the orchids we found, was a *floré de nacre*, the most beautiful orchid of all and one of the most rare. In the end, because I went to such unusual places, you see, I had almost the best collection of orchids in Caracas. I put them on bits of bark which I hung around the walls of the garden and they just grew and flowered for me, which they don't do for everybody. They cling, but they aren't parasites. They don't eat from the bark: they absorb their food from the rain. It's frightfully exciting because you suddenly see a little sort of swelling start and you know your orchid is going to flower.

So I returned to Caracas on the shell plane with Porfirio, two giant tortoises and my orchids – all of them in boxes. The Shell plane was very comfortable. You had a table and chairs like in a drawing-room. Peter and I – Peter was a bridge champion of Austria – decided to play bridge with Elizabeth, who was also very good at bridge and the Lebanese Ambassador who was bridge champion of the Lebanon. It was the most hairy journey, with the plane going bump, bump, bump in a terrific thunderstorm. If you've never played bridge with two national champions in a buffeted plane in the middle of Venezuela with a squawking parrot in a cardboard box at your feet, you can't have any idea what an absolutely fascinating experience this was, especially as Peter and I made grand slam after grand slam!

The story of Porfirio, of course, has ended happily. Not so the story of my two tortoises and my orchids. When the tortoises got back to England, Sid, the gardener, made a run for them and then, during the winter, on the advice of the local zoo, we put them in the garage and covered them with straw to hibernate, and they *seemed* to sleep but they died. An awful thing. I think they were eaten by rats. I should have taken the advice of Audrey Southborough, Moyna's mother-in-law, who kept a tortoise *she* brought back from Venezuela in the hot cupboard during the winter and it lived for ages.

As for my orchids, they all lived for me in Caracas, but, when we were going back in July '69, Geza Gyarfas, another Hungarian friend of mine, said, "You have so many, I'll pack them for you so you can send them by sea." I could have freighted them by air with the tortoises which were met at Heathrow by Kitty, my mother-in-law, and Sid but, alas, I sent them by boat to England with most of our luggage. We couldn't actually take them with us because we were travelling with Porfirio on an Italian liner to Naples. From there, before returning to Slepe, we were going to Gozo to stay in my new house, and then to Massalubrense to stay with Cecilia Foley, then to St. Moritz to stay with Monique de Nervo, and then to stay with Hupi and Blancie van Nispen who'd been moved to the Dutch embassy in Paris.

Anyway, in July '69, I said to Geza, "I'll pack up everything else but will *you* pack the orchids for me last thing so they don't hang about too long?" and he packed them in plastic in moss and put them in a crate and they were supposed to arrive in Southampton in three weeks with the rest of our luggage. But, because of a dock strike at La Guaira, our main luggage and the orchids didn't arrive till well after we got back to Slepe in September. The man who runs the orchid farm at Plush Bottom is a great friend of mine and he'd said he would collect all my orchids and keep them in his orchid house and give them to me when they were in flower. When they *did* arrive, I took the whole crate over to him, and all but four were dead, including my *floré de nacre*. I was offered eight hundred pound for that *floré de nacre* before I left Caracas, but I wouldn't sell it because I loved it so.

I had so many adventures in South America as a diplomat's wife. Apart from the war in France, I consider it the most exciting period of my life. When we got back from Bogotá in '67, we made great friends with Pepito Herrera, the one time Venezuelan Ambassador to Sweden, and his wife, and they invited me to lunch at their house with its gorgeous garden and swimming pool in the Valle del Tuy. "Elizabeth Taylor", – the girl Snowy fell for – took me because she was a friend of Pepito's daughter. All of us, including the daughter, were sitting in the garden having drinks before lunch, and Pepito's wife said she couldn't find her little dog anywhere. We went in to lunch. Still no sign of this little dog. After lunch, we all went out to look for it, and there, on the lawn, was this huge snake with a bulge in its tummy. Pepito rushed out with a machete, cut off its head and found the dog still alive inside. As I said, the Spanish name for such snakes is *tragavenado* which means "deer swallower". They spit out the horns and ingest the deer. It takes ages.

Still on snakes, I want to tell you about an incident involving the American Ambassadress in Caracas. The American Ambassadress gave her usual 4th of July party in '67. Afterwards we were going on to a barbecue given by Betty-Fox Vale and Bill, the American Military Attaché – Bill actually was a very good barbecue cook. Bill and Betty-Fox used to ring me practically every day and say, "This is Betty-Fox, Dodo, just to say hi!" But, at the 4th of July party beforehand, I had a long talk with the American Ambassadress about ham radio as she was a ham radio fan, and it so happened that my sister's husband in Australia was a ham radio fan, and used to get in touch – he still does – with a similar fan in Lytchett village to give us messages.

Anyway, a few days later, a very dramatic thing happened, and, thanks to the American Ambassadress being a radio ham fan, it ended happily. An

Indian child in the Llanos was bitten by a *coro-coro* and, when she got to hear of this, she radioed a man who ran a snake farm in Miami for advice. The *coro-coro*, you see, is supposed to be deadly. He said,"Well, I've been bitten by *coro-coros* on my farm and I've survived. Working with snakes I've built up a resistance. If you can get me to Venezuela, I'll give my blood to the child and see if it gives him the anti-venom."

So the American Air Attaché in the Embassy flew his own plane to Miami, picked this man up and took him back to Caracas, and then the Venezualan Army flew him with an army doctor in a helicopter to this child in the Llanos and the doctor gave a blood transfusion and the child survived.

Afterwards, President Leone, who I loved so dearly, asked the American Ambassadress what he could give this snake farmer in exchange. Would he like a decoration or money? But the farmer said all he would like was that the child give blood to a blood bank every year so that anybody bitten by a *coro-coro* could have a transfusion.

Personally, I'm not frightened of snakes. We were once driving through the Llanos in the Land-Rover and we came across an anaconda in the middle of the road and, thinking it was a fallen tree, we drove over it. As we drove over it, its tail came up and took the spare wheel off the roof. I said, "I don't mind snakes. We don't want to be without a spare wheel so I'll go back for it." Ortez, our chauffeur, wouldn't let me: he pushed me out of the way and went back for it himself. He was lucky the anaconda didn't wrap itself around him and squeeze him to death.

Boca Seca was an island just beyond Puerto Caballo, the Venezuelan Naval base, several hours drive from Caracas. The island was owned, by virtue of twenty years tenure, by a multi-millionairess. She was one hundred per cent German and was the representative for Volkswagon in Venezuela. Blancie introduced me to her. She's still alive, but she's very old and rather ill. She's devoted all her life to the Indians in South America and has taken marvellous films of them and written a book about them with her daughter. She ventured into parts of the Interior nobody else has ever been, and she knew the Caribbean backwards. She really took over Boca Seca because of its coral. It has the most beautiful coral I've seen anywhere in the world, and that includes San Andres and Trincomalee. After my first visit I went there as often as I possibly could because I fell in love with it.

The first time I went there was for a weekend with the van Nispens and their children and Chipps and Bruce and Jamie and Carol. We went out in a launch. There was nobody else on the island at all. It was completely wild and there was no water on it – that's why it's called Boca Seca ("Dry mouth"). As

I'm a great water fiend, I insisted on taking four great bidons of water on the launch with us apart from our soft drinks and limes and wines. Blancie pulled my leg about it. She said, "My God, Dodo! Aren't you going to have whisky the whole time you're there?" Otherwise we only took biscuits because we knew we could fish for our meals and cook what we caught over a fire on the beach.

The owner had made a hut with three bedrooms and a terrace out of Volkswagon packing cases whose foam-rubber lining she used for chairs and beds. The children slept outside in hammocks slung on the terrace. It was all very primitive, but frightfully comfortable. We swam all day and had a camp fire of driftwood to cook our fish.

This was the sort of life I loved in Venezuela. Bruce and I often used to stay with Venezuelan Generals and Admirals and people in their shacks on the coast – they invited us because they knew we wouldn't mind roughing it. For instance, an Air Force general and his wife took us out to their shack on an island near Catya. The mangroves there were absolutely *covered* with oysters. Bruce spent a whole afternoon opening them with a knife. I'm sure I ate ninety. I trod on a sea urchin, I remember. Some Air Force officers, all terribly high and making terribly rude gestures and saying, "She loves the candle!", melted a candle and poured wax on my foot – the wax takes away the inflammation and the sea urchin's spikes get stuck in the wax and you can pull them out.

Anyway, at Boca Seca, everybody had laughed about my four bidons of water but, on the last day, the men were jolly glad to use what was left to shave with. After three days in the wild it's awfully painful shaving with sea water which won't lather. So I got full marks for that.

Another island we stayed on was Orchilla. According to Chipps, the former dictator of Venezuela used it as a hunting ground for girls. Girls flown in from Cuba were let loose every Friday night and, next morning, the Cabinet would arrive and set off on motorbikes and chase them with airguns and have sex with them in the dunes. Admiral Carbonell, the Minister of Defence, and his wife, once lent me their bungalow on Orchilla and I went there by a Naval plane with Bruce and Jamie and Kitty, my mother-in-law, who had flown out to stay with us too.

It was the most gorgeous holiday. One night the Naval chap who ran the place gave us gloves, and the eight of us, paddling in a line, picked up langoustas with our hands. The Naval chef then cooked them for us and they were absolutely delicious. By day, of course, we swam. The water was crystal clear. One afternoon Kitty was bobbing around wearing that mask thing you use to look at coral and, as Jamie and I walked along the jetty, he suddenly shouted, "Look, Mummy! Granny Kitty's being followed by barracudas!" He dived in at once and they went away because of the splash. There were *three* of them!

Clive Russell introduced us to a couple called Pippinger in Caracas. He was an American businessman and she, Josie, was a Venezuelan. The fishing fields off La Guaira are some of the best in the world, and Josie had her own fishing boat for deep sea fishing. She said to me, "Would you and your husband and the children like to come fishing with me?" I said, "We'd simply adore to."

So we all went out, but it was choppy and Chipps was seasick and Jamie was seasick, so another boat came to fetch them back to Camuri Grande where they went swimming, and Josie and I continued on with Bruce. Suddenly we saw a floating log. Josie said, "I bet there's some fish off that log" and, sure enough, we got into a shoal of dorados, lovely, lovely fish which are golden and go blue when they're dead, huge great things, bigger than salmon. You're in your seat with your rod strapped to you, and you throw your line and the boatman does all the manoeuvring, following the fish till you pull it in, but, in this case, the dorados were so numerous that, when I threw in my line, I caught one at once – by the tail! In fact, then we caught so many dorados between us we had to stop fishing early or the boat would have sunk. I gave mine to friends including Mel de Liefde, who had a big freezer, and to Francesca next door who made us delicious cold *sancotcho*.

The next week Josie invited me and Bruce to go out fishing with her again. I simply adored it: it was great fun because I liked Josie so much. First, we had a picnic on board this lovely boat of hers, just the three of us and the boatman and his assistant. Then, after Josie had fished for about an hour and caught nothing, she handed the rod to me. I sat down, took the rod, and, almost immediately, hooked a blue marlin. The boatman got terribly excited and, talking very quickly, rushed back, shoved his assistant from the wheel to sit at it himself, and he and I together fought that blue marlin for an hour – you can't do it by yourself, you see. Josie, who'd been fishing for years, said, "Dodo, you *are* lucky! I've never caught such a big one in my life." It was ninety kilos, a hundred and eighty pounds, bigger than Hemingway's! Twelve stone! More than *I* weigh! And it was longer than me, too – three metres at least. Absolutely incredible.

While I was still fighting it, I looked round, and Bruce was quite white. He flung his arms around me; he thought I was going to be taken away by the marlin, and I could have been, I suppose, but for the boatman being so good the way he quickly followed the fish every time it jumped and pulled. I had backache for a week! When we'd landed and done the weighing, we asked everybody at the Puerta Azul Club, where the launch was moored, for a camera, as mine was at home, but the sad thing is nobody had one so there's no photographic record of me with my blue marlin. As it was too big to bury, we gave it to fishermen for bait.

Egon Herbig, the embassy doctor, used to fly us to a bit of land he had on the coast where he'd built a hotel for the Military as a means of extra income. One day, we went for a swim there after lunch, and the sea was full of jelly fish. Herbig said, "Oh, don't bother about them. They're not the sort that sting." At that moment, I was stung on the left arm by a Portuguese Man of War! He said, "You'll have a weal until the day you die," but I put on my marvellous Anthisan stuff and the weal had gone in half an hour. Anthisan was something I just couldn't have done without.

Herbig had settled in Venezuela with his German wife and three daughters because he loved the jungle and he loved the Indians, many of whom were his patients. He used to take Bruce and me to extraordinary places in the heart of the jungle, when he was visiting them, often letting Bruce take the controls. The Indians had cut little landing strips specially for Herbig. Once we managed to land with great difficulty on a strip that was very overgrown. After looking around, Herbig said, "Oh, dear! I'm afraid my Indians have moved on to other hunting grounds!" I said to him, "But how on earth are we going to get away from here?" "Oh, that's all right," he said, and he jumped in front of the plane, lit a match to set fire to the runway, jumped back in his seat and took off through the flames quite dramatic, actually. He was crazy but such fun.

Eventually he was killed with his wife and two of his daughters coming into land at Caracas. Airliners come in at La Guaira down at the coast, as Caracas is high up in a sort of a bowl with mountains rising all round it, but there's a little airport up in Caracas for Cessnas and helicopters.

This reminds me of the U.F.O. Bruce and I saw in 1968. We were sitting by the swimming-pool and suddenly we saw something that looked exactly like a flying saucer, silhouetted against the lovely mountain, the rainforest, only five minutes from the house, where I sometimes used to go to pick orchids. We were used to seeing planes from the terrace and we knew the sounds they made, but this wasn't a plane: It was round and silver and it went terribly quickly without making any noise at all. Unless it was a secret weapon of the Russians or the Americans, there's no question but that it was a U.F.O. My eyes were better in those days and I *saw* it, and Bruce saw it, too. And, as I say, it wasn't still, so it couldn't have been a trick of the light.

I must now tell you about two places – Tovar and Angel Falls. Tovar is fascinating. During the nineteenth century, a religious sect in the mountains of Germany was being persecuted and they escaped in a boat and landed in Venezuela where whoever was in charge at the time said, "O.K. You can have some land and settle here, but you must keep to yourselves." They'd brought chickens and bees and seeds and things, so they walked over the mountains to Tovar, and there they settled because it reminded them of home. Indeed the landscape *is* very like Bavaria – it's got pines and blackberries and it's high enough to have a non-tropical climate. They made a completely German village with a little pepperpot church and a bakery and pigs for their *Bratwürst* and *Leberwürst* and they intermarried for generation after generation because there was no road to them: they were completely cut off. And then, before the Second World War during the dictatorship of Gomez, while an escape route was being built out of Caracas to the sea in case the road to La Guaira was blocked by revolutionaries, the Colonia Tovar, which nobody till then knew about, was discovered, and now it's a tourist resort.

The colonists didn't even speak Spanish when they were discovered, and, though they speak some Spanish now because of the tourists, they still speak German among themselves. It's quite extraordinary to find this little bit of Germany where everyone is blue-eyed and fair-haired in the middle of a tropical country.

When John Cronin, the M.P. for Loughborough, came to stay with me in '68, I took him to spend a day at Tovar. On the way back, completely without meaning to – I always lose my way: I've *no* bump of locality – I managed to get into the university which was closed because of the usual gun battle between the students and the Army, and, the next thing we knew, two guards were pointing machine guns straight at us and I had to stop. They insisted on sitting in the back of the car with their guns resting on our shoulders until we'd driven out again. John said, "They simply won't *believe* this when I get back to the House of Commons!"

I was using the Jaguar. In Caracas we had our old Ford Consul, a Jaguar and a Land-Rover. We'd imported the Consul – the Land-Rover came with the job – but we were allowed to import one new car tax free during our three year term, so we imported a grey E-type two seater Jaguar, a divine *décapotable*, for two thousand pounds. We sold it for four thousand pound before we left so we would have enough money to buy a new car afterwards.

Chipps used to drive with his chauffeur either in the Consul or the Land-Rover so the Jaguar was really my car. I usually don't really care two hoots about cars but this car thrilled me because it went frightfully fast, it was terribly comfortable and it was sexy – you couldn't stop at a red light without somebody picking you up.

Anyway, I was taking Bruce from the Spanish school one day and we got to a red light and I stopped. Some Secret Police, who were going in my direction in their big American car, bumped my divine, my precious, Jaguar as they passed, ignoring the red light. I was hopping mad. So I didn't bother about the red light either: I *chased* them, with Bruce shouting instructions. I knew where the Secret Police Headquarters was so, short-cutting them through the University, we went straight there and arrived at the same time. The Major came down. I said, "Look at it! My new car! Your men bumped it, hit and run! I'm Diplomatic! My name is Dodo Selby Bennett. I'm the British Military Attaché's wife!" He said, "Señora, I'm most terribly sorry. Take it to your garage and have it mended and we will pay the bill." Then he angrily turned to his men. "You allowed yourselves to be overtaken by a woman!"

The Secret Police did awful things like hold Cubans' heads in buckets, tortures I disapproved of. I hope they got *their* heads held in buckets.

Angel Falls, Canaima, is the highest waterfall in the world. It falls three thousand feet over the edge of a high table mountain in South East Venezuela, which the Indians think of as a god and where the film *The Lost World* was made with all those pterodactyls and other extinct animals. It's an extraordinary plateau, a completely wild place standing in the middle of the landscape, which you can't get to except in an aeroplane. The story goes that, in the Twenties, there was a chap called Jimmy Angel who bummed around the bars of Panama, making a living by hiring out a little aeroplane. One day a chap said to him, "Will you take me to a plateau where there's a river full of diamonds on the condition that I, only, read the map?" Jimmy agreed so they both got into his little plane and chugged off. Eventually they landed on this plateau and Jimmy Angel began to oil his machine and whatever while the other man disappeared. After about three hours he came back to Jimmy with a suitcase full of diamonds and asked to be taken back to Panama. Jimmy received five hundred dollars for the trip, an awful lot in those days and, ever after that, Jimmy tried to find that plateau on his own. Finally, when he did so, his plane crashed – you can still see it there on top. It took him weeks and weeks to find a way down from the plateau to Canaima and civilisation but, on the way down, he saw this eerie waterfall, falling from the plateau, and that's why it's called Angel Falls.

In '68, Hugh and Antonia Fraser were staying in Caracas with Sir Raymond Smith and his wife Dorothy. Raymond was an agent for various companies and Hugh, being an M.P. and something to do with the Ministry of Aviation, was on an official visit and, just like Chipps, trying to sell things to South America. I had a lunch party for the Frasers – they were cousins of mine, and Hugh's sister, Veronica, was married to Fitzroy Maclean whom I fought at Lancaster.

Brigadier Warburg, Tom Warburg, was staying with us at the time. He was the one that came out for the Army, like Snowy and Mick came out for the Navy; he was Chipps' Army contact with the Ministry of Defence and, like them, he stayed with us several times. Tom was a darling and I simply adored him. He had a face that never changed. He looked frightfully serious and terribly pompous, but he wasn't in the least. Bruce had these stick-on darts, you know, with rubber on the end, that you fire at things with a sort of pistol, and Tom once found one of these in the garden and stuck it on his forehead. I had some frightfully important admirals and people coming in to see Chipps to talk about a forthcoming fleet visit and, for a time, I was so preoccupied that I never noticed that Tom had this thing on! He was a very funny man.

Anyway, it was agreed that about ten of us would go in the Shell plane for a couple of days to a safari camp in Canaima near Angel Falls which we flew right underneath on the way. Poor Hugh, he was absolutely scared stiff: even though he was in the Ministry of Aviation, I've never seen anybody look more terrified. Chipps was terrified too, but Antonia and I *enjoyed* the experience. I took a lovely photo of her and Tom at Canaima by a waterfall below which we all swam when we weren't watching birds and animals in the jungle and looking at the millions of other waterfalls nearby.

Hugh and Antonia Fraser at Canaima.

I also took a photo of Patricia Redman's grave. Patricia was the wife of Anthony Redman, Chipps' predecessor in Caracas and, as she died at Canaima and loved it so, Anthony had arranged for her to be buried there. I sent a copy to Anthony who was now living in Minorca. I must say, when I saw this jungle grave, which was kept very tidy by the owner of the camp, I thought how lucky she was to be buried there. I felt rather an affinity with her, not only because we both loved the jungle so, but also because she looked so like me and, when I first arrived in Caracas, you remember, Nina Pocock thought she *was* me, that I was her ghost.

Another person who stayed with me in Caracas was Ian Farquhar. Ever since I met Howard at Ian's wedding, I've seen Ian on and off throughout my life. In Caracas, he stayed with me twice, actually. The second time, in '68, was the time of the Devil Dances of Yare, that extraordinary mixture of Catholicism and Indian superstition. The Catholic Church has always gone along with the heathen religions. In Roman days it superimposed the Virgin Mary on Venus, and it did the same sort of thing with the Indians in South America. In Yare, there was this annual ceremony when the Indians went to Mass and then did dances, frightfully sexual, dressed in devil masks and blowing pipes and things, before getting drunk and going round raping. I've a devil mask of Yare here in the house. It's got red cheeks and horns and ears and a very long nose. It looks terribly like my father-in-law Andy, the judge. To be raped by somebody wearing that must have been quite terrifying. Anyway, Ian and I watched some of this dancing in the streets which goes on all over the town for most of the day, and then we drove to Puerto Caballo where we spent the night before taking a launch out to Boca Seca.

In May '69 – Bruce had gone to the crammer's in Berkshire and, as we were leaving Caracas in July, Maria had already started on the packing – we went to say goodbye to our other parishes of Colombia, Panama and the Dominican Republic. As always we were always thinking of pennies – all my life I've been thinking of pennies – and in Panama we made enquiries and discovered it was just as cheap to fly to Santo Domingo via the Central American Republics and Mexico as to fly there direct. So up we went to Mexico through Central America. We were both dying to explore. Chipps and I are great explorers. That's why I've loved being married to him. That's why I've had such a marvellous Cook's Tour and travelled the world as Daisy Carter predicted, getting at the *heart* of countries and not just sitting around in hotels. We both agreed terrifically about that and we both learned languages very easily and it was all great fun.

Anyway, after Bogotá and Panama City, we flew each step of the way to Mexico. We went to Costa Rica, where we went into the volcano which blows up occasionally. You could smell the sulphur which was still burning and even more extraordinary than Vesuvius. Then we went to Nicaragua, Honduras, Salvador and Guatemala. Salvador was having a sort of revolution so we were frightfully guarded at the airport, but I managed to buy some divine hand-embroidered tablemats there.

In Mexico City, though we were staying in a hotel, we were welcomed at the airport by the Military Attaché, called Colonel Shackleton, a cousin of Eddie Shackleton, Lord Shackleton, my old friend. When we arrived they looked in my passport and they said, "You can't land. Your vaccination for smallpox is out of date." It was out by one day. It never *dawned* on me to check. We were Diplomatic, we had Diplomatic passports, the Military Attaché was waiting for us outside the barrier, but they said, "NO, no, you cannot land. You must be vaccinated." One day out! Ridiculous, but I could see the régime here was very particular about regulations.

Chipps was all right but I knew that I couldn't get through that barrier and go and have dinner with the Military Attaché until I was vaccinated. So I went into a room where there was a terrific sort of *gauleiter* woman, an enormous great woman in a filthy dirty white coat, holding a needle and the vaccine, and a queue of about twenty people behind me who hadn't got up-to-date vaccinations either. I was at the front because I was a diplomat and, seeing this *gauleiter* in her filthy dirty clothes, I produced a box of matches from my bag, took the needle out of her hand, and lit a match and let it burn under the needle until it went out. Then I said, "Now you can vaccinate me – in my leg," which she did.

The funny thing was the next man in the queue said, "Señora, could I borrow your box of matches?" and the whole queue followed suit. I think I saved a few lives that night. At dinner, the Military Attaché's wife told me that *she* had to be vaccinated on arrival and she had a poisoned arm for six weeks. I said, "Do you mind giving me a hot kettle? I'm going to take the vaccine all out," and I took it all out, using a handkerchief as a hot fomentation.

When we woke in our hotel next morning, the first thing I said to Chipps was, "I'm going to look in the telephone directory and see if there are any Turnbulls." Mexico was the country of my Turnbull ancestors, the main reason *I* was dying to explore it. As I said, my great-grandmother on my father's side was Mejia de Turnbull of Puebla, Mexico. A younger Turnbull son, a relation of the Percys, went out to Mexico to make his fortune and he married a Miss Mejia, the sister of General Mejia who was shot with the Emperor Maximillian. For some reason, their daughter, Bernarda Mejia de Turnbull, came over to England and, after attending lessons with Edward VII, eventually married my great-grandfather Lees, and their son was my grandfather, Sir Elliot Lees.

I looked in the Mexico City telephone book and found "W. Turnbull" so I just dialled the number and said, "Could I speak with the Señora?" She said, "I *am* the Señora." I said, "Before I married, my name was Dodo Lees." She said, "Are you the granddaughter of Sir Elliot Lees, Bart., M.P.?" I said, "Yes, I am." She said, "My husband is your Cousin Walter. I'll send the chauffeur with the car for you straight away." So I rang up Colonel Shackleton, the Military Attaché, and said, "We can't have lunch with you today. We're having lunch with my cousins."

We absolutely fell on each other's necks! Walter – his wife's name was Carmen – was by now eighty-seven. In fact, he died six months after my visit. I think he was so excited to see this English cousin of his that it killed him. He'd run the American Fruit Company in Central America for years so he was quite a rich man.

Walter and Carmen lent us their car and their chauffeur until we left Mexico in four days' time. We went, of course, to all those gorgeous places like the Temples of the Moon and the Temples of the Sun, but we also went to Puebla where, after lunch at her flat, Walter's cousin, my cousin, Maggie Zapata, took us to see the family's town house and *hacienda*. The *hacienda* had been given to the Indians after the revolution. They ran the farm very well but its house, a lovely old Scarlet O'Hara house, was rather falling to pieces. The town house in the city of Puebla was now a hotel.

Chipps said he never thought when he married me in the church in Poole that he'd have a Mexican cousin called Zapata! Actually, I'm sure I've *Aztec* blood – that's why I'd always such an affinity with the Indians. The funny thing is that, though my mother called me Dolores after my Weld grandmother and Our Lady of Dolores, she was unwittingly calling me after the Mexican Revolution which was Communist. A priest went out onto a balcony of little Mexican village called Dolores and cried, "*Viva Mexico*!": *La Grita de Dolores* – the cry of Dolores – was when the Mexican Revolution began. Maggie also showed us the statue of Zaragossa below which the name of my great-great uncle, General Mejia, is inscribed because he fought for him. Chipps took a photo of Maggie and me on the steps. We might have been twin sisters: we looked *exactly* alike, though she was about ten years younger. The photo, alas, was in a suitcase which was stolen from us in Rome when we were staying with Cecilia Foley.

From Mexico, we went to Santo Domingo and stayed with the Bells at the embassy, the one with the water shortage and the spare bedroom, our bedroom, where Graham Greene wrote the *Comedians*. Though Chipps wasn't accredited to Haiti, we decided to go over to Haiti for a jolly, and, it so happened, the British Consul, who was also the Shell representative, arranged for us to stay in the same small hotel in which in the *Comedians* the hero arrives to find a corpse floating in the swimming pool and next morning sees the garden swarming with "Tonton Macoutes", the secret police, lurking behind bushes.

The hotel seemed to be an exact copy of the one in the film, except when we arrived there was no corpse in the pool. But next morning, Chipps was delighted to see a couple of "Tonton Macoutes", complete with suits and dark glasses, lurking behind bushes in the garden. He rushed down and asked them if they really were "Tonton Macoutes", or were just paid by the hotel to give a little atmosphere.

They were fuming and they angrily proclaimed that they were real Tonton Macoutes and I thought that Chipps was going to be shot.

It was a terribly civilised hotel. We had marvellous French food and, in our room, there were flowers and a fridge full of cold drinks. I do want to make the point that, apart from the terror and the voodoo, Haiti was frightfully attractive. I mean, every house and every hut was beautiful. There were even artists painting in the streets. It was like being in the South of France. But, as I say, there was terror too.

We were attending the Consul's party to celebrate the Queen's Birthday when suddenly we saw tanks arriving and Tontons Macoutes climbing up the trees outside with their *mitraillettes*, their machine guns, and in strode Papa Doc and stood in the most awkward place possible, between the sliding doors which separated the food from the guests. As he hadn't been appeared at any other diplomatic functions for a long time, and had chosen to attend the Queen's Birthday, the French ambassadress went up to him and said, "*Je crois que ça va* . . . I think this is going to cause some jealousy, Monsieur Le Président!" to which he replied, "That's exactly what I hope, Madame!"

The next day, when we went on the beach for a sort of sun party, Tonton Macoutes were around us *everywhere* because a Minister was swimming. One of them was half asleep in a deckchair and Chipps – I promise you this is a true story – coolly picked up his *mitraillette*, looked at it and said, "Chicago, 1929. Not a bad year for Thompson sub-machine guns!" Chipps certainly has a lot of guts. The man was furious. Clearly no one had ever touched his precious gun but he did nothing when Chipps returned his weapon.

We returned to Caracas for our *despedidas*, the farewell parties in our honour. In fact, we were given one every night for six weeks before leaving – very exhausting. It was rather embarrassing because other diplomats who were leaving had practically none.

The divine Mel de Liefde said to us, "Put everything in cases and come and stay with Joost and me in the Shell residence for a month. Otherwise you'll be dead," so we stayed with them for a month – they actually let us use their bed. Our successors-to-be decided to take over our tenancy and move in early, but unfortunately they didn't keep our darling servants, Franklin and Maria.

Herbig, at his *despedida*, showed us films he'd taken in the Islas Galapagos. And, for his, my darling Braithwaite put up a special screen in his lovely garden and showed *To Sir with Love* – Sidney Poitier, the star of the film, arranged for a copy belonging to a friend of his to be sent specially from the States. It was an awfully cold night and my host went inside and took the most gorgeous Guianan bedspread off his bed to put round me as a shawl and said I could keep it. Unfortunately that, too, was in the suitcase which was nicked in Rome.

Frankly, the reason for our incredible amount of *despedidas* – they were given for us by everyone almost from the President downwards – was that our stint in Venezuela had been a *succès fou*. And not just Venezuela. I mean, who else but Chipps would have arranged, during exercises between the two Navies, for the Commander of the Colombian Fleet, who was rather ashamed at the state of his ships, to fly his Admiral's flag from a British frigate and then to take command of the combined force from its Ops Room? Such a thing was unheard of! The Americans wouldn't have dreamed of allowing it! And who else but Chipps would have the brilliant idea of founding a Nelson Club for Venezuelan Navy Officers who had been trained in England, and British ex-Naval officers doing business in Caracas? The first meeting was at our house. The second meeting was in a sham English pub called the White Horse, run by two Hungarians. I remember the latter for two reasons. Firstly, to go with our drinks inside the pub before sitting down to dinner out on the patio, I invented tiny little Scotch eggs made with gulls' eggs, breadcrumbs and a sort of ham mousse called *diabolita*. Secondly, during dinner, the lights went out and there was a terrific burst of gunfire from outside. Admiral Carbonell, later the Venezuelan Minister of Defence, quickly put his hand in his pocket, then turned to me and said, "Oh dear I could be courtmartialled. I've forgotten my gun, I'm supposed never to be without it." When men meet men in Venezuela and clasp their hands round one another, it's not just Latin exuberance, it's also to feel if the other's got a gun.

One Venezuelan Admiral was so aware of his limitations that he got cold feet when he was supposed to exercise with a Task Force of ours coming through the Caribbean. Word even got round that he wouldn't dare to take his ships out to sea with ours at all – this after endless diplomacy and advance planning by Chipps. So Chipps told me to go on a roof in Puerto Caballo at eight o'clock in the morning and see what happened. I went up on the roof and I saw three Venezuelan destroyers leaving harbour with the Royal Navy ships. I thought, "Thank God!" But the Admiral *had* opted out, claiming he was ill.

Darling Felix Mendosa, who was only a Captain then, had taken command solely to back Chipps up. From that moment Felix was our friend, and we're *still* great friends – he has a house in Richmond. His wife, Patricia, was English. They met when he was visiting Barrow-in-Furness as a young Naval officer, training in England. Later, after he'd got to the top of the Naval tree, he came as Venezuelan Ambassador to London and I was very involved with him when I tried to get Venezuelan oil for Malta . . .

To give you an idea of how highly Chipps was thought of in Caracas, when, afterwards, he was in the City and we went to a Party given by Sir Raymond Smith for Admiral Carbonell at Claridge's, I remember Admiral Carbonell saying in front of an admiral of our Ministry of Defence that Chipps was the best Naval Attaché Caracas had ever had. The irony is that this particular British admiral had never much appreciated Chipps . . .

Chipps and Dodo with Officers of the Venezuelan Navy on board H.M.S. Zest.

On the ship from La Guaira to Naples, Porfirio's cage had to be up on deck just like Bliss's on the journey out. In the cage next to his were about twenty parrots belonging to a priest who was taking them to sell in Spain. They were sad-looking and terribly mangy. I thought, "Oh gosh, they've probably got ghastly diseases which I don't want given to Porfirio!" so I spoke to the sailor in charge and he said, "Don't worry. I won't give him the same feeding bowl." He absolutely *adored* Porfirio and we were both terribly sorry for these mangy creatures and felt they wouldn't have the happy life Porfirio was going to have with me. I mean, even on board ship, I took Porfirio out of his cage every day and walked him round the deck on my finger.

Jamie and Bruce, now fifteen and eleven respectively, were both in England. Bruce was to join us in Gozo, but Jamie had been put on a plane by Moyna Hopwood to stay with Paul and Henriette Vieilhomme in St. Tropez. Henriette planned to drop Jamie in Nice so he could join us when we called in there. Unfortunately our annoying Italian captain arrived in Nice at six o'clock in the morning instead of eight in the evening, so, when Henriette arrived with Jamie, we'd already sailed, but we sent her a cable from the bridge and she put him on a plane so he could catch up with us at Naples.

At Naples, after collecting Jamie and a new car arranged for by Chipps, we drove down through Calabria in no time at all as it now had a motorway. Then, from Syracuse, we crossed in the ferry to Malta, and on to Gozo where my house, already vacated by my tenant, was waiting for us with my darling maid, Josephine, and my marvellous gardener and my marvellous lawn, sown with seeds from the Mesa. We spent the whole of August swimming and boating, and I, of course, was also very busy setting the house in order and making a report on tourism for the Prime Minister.

Then it was back to Slepe Green via Rome, St. Moritz, Paris, Le Havre and Southampton. In Rome, as I've already said, we lost a suitcase – while we were dining in Trastevere with Cecilia Foley and her boyfriend Riccardo de Laurentis: our car was broken into. Otherwise we had no mishaps. And Porfirio was so *adaptable*! It was snowing when we were staying with Monique at St. Moritz but he was perfectly happy. At the ferry in Le Havre, I said to Chipps, "I've all the papers for Porfirio but the children are tired and there's going to be endless chit-chat. I'll hide him under my fur coat." And that's what I did: I smuggled him into England.

We arrived back at Slepe Green in early September. It seemed we'd been away for years and years instead of only three.

Part 12

Swan Song

Chapter 37

SONS

So we've reached '69. Yes, I was only forty-nine, forty-nine! When I was a girl, I always said I wanted to die when I was thirty-five, though I'd have missed an awful lot. But things began to get boring in my fifties, or perhaps I should say "less fun" – to be bored is an awful confession of stupidity.

On my return from Caracas, Eddie Shackleton asked if I wanted him to recommend me to Wilson for a peerage. I said, "Honestly, I don't think so. I don't quite know if Chipps is going to be merchant banking in the city or if he's going back to South America to represent British companies. I've always followed him and, if he goes abroad again, I'll have to pack up and go with him. I don't want to be a Baroness in name only. If I do the job, I want to do it properly." I might have been on the hop all the time, and I didn't want to be like Lady Falkender who never seems to open her mouth.

Perhaps I made a mistake. The only thing I've really regretted in my life is not to have been elected as a Labour MP, but I gave that up to marry Chipps. It's wonderful to see Jamie and Bruce now settled in careers of their own.

In the middle of the Christmas term at Eton they have "long leave" which is a holiday of about a week, and I decided this would be a good time to have a party for Jamie. My children knew very few local children and I wanted them to have some social life in Dorset, like I did when I was young. So I rang up John Mansel, my old friend and dancing partner since childhood who lives at Smedmore, and I said, "John, look in your "Was-a-book' and tell me all our mutual firends who've got children of fifteen or thereabouts." We call *Burke's Peerage* the "Was-a-book" because my mother's generation used to say about people we'd just met. "oh, his mother was a This and his grandmother was a That . . ." We thought this terribly funny, actually, and used to pull their legs about it like mad.

Anyway, John looked through his Was-a-book and, with his help, I compiled a list of about sixty young things to come to Jamie's party, including the sister of Alistair Jackson, the master of the South Dorset Hunt to whom Chipps was now whipping-in and, also the daughter of Meryl Thompson who I'd stayed with in Kuala Lumpur. Everyone was about

Jamie's age and the idea was that, after dropping them here, the grown-ups would go over to Slepe House where Kitty would give them dinner.

It was a whale of a party. Mrs. Bradford and I did the eats and we had a huge buffet in the drawing-room and what we call the 'old room' – the one with the corner seat where we have the television and usually eat at night – and the dining-room was cleared for dancing to tapes arranged by Jamie.

The day before the party, Kitty said to me, "There's a wartime girlfriend of Chipps' called Stella Barrow who's just come to settle in Dorset and I believe she's got a daughter of Jamie's age." So I rang up Stella and arranged for her daughter, 'Scilla, to come to the party – John Templeton-Cotill's sister Rose, actually, drove her over as they were friends. So this fair, slim, charming, pretty girl arrived and everybody danced and the party was a great success and, the next day, Jamie said to me rather sheepishly, "Do you think we could ask Miss Barrow to lunch on Sunday, Mummy?"

That's when their romance really started and, when 'Scilla came out to Gozo with us the next year for the summer hols, the pair of them just walked round hand in hand all day long. A year later, though he hadn't got the results, Jamie had passed all his "A" levels and could leave Eton. He didn't want to go to university. He wanted to get on with his life and marry 'Scilla. He was only just seventeen and she was still sixteen. Romeo and Juliet. Sweet.

4th June at Eton, 1970.

Dodo, Priscilla Barrow, Jamie, Bruce and Chipps.

Jamie's last few years at Eton weren't entirely happy. At the end of one of his holidays in Caracas, I gave him a miniature bottle of rum. This he put quite openly on the mantelpiece of his study, and the boys' maid reported the fact she'd seen it to his house master. His first house master, darling Peter Lawrence, "Wetty Lawrence", whose six page letters, along with Moyna Hopwood's, were such a help to me that I never felt I was far away at all, had left, and a new man had taken over. This new house master had it in for Jamie. He rang up Moyna and Mike Hopwood, because they were standing in loco parentis, and said, "Come and remove Jamie. I'm sacking him," whereupon Mike got straight in his car and faced him, insisting that Jamie see the headmaster, Chevenix Trench who, instead of sacking him, gave him six of the best. Jamie took his "O"s the next day and passed them all, but it was entirely due to Mike that his life wasn't ruined.

You can see, though, why he wasn't frightfully keen on education after Avisford and Eton! That's why he did his "A" levels terribly young and, though he was offered a place at Oxford, decided to get a qualification for life as soon as possible, motivated by the fact he wanted to marry 'Scilla.

I remember getting back with Chipps in early '72 from a skiing holiday with the Ruck-Keenes and Jamie presenting us with a sort of fait acompli. He'd been to see my old boyfriend, John Sherbrooke, who was our solicitor in Swanage, and said to him, "I think I want to be a solicitor," and John had agreed to take him on. Meanwhile Chipps said he would finance him to learn languages on the Continent, just as he himself had done in the Navy. He came back speaking fluent French, Spanish and Italian – Chipps' languages. Then he read Law at Guildford College, became an Officer in the Royal Wessex Yeomanry, and did his articles both with Theodore Goddard in London and with John's partner, Alex Thavenot, at their Wareham office where he's now a partner himself.

Jamie, actually, is also a very talented artist. When he was an articled clerk in London, he was so badly paid he did sketches in his lunch hour and sold them for twenty-five pounds each – people were queuing up to buy them. And, when Conches-en-Ouche and Wareham twinned in '78, the Mayor of Wareham gave one of Jamie's watercolours to the Mayor of Conches where it now hangs in its Hotel de Ville.

When I told Michael Jennings, the headmaster of Avisford, that I was not sending Bruce to prep school on the advice of Dr. Bill Whiles, who had told me he was dyslexic, he said, "You need your own head examining for sending him to a trick cyclist!" But look where Bruce has got now! He's a re-insurance broker at Lloyds and does a lot of their foreign accounts all over Europe and Eastern Europe, travelling to Yugoslavia, Czechoslovakia,

Poland and Russia and also to Brussels, Italy and France. Not only that, he's climbing up in the political world, and on my side! After his "A"s at Harrow, he went to Bournemouth University to read Law and Politics. We gave him a motorbike and, as my mother was getting very old and starting to fall about, he agreed to live with her to be a grannysitter at night, first at Shepherd's Cottage, Winterborne Whitechurch, and then in one of our farm cottages, when I persuaded her to come here in '78, two years before she died.

In his second year at college, Bruce was elected President of the Students' Union. By then he was very active in the local Constituency Labour Party because I had gradually handed over my activities to him. Politics is in his blood. He failed his degree the first time, but the Director of the college said he could take it again because he was dyslexic. Before cramming for this second sitting he had a gap. His Italian was O.K. because we used to send him to stay with his Godparents, Nella Garronska and Cecilia Foley, and Lulu Guerra de Boekstyns' widow, Neni, in Italy, and his Spanish was fluent because of being educated at the Spanish School in Caracas, so we sent him to France to brush up his French – as an internationalist, I'm a great believer in children learning languages and I think you have so much more fun when you go away.

First he went to Normandy and helped a farmer with bringing in the potatoes, but he came back with such a terrific Norman accent we then sent him to Paris where he did a short course at the Sorbonne and took a diploma. I remember that winter we picked him up in Paris and took him skiing with us in Megève and Zermatt. I always loved skiing with Bruce. He never made me feel I must keep up with him and he helped me when I fell down. He gave me greater confidence and, as a result, I skied better whenever he was with me.

Well, then he went back to college and got his degree. Like me, his Godfather, Sir Joseph Weld, who was Lord Lieutenant at the time, had never seen a graduation ceremony before, so we took Joe along and he had a very matey time – he knew a terrific lot of the people there in their official capacities and many of the Labour councillors had been great supporters of mine when I stood for Bournemouth East and Christchurch.

Bruce was then out of work for six months. Oh it was awful! I wrote to all my friends and Chipps wrote to all his friends. Bruce went to interviews every week, and he got more and more depressed and my heart was absolutely breaking. I think unemployment is the most dreadful thing. I thought so in the Thirties and that's why I became a Socialist as you know, but, when it happens to your own son, it's simple frightful.

Luckily, one of the people I wrote to was Fred Warner, the one I dined with when Burgess and Maclean flitted to Russia. Since then he'd married and had children and been Ambassador in Tokyo. Anyway, he now lived in Dorset and, as I'd known him since I was a child, I wrote to him and said, "Can you help Bruce?" and he got him an interview at Fenchurch the Insurance brokers. Just before Christmas, the personnel chap at Fenchurch rang me up and said, "I've got good news for your son. We're taking him on."

He was two years in Fenchurch and he learned a very great deal, but he wasn't getting any further and his salary was very low. So he answered an advertisement from Harris and Dixson – also insurance brokers – went for an interview and got a job with them as an international re-insurance broker.

At twenty-five he was elected as the youngest ever director of the London Co-op but, because of his age, he was only elected for a year. When he came up to re-election he said to me, "Mummy, I'm never going to get in, because not only are the Conservatives and the SDP running a campaign against me, so are the Communists and the *Morning Star*!" Well, he came top of the poll, so now he's hoping to get a constituency.

Chipps, who looks rather respectable, went to the offices of Harris and Dixson where Bruce introduced him to the directors, and they immediately started saying things like, "Well, Bruce, we thought you were educated in the Gorbals! We didn't expect your father to look like this!"

Jamie, of course, being a solicitor, can't be actively political as it wouldn't do his job any good at all. But I suspect he's also on my side. Chipps, I needn't tell you, is Tory through and through.

Chapter 38

Back To Venezuela

After several years in banking and shipping in the city, Chipps joined up with some friends in Cracas to represent a lot of major English firms in Venezuela, people like British Shipbuilding, and G.K.N. and B.T.R. So we went out to Caracas twice – in '79 and '81 – and stayed at the Intercontinental. It was great fun seeing all our favourite haunts again. Our room would be full of flowers when we arrived and friends were constantly ringing up to ask us to dinner, to lunch, to this and to that. On the first trip we flew via Barbados and a friend of mine, David Martin, whom I'd last seen in the Bitter Lakes and who now lived there, showed us all round the island – lovely sand and coral and palms and sandpipers: a most charming place.

When Chipps was there previously, to arrange a Naval visit, he discovered that his hotel was an establishment stuffed full of frustrated Canadian women who had flown over to have fun with black men. Specially chartered plane loads came for a week at a time, but the British Embassy hadn't a clue what was going on and had booked him in too. But Chipps soon found that the women weren't interested in a white man!

Colonel Drax, an ancestor of our Dorset friends, planted the first sugar plantations in Barbados and Jamaica during the seventeenth century. There's still a Drax Hall in both islands and we saw the one in Barbados, a beautiful old house with a lovely Georgian staircase where the overseer lives. Actually, Wol and Pam Drax bought their own private house in Barbados five or six years ago. They go out once a year, and, while Wol copes with his business interests, Pam is on holiday.

Each of our business trips to Caracas lasted two or three weeks and we could have parties there in the house of Chipps' partner, Roger Silver, for the people they hoped to do business with. Chipps was apparently doing very well indeed and had various large contracts just coming off when the Falklands War started in '82 and the President of Venezuela went on television and said, "We will do no further business with England." So, of course, Chipps' business folded. Alas!

One of the firms Chipps represented produced Reverse Osmosis plants and I got the literature and sent it to Dom Mintoff in Malta because of his water shortage. The firm offered me a commission but I said, "No, I'm not going to recommend you, but I will send him your literature as I think Reverse Osmosis is a good idea" – I never accept commissions or anything, and that's why my advice is so often taken. In fact, Dom shopped around and bought a plant from another country.

After the Falklands War, I tried very hard to get Dom cheap Venezuelan Oil. Malta, of course, was now independent and Dom said, "The best thing is to have a Consul in Caracas," and he asked me for names. So I asked my friend Admiral Felix Mendosa, the Venezuelan Ambassador in London, for advice and we whittled down a list to ten names and sent them to Dom who selected another friend of mine, an international lawyer. Dom then applied to the Venezuelan Government to appoint him as Maltese Consul in Caracas. Eventually the reply came back that Malta was already represented in Caracas. Well, Dom and I knew this wasn't so and I found out from Felix that they were referring to the Embassy of the Sovereign Order of the Knights of Malta in Caracas, who were all Italian business men and not representative of the Maltese Government in any way! We explained the mistake and our nominee was agreed and sent, but unfortunately, the negotiations for cheap oil fizzled out. The reason, I'm afraid, was political. Though independent, Malta was still associated in the Venezuelan mind with England, so Dom had to get his oil from Saudi Arabia.

Chapter 39

Malta and Mintoff

1970 I had decided to build an upstairs to my house in Xlendi and the mason and all the village came to me and said, "Mrs. Dodo, we'll do the work for you but we can't do it in three weeks like last time. It'll take at least a year because we're busy building marble palaces for English people up on the cliff." The next day I said to Johnnie, my gardener, "Who are these stupid English people building palaces on the cliff?" and he said, "I don't know the names of all of them but one's called Mr. Carroll Fitzgerald" Carroll Fitzgerald, my former fiancé!

Monique had flown over to stay with me – she'd brought her cook and her maid with her so we were living in absolute luxury – and, needless to say, we immediately went up to see Carroll. But he'd just married somebody who was very jealous, so he wasn't allowed to see us on that occasion. How ridiculous. But now his wife and I are great friends so he's allowed to trundle down and have a drink in my garden . . . No, nothing more. All he can really do is swim in his lovely salt water pool or read!

The following year, 1971, Dom Mintoff was back in power and was insisting on reviewing his defence pact with Britain. John Templeton Cotill had written to me saying, "Darling Dodo, when you come out this year, get in touch for God's sake. I'm now Flag Officer Malta and Commander British Forces Malta, and I'm dying to talk to you" – he'd been Chief of Staff in Singapore, negotiating for Heath about defence with Lee Kuan Yew and was now doing the same thing with Dom. Eventually I got in touch with him using the phone at the police station at Xlendi – I wouldn't have one in the house there. John came over to Xlendi in his Admiral's barge and stayed a weekend, which was great fun because he could take Chipps and the children and me round the islands, and feed us with lovely recipes he'd taught his Maltese stewards how to prepare. At one point, while the others were lazing on deck, John and I went for a swim and he said, "Look, Dodo, you've got to do something for me about these defence talks. I asked to call three months ago and I haven't had a peep from the Prime Minister, and nor has the Brigadier nor the Air Force Commander."

I rang up Martin Zammit, Dom's Private Secretary, and made an appointment to see Dom at the Auberge one morning at eleven when I said, "Now Dom, you've absolutely got to meet your Flag Officer! He was Chipps' and my best man!" Dom said, "Oh, Dodo, you know I don't like the Services!" I said, "But John's not a typical admiral. He's been Naval Attaché in Russia, he's intelligent, he's got a house in France and he speaks lots of languages . . . "Well, would he come in civilian clothes?" I said, "He'll come in a bikini if necessary!" So Dom said, "All right. You can tell his Flag Lieutenant to ring up Martin and I'll see him at eleven o'clock tomorrow."

So off I went and caught the ferry back to Gozo and rang John and said, "You're seeing Dom at eleven o'clock tomorrow morning in a bikini!"

So John put on a sort of South of France shirt and sort of South of France trousers and walked by himself up the steps and into the Auberge de Castille to meet Dom who was dressed, as they always are in Malta, in a suit and tie. He said, "But Admiral, you haven't got a jacket!" and John said, "Well, Dodo told me to come in a bikini and I thought this was the next best thing!" Of course, they made terrific friends. Dom said, "I can give you a quarter of an hour" and, after two and a half hours, John made the biggest sacrifice he's ever made for England: he shared Dom's lunch which was a thermos of tepid tea and a doughnut.

Soon afterwards, I was swimming again with John and he told me that Dom's last telegram to Heath was really too rude. He thought negotiations were going to be broken off – it was all to do with the amount of rent for British bases. I said, "I'll ring Dom tonight!" He said, "Yes. He must send a more conciliatory telegram or it's the end of negotiations."

You see, John was frightfully on Dom's side, he really was. He adored Malta and he adored the Maltese, and they adored him. And, although I expect he votes Tory, he's not a very Tory person. So I went into the police station that night and I got straight through to Dom, which isn't always easy. I said, "Dom, your last telegram to Heath was too rude. You must send a more conciliatory one." Dom said, "What the hell is this? Diplomacy on the telephone from a police station in Xlendi and a woman to boot!" I said, "Dom, I'm giving you a message. If you could be a little more conciliatory, somebody might come out." He said, "Who will come out? The Holy Ghost?" I said, "Dom, this is a message." He said, "Who's it from?" I said, "Mickey Mouse" and hung up, and that's how the terrific story started that there was a spy known as Mickey Mouse in Malta.

But Dom did send a telegram to Heath, and Lord Carrington came out and negotiations appeared to be as merry as a marriage again. N.A.T.O. pulled out of Malta in August and, though it wasn't until eight years later, in 1979, the British finally had to leave too.

There were still plenty of hiccups however. I remember John ringing me up in Slepe Green while I was cooking the turkey one Christmas Eve. He said, "Look, if you don't make the same telephone call you did last time we're going to be kicked out of the island completely." So, in between basting the turkey, I tried to ring Dom in Malta but the lines were engaged. I didn't get through and all our Services were kicked out, all our radars had to be dismantled . . . But Dom remained awfully sweet to John. He intimated that, after he had left officially, he could sneak back through the V.I.P. room in the airport terminal and hide in his old official residence, the Villa Portelli. John had three days quiet sleep and then the Services came back again! A little later, when John left the Navy, Dom offered him the job – he didn't take it – of running all his shipyards, which shows how much he liked him personally.

Dom didn't only expel the British Services: in 1981 he expelled the Libyans, every single one of them. He'd always believed he would find oil and finally he did find oil on Malta's side of the median line between Libya and Malta. So he put it out to tender, and Texaco got it and hired an Italian drill and they dug and the oil gushed. But although the oil was on Malta's side, a Gadaffi gunboat was there next morning with its guns pointed at the rig and a message: "If you don't plug that hole and go away at once we'll open fire".

As they were unarmed, they ran like riggers. I happened to be having breakfast with Dom the next morning and he was as white as a sheet and constantly on the phone telling his police and the Army to put oil drums anywhere Libyan troop carrying planes might land. Dom and Gadaffi had recently been great buddies, but then they'd argued as to the exact position of the median line and Dom considered this oil to be on his side and Gadaffi considered it was on his side. Then Gadaffi had agreed to send the matter to the International Court at the Hague for adjudication, but he'd come over to lunch with Dom and refused to sign the necessary documents, and reneged on his promise. Moyra, Dom's wife, told me about that lunch. Gadaffi arrived with twelve bodyguards, and Moyra, who was preparing the *fenek*, the rabbit, said, "I haven't enough food for this many." So Dom explained the situation to Gadaffi who sent all, except one, of the bodyguards away. Gadaffi then insisted on going upstairs to Dom's bedroom to pray and he spent so long praying that Moyra had to send someone to ask his remaining bodyguard, who was on duty outside the door, when he was coming down to eat. Apparently he raised his hand with five fingers. Then Moyra's friend came down and said to Moyra "I do not know. He may take five minutes, five years or five centuries!" Then, when at last he came down, he refused to be photographed with wine on the table. Rather undiplomatic. Dom loves to make his own wine and offer it. He used to waterski over to John and me with bottles of his wine when we were on the barge . . .

Anyway, back to the gunboat incident. Dom finally went on Television and said that all Libyans had to be out of Malta by four o'clock that afternoon, and by the time they'd got their wives, their concubines, their children, their nannies, their animals, their antiques, and their clothes onto their transport planes, they could only fit in one of their total of twenty helicopters. So Gadaffi came on Libyan television that night and said, "In view of our past friendship with Malta, we are donating nineteen helicopters to the Maltese." The matter of the oil isn't resolved yet, though Dom won his case in The Hague.

I hope I've convinced you how very much wrapped up I am in the fate of Malta. But the success of tourism there has been my main achievement. Dom was against it at the beginning. He said he didn't want a nation of waiters, but he came to realise, of course, that it was his salvation. In fact, for five years, I tried in my reports to persuade him and Bonnici, the new Prime Minister, to bring in a Tourist Pound – you go out at present with one hundred pounds and you get about sixty Maltese Lira, which is what the old Maltese Pound is now called. This is too little even though what you buy in Malta is sometimes cheaper than in England. You can't raise the standard of living and increase the Old Age Pension and improve health without the wherewithal to do it, but the unfavourable rate of exchange may be deterring visitors.

I was probably the first person in Malta or Gozo to install ceiling fans of the really good old-fashioned Singapore type all over my house. They make the whole difference. So, when I had an awful lot of complaints that the airport was terribly, terribly hot, I said to Bertie Hyzler, the Minister for Health, "Look, Bertie, I've told Dom in my report that he must have ceiling fans in the airport," and, after visiting the airport one Thursday, he said to me, "You're talking nonsense, Dodo. The airport isn't at all hot." I said to him "Go when you're not expected." I was amused to see in the *Times of Malta* next day that ceiling fans were to be installed, and its thanks to them that arrival at the airport is now bearable.

Whenever he thought I was talking sense, Dom did what I wanted within a couple of days. He's dynamic and that's why I called him "Dynamic Dom" in my publicity when I started Tourism.

There's only one person I know who doesn't like fans and that's Johnnie, my gardener. Every time he comes in from the garden for a cup of tea, he turns off the fan. But he asked me one day where he could buy one. They were now being imported in large numbers so I said, "Anywhere. But why," I said, "do you want a fan, Johnnie? You turn this one off every time you come in." "Oh, it's not for me," he said, "It's for my cows." He lives in an old arched farm house in a room next to his cows and, if ever you were to go up there, you'd see the cows have a fan while Johnnie hasn't!

When Borg Olivier was Prime Minister during my absence in South America, Poulson, the architect – Reggie Maudlin's chum – built a huge hospital in Gozo with air-conditioning. Well, the Maltese don't like air-conditioning: they think it will kill them. We had this absurd air-conditioned hospital in Gozo where there were no specialists because they lived in Malta. So Dom got rid of the air-conditioning and flogged it to Gadaffi and cut the hospital down to size, with one operating theatre and a surgeon there permanently in the summer. There's also a very good Casualty department, which is very necessary because the tourists are always falling and hurting themselves on rocks and things.

Now, of course, they have more surgeons and it's because of me, actually, that there are helicopters to take the specialists from Malta to Gozo when someone is really ill, or to take patients if necessary from Gozo to St. Luke's Hospital in Malta. This is because, on a skiing holiday in Kitzbuhel, I met a great friend of mine, Wernie von der Schulenberg, the man whose father tried to kill Hitler – he and his wife Dorlie used to come to Boca Seca with us when we were in Caracas. One evening, Wernie said to me, "What are you up to now, Dodo?" I said, "Well, my best man is Flag Officer Malta where I'm frightfully involved in everything."

Wernie, who now had the Mediterranean Desk at Bonn, said, "What's all this balls about Dom wanting his own Navy and Air Force?" I said, "I can tell you exactly what he wants them for. He wants helicopters to fly specialists and patients to and from Gozo, and he wants helicopters and patrol boats to stop the drug traffic – drugs are coming from Turkey and being trans-shipped in the Bay of Dwejra and then going on to Marseilles to be processed for America. And I want him to have helicopters and patrol boats to spot oil slicks and patrol boats to spray them with detergent. I also want him to have patrol boats to stop Sicilians poaching Malta's lifeline, namely, its fish." He said, "Well, Willy Brandt put this matter of Malta having a 'private navy and air force' on my desk last week and, now that you've explained everything, Dom will get what he wants." Dom was a great friend of Willy Brandt's who, of course, I also knew because I'd met him in Compiègne with Denis Healey at the Socialist Seminar in 1950.

I'm especially glad to have played a part in getting Dom and Moyra together again after they'd separated. She left him when he became so terribly anti-British after his battle with the Conservative Government and Heath over the rent for British bases – I was one of the few of her English friends she was allowed to see. When she left him, Dom thought she'd come back in a fortnight, but she went back to England and, having been a V.A.D. during the war, was able to get herself a job as an assistant night nurse in a hospital in Sussex. She lived in a bed-sit and dressed in jumble clothes. At the time Prince Charles came out and stayed with John Templeton Cotill at the Villa Portelli, I said to John, "Do ask Prince Charles to try to get Moyra back with Dom as I think it's so important for Malta." John did this and Prince Charles had a word with the Queen who invited Moyra to lunch with Dom when he was over to smooth things out a bit with Heath at Chequers. I gather the Queen pushed them into a little side-room together and said, "I'm sure you'll want to speak to one another privately." Well, Moyra agreed to come back to Dom on her own terms, one of which was that she should be allowed to see whatever friends she wanted to. They returned that night. When Dom got back on the Saturday with Moyra he arranged a party the next day to which he invited John and me.

The party was held at a little cinema in Valletta where the priests censored films so they could be shown to good Catholics. Dom often took that cinema over on Sundays and we, that is his friends and his Cabinet, used to have buffet drinks there before watching a film. Dom thought of these Sunday parties as rather smart. It was lovely seeing Moyra again, and she and I sat at the back and she told me all her experiences and how glad she was to be in Malta again. And, even though she's English, a de Vere Bentick, the Maltese adore Moyra. I could understand, though, Dom's anger with the British and their usual meanness with money. Borg Olivier's Government had left the country absolutely bankrupt. Dom hadn't enough money to pay the police or the civil servants, let alone put up the Old Age Pension as he'd promised in his election speeches.

Under Borg Olivier, while I was in South America, there was a huge boom in tourism and people were letting absolute pigsties for vast sums to foreigners who didn't know the conditions till they arrived. I was afraid of typhoid, so I recommended that no one be allowed to rent their property without having their facilities inspected and being put on an official register. I also recommended that, as there were no rates, people who put up tourists should pay a tax which could go towards better drainage and sanitation generally. Both recommendations were implemented, and the tax was set at two-hundred and fifty Maltese pounds, so that put an end to the cowboys.

I didn't always get what I wanted from Dom easily. In the early Seventies I was frightfully keen on having a marvellous hotel at Ta' Cenc built by Massimo Igliori, the Italian entrepreneur who did the Costa Smeralda for the

Aga Khan. But Dom, being a Socialist, delayed the project as being too luxurious and also because Massimo was Italian and not Maltese. I liked it from the point of view of taste – it was pretty and made of the local stone and I also knew it would attract rich foreigners who would buy the local lace and provide employment.

Anyway, I at last persuaded Dom to let the project continue. Then, a few years later, because of the water shortage – this was before reverse osmosis – Dom introduced a rule that swimming-pools must only have salt water. Now, Massimo's hotel had a very big swimming-pool, all done with fresh water, and he would have to completely re-plumb it, so he said, "Dodo, can you help me?" I said, "Yes, if I have the ammunition." So I went to his manager and asked for what I considered the most relevant details, then wrote in my report to Dom, "They employ one-hundred and twenty Gozotans for ninety guests," and Massimo was allowed to continue with fresh water.

When Massimo wanted his hotel to have a private beach, Dom at first said no. But I thought the tone of the guests so good for tourism that I said, "If I persuade him to build a new road from Ta' Cenc to Mgarr Xini will you then let him have his private beach?" and Dom complied.

Massimo was a great friend of mine and I really did help him enormously. He fell in love with Gozo and he wanted to die there but unfortunately his family took him back to die in Naples.

One thing Dom and his Party – me too – entirely agreed on was the need of a National Health Service for Malta but, as with Nye Bevan in England, the doctors were absolutely bloody-minded and stuck out for everything they could. I remember sitting in the Auberge with Dom and saying, "Nye found it difficult. Don't lose your temper." He said, "I never lose my temper! I never lose my temper!" I said, "What are you doing now?" Anyway, he kept his temper and got the National Health Service through. But, when the doctors insisted on only doing one year as houseman before becoming a registrar unlike the two years in England, a system Dom preferred, he did lose his temper and a lot of his doctors left. So he got on a plane and went to Czechoslovakia, Yugoslavia and Poland and brought back some frightfully good doctors from there instead.

The Maltese, especially the Gozotans, didn't really want foreigners but in fact they have improved the medicine enormously. For instance, a Polish lady doctor has alleviated Malta's endemic kala-azar fever problem – Gerald de Trafford's wife, Charlotte, and also their son, Jasper, were cured of this thanks to her accurate diagnosis.

My darling orthopaedic surgeon, Nick Vere-Hodge of Poole, had set my leg four times and used to treat Chipps even on a Saturday afternoon every time he fell off his horse out hunting. He had just come back from Egypt where he helped Mrs. Sadat start her marvellous hospital near Cairo. He told me he'd love to do something for Malta but, this time, without charge. So I said to Dom, "Would your Health Service like the help of this marvellous orthopaedic surgeon? He's prepared to do it, just for expenses, for a couple of months in the winter." Dom said, "Yes, I jolly well would!" But, after the huge row with the B.M.A. when Dom got all his foreign doctors, Nick changed his mind. He hadn't yet retired and it would have been too controversial.

Dom retired last year but he still has a job – he runs the Central Bank – and is very much a power in the land so I shall continue to do favours, receive complaints and write reports like an ombudsman – he has briefed the new Prime Minister.

A delegation came one day to the door of my house in Xlendi and said, "You must go to the police station. There isn't a toilet in the cell." I said, "I'm not sure but in England I think we use a bucket, but I'll go and look all the same." So I went round to the police station where it took the policeman about half an hour to find the enormous medieval key to the cell. It was a small cell, empty save for a very comfortable-looking divan, which appeared to be extremely well used, presumably by the policeman. But the delegation were right: there was no bucket. Before leaving, I walked over to the window, found that I could take down the iron bars, opened the windows and stepped on to the quay. "Oh!" I said, "What's the worry? Prisoners can go to the public loo next door!" The policeman looked at me. He said, "Mrs. Dodo, you are clever! I've been here sixteen years and I've never noticed the builder forgot to cement in the bars." And the fascinating thing was that the prisoners had always apparently returned to their cell after using the public loo! This was at the time when Dom was being accused of being a dictator and running a Police State!

The following year, Dom issued the police with guns. I was cashing some travellers' cheques at the bank in Valletta when I noticed a policeman hiding what must be a gun in a paper bag in his trouser pocket. I said to him, "Do you know how to use that thing?" He said, "We've had a half hour lesson." I said, "Haven't you holsters?" He said, "No, Mrs. Dodo. Please try to get us holsters." So the police were issued with holsters. How? Because I rang up Dom and said, "If you don't issue your police with holsters, they'll shoot their own balls off!"

I help in every way I can. About four years ago, I noticed a dustman in Xlendi removing rubbish from the rocks with his hands, so I gave him a pair of tongs. Now all the dustmen have them.

I must just say a few more words about Dick Crossman, who I knew of course from the Round Table Conference on Malta and often met afterwards at the House of Commons. Dom liked Dick very much, and lent him his summer house near Marsaxlock so that he and Anne and their two children could come out to have their summer hols. It was in 1973, a year before he died, the year before Wilson won the election. I was talking to Moyra on the phone about something or other and she happened to say, "Oh, Dick's here with his family." I said, "Do tell them I'd love them to come to lunch." So Dick rang me up at the police station and said they were coming on such and such a ferry. I was alone at the house and it was May or early June because we had strawberries. The wild strawberries of Gozo are the best in the world; they're like those of France and Ireland, only bigger, or so Dick said. He'd never had them before.

Anyway, they came over and, oh, Dick did bully me. He said, "Tell me the history of your island," and, of course, I never can remember. He said, "How old is Gigantija?" I said, "I think it's 2,900 B.C." He said, "You ought to know!" Well, after lunch, served by my maid Josephine in my divine house, we all went for a long walk over to Fungus Rock where a fungus grows which is frightfully good for blood pressure – when he was a Minister, Dick had once done a survey on this fungus, and the Marines had climbed the rock to collect it for him, using chains and ladders. I remember Dick saying to me, "The only Minister Wilson ever left long in office, Dodo, was your chum Denis Healey, and that was because he thought he was the least threat to him." How I wish Denis was running the Party now! Anyway, the following year Dick died of cancer. Then his son hanged himself in the barn of Anne's farm. Young people do suffer.

Chapter 40

SETTLING DOWN IN DORSET

In '72, when Idi Amin kicked the Asians out of Uganda, they came to England with very little warning and the W.V.S. asked me to help put up some of them at the old army camp in Piddletrenthide – it was empty and we prepared it in a hurry. They arrived with nothing. They weren't allowed to take any money; all their jewellery had been taken off them at the airport in Uganda and they were just herded over here like cattle. My friend, Damaris Mansel, was very important in the WVS and had a lot to do with getting the camp ready. John and Damaris Mansel live at Smedmore on the Isle of Purbeck. The first oil to be found in England was on their land. Rhys Mansel, John's father, always used to say, "I'm going to be a multi-millionaire because we're going to find oil at Kimmeridge" – Kimmeridge is their own beach and its cliffs are oily shale. Indeed oil was found on land of theirs near Smedmore, but the sad thing is that, by the time they found it, minerals had been nationalised and he didn't get a penny. I think, actually, B.P. do pay John something. They do his drive up regularly for their lorries and so on, but he's certainly not a multi-millionaire . . .

Anyway, I rang up Damaris about this camp for the Asians and I said, "Can I help? Do you need a nurse? What do you need?" She said, "Yes you can help. I'll give you a W.V.S. overall and you can go over and ask the woman running the camp what she'd like you to do." Well, I'm not a member of the W.V.S. but she gave me one of their green overalls, and off I went and the woman in charge asked me to cope with the kitchen arrangements. So I said to the head man, the Asians' representative, "Look, I'm the one who's going to see that the kitchen arrangements and the food are O.K. Wouldn't the women prefer to cook for themselves?" He said, "Yes, that's what they'd really like to do." I said, "Well, you, give me a list of everything they want – rice, chillies, that sort of thing – and I'll get it." So he gave me a list and I got in touch with the army at Bristol who sent lorries with all the food they needed, and they cooked for themselves the whole time they were there.

The Asians, in fact, were frightfully happy at Piddletrenthide. There was no colour bar whatsoever in the Piddle Valley. They were invited out to drinks in the pub, and all Damaris' friends brought over flowers and masses of clothes. We had a sort of open stall for all these jumble clothes – shoes and everything – and everyone could try them on and choose what they wanted for free. Unfortunately, after about six weeks, they were moved to another camp near Bristol. They didn't want to leave, but the powers that be thought that, as it was coming on to winter and the camp only had outside loos, they should go elsewhere for the sake of the tiny babies and the very old.

I got a letter, actually, from their head man about a year later saying that every single one of those people were now settled and had their own businesses or were working for relations: none of them were left in camps. In a year, that's extraordinary. That's why Asians are unpopular, let's face it – they do work hard and make money.

Otherwise "county" life just went on as before. There were a couple of rather amusing Hunt Shows run by the Master's wife, Tessa Jackson, at Bovington Camp. In one sketch I was with the Secretary of the Hunt, Mike Dangerfield, at a cocktail party being frightfully catty about the people around us, well-known people in the Hunt. And Chipps and I repeated that "milkman" sketch we'd done all those years ago for Concert Parties – the one where he creeps back after a dreadful row, puts his hands over my eyes and gives me a passionate kiss, and I say, "Only one pint today, thank you, milkman!"

In the winter of '77 about six of the Forêt de Bretonne Hunt came over to hunt with the South Dorset. That was fun. They brought their gorgeous French horns – and their wives. One was called Bernard Healey, another Lepinard. The Forêt de Bretonne is near Le Havre on the road to Rouen. When we went back to hunt with them, Chipps and I stayed with Bernard Healey and his wife. And when we went skiing in Megeve we generally went via Le Havre so as to have lunch with them. When the hunt members of the Forêt de Bretonne first came to Dorset, they stayed at the Crown Hotel in Blandford.

There was a party for them, at Plumber Manor, a hotel and restaurant near Blandford. It went on rather a long time and we were all in terribly good form. Chipps, and the Master, Alistair Jackson, played "Rule Britannia" on these lovely French horns. Apparently the French, when they got back to the Crown Hotel, marched up and down the corridors playing their horns. The Crown said they could never stay there again, so they always stayed with me.

When we hunted with them a month or so later, they awarded Chipps *Les honneurs* – the slot, a hoof of the deer they killed. The Forêt de Bretonne is a stag hunt so. At the end of the hunt, the hounds surround the stag and hold it at bay, and then one of the hunt kills it with a sword – the *coup de grâce.*

I've now given up riding altogether. I hunted Chipps' horses until about ten years ago and I rode James' pony until five years ago when he died. I've stopped mainly because my eyes have become too bad.

Chipps' horses are always so enormous. At my age I honestly don't want to fall off a seventeen-hand horse. You do rather lose your nerve as you get older. When you're younger, you're braver. When you're older, you think, "If I break something I'll be in plaster for two months" which is such a bore. But I skied till quite recently. I don't go down black runs anymore, I go down the blue ones. Jamie at present has a huge horse called Spartacus (which he shares with Bruce when he's down here). 'Scilla has her own horse so they hack together.

Jamie married 'Scilla on 22nd April, 1978. They were both twenty-three. Her parents live at Marnhull and they had a marquee outside their house. The Catholic church at Marnhull is about as big as my drawing-room and obviously wasn't going to be big enough for four hundred guests, so they had the wedding in the Protestant church. The Protestant parson read the service and Father Pedrick gave the blessing – all very ecumenical, rather nice. And Jamie invited his Wessex Yeomanry Sergeants who crossed swords when he and 'Scilla came out of the church, and he had a lovely bagpipes' chap to play.

Jamie and 'Scilla's Wedding, 1978.

The Yeomanry helped put up the marquee for the reception and Cecil Dowell, the Terrierman for the South Dorset Hunt, acted as Master of Ceremonies, wearing Chipps' red hunt evening tailcoat. Now he's Jamie's gamekeeper and my invaluable gardener and handyman.

Naturally, because she was paying, Stella had to restrict the amount of our guests so I made out three lists – relatives, friends and refusers. Luckily a lot of our Dorset friends were mutual friends so they went on her list. When I gave her my list of refusers, I said, "These are friends of mine in Rome and Paris and South America. It's certain they won't come but they must be asked." Actually, an awful lot of them came over, including Jean de Villeyre and his daughter, and Monique de Nervo, of course, who is Jamie's Godmother. Darling Monique. She's grey now, but she's still pretty and well-dressed and vivacious . . . So, in fact, it was an international wedding. Ian Farquhar was there and, of course, Chipps' Bennett relations who came down from Norfolk, Suffolk, and all over England. Ian and Monique stayed with me at Slepe Green, but several guests, including Jean and his daughter and my brother Mike and his wife, stayed at the Farm House which I was then letting, whenever I could, as a Holiday Home.

After the reception, Jamie and 'Scilla went away on a tractor. They spent their honeymoon at Cecilia Foley's house in Massalubrense overlooking Capri – Jamie did some lovely paintings of the Bay of Naples and Positano and so on. Then they came back to their first home together – the Granary Flat which Bruce has now but which I'd done up for Jamie when he was seventeen. Then Chipps leased the Farm House to Jamie and they moved in there. Andrew was born on the 3rd September, 1982, and Nicholas Harry was born on 31st July 1986.

I love being a grandmother. Though I think babies are very sweet, I'm not crazy about them until they begin to talk, so Andrew I adore. We get on terribly well. He has his own private ginger biscuit tin which he hides because otherwise "Grandpa will nick them"! I think I've also told you that only boys are born at Slepe. Even the farm labourers who were here always had boys. I still maintain it's because of the healthy unchlorinated water which comes from our deep well. I said to Jamie, "If you want a girl you'll have to go to Gozo for 'Scilla to conceive it. She certainly won't conceive it at Slepe Farm."

Chipps and his grandson, Andrew, 1988.

I gave forty of our gucsts lunch at my mother's Domesday cottage in Winterborne Whitechurch before we went to the wedding – Winterborne Whitechurch is nearer to Marnhull than we are. We did the food and took it over. My mother was a great party giver and it was the last party she ever gave in her own home because, very soon after that, she came to live at one of the cottages on Slepe Farm so I could care for her. I'm so glad she came with us to Gozo only a few years before. She absolutely loved Xlendi and the whole village adored her and called her "Mummy". As she was such a holy woman she insisted on walking up to Mass every morning though she was crippled with arthritis. She even went on my boat. I owned a little fishing boat then, which I've now sold to a fisherman who lets me use it as if it were still mine, and we got my mother into it somehow and Glen Martin, who owns the St. Patrick's Hotel, rowed us out to see the sunset and do some fishing. She was thrilled, of course, to meet her cousin Cecilia de Trafford and all her family.

It was terribly difficult to persuade my mother to come to live here, on

Slepe Farm. She loved her cottage – it was on "Aunt" Vivian Pleydel-Railston's Whatcombe estate and she'd lived in it since the war, and she loved her independence. I think the main reason she agreed to move was the fact that she was burgled. She went to stay with a friend of hers, Mary Thompson, in Wales, and she got John Miners who owns the Forge Garage in Winterborne Whitechurch to drive her in one of his cars. John is a very old family friend. We've known him since he was a boy. He was an only child and he lived with his mother in the lodge of Whatcombe House. When I had my coming out dance, which was rather lavish, it was the first time this little boy had seen me in evening dress. Anyway, John and I are great, great friends and he adored my mother and he drove her to Wales. By then she wasn't driving her Morris Minor any more and I had it. I've still got it. Well, the day before she left, she gave her jewellery to her darling Lynda to keep, and the silver she gave to Bernard, Aunt Vivian's butler, who'd been looking after her in his spare time for years and years. Next morning, when Lynda went in to clean the best furniture, she found that everything of value had gone.

There's a lay-by in the main Dorchester-Blandford road near Winterborne Whitechurch called Fancy's Lay-by because Fancy, an old age pensioner who did odd jobs and things, used to leave his van there, and, one night when he drove in, another van was occupying 'his' lay-by. So he found a piece of paper and pencil, took the number of the van, walked up to a public phone box and rang the local bobby and said, "There be a van in my lay-by." The bobby said, "It's not really your lay-by, Fancy – it's a public lay-by. I can't arrest a man for stopping there" and hung up. But, when Lynda rang the police to tell them Mrs. Lees' good bits of furniture had gone, they immediately got on to Fancy who gave them the number of the van he'd seen, and they watched out for it at all the ports of England.

They found the culprits at Felixstowe, actually. They waited until they'd put my mother's furniture into a container and, when it was going on board, they pounced, and recovered everything. Those men may still be in prison. The police not only got them: from the bills of *lading* they discovered the names of the three antique dealers in Amsterdam to whom the stolen goods were going, so Interpol was able to pounce on them as well. They found things that had been missing from museums and *châteaux* and God knows what for years and years.

Anyway, my mother came to live in a cottage at Slepe Farm, where, in the garden, I put a mobile home for Mrs. Young, a cook/housekeeper, and a bird table so she could sit and watch the birds she loved so much for hours on end. Then, a week before she died, she fell.

Mrs. Young, rang me up at seven o'clock. In the morning and said, "I've just gone in to get your mother's breakfast and she's on the floor and I can't move her." So I rang the doctor at once and by the time I got over he was there. He said it was essential she go into hospital for an investigation as she'd had a slight stroke, but the three of us couldn't move her – being a heavy woman with arthritis, she was a dead weight. I rushed down to the farm to get Jamie who was in the middle of rescuing a cow that had fallen into the slurry pit. I said "Jamie! Quick! You must come! Mummy's fallen on the floor and we can't move her!" He said, "But I've a cow in the slurry pit!" I said, "Jamie, your grandmother is far more important than a cow! Come quickly!" So he rushed up to her cottage, picked up my mother like a baby, and put her on the bed. Well. She kept saying to Mrs. Young, "Don't let Dodo put me into hospital because I'll never come out!" But Mrs. Young said, "I think Dodo must. She couldn't live with her conscience if she didn't," and persuaded her to go.

She was in Poole General, the Cornelia of which she'd been a governor in the dim, distant past. I put her in a public ward. If you're old and really ill, you're better nursed in a public ward, certainly at Poole. And she had people all around her who knew her, who had lived in Lytchett Minster or who had been tenants or tenants' relations on the Lees' estate; the patient in the next door bed was a former tenant's niece. I went every day and, with the permission of the sister, blanket-bathed and nursed her. She was there a week and, after doing a barium meal to see everything was all right, the doctor said, "She is so well I can't let her have the bed any more. You can take her out at three o'clock tomorrow afternoon."

So I went to Bournemouth with 'Scilla, who was just moving into the Farm House, to buy a Moffet cooker and then returned to pick up my mother. Mrs. Young was already at the hospital. She had packed for her and my mother was ready, siting to leave, and, at a quarter to three, just before 'Scilla and I arrived, she had a heart attack and died. Mrs. Young said to me that the doctors and nurses, seven in all, came round her, so, if she could have been saved, she would have: there was no way would she have been saved at home. Oh, how I adored my mother . . .

Father Pedrick took the funeral service in the Catholic church, Our Lady of Lourdes, in Blandford. The same Father Pedrick who married Chipps and me and baptised our children, married 'Scilla and Jamie, and baptised our grandsons. My mother had told him exactly how she wanted the service done, with a Latin Mass and with certain prayers she'd chosen. She was buried in the Catholic Corner of Blandford's Protestant graveyard. I hate funerals but I had to attend. My brother, Mike, came over from Ireland so he and I and Chipps and the children were together. And Mike's daughter, Christine, came down from London. And my father's only surviving sister, Aunt Nancy, came down from Surrey.

Aunt Nancy was absolutely extraordinary. She was ninety-five when she died and looked younger than me.

We ourselves were burgled two years ago. It was a blustery winter's night. Chipps had a cold and was in his room and I was in mine, and I woke up and went to the loo, turning on the landing light. I hadn't a clue we were being burgled, but I must have frightened away the burglars because, the next morning, we found all my decanters and all my silver on the dining-room table ready to pack, including a silver framed photograph of my mother. They'd taken every other silver-framed photograph – all from off the piano in the drawing-room – and also the Dresden china, left us by Kitty, in my Sheraton desk. We called the police but they've never found the burglars or the stolen property.

The only thing I really miss, apart from a photograph of Howard, is an old silver Venetian jug of my mother's, once used for the Host in Mass. The top of it was for the water, and the bottom, which sort of screwed on, was for the wine, and the handle was a naked woman with a gorgeous bosom – she was leaning backwards, and all around her were satyrs. That jug was unique: I've never seen another like it in the world. Naughty old Venetian priests!

When the Police Inspector came, he looked at Pride and Prejudice in the recess of the staircase, the Peking temple dogs the Mandarin gave to Grandpa Radcliffe, and he said, "I dusted those for nine months!" They'd been two of the pieces stolen from my mother, you see, and they'd had to stay at the police station until the trial. They'd been wrapped in my mother's eiderdown so they wouldn't be damaged. Those burglars knew exactly what they were doing. Among the other items they took were her French inlaid commode, her antique bookcase and her antique sewing-box. It emerged at the trial that they'd been round Winterborne Whitechurch asking people it they'd any old clocks for sale, and a villager said, "Well, I haven't but perhaps Mrs. Lees has." So, when they got to my mother's cottage and saw it was empty, they broke in.

If I knew l was going to die very soon, I'd go on a world cruise, and to hell with it – I'd like to die at sea or, preferably, *in* the sea.

I *hate* growing old. Most of my childhood was fun, and most of my teenage was fun. My twenties were partly fun and partly not fun – I was growing up and making my life. But, goodness, I had fun in my thirties, and, goodness, I had fun in my forties. My fifties were less fun, and to be in my sixties is murder. It's jolly difficult coming to terms with being fatter and not being madly attractive to rampant men when you go to a party.

Dodo and Porfirio.

I still, of course, give and go to parties, though I told all my friends I'd be in purdah for three weeks to do this book. In fact, I've had to turn parties down. But there'll be others.

The old days *were* much more fun. Not that I don't make the most of each day now. Every day's different and I refuse to stick to a routine. If I had a routine I would die of boredom. Moyra Mintoff, when she trots over to Gozo to see me, always says, "You are marvellous, Dodo. You're always laughing." I laugh and, sometimes, I rebel. I may be learning how to come to terms with growing old but I shan't become serene: I shall continue to *pêter le feu* – an expression that doesn't sound so bad in French!

Last Christmas Eve, we were hit by another car and the whole of the passenger side was staved in; I was thrown against Chipps and our car was a write-off. If I'd been wearing a safety-belt I'd have been killed. I've got a special doctor's certificate to say that I needn't wear one. I haven't felt safe in a safety-belt since an accident in Caracas when I was in the driver's seat and thrown onto my shoulder on the other side. After dropping two people who'd been working in my house doing some carpentry, I was stationary in a one-way street and a car came down the wrong way. The driver was uninsured and he'd stolen the car. And I'd have been killed, of course, in the war if I'd been wearing a safety-belt when my ambulance was blown up by a mine. I'll put a safety-belt on if Chipps is driving like a maniac on an *autobahn* or something but, even then, I keep my finger on the button.

I wonder which one of us will see the other out. I shall never leave him, except through death. I sometimes sing to him "Let Him Go, Let Him Tarry" and that maddens him but, good God, who else would care for his bad back? Who else would keep me on the straight and narrow? After you've been married to someone for so many years, you've sort of got used to them; they're part of you. It's a strong thing, marriage. You can get over problems with time – that's why I don't approve of divorce. I would advise any young person to marry for love like I did, and jolly well make it work.

It would help if Chipps wasn't so tidy. As he's used to living in a tiny cabin, everything's always in its place and he knows where it is – he thinks he knows, anyway. He gets terribly irritated by what he thinks is my sluttishness. And I get terribly irritated by his continuously throwing things out. I like a washing-up brush to be nice and soft for brushing bits off the plates before I put them in the machine. But, as soon as a brush is nice and soft, he says it's old and tatty, throws it out and buys a new one which, of course, takes another six months to become soft and then he throws that out. Whatever he thinks is tatty, he simply throws out – my favourite cushion, a washing-up bowl, a bucket, anything.

But that's just a matrimonial *problem*. I still love him. Though there are people I've never got on with, I've never hated anybody, except perhaps Cynthia, Chipps' stepmother, and, even in her case, 'dislike' is probably the better word. I'm sure there are lots of people who hate or have hated me but I don't think I've consciously done them harm. I've taken people's boyfriends away. That I have done. But they were more attracted to me, than I was to them. It's just a thing that happens. You go to a party, your eyes meet and they're your slave. Especially when you're a virgin. I was accused, before I was seduced in France, of being a cock-teaser. But I was so innocent I hardly knew what that meant. I'm still rather innocent about sex. All I really know is what Chipps has taught me. Carroll Fitzgerald wasn't much help in that direction – he'd go to sleep in the middle.

The reason I didn't like Chipps' step-mother is the fact that she took Andy, Chipps' father, away from Kitty. The story of Kitty's marriage is rather fascinating, actually. As a young woman Kitty Selby Ormond was very pretty, very attractive, and a great friend of the Duke of Windsor and Lady Cunard. In fact, she used to lend the Duke, when he was Prince of Wales, her flat in Endsleigh Gardens, London, for his fun and games. Anyway, she married somebody much older than herself called Jordan Walker and they had a son called John. Now the extraordinary thing is that, when John was five, her brother, Pat Selby Ormond, and my father-in-law, Andy Bennett, and her subsequent third husband, Geoff Pittar, were all at Pembroke College, Cambridge, at the same time – all were eight years younger than she was. Well, she went down to Cambridge for May Week – I think she was a bit bored with old Walker and she met Andy at the Ball and they fell madly in love, just like that. But she said to Andy, "I've got a five year old son, I can't leave my husband." So Andy said, "We won't communicate with each other for six months, but if, after that, we still feel the same way about each other, we'll meet under the clock at Selfridge's."

Well, they met under the clock at Selfridge's and they went to Paris that night and they lived in Paris where, as well as being an English Barrister, he passed his *license es droit* to become a French lawyer. They were so frightfully hard up – because Walker, naturally, cut her off without a shilling – that she had to run a hat shop. After five years, he divorced her, and Andy and she were married in the British Embassy. In fact, when Chipps was a young Naval officer, he went to the Embassy to check if he was legitimate and he discovered that he was.

Unfortunately, when Chipps was only about five, this Cynthia I disliked – she's dead now – got Andy in her clutches. He was going off to spend a weekend with her on some false pretext and, being frightfully absent-minded like all clever lawyers, he picked up the wrong case, which contained Chipps' baby clothes, and left behind the case which contained going-away things which warned Kitty of what was really happening, and she sued him for divorce. In court the Judge said, "This is absurd. It's obvious you're both still in love. You must get together again," and they looked at each other, rushed across the court and fell into each other's arms and said, "We won't divorce." At which point Cynthia got up at the back of the court and said, "You've got to! I'm having a baby!" Well, she didn't have a baby for several years.

After her second divorce, Kitty married Geoff Pittar who was now Secretary of I.C.I., in Billingham, and who'd also fallen in love with her during that May Week Ball at Cambridge. He'd waited for all those years without ever looking at another woman. His family invented the petard – the explosive used for everything from hand grenades to fireworks and the name gradually became Pittar. They were Huguenot and they came over to England at the time of the troubles.

As Kitty had custody of Chipps, it was Geoff and she who really brought him up, and he spent a lot of his childhood at Dorrea, Kitty's father's house in Saint-Jean-de-Luz, as Geoff had to give up his I.C.I. job and go to a sanatorium in Switzerland due to T.B.

Then, at the outbreak of war, Geoff bought Slepe House and Slepe Farm because the doctor said he couldn't go back into the army, and that farming would be good for him. He farmed here and ran the A.R.P. and the Home Guard in Lytchett throughout the war. And that's when I met Chipps – while he was about to go to Marlborough. He then went on to Dartmouth as a Public School Entrance.

Have I any other ambitions? Only to be twenty-one again! . . . No, I'm not maintaining a façade. Life would be awfully dull if one never giggled. Having fun is a part of it.

Do I care what people think of me? I care about what the people I love think of me. When Chipps ticks me off, I care about that. If Anne Russell, Anne Swinton-Lee, my old fellow *ambulancière* says, "You really are being a pill, Dodo!" I care about that. And my dear friend, Mrs. Bradford, who's worked for me for so many years, if she ticks me off – and she ticks me off like crazy – I care about that. But, if you mean 'Do I care what the world thinks of me?' no, I can't say that I care frightfully, either about what it thinks or what it says.

I mean, I've always stood out like a sore thumb in Dorset. There was I, a Socialist, with a very Conservative mother and a very Conservative family generally, but it never worried me. Even now they all say, "She's a Socialist who sent her sons to Eton and Harrow," but that brushes off. I know I've done what I could to help people – and I hope I'll go on doing it. I've done a lot to help Malta. I helped a lot of people in the war. I do think that, when a man is dying on the field of battle and a pretty girl cuddles him and gives him a morphine injection and eases him into the next world, well that must be a bonus for him. I remember an Italian at Shenley who was blinded and, when I used to go in on night duty to see if he wanted something to send him to sleep or a glass of water, he used to say, "It's like having my mother here" . . .

I must go and say goodnight to Porfirio.

Goodnight, Porfirio. Shall I tickle your tummy? Give me a kiss. I do love you, my darling, my lovebird. Goodnight, my precious. Yes, you *are* my precious . . .

Slepe Green, 1988.

Epilogue

BY CHIPPS SELBY BENNETT

Dodo died on 26th August 1991, a few days after returning from a visit to her beloved Gozo She had known that it would be for the last time. She left behind the manuscript of this book which I previously had not read. I found it fascinating and was determined to have it published.

Dodo had a wretched last few years. However, I like to remember the tall, quick-witted, vivacious, caring, and striking looking young woman from Dorset who, as she describes in this book, so fascinated politicians and tycoons, generals and admirals, ambassadors and relations from all over the world, as well as innumerable friends from all walks of life, from Paris to Panama, from Haiti to Hong Kong, from Malta to Caracas, from the Rhine to the Amazon – and who fascinated me from the age of thirteen.

Fulsome Obituaries appeared in the *Times*, *Telegraph*, *Guardian* and *Independent*, as well as in the local Dorset newspapers, and even in *Horse and Hound* and *The Times of Malta*. The Press were clearly fascinated by a woman who had led such a full life. They described how she had met Hitler as a young girl, how she was decorated with the Croix de Guerre and Bar for her war-time exploits, how despite her upper-class connections she had stood for Parliament as a Labour candidate, whilst strongly supporting fox hunting, how she had influenced Dom Mintoff and how she had travelled all over the world following me. Although highly intelligent, she had had virtually no formal schooling. However, she was very well read and a brilliant linguist.

Her funeral Requiem Mass was held at the Weld family private chapel, set in the grounds of Lulworth Castle which she describes in this book. Father Alexander Sherbrooke, the son of John Sherbrooke, officiated and her cousin Colonel Sir Joseph Weld himself served Mass. Humphrey Weld of Chideock, her closest Weld relation, was in the front row, together with Colonel Michel Perrodon, in full uniform, representing the French Army. Her coffin was draped in the Tricolour. on it lay her Croix de Guerre and Bar, the red Chechia cap of her old Regiment, the *6ième Régiment d'Infanterie Coloniale*, and a single white rose with a card, "Darling Dodo – With So Much Love. Life was never dull with you – Chipps".

A week later, there was a Service of Thanksgiving for her life, in Lytchett Minster Church. The front row was occupied by representatives of her main interests in life: Colonel Perrodon, representing the French Army who read a letter of tribute from the French Ambassador; the Maltese High Commissioner who read a Maltese poem; two senior County Councillors representing the Labour Party; Sir Stephen Hammick, the Chairman of the Dorset County Council; and Edward Knowles, the Master of the South Dorset Hunt. Her two sons, Jamie and Bruce read the lessons.

Her cousin, Sir Thomas Lees, in an outstanding address, stressed Dodo's three outstanding qualities: her innocence, her courage and her faith. He quoted from Wol Drax's letter to Chipps, "Who else would one ever expect to see at the end of a fuel hose whilst refuelling at sea in the middle of a Fleet Exercise in the China Seas? Who else would appear from behind a screen at the end of an after-dinner talk by Mountbatten to the Chatham Dining Club, notebook in hand and representing the *Daily Express*?"

He also quoted a letter from Admiral John Templeton-Cotill, "I admired her as much as I was fond of her. It was she who was at the bottom of the Maltese Settlement in 1972. I played a modest, but I think an important, part as the only Englishman with whom Dom would talk without pretence. And Dom would never have bothered with the local Admiral – in his eyes a conventional stuffy – if Dodo had not given me the entree." He also quoted from a letter from Tony Palamountain: "I shall always remember meeting her by chance in London. She had just joined the French Army. I was in the A.T.S. – collar and tie, hair well above the collar, etc. Dodo wore an open-necked khaki shirt with short sleeves – it was Summer – a double string of pearls, her hair hanging down her back and a black fore-and-aft cap with the gold Cross of Lorraine. "Darling, how lovely. Come and have lunch. we'll go to Claridge's Causerie", and she transported me out of my drab world. Dodo, Tom Lees said, transported lots of people out of their drab worlds.

Many of the people who featured in this book came to one of the Services or wrote to me: V.A.D.'s, Sir Harold Hood and Ian Farquhar from her war-time days in London; Sid Chappell, Violet Bradford and other friends from Lytchett; Monique de Nervo, and an Officer who had served with her in the *6ieme R.I.C.* from France; Peter Bence-Trower and Reggie Fitzgerald from *Battleaxe* days; Michael Saunders-Watson, "Snowy's" Flag Lieutenant; the Dolanyi's from Caracus; Cecilia Foley and Nella Gavronska from Rome; Ann Swinton-Lees (now Mrs. Martin Russell) her fellow *ambulancière* and close friend; Kay, Dodo's great rival on the journey down to St. Jean de Luz. The list is endless.

A month later, another moving Service was held in the little Church of

Xlendi, in Gozo. It had been arranged by Gerald de Trafford, the son of Dodo's great friend Cecilia. Dom Mintoff was abroad, but Moyra, his English wife, was there. Afterwards, I gave Dodo's ring, "Howard's ring", to Josephine who had been Dodo's loyal maid and friend in Xlendi for twenty-five years. It seemed a suitable end to Dodo's favourite piece of jewellery which had travelled with her all over the world.

Most of her ashes now lie in the Lees' family grave in Lytchett Minster next to a Memorial to her great childhood friend, her cousin James Lees. A simple stone plaque is engraved:

DOLORES (DODO) SELBY BENNETT
CROIX de GUERRE and BAR
DAUGHTER OF CAPT BERNARD LEES
BELOVED WIFE OF
CMDR H SELBY BENNETT R.N.
1920 – 1991

Afterwards, some of her ashes were scattered in the sparkling waters of Xlendi Bay, off "Dodo's rock" and in the Blue Grotto. Others were also scattered in the wild cottage garden of Slepe Green where her parrot, Porfiro, still flies up onto the thatched roof vainly crying:

"Dodo! . . . Dodo! . . . "

He's not the only one.

Slepe Green, 1992.

Slepe Green

DODO LEES

Dolores ("Dodo") Selby Bennett, née Lees, nurse with the wartime Maquis, politician and journalist, died on August 26 aged 71. She was born on April 20, 1920.

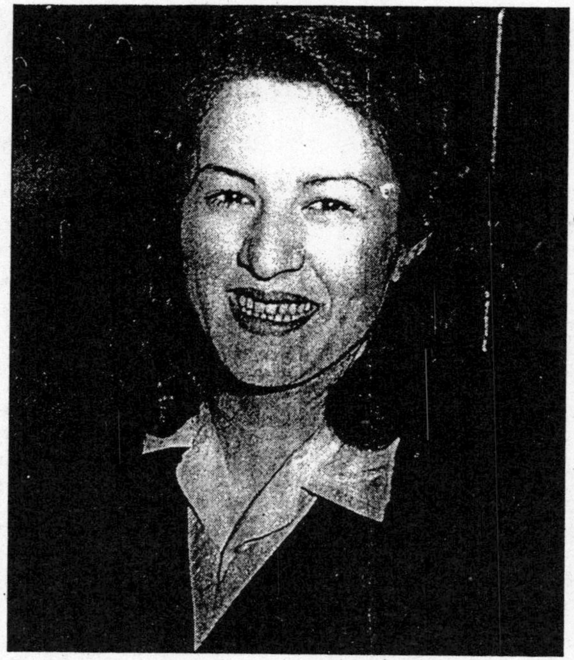

DODO Lees led an extraordinarily varied life. Born into two well-known Dorset land-owning families, the Leeses and the Welds, she was determined to see more of life than the county of her birth. As a girl journalist before the war she was taken by friends to meet Hitler, but when German troops marched into Czechoslovakia in March 1939 she lent her passport to Jews in Prague to enable them to escape.

During the war she worked as a Voluntary Aid Detachment (VAD) nurse in various hospitals but for D-Day she took advantage of her family connection with the Chief of the Imperial General Staff, Lord Alanbrooke, to persuade Ernest Bevin, the Minister of Labour, to allow her to join the French Red Cross as an ambulance driver.

She served with the 6th Colonial Infantry Regiment in the French First Army and saw service in the battle of the Colmar Gap and during the Rhine and Danube campaigns, subsequently taking part in the liberation of Dachau concentration camp and tending the inmates. In the winter of 1944-45, hearing that the Resistance fighters in the Vosges mountains were in need of medical assistance she crossed the German lines, disguised as a civilian, and lived with the Maquis in a cave. She was awarded the Croix de Guerre and Bar for rescuing wounded men under fire and in minefields.

After the war, by now a well-known figure in the French Army, she was, despite her British nationality, made an officer and appointed personal staff officer to Marshal Leclerc, the dashing French soldier who had commanded French armoured units on D-Day and accepted the surrender of German-occupied Paris in August 1944. Leclerc was at that point going to Indo-China as commander-in-chief, but when he was killed in an air crash in Algeria in November 1947 Dodo Lees was seconded to the French Foreign Office and sent to make a series of lecture tours in America, informing audiences in the United States of the French attitude to the Marshall Plan.

She and Hitler shared the same birthday, April 20; indeed he had had the impertinence to tell her that on that score she would make a fine public speaker. In the event – an event Hitler could not possibly have foreseen – she joined the Labour party, much to her family's dismay, and fought Brendan Bracken in Bournemouth East in 1949. She also nearly unseated her cousin, Sir Fitzroy Maclean, another wartime hero, in Lancaster in 1951. In 1953, a week before her marriage, she was offered a safe Labour seat. However she felt that a political career was incompatible with following her future sailor husband around the world. In 1955 following her husband's destroyer to Malta, where the influential Strickland family were her cousins, she was virtually co-opted into the government by Dom Mintoff, the prime minister.

He put her in charge of starting tourism; thus she made a contribution to the extraordinary change in Malta's standard of living. She kept a house in Gozo and remained a confidant of Mintoff and of his English wife, and played a key role in restraining many of his anti-British excesses when he was elected prime minister again in 1971. Rear-Admiral John Templeton-Cothill, the commander of British forces in Malta, had been best man at her marriage and she was able to ensure a close, if discreet, liaison between these two men throughout the period when Mintoff was outwardly seeking to throw the British out of Malta.

Meanwhile, back in Dorset, in 1962 she played a key role in ensuring the election of the Labour candidate Guy Barnett to what had always hitherto been regarded as the safe Conservative seat of South Dorset.

In 1966 her husband, Commander "Chipps" Selby Bennett, was appointed defence attache in Venezuela, Colombia, Panama and the Dominican Republic. For the next three years she travelled extensively in Latin America, parts of which were then threatened with Cuban-based uprisings.

Dodo Lees was a highly intelligent, but also warm hearted and attractive, woman who took her own line – such as fiercely defending foxhunting in Labour circles. She even canvassed against her husband in 1989 when he successfully stood for the Dorset county council – as a Conservative. She spoke many languages and regarded both France and Malta as her second countries.

She leaves her husband and two sons.

Dodo's Outline Family Tree

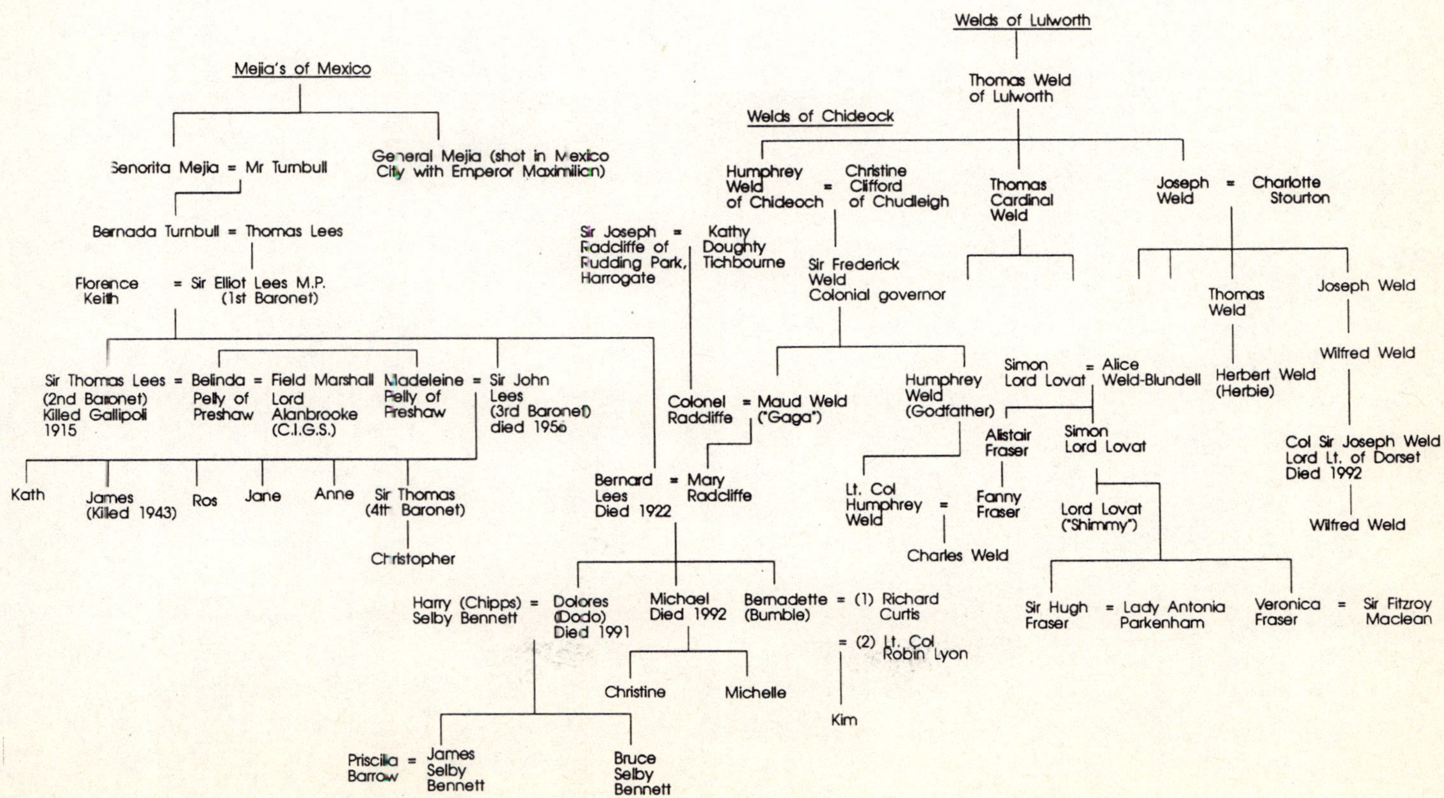

INDEX

A

Abel Smith, Lady May, 241

Abrahams, Jack, 223, 224

Ackerman, Air Marshal, 125

Addeley, Peter, 270

Agnew, Mark, 203

Al Saud, Mohammed, 293, 294, 296

Amin, Idi, 347

Amory, Julian, 202, 205

Arias (later President of Panama), 292, 299

Attlee, Lord, 166, 175, 176, 202

Aumeron, Colonel (later General), 107, 114

Austen-Leigh, Reverend, 187

B

Baker, Bea, 137

Bandon, Air Marshall "Paddy", 235, 250

Barkley, Alban, 137

Barrow, Stella, 97, 332

Barthelet, Colonel "Boulaya", 98

Bearsted, Lord, 283

Beaumont, Baroness Mona, 23, 42, 57, 65, 67

Beaverbrook, Lord, 64, 159, 160

Beck, Baroness Ditty, 227

Beck, Fritz, 228

Beckhoff, Susan, 294

Begg, Admiral Varyl, 238, 251, 252, 253

Bell, Ian, 300, 301

Bell, Ruth, 300, 301, 302

Bell-Salter, Admiral, Columbian Navy and Commander R.N., 307, 308

Bence-Trower, Captain Peter, 196, 263, 360

Bence-Trower, Sheena, 196, 197, 209, 210, 261, 263

Benn, Anthony Wedgwood "Wedgie", M.P., 264

Bennett, Mr Justice "Andy" C.H.A. Bennett Q.C., 92, 181

Bernadotte, Prince of the Netherlands, 119, 123

Best, Commander Rupert, 308

Bevan, Nye, 19, 189, 202, 203, 265, 274

Bevin, Ernie, 78, 107, 153, 162

Blum, Leon, 37

Bond, Mark (later General), 35

Bone, Charles, 202

Bonnici, Mr., 341

Boris, King of Bulgaria, 49, 51

Bossom, Doric, 69, 70, 71, 74, 145, 187

Bossom, Sir Alfred, 70

Bowyer, Brian, 253, 255

Bracken, Brendan, 163, 165, 166

Braddock, Bessie, 166, 175, 176

Bradford, Mrs. Violet, 332, 358, 360

Braithwaite, Ambassador E.R., 295, 296, 325

Brandt, Willy, 167, 342

Britten, Pat, 63, 66

Brooke, Field Marshal, Sir Alan "Uncle Alan" (later Lord Alanbrooke), 53, 62, 78, 236

Brookings, Isobell, 144

Bruce-Haye, Brigadier "Beloved", 76, 80

Burgess, Guy, 159, 335

Busiri-Vici, Assia, 215

C

Cabot Lodge, Henry, 276

Cabot Lodge, John, 276

Cachin, Charles, 147, 220

Cachin, Ginette, 147, 213

Cahen d'Anvers, Gilbert, 212

Cairo, Jim, 198, 256

Canez, Bishop, 290

Carbonell, Admiral, 315, 325, 326

Carrington, Peter, 241

Carter, Daisy, 107, 148, 321

Cassar, Anthony, 203

Castle, Barbara, 166, 175

Cecil, Lord Robert "Bob", 166

Chappell, Sid, 262, 263, 280, 360

Charles, Prince of Wales, 343

Charnier, Jacques, 147

Chudleigh, Lord Clifford of, 194

Churchill, Sarah, 26

Clydesdale, Douglo (later Duke of Hamilton), 23, 44, 250

Cobham, Sir Alan, 38

Cole, Val, 54

Colfox, Lady "Aunt Mamie", 18, 37, 43, 54, 159, 164

Colfox, Sir Philip, 18, 184

Comyns, Betty, 58

Coningham, Sir Arthur "Mary", 75, 77, 79, 84, 86, 88, 89, 94, 95, 106, 127, 128, 141, 142

Coward, Noël, 89, 127

Crichton, Barbie, 68

Cronin, John, M.P., 176, 280, 318

Crossman, Richard "Dick", M.P., 203, 346

Cunard, Lady, 356

Curtis, General "Squeaker", 63, 84, 107

Curtis, Lawrence, 142

D

d'Aimbert, Captain Pierre, 104

d'Allières, Buddy, 87, 93

d'Hendrecourt, Vicomtesse, 37

d'Urcels, Duc, 37

Dalyell, Tom, 264

Dance, Mr., 19, 38, 44, 60

Dance, Polly, 163

Dangerfield, Mike, 348

Davies, Clifford, 162, 163

de Baudry d'Asson, Comte, 90

de Beauvau-Craon, Prince Marc, 131, 154, 222

de Brincat, Johnnie (Director of Agriculture in Gozo), 304

de Chargière, Jacqueline, 96, 110

de Crouy-Chanel, Conte Etienne, 156, 157, 187, 190, 201

de Crouy-Chanel, Contesse Jacqui, 156, 157

de Croy, Princess Aliette, 129

de Foucauld, Comtesse, 91
de Gaulle, Général Charles, 92, 93, 126, 282
de Guerra de Boeckstyns, Count Lulu, 217, 223
de la Rouchefoucault, Duc, 84
de la Tour du Pin, Madame, 126
de Langallerie, Fafa, 96, 118, 119, 123
de Lattre de Tassigny, Général (later Maréchal), 90, 108, 117, 126
de Laurentis, Riccardo, 327
de Liefde, Joost, 283, 310, 316, 325
de Liefde, Mel, 283, 284, 310, 325
de Linares, Général, 104
de Luna, Duke and Duchess, 227, 276
de Marmol, Baron Eduard, 37
de Meeus, Comtesse, 36
de Nervo, Baronne Monique, 86, 87, 89, 90-93, 102, 103, 106, 123, 124, 126, 129, 133, 134, 136-139, 146-149, 170, 181, 183, 184, 186, 190, 212, 222, 223, 249, 312, 327, 338, 350, 360,
de Nervo, Baron, 90
de Noailles, Duchess Geneviève, 134, 138
de Nunes, Senõra, 283
de Pentheny O'Kelly, Mrs., 42, 58
de Peyerimhoff, Madame, 91, 94, 106
de Salis, Comtesse, 78, 79, 83
de Trafford, Cecilia, 194, 195, 197, 201, 202, 205, 206, 216, 217, 218, 238, 257, 261, 271, 273, 274, 351, 361
de Trafford, Charlotte, 344
de Trafford, George, 257
de Trafford, Gerald, 274, 344, 361
de Trafford, Jasper, 344
de Villaverde, Marquesa, 220
de Villèyre, Jean, 91, 125, 126, 138, 222
de Vilmorin, Lulu, 124
de Voss, Kay, 26, 170, 236, 360
de Zuluetta, Anne, 206
Dennery, Etienne, 126, 132
Dennison Pender, Margaret, 68
Deschelrins, Christianne, 108
Dessert, Colonel, 90, 108
Devi, Sita, 170
Devonshire, Andrew Duke of, 66, 76
Diana, Lady (later Princess of Wales), 223, 224
Dick-Reid, Dr. Grantley, 24
Dilke, Alice, 65, 307
Dilke, Christopher, 307
Doan, Dorothy, 134
Dolanyi, Senõr and Senõra, 311, 360
Doughty Tichborne, Katty, 29, 64
Douglas, Air Marshal Sir Sholto, 128, 233
Douglas-Hamilton, Lord David, 47
Dowell, Cecil, 350
Drax, Admiral, 20, 26
Drax, Lady, 26, 59, 162
Drax, "Dor", 26
Drax, "Wol", 160, 262, 280, 336, 360
Drax, The Hon. Pamela "Pam", 250, 280, 336
Drummond-Hay, Lady Margaret, 23
Dubonnet, André, 89, 90, 115
Dubonnet, France, 89, 90, 115

E

Eisenhower, General Dwight, 94, 117

Ellis-Flint, Clough, 244

Ercklentz, Hima, 41, 48-54

Ercklentz, Irmgard "Irmchen", 41, 46-50, 52, 54, 71

Esterhazy, Prince "Bonde", 217

F

Fane, Anne, 73

Farquhar, Ian, 58, 61, 72, 76, 86, 166, 190, 272, 321, 350, 360

Fath, Jacques, 133, 139

Fennick, Moses, 205, 206

Fersen, Olga, 215

Fitzalan-Howard, Miles (present Duke of Norfolk), 23, 198, 199

Fitzgerald, Carroll, 93, 123, 132, 139, 144-146, 154, 186, 192, 338, 356

Fitzgerald, Commander Reginald "Reggie", 196, 209, 360

Fitzgerald, Diana "Di", 196

Foley, Lord, 156

Foley, Cecilia, 215, 223, 312, 323, 327, 334, 350, 360

Fonteyn, Margot, 26, 27, 132, 187, 299, 300

Forbes, Ian, 40

Fortcht, Willy, 39

Frank, Sir Howard, 75-80, 83, 85-87, 93-95, 113, 118, 125, 127, 134, 166, 177, 187, 190, 241, 250, 321, 354, 361

Frank, Lady "Nan", 75, 77, 79, 80, 86, 89, 94, 95, 127, 128, 177

Fraser, Lady Antonia and Sir Hugh, 319, 320

Freeman, Trifene, 261

G

Gadaffi, Colonel, 340-342

Galitzine, Prince Yurka, 273

Garbutt, Jack, 46, 50, 51, 249

Gavronska, Nella, 217, 223, 360

Getty, Paul, 224

Giusti, Mario, 217, 218, 222

Gladstone, Admiral, 238-240

Grantham, Admiral Sir Guy "Grannie", 195, 196

Greene, Graham, 26, 300, 324

Guillemand, Colonel, 83, 85

Gyarfas, Geza, 312

H

Haley, Tim, 69

Hamilton, Nina "Aunt Nina" Duchess of, 47, 71

Hammick, Sir Stephen, 360

Hampshire, "Paddy", 192

Hankey, Henry, 299

Hankey, Veronica "Vronny", 299

Hartington, Lord, 66

Healey, Denis, M.P., 167, 175, 279, 342, 346

Healey, Bernard, 348

Heath, Edward, M.P., 338, 339, 342, 343

Henegan, Mike and Mary, 235, 250

Henlein, Conrad, 49, 52

Herbig, Dr. Egon, 292, 299, 310, 317, 325

Herrera, Pepito, 313

Hodgkinson, Hugh, 270

Hogg, the Titchborne Claimant, 29

Hohenzollern, Heinrich, 52

Holland, Mr., 163

Hood, Sir Harold, 43, 66, 67, 69, 77, 80

Hopwood, Michael (3rd Lord Southborough), 187, 266, 333

Hopwood, Moyna (née Chattey and later Lady Southborough), 131, 187, 188, 190, 235, 266, 283, 312, 327, 333

Howard of Glossop, Lord Bernard, 23

Hunt, Sir John, 35

Hutchinson, Mr., 233

Hutton, Barbara, 209

Hyde, Ronnie, 155-157, 160, 161, 249

Hyzler, Bertie, 341

I

Idris, Wynn, 143, 148

Igliori, Massimo, 343

Illingworth, Lady Margaret, 69, 71

J

Jackson, Alistair, 331, 348

Jackson, Tessa, 348

Jaeger, Lewis, 136, 142

Jennings, Michael, 264, 333

Jimenez, Commodore, 302, 303

Jocet, André, 89, 92, 106

Johore, Sultan of, 19, 235, 248-250

Jox, Monsieur, 130

Juan, Don, Pretender to Spanish Throne, 227, 228

K

Kemsley, Lady, 125

Kennedy, Katherine "Kick", 66, 76

Kennedy, James "Jimmy", 66, 67

Kent, Princess Marina, Duchess of, 89

Kent, Princess Michael of, 250

Kilmuir, Lord David, 202, 205

Kitson, Penelope "Bun", 224

Klotz, Pierre, 220

Knowles, Edward, 360

L

Lambe, Ivor, 46, 130

Langlais, Commandant Pierre (later Colonel), 90, 117, 118, 123

Law, Admiral Sir Horace, 243

Lawrence, Peter "Wetty", 333

Lawrence, T.E., 26

Laycock, Major General Sir Robert "Bob", 201, 203

Leclerc, General (later Maréchal), 118, 125, 126

Lee, Hilary, 68

Lees, Bumble, 15, 25, 36, 44, 63, 64, 70, 84, 86, 106, 107, 142, 173, 186, 246

Lees, Captain Bernard Percy Turnbull, 15

Lees, James, 18, 23, 35, 36, 38, 361

Lees, Katherine "Kitty" (Lady Nugent), 22, 30

Lees, Lady Florence, 15

Lees, Lady Madeleine "Aunt Maddy", 18, 23, 24, 26, 27, 35, 36, 44, 48, 54, 71, 107

Lees, Mary "mother", 15, 17-22, 24-29, 31, 35-38, 40-42, 47, 50, 51, 54, 57-60, 63, 65-69, 73, 76-78, 84, 87, 106, 107, 114, 123, 124, 126, 130-133, 136, 138, 145, 153-155, 162, 163, 168, 181, 187-190, 192, 193, 222, 224, 228, 233, 235, 261, 264, 294, 323, 331, 334, 351-354, 358

Lees, Michael "Mike", 15, 20, 25, 26, 30, 35, 38, 44, 62-64, 91, 106, 137, 144, 173, 218, 264, 350, 353

Lees, Sir Elliot, 15, 17, 163, 187, 323

Lees, Sir John "Uncle Jack", 15, 18, 23-25, 27, 28, 38, 43, 44, 47, 50, 51, 69

Lees, Sir Thomas "Tom", 18, 59, 225, 263, 360

Lennox-Boyd, Alan, 202

Leone, President of Venezuela, 295, 296, 304, 314

Lepinard, Monsieur, 348

Lewis, General Richard "Dick" and Nora, 131

Lincoln, Sir Anthony and Lady, 280, 284, 295, 297, 298, 303

Linklater, Eric, 212

Llewellyn, Lord Jay, 63, 64

Louis-Dreyfus, François, 102, 138, 139, 144, 146-149, 170, 177, 181, 184, 185, 223

Louise, Carole, 160, 161

Lovat, Lord "Shimmy", 173

Lyttleton, Moggy, 68

M

Maclean, Donald, 144, 159, 335

Maclean, Brigadier Sir Fitzroy, 64, 166, 174, 175, 176, 320

Maclean, Veronica (née Fraser), 64, 73, 174, 320

Macmillan Douglas, Tina (née Douglas Roberts), 39, 44, 45, 91

Madden, Captain Colin, 217

Malden, Diana "Di", 39, 45

Mancroft, Lord Stormont, 160

Mansel, Damaris, 347

Mansel, Elizabeth, 45

Mansel, John, 331

Mansel, Rhys, 347

Mansel-Pleydell, David, 193, 215

Martin, David, 199, 336

Martin, Glen, 351

Massigli, Odette, 156, 158

Masurel, Nanou, 212

Maudlin, Reginald "Reggie", 342

Maugham, Somerset, 249

Maxton, Jimmie, 45, 166

Maxwell Knight, Captain, 66, 67

Maxwell Stuart, Arthur, 23, 63

Maxwell Stuart, Madeleine, 63, 68, 74

Maxwell-Fyfe, David, 202

Mayer-Speir, Paul, 49

McCarthy, Desmond (later Admiral) and Agatha, 24

Mejia de Turnbull, Bernarda, 15, 322

Mendosa, Admiral Felix, 326, 337

Micaleff, Josephine, 275, 327, 346, 361

Miller, George, 128

Miners, John, 352

Mintoff, Dom, 52, 64, 65, 195, 201-206, 272, 273, 337-346, 359-361

Mintoff, Moyra, 201, 203, 340, 342, 343, 346, 355, 361

Mitford, Nancy, 26, 89

Mollet, Guy, 167

Monserrat, Anne, 194
Montgomery, Lord "Monty", 77, 79, 80, 83, 84, 85, 94
Morrison, Herbert, 163
Mountbatten, Iris, 39
Mountbatten, Lady Edwina, 87, 93, 250
Mountbatten, Lord, 123, 159, 360
Mowbray and Stourton, Lord William, 23
Muller, Elizabeth, 295, 310
Muller, Peter (Austrian Ambassador), 286, 303, 310
Musgrove, Group Captain, 293, 294

N

Nichols, Beverley, 156
Norman, Dick, 189, 224
Norrington, Captain, 228, 229, 238, 253
Northcroft, Evelyn, 79, 89, 131
Noyes, Alfred, 41

O

Ogilvy, Felicity, 228
Olivier, Borg, 201, 342, 343
Ormond, Elizabeth "Betty", 168, 169, 170, 181, 190, 210, 220
Ormond, Lieutenant Colonel Selby, 168
Ormond, Patrick Selby, 92, 357
Osborne, Sid, 183, 186

P

Palamountain, Toni, 153, 360
Palewski, Gaston, 89, 92, 126, 131
Paul, Gerald, 126-128, 130-132
Payachevich, Geza, 310, 311
Pedrick, Father, 181-183, 228, 349, 353
Peron, Eva, 147, 149
Perrodon, Colonel Michel, 359, 360
Perth, Lord, 202, 205
Petrelli, Cardinal, 193, 213
Phillips, Yootha, 58
Picasso, 147
Pinilla, José M., 299, 300
Pippinger, Josie, 316
Pittar, Geoff, 59, 60, 194, 225, 262, 357, 358
Pittar, Kitty (née Katherine Selby Ormond), 59, 153, 154, 189, 190, 193, 194, 225, 233, 263, 312, 315, 316, 332, 354, 356, 357
Pleydell-Railston, June, 42, 54
Pleydell-Railston, Vivian "Aunt Vivian", 19, 42, 43, 58, 123, 130, 131, 184, 193, 215, 352
Pocock, Mike, 283, 294, 310
Pocock, Nina (later Lady Bearsted), 283, 295, 298, 310, 321
Pope Pius XII, 183, 213
Posse de Rivas, Antonio, 281, 283
Posse de Rivas, Marisa, 281, 286, 297
Priestley, J.B., 156

R

Radcliffe, Lady Maud "Gaga", 15, 16, 22, 28, 29, 36, 41, 42, 45-47, 63, 95, 144, 160, 182
Radcliffe, Sir Joseph, 29, 354

Rawlinson, Peter, 76

Raymond, 25, 156

Redfern, Tommy, 69

Redman, Lieutenant Colonel Anthony, 282, 283, 301, 321

Redman, Patricia, M.P., 283, 321

René, Madame, 90, 96

Renkin, Jean and Marie, 37, 52, 53, 94, 212

Renkin, Nanette, 37, 53, 61, 94

Rex, Gräfin, 39, 91, 143

Rockerfeller, Nelson, 304

Roco, Captain, 97-102, 139

Rossie, Theo, 272

Rousseau, Ted, 134

Royle, Sir Arthur, 125

Ruck-Keene, Vice-Admiral Philip "Phil", 53, 155, 219, 270,

Russell, Clive, 307, 316

Russo, Jaime, 206

Rutland, Charlie Duke of, 76

S

Salvin, Herman, 30

Salvin, Annette "Nettie", 30, 31

Samuel, Peter, 283

Saunders Watson, Commander Michael "Mick", 297, 360

Savage, Alma, 131, 134, 135, 137, 140, 142, 144

Schleswig Holstein, Prince Hima, 48

Scicluna, Marquis, "Joe", 205, 206

Scott, George, 111

Selby Bennett, Andrew, 350

Selby Bennett, Bruce, 16, 36, 40, 41, 92, 138, 215, 222-225, 233, 257, 264-268, 276, 281, 284, 286, 292, 293, 305, 314-317, 319,-321, 327, 331, 333-335, 349, 350, 360

Selby Bennett, Jamie, 16, 40, 63, 68, 90, 92, 188-190, 192-197, 201, 206, 209, 211-213, 215, 218, 219, 222, 225, 229, 233-236, 238, 240-248, 250-257, 263-266, 276, 286, 293, 300-303, 305, 314-316, 327, 331-333, 335, 349, 350, 353, 360

Selby Bennett, Commander Harry "Chipps", 16, 24, 25, 28, 29, 38-41, 43, 59, 60, 63, 67, 87, 92, 93, 99, 148, 153-157, 167-170, 173, 174, 176, 177, 181-184, 186-194, 196-202, 206, 209-220, 222, 224, 225, 227-229, 233-238, 240-248, 250, 251, 253, 256, 261-268, 270-272, 275, 276, 279-285, 287-294, 296-301, 303-305, 307, 309, 314-316, 318-327, 331-336, 338, 339, 344, 348-350, 353-358, 359, 360

Selby Bennett, Nicholas Harry, 350

Selby Bennett, Priscilla "'Scilla" (née Barrow), 266, 332, 333, 349, 350, 353

Selkirk, Lord Geordie, 250

Seymour-Hayden, Captain Alan and Sally, 211

Shackleton, Lord "Eddie", 155, 175, 268, 322, 331

Shackleton, Colonel, 322, 323

Shacklock, Captain, 196, 198, 252

Shaw-Stuart, Molly, 40

Sheed, Frank, 131

Sherbrooke, John, 43, 50, 54, 58, 60, 68, 74, 76, 77, 280, 333, 359

Shinwell, Manny, 158

Signac, Paul, 147, 186, 213

Silver, Roger, 336

Smith, Sir Raymond, 319, 326

Smith, Lady, Dorothy, 319,

Snoy, Baron Raymond, 38, 53
Sollyflood, Peter, 144
Southborough, Lord Frank, 283, 294
Southborough, Lady Audrey, 283, 312
St. Cassia, Henry, 195, 196
Stacey, Mr., 60
Stack, Prunella, 44, 47
Stevenson, Adlai, 157
Stokes, Lord Richard "Dick", 157, 158, 175
Stourton, Cicely, 42, 43
Strickland, Mabel, 194, 203
Stringer, Brian, 54
Swinton Lee, Anne (later Mrs. Martin Russell), 78, 79, 83-88, 90-92, 94, 96, 104, 106, 108, 110-114, 116, 117, 124, 126, 153, 155, 157, 169, 177, 358
Swinton Lee, Brigadier Stanislake, 79, 106

T

Tedder, Air Marshal, 94
Templeton-Cotill, Rear Admiral John, 181, 183, 191, 195, 225, 250, 273, 308, 332, 360
Thatcher, Margaret (née Roberts), 166, 172, 173
Thompson, Sir Robert, 234
Thompson, Wing Commander Peter, 234, 293
Thompson, Meryl, 331
Tichborne, Roger, 29, 182
Townley, Commodore John "Snowy", 297-301, 303, 313, 320, 360
Trench, Chevenix, 333
Trinder, Tommy, 45
Troubridge, Sir Peter and The Hon. Lady Venetia, 250, 251
Trujillo, Senõr, 279, 300, 301
Tuffnell, Captain Mike and Patsy, 241, 245

V

Vale, Lieutenant Colonel Bill, 296, 303, 313
Vale, Betty-Fox, 296, 303, 313
van Nispen, Blancie and Hupie, 287, 310, 312, 314
Vasiltchikoff, Princess Irina, 215
Vaux, Lord, 22
Vere-Hodge, Nick, 344
Vernon, Peter, 198
Vieilhomme, Henriette, 91, 92, 128, 145, 147, 188, 190, 204, 210-212, 220, 327
Vieilhomme, Paul, 92, 95, 147, 188, 190, 210, 220, 327
von der Schulenberg, Wernie, 342
von Schuschnigg, Dr. Kurt, 142

W

Walker, John, 268
Wallis, Colonel, 72, 73, 74
Wallis, Frankie, 72
Warner, Sir Fred, 159, 334
Warrington, Captain, 197
Weidemann, Ed, 135
Weill, Berthe David, 134, 249
Weld, Cardinal, 213
Weld, Colonel Sir Joseph, 16, 87, 223, 334, 359
Weld, Humphrey, 15, 359

Weld, Sir Frederick, 16
Weld, Thomas, 16
Weld-Blundell, Mary, 41
Whiles, Dr. Bill, 266, 268, 333
Williams, Colonel Eric, 85-87
Williams-Wynn, Peggy, 156
Windsor, Duke and Duchess of, 128, 356
Wodehouse, P.G., 135

Y

Yates, Gilbert, 144
Young, Barbara and Hilary, 306, 309, 375
Young, Mrs., 352, 353

Z

Zammit, Martin, 338
Zapata, Maggie, 323
Zarubin, Ambassador, 158, 159
Ziegler, Philip, 306
Zingone, Luciano, 215, 218
Zwirski, "Zizi", 134